Classical General Equilibrium Theory

Classical General Equilibrium Theory

Lionel W. McKenzie

The MIT Press
Cambridge, Massachusetts
London, England

This book was set in Times New Roman on 3B2 by Asco Typesetters, Hong Kong and was printed and bound in the United States of America.

Library of Congress Cataloging-in-Publication Data

McKenzie, Lionel W.
  Classical general equilibrium theory / Lionel W. McKenzie.
     p.   cm.
  Includes bibliographical references and index.
  ISBN 0-262-13413-6 (hc : alk. paper)
  1. Equilibrium (Economics) 2. Equilibrium (Economics)—History. I. Title.
HB145 .M39   2002
339.5—dc21   2002023017

To the memory of my beloved wife of 56 years,
Blanche Veron McKenzie,
without whose faithful support the work could not have been done

Contents

Preface

General equilibrium theory in the modern sense was first developed in the second half of the nineteenth century by Francis Edgeworth, Alfred Marshall, and Léon Walras, most systematically by Walras. In the first half of the century some earlier moves in the direction of formal analysis of competitive markets using mathematics had been made by Augustin Cournot and Jules Dupuit. Then in the early twentieth century Vilfredo Pareto and Gustav Cassel added some additional formulations to this theory. However, the modern elaboration and rigorous development of general equilibrium theory from these foundations was begun in the 1930s and 1940s by John Hicks and Paul Samuelson, in the tradition of academic economics but with liberal appeal to mathematics, and by Abraham Wald and John von Neumann, from a rigorous mathematical viewpoint. Frank Ramsey in the late 1920s and von Neumann in the 1930s had laid the ground for optimal growth theory, which I relate to general equilibrium over time. However, the general equilibrium theory that this book is concerned to present was developed in the second half of the twentieth century primarily by Kenneth Arrow, Gerard Debreu, and me but with many contributions from others. In particular, Tjalling Koopmans should be mentioned for his activity analysis and optimal growth theory. Morgenstern, Samuelson, Hicks, and Koopmans were my teachers. Of the authors whose work is cited here Hiroshi Atsumi, Robert Becker, Sho-Ichiro Kusumoto, Leonard Mirman, Tapan Mitra, Anjan Mukherji, Kazuo Nishimura, José Scheinkman, and Makoto Yano were my students. I apologize to my many students whose valuable contributions to economics happened not to be relevant to this book. However, I must mention Jerry Green (1977) and Charles Wilson (1976) who were pioneers in the study of markets with asymmetric information. General equilibrium is far from the whole of economics.

I characterize the general equilibrium theory that I will discuss as classical to indicate that it is the theory developed in the 1950s and 1960s along with continuations in the period after that. It was then that theorists began to derive theorems in a more satisfactory way from the same basic assumptions and to provide natural extensions of the original results. The assumptions that I refer to, in the case of the existence, optimality, and turnpike theorems, are perfect foresight for each future state of the world, or equivalently one initial market in which all transactions are made for the whole future and for all states of the world. The traders in both models are assumed to continue to live throughout the period, finite or infinite, to which the market refers. On the other hand, for the stability theory which is the Walrasian tâtonnement, it is assumed that equilibrium is reached before transactions are made final. This theory received much attention in the 1930s, 1940s, and 1950s While not realistic, it gives an indication of the conditions for stability in the very short run. It may also be relevant to later theories of temporary equilibrium where the question of how expectations are formed is important.

In the literature after 1970 these assumptions were generalized in some fundamental ways. In the existence theory the case was treated of repeated markets in which assets including stocks, bonds, and money are traded. However, perfect foresight of future prices in each state of the world is still assumed. Thus what is achieved is the description of the relations between asset prices and other prices. These relations depend on asset payoffs for different states of the world whose objective probabilities are unknown and will be estimated differently by different traders (see Magill and Quinzii 1996). This elaboration of the model may be compared with the elaboration in optimal growth theory that retains the assumption of perfect foresight but examines the progress of capital accumulation in these circumstances leading to turnpike theorems. (See Becker and Boyd 1997 for many extensions of this theory beyond the scope of this book.) Perfect foresight means that the future state of the world is known. Thus the assumption is actually stronger than that used in the classical existence theory where trading takes place for goods that include a specification of the state in which they are to be delivered but perfect foresight of the future state is not assumed. In another direction the assumption that traders live through the whole future that is covered by the market is replaced by the assumption of an infinite sequence of overlapping generations. (See Balasko, Cass, and Shell 1980 for an existence proof.) In macro models of optimal capital accumulation uncertainty was introduced by Brock and Mirman (1972; see also Stokey and Lucas 1989). Finally in recent years much attention has been given in one sector models to chaotic paths of capital accumulation (see, for example, Majumdar and Mitra 1994; Nishimura and Sorger 1999).

This book does not attempt to cover these many amendments of the classical theory. It is aimed rather at presenting a detailed and rigorous treatment of the classical model itself in which proofs of the basic theorems are given step by step. This does not mean that the argument is easy. Every step of the proofs is given, but in many cases the individual steps require some elaboration by the reader to achieve a full understanding. I believe this is the only way to obtain a mastery of the method that will allow the student to go beyond what has been done already and derive new results. The class notes that are the original form of the material of the book owe a great deal to the suggestions of my students over the years. Also I am grateful to many of my former students for their assistance in removing errors and misprints from earlier versions of my manuscript. These are too numerous to list, but I owe a special debt to Kazuo Nishimura and Makoto Yano who used some of the chapters in their own general equilibrium seminars and to Hajime Kubota who came to Rochester during several summers to give my chapters their most careful reading. Of course, I know from experience that not all errors have been removed or ever will be removed, but I think that unfortunate circumstance should be laid at my door.

1 Theory of Demand

The two foundations of the theory of competitive markets are the theory of demand and the theory of production. This was made quite clear in the earliest mathematical formulation of competitive theory by Leon Walras (1874–77). His demand theory is based on consistent choice under budget constraints by a consumer acting independently of the choices of other economic agents. This is still the classical paradigm. The choices are derived from the maximization of a utility function given the budget constraints. Today an alternative approach is to introduce a binary relation, the preference relation, from which optimal choices under constraint may be shown to exist with or without the intervention of a utility function. However, in the classical theory a utility index is still used as a device to facilitate the derivation of the theorems on demand. A standard reference for this way of proceeding is the appendix of Hicks' *Value and Capital* (1939). On the other hand, Samuelson (1947) shows how the basic theorems on demand can be derived when starting from the demand functions that are assumed to exist and to satisfy a consistency condition. Finally a method was introduced by McKenzie (1956–57) in which these results are derived from a function of prices that gives the minimum income needed to achieve commodity bundles as good as a given bundle. We call this the direct approach, and this is the approach that we will treat as primary.

1.1 A Direct Approach to Demand Theory

We suppose there is a finite list of commodities that the consumer may enjoy, indexed from 1 to n. A commodity bundle may be represented as a point in $\mathbf{R}^n$, the Cartesian product of n copies of the real line with a Euclidean topology. The commodity bundle may contain negative as well as positive components. Negative components represent goods provided by the consumer, for example, various types of labor service, while positive components represent goods taken by the consumer. Let C be the set of commodity bundles that it is possible for the consumer to trade. In the space $\mathbf{R}^n$ a set S is closed if and only if $x^s \in S$ for $s = 1, 2, \cdots$, and x^s converging to x implies that $x \in S$ (see Berge 1963, p. 88). We make the following assumptions.

ASSUMPTION 1 C is not empty, and C is closed and bounded from below.

ASSUMPTION 2   A binary relation is defined on C that is denoted by $\mathscr{R}$ and referred to as a preference relation. We interpret $x\mathscr{R}y$ to mean that the commodity bundle x is *preferred* to y; that is, x as good as or better than y.

ASSUMPTION 3   The relation $\mathscr{R}$ is complete and transitive. That is to say, for any x and $y \in C$ either $x\mathscr{R}y$ or $y\mathscr{R}x$, or both. Also $x\mathscr{R}y$ and $y\mathscr{R}z$ imply $x\mathscr{R}z$.

It is clear that assumption 3 implies that $x\mathscr{R}x$ holds.

ASSUMPTION 4   The relation $\mathscr{R}$ is closed. This means if sequences of bundles x^s and y^s satisfy $x^s \to x$ and $y^s \to y$, and $x^s\mathscr{R}y^s$ for all s, then $x\mathscr{R}y$.

The form taken by the assumptions on preferences is influenced by the role they play in the theory of the competitive economy. For example, the assumption that the set of possible consumption bundles is bounded below is used in the proof that a competitive equilibrium exists. Additional assumptions will be needed for that proof, which will not be made at this point, for example, that the possible consumption set C is convex and that the preferences have a convexity property as well. Other assumptions will be used in other parts of the theory, such as smoothness of preferences to allow for continuous or differentiable demand functions in the theories of stability and comparative statics. But for most of this chapter we will make do with the assumptions we have just listed. With them it is possible to obtain all the basic classical theorems on demand in a rather general form and with economical proofs.

We also define the *preference correspondence R* on C by

$$R(x) \equiv \{z \mid z \in C \text{ and } z\mathscr{R}x\}.$$

In other words $R(x)$ includes all commodity bundles that are as good as or better than x. It is nonempty since it contains x. Define the *strict preference* relation $\mathscr{P}$ by $x\mathscr{P}y$ if and only if $x\mathscr{R}y$ and not $y\mathscr{R}x$. The *strict preference correspondence P* is defined on C by

$$P(x) \equiv \{y \mid y \in C \text{ and } y\mathscr{P}x\}.$$

$P(x)$ may be empty. We also define an *indifference relation* $\mathscr{I}$ by $x\mathscr{I}y$ if $x\mathscr{R}y$ and $y\mathscr{R}x$, and the *indifference correspondence* $I(x)$ is defined in the analogous way to $R(x)$ and $P(x)$. I should mention here that in chapter 5, we will introduce the assumption that $R(x)$ is the closure of $P(x)$ at points x of C for which preferred bundles exist. This assumption is stronger than assumption 4 because it excludes thick indifference sets $I(x)$ except at points of satiation.

The effect of combining $\mathscr{P}$ and $\mathscr{R}$ is given by

LEMMA 1 $w\mathscr{P}z$ and $z\mathscr{R}x$ implies $w\mathscr{P}x$. Also $w\mathscr{R}z$ and $z\mathscr{P}x$ implies $w\mathscr{P}x$. Finally $w\mathscr{P}z$ and $z\mathscr{P}x$ implies $w\mathscr{P}x$.

Proof $w\mathscr{R}x$ follows from $w\mathscr{P}z$ and $z\mathscr{R}x$ by transitivity of $\mathscr{R}$. Suppose $x\mathscr{R}w$ held. Then $z\mathscr{R}x$ and $x\mathscr{R}w$ implies $z\mathscr{R}w$ by transitivity of $\mathscr{R}$, but this contradicts $w\mathscr{P}z$. A similar argument proves the second proposition. The third proposition is an immediate implication of either of the first two.   ∎

Let $\mathbf{R}_+^n = \{p \in \mathbf{R}^n \mid p \geq 0\}$. (In our use of $\geq$ and $\leq$ between vectors of $\mathbf{R}^n$ the inequality applies to each component of the vectors taken separately.) For $x \in C$ and $p \in \mathbf{R}_+^n$, the *minimum income function* $m_x : \mathbf{R}_+ \to \mathbf{R}$ is defined by

$$m_x(p) \equiv \inf\{pz \text{ for } z \in R(x)\}.$$

Since $R(x)$ is not empty and C is bounded below, it is clear that $m_x(p)$ is well defined for $p \geq 0$. The minimum income function is illustrated in figure 1.1. If negative prices are allowed, for $m_x(p)$ to be well defined, it would be necessary to assume that C is bounded.

Define the *budget set* $H(p,m)$ for $p \in \mathbf{R}_+^n$ and m a real number by

$$H(p,m) \equiv \{z \mid z \in C \text{ and } pz \leq m\}.$$

The *demand correspondence* $f(p,m)$ is defined for $p \in \mathbf{R}_+^n$ and m a real number by

$$f(p,m) \equiv \{x \mid x \in H(p,m) \text{ and } z\mathscr{P}x \text{ implies } z \notin H(p,m)\}.$$

With these assumptions and definitions we are able to prove the preliminary results that lead up to the properties of consumer demand as described in the classical theory. It is a fundamental fact about this theory that it completely isolates the consumer from society except for his participation in the market. That is, his preferences are not dependent on the choices of other persons. This is an abstraction from reality, but it is an abstraction that makes the theory possible in the general form in which

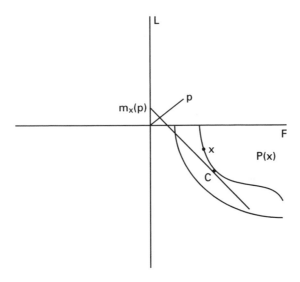

Figure 1.1
The goods are labor (L) and food (F). Labor is numéraire. $m_x(p)$ is the minimum income needed at prices p to reach the preference level given by the consumption vector x.

we study it. It is interesting that the originator of the theory, Léon Walras, was influenced by the theory of static equilibrium in classical mechanics. According to Jaffé (1954) he was familiar with the book by Poinsot (1803) in which the theory of statics in mechanics is derived from axioms. In a similar manner the theory of the competitive market is derived from axioms in *The Theory of Value* by Debreu (1959). In this book I will continue the practice of deriving theory from a set of axioms or assumptions.

Let us first prove some simple properties of R, m_x, and f. The *graph* of a correspondence Φ, which maps X into Y, is the set $\{(x, y) \mid x, y \in Y$, and $y \in \Phi(x)\}$.

LEMMA 2 (Berge 1963, p. 111) *Assumption 4 is equivalent to assuming that the graph of the correspondence R is closed.*

Proof Make assumption 4. Let $x^s \to x$ and $y^s \to y$ where $x^s \in X$, $y^s \in Y$, and $x^s \in R(y^s)$. Since C is closed by assumption 1, $x \in C$ and $y \in C$. By the definition of $R(x)$, we have that $x^s \mathcal{R} y^s$ for all s. Therefore $x \mathcal{R} y$ by assumption 4 and $x \in R(y)$. The converse implication is obvious.   ∎

LEMMA 3 *m_x is positive homogeneous of degree 1, concave, and continuous.*

Proof The equality of $m_x(tp)$ and $tm_x(p)$ is immediate from the definitions when $t \geq 0$. This is positive homogeneity of degree 1. To prove concavity, let $p = tp' + (1 - t)p''$, $0 \leq t \leq 1$. For any $\varepsilon > 0$ there is $z \in R(x)$ such that $m_x(p) > pz - \varepsilon$. In other words, for this z and ε,

$$m_x(p) > tp'z + (1 - t)p''z - \varepsilon.$$

Therefore, by definition of m_x,

$$m_x(p) > tm_x(p') + (1 - t)m_x(p'') - \varepsilon.$$

Since this holds for all $\varepsilon > 0$, we have

$$m_x(p) \geq tm_x(p') + (1 - t)m_x(p'').$$

This is concavity for m_x.

For $p > 0$ the continuity of m_x follows from its concavity (Fenchel 1953, p. 75; Rockafellar 1970, p. 82). A general proof for $p \geq 0$ is given in appendix A. ∎

Figure 1.2 illustrates the concavity of m_x.

LEMMA 4 *For any $p > 0$ and $x \in C$, $m_x(p) = pw$, for some $w \in R(x)$.*

Proof $H(p,m)$ is closed as the intersection of closed sets (Berge 1963, p. 68). Consider the set $B_x = R(x) \cap H(p,px)$. B_x is the set of preferred points that cost no more than x. B_x is not empty, since it contains x (recall that we are using the term "preferred to" to mean "as good as or better than"). B_x is compact as the intersection of a closed set and a compact set. Therefore pz assumes its minimum value at some $w \in B_x$ (Berge 1963, p. 69). ∎

If $p > 0$ does not hold, the infimum that defines $m_x(p)$ may not be attained as figure 1.3 illustrates.

LEMMA 5 *If $p > 0$, $H(p,m)$ is compact. If $H(p,m)$ is not empty, $f(p,m)$ is not empty.*

Proof Consider $B_x^v \equiv R(x_v) \cap H(p,m)$, $v = 1, \cdots, k$. Since the relation $\mathscr{R}$ is complete and transitive, by assumption 3, there is a function $v(j)$ such that $B_{x_{v(1)}} \subset B_{x_{v(2)}} \subset \cdots \subset B_{x_{v(k)}}$, where $v(j)$ maps $\{1, \cdots, k\}$ onto itself. In other words, the sets B_{x_v} are nested. Therefore $\bigcap_{v=1}^{k} B_{x_v} =$

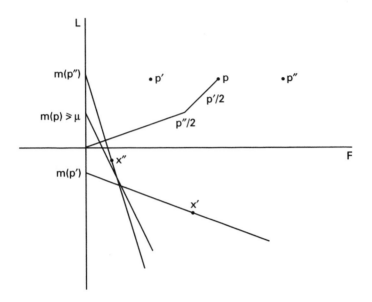

Figure 1.2
Given the values of $m(p')$ and $m(p'')$ the smallest possible value for $m(p)$ is μ. The consumption bundles x' and x'' are indifferent.

$B_{x_{v(1)}} \neq \emptyset$. Thus any finite subset of the collection $\{B_x\}$ for $x \in H(p,m)$ has a nonempty intersection. Since $H(p,m)$ is compact, $\bigcap_x B_x$ for $x \in H(p,m)$ is not empty (Berge 1963, p. 69). However, y in this intersection implies that $z \notin H(p,m)$ if $z\mathscr{P}y$, so $y \in f(p,m)$. Also $z \in H(p,m)$ and z not in this intersection implies that $y\mathscr{P}z$ and $y \in f(p,m)$, so $z \notin f(p,m)$. Thus $f(p,m) = \bigcap B_x$ over all $x \in H(p,m)$ and $f(p,m) \neq \emptyset$. ∎

In order to state the next three lemmas, it is convenient to introduce two assumptions that are only made when they are explicitly mentioned.

ASSUMPTION 5   Local better point. Given $x \in C$, let U be an arbitrary neighborhood of x. There is $x' \in U \cap C$ with $x'\mathscr{P}x$.

ASSUMPTION 6   Local cheaper point. Given $x \in C$ and $p \geq 0$, $p \neq 0$, let U be an arbitrary neighborhood of x. There is $x' \in U \cap C$ and $px' < px$.

Assumption 5 is an assumption of local nonsatiation for a particular consumption bundle x. Assumption 6 says for a particular commodity bundle x and a particular price vector p there is a possible consumption that is nearby and cheaper. Now we may state

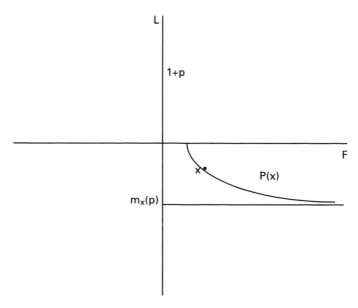

Figure 1.3
The infimum of pz is not attained over $P(x)$.

LEMMA 6 *If assumption 5 holds for $x \in f(p,m)$, then $px = m$. If assumption 5 holds for all $z \in f(p,m)$ and $x \in f(p,m)$, then $px = m_x(p)$.*

Proof The definition of $f(p,m)$ implies $px \leq m$. Suppose $px < m$. Then there is a neighborhood U of x such that $z \in U \cap C$ implies $pz < m$. Therefore, by assumption 5, there is $w \mathscr{P} x$ and $pw < m$. This contradicts the definition of $f(p,m)$, so $px = m$. If there were z with $z \mathscr{R} x$ and $pz < m$, then by a repetition of the preceding argument there is $w \mathscr{P} z$ and $pw < m$. Then $w \mathscr{P} x$ by lemma 1. This contradicts the definition of $f(p,m)$. Therefore $m = m_x(p)$. ∎

Lemma 6 says that local nonsatiation at a point $x = f(p,m)$ of the demand set implies that all income is spent and that local nonsatiation throughout the demand set implies that income m is minimal for the level of preference achieved. We next establish conditions under which purchases made at income levels $m_x(p)$ lie in the indifference set containing x. Recall $x \mathscr{I} y$ if and only if $x \mathscr{R} y$ and $y \mathscr{R} x$.

LEMMA 7   *Let $z \in f(p, m_x(p))$. Suppose that assumption 6 is satisfied at (z, p) and $p > 0$. Then zIx.*

Proof   By definition of f,

$$pz \le m_x(p). \tag{1}$$

By lemma 4, since $p > 0$, there is $w \in R(x)$ for which $pw = m_x(p)$. But by definition of f, $w\mathscr{P}z$ does not hold. Then, by definition of $\mathscr{P}$, either $w\mathscr{R}z$ does not hold or $z\mathscr{R}w$ holds. However, by completeness, if $w\mathscr{R}z$ does not hold, $z\mathscr{R}w$ must hold. Also $w \in R(x)$ implies $w\mathscr{R}x$. Therefore, by transitivity, $z\mathscr{R}x$.

By assumption 6 there is a sequence $\{z^s\}$, $z^s \in C$, and $z^s \to z$, such that

$$pz^s < pz. \tag{2}$$

Together (1) and (2) imply $pz^s < m_x(p)$, so $z^s \notin R(x)$. Thus by completeness $x\mathscr{R}z^s$. Since by assumption 4 the preference relation is closed, $x\mathscr{R}z$. This together with $z\mathscr{R}x$ implies $z\mathscr{I}x$.   ■

Lemma 7 shows that it is the assumption of a local cheaper point that leads bundles demanded at minimum cost $m_x(p)$ to lie in the indifference set for x. See figure 1.4. This fact plays a critical role in two later proofs, the proof that a Pareto optimum may be realized as a competitive equilibrium, and the proof that a competitive equilibrium exists.

Let $\mathbf{R}_{++}^n = \{p \in \mathbf{R}^n \mid p > 0\}$. We define the correspondence $f_x : \mathbf{R}_{++}^n \to C$ by

$$f_x(p) \equiv f(p, m_x(p)).$$

Let $z \in f_x(p)$. Over a neighborhood of p for which $f_x(p)$ satisfies assumption 6, $f_x(p)$ is a *compensated demand correspondence*. The correspondence $f_x(p)$ associates prices with bundles in the indifference set of x, which may be demanded at those prices given appropriate incomes. Of course, some bundles in $I(x)$ may not be bought at any prices and incomes if the sets $R(x)$ are not convex. Also if the indifference set is thick, some bundles that are indifferent with x may be too expensive to buy at $m_x(p)$. We may now approach the proof of the major theorems on demand. When $f(p, m)$ or $f_x(p)$ are single element sets over a neighborhood, f and f_x may be regarded as ordinary functions, and they may have derivatives over the neighborhood.

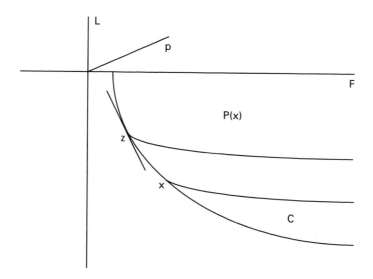

Figure 1.4
Although $z \in f(p, m_x(p))$, z is preferred to x. However assumption 5 is not met.

LEMMA 8   *Suppose $p > 0$ and assumption 5 holds at $f_x(p)$. Then, if the derivatives exist,*

$$p \cdot \left(\frac{\partial f_x(p)}{\partial p_i}\right) = 0, \qquad i = 1, \cdots, n.$$

Proof   We may assume that f_x is a function. Then there is $z = f_x(p)$. By lemma 4, there is $w \in R(x)$ such that $pw = m_x(p)$. I claim that $z \in R(x)$. Suppose not. Then $x \mathscr{P} z$. Since $w \mathscr{R} x$ and $x \mathscr{P} z$, it follows that $w \mathscr{P} z$. Since $pw = m_x(p)$ and $w \mathscr{P} z$, z cannot be a value of $f_x(p)$. This is a contradiction. Therefore $z \in R(x)$.

Let $y = f_x(q)$. For q near p, we have that $q > 0$, so $y \in R(x)$ by lemma 4 also. By definition of $f_x(p)$, $pz \leq m_x(p)$. On the other hand, $y \in R(x)$ implies that

$$m_x(p) \leq py = p \cdot f_x(q).$$

But lemma 6 implies $pz = m_x(p)$. Thus $pz = p \cdot f_x(p) = \min p \cdot f_x(q)$ for q in a neighborhood of p. Then, if the derivatives exist, it follows from the necessary conditions for a minimum that

$$\frac{\partial(p \cdot f_x(q))}{\partial q_i} = p \cdot \frac{\partial f_x(q)}{\partial q_i} = 0, \qquad i = 1, \cdots, n,$$

at $q = p$.   ■

LEMMA 9   *Suppose that $p > 0$, and assumption 5 holds at $f_x(p)$. If the derivatives exist, $\partial m_x(p)/\partial p_i = f_{xi}(p)$, and $\partial f_{xi}(p)/\partial p_j = \partial^2 m_x(p)/\partial p_j \partial p_i$, $i, j = 1, \cdots, n$.*

Proof   The lemma is implied by the following series of equalities

$$\frac{\partial m_x(p)}{\partial p_i} = \frac{\partial(p \cdot f_x(p))}{\partial p_i} = f_{xi}(p) + p \cdot \frac{\partial f_x(p)}{\partial p_i} = f_{xi}(p).$$

The last equality is justified by lemma 8. As this formula suggests, the existence of the first partial derivatives of m_x at p requires that f_x be single valued there but not that it have partial derivatives there.   ■

Figure 1.5 illustrates the proof of lemma 8. The first basic fact about demand correspondences is their homogeneity.

LEMMA 10   *The demand correspondence $f(p, m)$ is positively homogeneous of 0 degree in (p, m). The compensated demand correspondence $f_x(p)$ is positively homogeneous of 0 degree in p.*

Proof   The homogeneity of $f(p, m)$ is immediate from the definitions. For $f_x(p)$ we have the following series of equalities

$$f_x(p) = f(p, m_x(p)) = f(tp, tm_x(p)) = f(tp, m_x(tp)) = f_x(tp)$$

for all $t > 0$. The second equality uses the first part of the lemma and the third equality uses lemma 3.   ■

The more subtle results of demand theory for a compensated demand function are contained in the first theorem. Define the *n by n substitution matrix $S_x(p)$* by $S_x(p) = [\partial f_{xi}(p)/\partial p_j]$, $i, j = 1, \cdots, n$.

THEOREM 1   *On assumptions 1 to 5, for any $x \in C$, $S_x(p)$ exists for almost all $p > 0$. Moreover*

i. *$S_x(p)$ is symmetric.*

ii. *$z^T S_x(p)z$ is negative semidefinite.*

iii. *$p^T S_x(p) = 0$ and $S_x(p)p = 0$.*

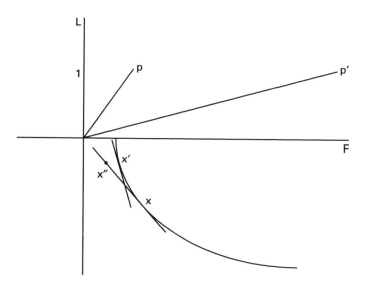

Figure 1.5
$p(x'' - x) = 0$ and $p(x' - x)$ converges to 0 as x' converges to x. Thus $p \cdot D_p f_x(p) = 0$.

Proof By lemma 9, $S_x(p) = [\partial^2 m_x(p)/\partial p_j \partial p_i]$ when the derivatives exist. By lemma 3, $m_x(p)$ is concave. Therefore the second differential of $m_x(p)$ exists almost everywhere in the interior of the positive orthant (Fenchel 1953, p. 142; Alexandroff 1939). By Young's theorem, the existence of the second differential implies that

$$\frac{\partial^2 m_x(p)}{\partial p_i \partial p_j} = \frac{\partial^2 m_x(p)}{\partial p_j \partial p_i},$$

or $S_x(p)$ is symmetric. (For the case where the second derivatives are continuous in a neighborhood, see Wilson 1911, p. 102.) The concavity of $m_x(p)$ from lemma 3 implies that the second differential is negative semidefinite. Finally (iii) follows from lemma 8 and (i). Of course, (iii) may also be derived from lemma 10 and (i). ∎

The fundamental theorem for the demand function $f(p, m)$, sometimes referred to as the Walrasian demand function, is that the price derivatives may be decomposed into a substitution effect and an income effect. Here the substitution effect is the derivative of the compensated demand function, which is sometimes referred to as the Hicksian demand function. It should be recalled that $f_x(p)$ is a compensated demand function if assumption 6 is met but not necessarily otherwise. It may happen that $f_x(p)$ is strictly preferred to x. See figure 1.4. The decomposition is called the Slutsky relation for its discoverer (Samuelson 1947, p. 103).

THEOREM 2   *Let assumptions 1 through 5 hold at $f(p,m)$. If $p > 0$ and the derivatives exist, and $p > 0$,*

$$\frac{\partial f_{xi}(p)}{\partial p_j} = \frac{\partial f_i(p,m)}{\partial p_j} + f_j(p,m) \cdot \frac{\partial f_i(p,m)}{\partial m}, \qquad i,j = 1, \cdots, n,$$

where $x = f(p,m)$. If assumption 6 holds $f_x(p)$ is a compensated demand function.

Proof   By lemma 6, $px = m = m_x(p)$. By the definition

$$f_{xi}(p) \equiv f_i(p, m_x(p)). \tag{3}$$

Therefore

$$\frac{\partial f_{xi}(p)}{\partial p_j} = \frac{\partial f_i(p, m_x(p))}{\partial p_j}$$

$$= \frac{\partial f_i(p,m)}{\partial p_j} + \left(\frac{\partial f_i(p,m)}{\partial m}\right)\left(\frac{\partial m_x(p)}{\partial p_j}\right)$$

$$= \frac{\partial f_i(p,m)}{\partial p_j} + f_j(p,m)\left(\frac{\partial f_i(p,m)}{\partial m}\right),$$

where the derivatives are evaluated at $m = m_x(p)$.

The last equality is implied by lemma 9. That $f_x(p)$ is a compensated demand function when assumption 6 holds is implied by lemma 7.   ∎

Define the *gross substitution* matrix F, a function of p and m, by $F = [\partial f_i(p,m)/\partial p_j]$, $i,j = 1, \cdots, n$. Let $Y = [f_j(p,m) \cdot \partial f_i(p,m)/\partial m]$, $i,j = 1, \cdots, n$, be the matrix of income effects. Then the Slutsky relation may be expressed succinctly by $F = S - Y$, where it is understood that the matrices depend on p and m in the ways described. It is worth noting that negative semidefiniteness will hold for F on the subspace $(f(p))^{\perp}$ orthogonal to the demand vector, since on this subspace $Yx = 0$. As we will see later there is a generalization of this property to market demand so long as the number of consumers is smaller than the number of goods.

COROLLARY   *If the vector of price changes v lies in the orthogonal subspace of the demand vector $f(p,m)$, then $v^T F v \leq 0$. That is, F is negative semidefinite on this subspace.*

Proof   The corollary follows from the fact that $Yv = 0$.   ∎

The most striking feature of the direct approach to demand theory is the very great latitude given to the set of possible consumption bundles. For example, the theory is applicable to consumption sets containing indivisible goods. Of course, the derivatives of the demand for indivisible goods with respect to the prices will always be zero when they exist, but this does not interfere with the use of the matrices F, S, and Y, which may contain many nonzero entries for goods that are divisible.

1.2   Demand Theory without Transitivity

It may be thought that it is not reasonable to assume that the relation $\mathscr{R}$ is transitive, since such consistency is usually not observed in practice. Moreover the completeness of $\mathscr{R}$ may be called into question. On the other hand, if the consumer cannot compare two bundles, it seems quite reasonable to treat them as indifferent in his sight. However, indifference does not enter the definition of demand we are using. Thus it is sufficient to take the strict preference relation $\mathscr{P}$ as primitive and define the correspondence R by means of the correspondence P,

$$R(x) \equiv \{z \in C \mid \text{not } x \in P(z)\}.$$

We also define the correspondence L by

$$L(x) \equiv \{z \in C \mid x \in P(z)\}.$$

The value of the correspondence L at x is called the *lower section* of P at x.

Replace assumptions 1 through 4 in this section by

ASSUMPTION 7 C is not empty and C is convex, closed, and bounded from below.

ASSUMPTION 8   A binary relation is defined on C denoted by $\mathscr{P}$ and referred to as a relation of strict preference.

Let A be a set of points in R^n. Then *convex hull A* is the set of all convex combinations of members of A. That is, the set of all sums $t_1 x_1 + \cdots + t_n x_n$ in which $x_i \in A$, $t_i \geq 0$, $\sum t_i = 1$, where n is arbitrary.

ASSUMPTION 9 $x \notin$ convex hull $P(x)$.

ASSUMPTION 10   The correspondence P has open lower sections relative to C.

Note that $R(x)$ is the complement of $L(x)$ in C, and therefore $R(x)$ is closed.

We wish to prove with these assumptions that the demand correspondence $f(p,m)$ is not empty, a result due to Sonnenschein (1971). The new assumptions are weaker in that transitivity is dropped and continuity is weakened. However they are stronger by the introduction of convexity conditions. Denote by $K(A)$ the convex hull of a set A. We will need a lemma of Knaster, Kuratowski, and Mazurkiewicz (KKM) (Berge 1963, p. 172).

LEMMA 11   *Let $A = \{a_0, a_1, \cdots, a_r\}$ be an arbitrary collection of $r+1$ points in $\mathbf{R}^n$. Let $\{S_0, S_1, \cdots, S_r\}$ be a collection of closed sets, and $I = \{0, 1, \cdots, r\}$. Assume that for all $J \subset I$, the convex hull $K(\{a_i\}_{i \in J}) \subset \bigcup_{i \in J} S_i$, then $\bigcap_{i \in I} S_i \neq \emptyset$.*

THEOREM 3   *Under assumptions 7 through 10, the demand correspondence $f(p,m)$ is not empty for $p > 0$ and $H(p,m) \neq \emptyset$.*

Proof   Let $\{x_0, x_1, x_2, \cdots, x_r\}$ be an arbitrary set of $r+1$ points in $H(p,m)$. Let $I = \{0, 1, \cdots, r\}$. Let $J \subset I$. Define for $w \in H(p,m)$ the set $B_w = R(w) \cap H(p,m)$. This is the set of commodity bundles in $H(p,m)$ that are as good as w. Thus $z \notin B_w$ implies $w \mathscr{P} z$. I claim that

$$K(\{x_i\}_{i \in J}) \subset \bigcup_{i \in J} B_{x_i}. \tag{4}$$

Suppose not. Then there is $z \in K(\{x_i\}_{i \in J})$ such that $z \notin \bigcup_{i \in J} B_{x_i}$. But this implies $x_i \mathscr{P} z$ for all $i \in J$. Since $x_i \in P(z)$ for $i \in J$, we have $K(\{x_i\}_{i \in J}) \subset$ convex hull $P(x)$. Thus $z \in$ convex hull $P(z)$ in contradiction to the assumption 9. Therefore (4) holds. The B_{x_i} are closed as the intersections of closed sets. Apply the lemma to establish that $\bigcap_{i \in I} B_{x_i} \neq \emptyset$.

But $p > 0$ implies that $H(p, m)$ is bounded and thus compact by assumption 7. So $H(p, m)$ has the finite intersection property (Berge 1963, p. 69). Since B_z is closed for $z \in H(p, m)$, as an intersection of closed sets, and the x_i are arbitrarily chosen points of $H(p, m)$, the finite intersection property implies that $\bigcap_{z \in H(p,m)} B_z \neq \emptyset$. Let x lie in this intersection. Then $x \mathcal{R} z$ holds for all $z \in H(p, m)$, so $z \mathcal{P} x$ implies $z \notin H(p, m)$, and $x \in f(p, m)$ by the definition. ∎

The loss of transitivity has required a new and somewhat more difficult proof that the demand correspondence is well defined for $p > 0$. Also lemma 7 can no longer be proved, so $f_x(p)$ may not be characterized as a compensated demand function even though assumption 6 holds. Otherwise, the theory expounded in section 1.1 is unchanged. In particular, $f_x(p)$ is well defined for $p > 0$ since $R(x)$ is closed. We may remove the condition $p > 0$ if C is taken to be bounded and therefore compact.

1.3   The Classical Theory

In the classical theory, rather than a preference relation, the point of departure is a utility function $u(x)$ defined on the relevant part of the commodity space. Then the demand correspondence is derived by maximizing this function over the budget set $H(p, m)$. Often in the formal development the set of commodity bundles that the consumer can trade is assumed to be the positive orthant of $\mathbf{R}^n$. However, we will find that it is positive prices that permit the analysis to proceed, while commodity bundles that are traded can be allowed to contain negative quantities of goods, to represent goods that are provided by the consumer, as well as positive quantities to represent goods that are taken. On the other hand, the analysis is confined to the interior of C to avoid the complications that occur on the boundary. We will find in the classical approach one loses the advantages that come from the use of the concave function $m_x(p)$. To compensate for this loss, it is assumed that the commodities are divisible and that the utility function is quasiconcave. A continuous real-valued function g defined on $\mathbf{R}^n$ is quasiconcave if $g(x) = g(y)$ implies $g((x + y)/2) \geq g(x)$. It is strictly quasiconcave if this inequality is strict whenever $x \neq y$. In developing the classical theory we will use the following assumptions.

ASSUMPTION 11 (Free disposal)   The set of possible consumption bundles $C \subset \mathbf{R}^n$ is convex with a nonempty interior. Also C is closed and bounded from below. If $x \in C$, then $y \in C$ for $y \geq x$.

ASSUMPTION 12 (Monotonicity)   A utility function u is defined on C. We interpret $u(x) \geq u(y)$ to mean $x\mathcal{R}y$ and $u(x) > u(y)$ to mean $x\mathcal{P}y$. For any x and $y \in C$, $x \geq y$, and $x \neq y$ implies that $u(x) > u(y)$.

ASSUMPTIONS 13 (Smoothness)   The function u is continuous and strictly quasiconcave in C and at least twice continuously differentiable in the interior of C. Also $\partial u(x)/\partial x_i > 0$, $i = 1, \cdots, n$.

In section 1.1 we derived the function $m_x(p)$ from the preference relation $\mathcal{R}$ and used that function to derive theorems on demand. It is also possible to derive a utility function $u(x)$ from the relation $\mathcal{R}$ (Debreu 1954). Moreover, given some smoothness properties for $\mathcal{R}$, the function $u(x)$ will be continuously differentiable (Debreu 1972).

The classical definition of the demand correspondence $f(p,m)$ is

$$f(p,m) = \{x \mid x \in H(p,m) \text{ and } u(x) \geq u(y) \text{ for all } y \in H(p,m)\}.$$

Since $u(x)$ is strictly quasiconcave by assumption 13, the demand correspondence is single valued and defines a function. In the presence of a utility function this definition is equivalent to the definition given earlier.

LEMMA 12   *Under assumptions 11 through 13 the demand function $f(p,m)$ is well defined for $p > 0$ and $H(p,m) \neq \emptyset$.*

Proof   Since $H(p,m)$ is compact, by lemma 1.5, the supremum is attained for a continuous function (Berge 1963, p. 69). Since u is strictly quasiconcave the supremum is attained at a unique point. Thus $f(p,m)$ is well defined when $H(p,m)$ is not empty.   ∎

From the definition of $f(p,m)$ if x is the value of demand for a particular choice of p and m, the set $H(p,m)$ and the set $P(x)$ are disjoint. Therefore in the interior of C where the first derivative $Du(x)$ of u exists, for any variation z of x such that $pz = 0$, it must be that $x + z \notin P(x)$. Thus $Du(x) \cdot z \leq 0$. Since $-z$ is also a variation that remains in C, it follows that $Du(x) \cdot z = 0$ whenever $pz = 0$. This implies that $Du(x) = \lambda p$ for some real number λ. See proposition 1 in section 2.5. But monotonicity implies that λ is positive. This assumption also implies that all income is spent or $px = m$. Thus the following conditions must hold at a value x of $f(p, m)$ when x lies interior to C,

$$Du(x) - \lambda p = 0,$$

$$px - m = 0. \tag{5}$$

The fact that $x + z \notin P(x)$ for $pz = 0$ also implies that $Du(x) \cdot z + 1/2z \cdot D^2u(x) \cdot z \leq 0$ for $pz = 0$, where $D^2u(x)$ is the Hessian matrix of u and defines the second differential of u at x. Since $Du(x) \cdot z = 0$, this means that the quadratic form defined by $D^2u(x)$ is negative semidefinite on the hyperplane $H(p) = \{z \mid pz = 0\}$ when x is a value of $f(p, m)$ interior to C. If $D^2u(x)$ is continuous and negative definite on $H(p)$, we will say that x is a *regular value* of $f(p, m)$. Let $U = [u_{ij}]$. The *bordered Hessian* of u at $x = f(p, m)$ is given by $\begin{bmatrix} U & -p \\ -p^T & 0 \end{bmatrix}$, where $U = [u_{ij}]$, $i, j = 1, \cdots, n$, and $u_{ij} = \partial^2 u / \partial x_j \partial x_i$.

LEMMA 13   *If the Hessian matrix of u at x is negative definite on $H(p)$, where $x = f(p, m)$ for $p > 0$, the bordered Hessian of u at x is nonsingular.*

Proof   Let the Hessian matrix U be negative definite on $H(p)$. Suppose the bordered Hessian is singular. Then

$$\begin{bmatrix} U & -p \\ -p^T & 0 \end{bmatrix} \begin{pmatrix} z \\ \lambda \end{pmatrix} = 0 \qquad \text{for some} \quad \begin{pmatrix} z \\ \lambda \end{pmatrix} \neq 0. \tag{6}$$

Suppose $z \neq 0$. If $\lambda = 0$, then $[u_{ij}] \cdot z = 0$. Since $pz = 0$ from (6), this contradicts the assumption of a negative definite Hessian on $H(p)$. Thus we may set $\lambda = 1$. Then $[u_{ij}]z = p$ and $pz = 0$, so $z^T[u_{ij}]z = pz = 0$, which again contradicts the assumption that the Hessian is negative definite on $H(p)$ if $z \neq 0$. However, $z = 0$ implies $\lambda = 0$ from (6), which contradicts $(z \ \lambda) \neq 0$. Thus the bordered Hessian must be nonsingular. ∎

Lemma 13 allows us to prove that the demand function is smooth at regular values, a result that was not available under the weaker assumptions of section 1.1.

THEOREM 4   *Under assumptions 11 through 13, the demand function $f(p, m)$ has continuous first derivatives at regular values.*

Proof   Observe that the bordered Hessian is the Jacobian matrix of the equation system (5) when x and λ are the dependent variables. Let $x' =$

$f(p', m')$ be a regular value of f, and let λ' be the corresponding value of λ in equations (5). Then by the implicit function theorem (Dieudonné 1960, p. 265) there exist functions $h_i(p, m)$, $i = 1, \cdots, n$, and $h_0(p, m)$ defined over a neighborhood W of (p', m') such that (5) is satisfied for $x = h(p, m)$ and $\lambda = h_0(p, m)$ and $h(p', m') = x'$, $h_0(p', m') = \lambda'$. Moreover these functions have continuous first partial derivatives in W.

We must show that $h(p, m) \equiv f(p, m)$ for (p, m) in W. Consider $Du(x)$ for $x = h(p, m)$. Since u is strictly quasiconcave, $Du(x)$ strictly supports the convex set $R(x)$. That is, $Du(x) \cdot z > 0$ for $z \neq 0$ and $x + z \in R(x)$. This implies by (5) that $pz > 0$ for $x + z \in R(x)$. Since by (5) it also holds that $px = m$, the conditions are met for $x = f(p, m)$ by the definition of f. ∎

From the proof of Theorem 4 we know that conditions (5) are satisfied by the demand function in the neighborhood of a regular value. Therefore we may study the variation of demand with price and income by differentiating (5) totally. This gives

$$\begin{bmatrix} U & -p \\ -p^T & 0 \end{bmatrix} \begin{pmatrix} dx \\ d\lambda \end{pmatrix} = \begin{pmatrix} \lambda\, dp \\ x\, dp - dm \end{pmatrix}. \tag{7}$$

Therefore

$$\begin{pmatrix} dx \\ d\lambda \end{pmatrix} = \begin{bmatrix} S & -v \\ -v^T & w \end{bmatrix} \begin{bmatrix} \lambda I & 0 \\ x^T & -1 \end{bmatrix} \begin{pmatrix} dp \\ dm \end{pmatrix}, \tag{8}$$

where

$$\begin{bmatrix} S & -v \\ -v^T & w \end{bmatrix} = \begin{bmatrix} U & -p \\ -p^T & 0 \end{bmatrix}^{-1}. \tag{9}$$

Consider that

$$Du(x) \cdot dx = \sum_1^n \left(\frac{\partial u(x)}{\partial x_i} \right) dx_i = \lambda p\, dx \qquad \text{by (5).}$$

Since $m = px$ from monotonicity, differentiation gives

$$dm = p\, dx + x\, dp. \tag{10}$$

Therefore $Du(x) \cdot dx = \lambda p\, dx = 0$ implies $dm = x\, dp$. This is the compensation dm required to hold utility constant after the price change dp.

Substituting in (8), we find that $Du(x) \cdot dx = 0$ implies $dx = \lambda S\, dp$. As we have seen, $\lambda = 0$ is not possible if x is regular. Thus λS is the substitution matrix $[\partial f_{xi}(p)/\partial p_j]$, where f_x is the compensated demand function at x. Also by (8), $dp = 0$ implies $dx = v\, dm$, so v is the vector of derivatives of demand with respect to income $\partial f_i(p,m)/\partial m$. Multiplying the matrix on the left in (9) by its inverse on the right, we obtain $pv = 1$; that is, $p \cdot \partial f(p,m)/\partial m = 1$. Finally by (8) if we put $dm = 0$, we obtain

$$dx = \lambda S\, dp - (x\, dp)v,$$

which is the Slutsky relation of theorem 2 in matrix form.

The relations of theorem 1 are also implied by (8) for regular values of $f(p,m)$. We may prove

LEMMA 14   *If x is a regular value of f at (p,m), the substitution matrix S at (p,m) is symmetric and satisfies $p^T S = 0$. Also S is negative semidefinite of rank $n - 1$.*

Proof   The symmetry of S is immediate from the symmetry of U. To see that $Sp = 0$, consider

$$\begin{bmatrix} S & -v \\ -v^T & w \end{bmatrix} \cdot \begin{bmatrix} U & -p \\ -p^T & 0 \end{bmatrix} = \begin{bmatrix} I_n & 0 \\ 0 & 1 \end{bmatrix}. \tag{11}$$

Then $p^T S = 0$ follows by symmetry of S. This leaves the negative semidefiniteness and rank of S to be proved.

From (11) we derive $SU + v \cdot p^T = I_n$. Thus $SUS + v \cdot p^T S = S$. Since $p^T S = 0$, we have $SUS = S$. Also $p^T Sy = 0$ for all $y \in \mathbf{R}^n$. Since U is negative definite on all $x \neq 0$ that satisfy $px = 0$, we find that $y^T Sy = y^T SUSy \leq 0$, In other words, S is negative semidefinite.

The bordered substitution matrix is nonsingular as the inverse of the bordered Hessian. However, the bordered substitution matrix may be expanded by its last row and last column where $v_i v_j$ for $i, j < n$ multiplies the minor of S with the ith column and the jth row eliminated, with an appropriate sign, and w multiplies $|S|$. We know from lemma 13 that the bordered Hessian is nonsingular. Also we have proved above that $|S| = 0$. If all the $n - 1$ minors of S were 0, it would be implied by the expansion described that the bordered substitution matrix was also 0. Since this would be a contradiction, some $n - 1$ minor is not 0 and therefore S has rank $n - 1$.   ∎

COROLLARY $z^T S z = 0$ *if and only if* $z = \alpha p$.

Proof   Since S is symmetric, the characteristic vectors on the left are transposes of characteristic vectors on the right with the same characteristic values. Moreover the characteristic vectors belonging to different characteristic vectors must be orthogonal, and those belonging to the same characteristic value may be chosen to be orthogonal. Let $z = \sum_{i=1}^{n} \alpha_i z_i$, where the z_i are the orthogonal characteristic vectors. Then $z^T S z = \sum_{i=1}^{n} \alpha_i^2 \beta_i z_i^2$, where the β_i are the characteristic values. Since S is negative semidefinite, the β_i are nonpositive. Therefore $z^T S z = 0$ if and only if $\alpha_i^2 \beta_i = 0$ for all i. But $\alpha_i^2 \beta_i = 0$ if and only if $\alpha_i \beta_i = 0$, or $S z = \sum_{i=1}^{n} \alpha_i \beta_i z_i = 0$. Since p is the only characteristic vector, except for nonzero multiples of p, with the characteristic value 0, it follows that $z^T S z = 0$ if and only if $z = \alpha p$.   ∎

A remarkable condition has been found by Mitiushin and Polterovich (see Mas-Colell 1991, p. 282) that implies that the gross substitution matrix $F = [\partial f_i(p,m)/\partial p_j]$ is negative definite. In the language of choice under uncertainty, the condition is that the coefficient of risk aversion, which is defined as $-x^T [u_{ij}(x)] x / x D u(x)$, be less than 4.

THEOREM 5   *Make assumptions 11 through 13. If* $-x^T [u_{ij}(x)] x / x D u(x) < 4$ *for all* $x \in$ *interior* C, $x > 0$, *where* $x = f(p,m)$, *then* $[\partial f_i(p,m)/\partial p_j]$ *is negative definite.*

Proof   See appendix E.   ∎

Note that income is held constant as prices are changed in theorem 5. If all consumers have their coefficient of relative risk aversion less than 4 and the incomes of all consumers remain constant, the market demand function satisfies the Law of Demand, since the negative definite property for matrices is preserved under summation. Mas-Colell points out that if the income of the ith consumer is derived from the sale of initial resources ω_i and $\omega_i = \alpha_i \omega$ where ω is the vector of total resources in the economy and $0 \le \alpha_i \le 1$, then the individual consumer has a constant income if the total income of consumers is constant. Thus under these conditions the Law of Demand holds for the market demand function between price vectors p and q if all consumers satisfy the condition on relative risk aversion and $p\omega = q\omega$.

When a utility function is available, the minimum cost approach to demand theory can be rephrased with $m_x(p)$ replaced by $m_u(p)$ and $u = u(x)$. $m_u(p)$ is defined by

$$m_u(p) \equiv \inf pz \qquad \text{for } u(z) \geq u.$$

We may also write the compensated demand function as $f_u(p) = f(p, m_u(p))$. Under the assumptions of this section assumptions 5 and 6 are always met in the interior of C. Thus lemmas 6 and 7 hold there. Also the differentiability conditions of lemmas 8 and 9 hold at regular values of $f(p, m)$ by theorem 4. Finally theorem 4 implies that the conditions of theorems 1 and 2 are met at regular values.

It is useful to define an *indirect utility function* $v(p, m)$ by

$$v(p, m) \equiv u(f(p, m)).$$

Demand theory using the indirect utility function was developed by Roy (1947). A relation often referred to as Roy's identity is proved in

LEMMA 15   *Assume that $x = f(p, m)$ is a regular value, then*

$$f_i(p, m) = -\frac{\partial v(p, m)/\partial p_i}{\partial v(p, m)/\partial m}, \qquad i = 1, \cdots, n.$$

Proof   By the definitions $u \geq v(p, m_u(p))$ must hold. Since the cheaper point assumption holds, if the inequality were strict, continuity of u would imply that $m_u(p)$ was not minimal. Therefore equality must hold. By theorem 4, regularity allows differentiation of both sides with respect to p_i with u constant. This gives for $m = m_u(p)$

$$0 = \frac{\partial v(p, m)}{\partial p_i} + \frac{\partial v(p, m)}{\partial m} \cdot \frac{\partial m_u(p)}{\partial p_i}. \tag{12}$$

Also $p \cdot \partial f_u(p)/\partial p_i = 0$ by the analogue of lemma 8, and $m_u(p) = p \cdot f_u(p)$ by definition. Therefore

$$\frac{\partial m_u(p)}{\partial p_i} = f_{ui}(p) + p \cdot \frac{\partial f_u(p)}{\partial p_i} = f_{ui}(p). \tag{13}$$

From (12) and (13) we obtain, for $m = m_u(p)$,

$$\frac{\partial v(p, m)}{\partial p_i} + \left(\frac{\partial v(p, m)}{\partial m}\right) \cdot f_{ui}(p) = 0.$$

Since $m = m_u(p)$, we may replace $f_{ui}(p)$ by $f_i(p, m)$ to obtain

$$\frac{\partial v(p,m)}{\partial p_i} + \left(\frac{\partial v(p,m)}{\partial m}\right) \cdot f_i(p,m) = 0. \qquad \blacksquare$$

This is essentially the result obtained earlier (see lemma 9) that the rate of compensation per unit price change that will hold utility constant when the price of the ith commodity changes is the quantity of that commodity bought. However, it is now expressed in terms of the indirect utility function.

1.4   The Method of Revealed Preference

A further approach to the theory of demand is to postulate demand functions themselves as the objects given and to impose consistency conditions on them. This approach was pioneered by Samuelson (1947). The demand function $f(p,m)$ is defined for all (p,m) such that $p \in \mathbf{R}^n$, $p > 0$, and $m \in \mathbf{R}^1$ with $m > \min px$ for $x \in C$. We will make

ASSUMPTION 14   If $x = f(p,m)$ and $y = f(q,m')$, then $y \neq x$ and $px \geq py$ implies $qx > qy$.

ASSUMPTION 15   The demand function $f(p,m)$ is continuous.

ASSUMPTION 16   If $x = f(p,m)$, then $px = m$.

Assumption 14 is called the Weak Axiom of Revealed Preference. It was stated by Wald (1934–35) and used to prove a theorem on existence of competitive equilibrium. Let $\Delta x = y - x$ and $\Delta p = q - p$. Then the weak axiom may be stated alternatively as

$$p \cdot \Delta x \leq 0 \quad \text{implies} \quad (p + \Delta p) \cdot \Delta x < 0 \qquad \text{if } \Delta x \neq 0. \tag{14}$$

LEMMA 16   *Assumptions 14 and 16 imply that $f(p,m)$ is positive homogeneous of 0 degree.*

Proof   Let $q = \alpha p$ and $m' = \alpha m$, where $\alpha > 0$. Then $\alpha px = \alpha m = m' = qy = \alpha py$ by assumption 16. Therefore $px = py$, which implies $qx = qy$. This contradicts assumption 14 unless $x = y$. $\qquad \blacksquare$

Define a relation $\mathscr{D}$ by $x\mathscr{D}y$ if and only if there is a price vector p and an income m such that $x = f(p,m)$ and $px \geq py$. The weak axiom amounts to assuming that $\mathscr{D}$ is antisymmetric. That is, $x\mathscr{D}y$ and $y\mathscr{D}x$

implies $x = y$. A weak weak axiom may also be stated. Define $\mathscr{D}'$ by $x\mathscr{D}'y$ if and only if there exists a price vector p and an income m such that $px > py$. Then the weak weak axiom states that $x\mathscr{D}'y$ implies $\sim y\mathscr{D}'x$; that is, $\mathscr{D}'$ is asymmetric.

We may define a function in the theory of revealed preference analogous to the compensated demand function. Suppose $x = f(p,m)$. Define $\bar{f}_x$ by

$$\bar{f}_x(q) \equiv f(q, qx).$$

The function $\bar{f}_x$ describes the offer surface from x, a construction often used in the theory of international trade. This contrasts with the function f_x defined earlier, which under classical assumptions takes its values on the indifference surface through x. In the theory of revealed preference the indifference surface is not defined. However, if the function $\bar{f}_x$ is applied in the classical theory, at the price p where $x = f(p,m) = f_x(p) = \bar{f}_x(p)$, the offer surface and the indifference surface are tangent. Sometimes $\bar{f}_x$ is referred to as the *overcompensated demand function* and its use to derive a Slutsky relation is referred to as the method of overcompensation. Figure 1.6 illustrates the relationship between the compensated and the overcompensated demand functions. Let the n by n matrix $\bar{S}_x(p) = \partial\bar{f}_x(q)/\partial q$ evaluated at $q = p$. Recall that $x = f(p,m)$. That is, if the derivatives exist $\bar{S}_x(p) = [\partial\bar{f}_i(q, qx)/\partial q_j]_{q=p}$ where $x = f(p, px)$.

THEOREM 6   *Make assumptions 15 through 16. When the matrix $\bar{S}_x(p)$ is well defined, it satisfies*

i. $\bar{S}_x(p)$ *is negative quasi-semidefinite with rank* $\leq n - 1$.

ii. $p^T \bar{S}_x(p) = 0$ *and* $\bar{S}_x(p)p = 0$.

Proof   Let $y = f(q, qx)$ and $x = f(p, px)$. Then $qx = qy$ or $q \cdot \Delta y = 0$. By the weak axiom (14), $q \cdot \Delta y = 0$ implies $(q + \Delta q) \cdot \Delta y < 0$, provided that $\Delta y \neq 0$. Therefore $\Delta q \cdot \Delta y = \Delta p \cdot \Delta x < 0$ for $\Delta x \neq 0$. Let $\Delta p = \delta z$ where $\delta > 0$. As $\delta \to 0$, $\Delta x \to (\partial f(p, px)/\partial p)\Delta p$ and $\Delta p \cdot \Delta x \to \delta^2 z^T (\partial f(p, px)/\partial p)z < 0$, when $(\partial f(p, px)/\partial p)z \neq 0$. However, the positive homogeneity of $f(p, px)$ of zero degree by lemma 16 implies that $(\partial f(p, px)/\partial p)z = 0$ if $z = \alpha p$. (See appendix C.) Since z is arbitrary, $\partial f(p, px)/\partial p = \partial\bar{f}_x(p)/\partial p = \bar{S}_x(p)$ is negative quasi-semidefinite with rank $\leq n - 1$. (The prefix "quasi" means that the matrix is not required to be symmetric.)

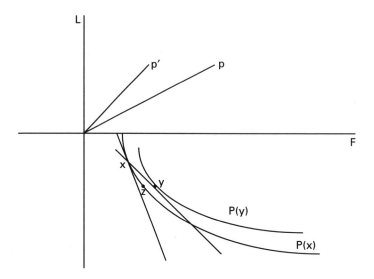

Figure 1.6
$y = f(p', p'x)$ and $y \in P(x)$. $z = f(p', m_x(p'))$ and $z \in I(x)$. $x = f(p, px)$.

Consider the offer curve from x, that is, $\bar{f}_x(q) \equiv f(q, qx)$, where $x = f(p, px)$. Putting $m = qx$, we have

$$\frac{\partial \bar{f}_{xi}(q)}{\partial q_j} = \frac{\partial f_i(q, m)}{\partial q_j} + \frac{\partial f_i(q, m)}{\partial m} \cdot f_j(p, px). \tag{15}$$

Differentiating the budget equation $q \cdot f(q, m) = m$ with m constant gives $q \cdot \partial f(q, m)/\partial q_j = -f_j(q, m)$. Also differentiating the budget equation with q constant gives $q \cdot \partial f(q, m)/\partial m = 1$. Then multiplying (15) through by q_i and summing over $i = 1, \cdots, n$ gives $q \cdot [\partial \bar{f}_x(q)/\partial q_j] = -f_j(q, m) + f_j(p, px) = 0$ at $q = p$. In other words, $p^T \cdot \bar{S}_x(p) = 0$. As mentioned earlier, $\bar{S}_x(p) \cdot p = 0$ is implied by the positive homogeneity of $f(q, qx)$. ∎

Note that the properties of $\bar{S}_x(p)$ (where $x = f(p, px)$) correspond to those of $S_x(p)$, when a preference order is present (where $x = f(p, m_x(p))$), as stated in theorem 1 except that $\bar{S}_x(p)$ has not been proved to be symmetrical nor of rank $n - 1$ for regular values. In fact, as Gale (1960) showed by example, $\bar{S}_x(p)$ may not be symmetrical). However, there is an important difference between $S_x(p)$ and $\bar{S}_x(p)$. The substitution matrix $S_x(p)$ is defined for any $p > 0$ and any $x \in C$ for which the derivatives exist, while $\bar{S}_x(p)$ has been defined for any $p > 0$ and $x = f(p,px)$ for which the derivatives exist. A broader definition of $\bar{S}$ does not appear to have any uses. On the other hand, when both $\bar{S}_x(p)$ and $S_x(p)$ are well defined and $x = f(p,px)$, they are identical. This is clear from a comparison of (15) with Theorem 2. In this case $\bar{S}$ is symmetric. It may be shown that the converse is also true. If $\bar{S}_x(p)$ is symmetric for all $p > 0$ then a relation $\mathcal{R}$ exists satisfying assumptions 1, 2, 3, and 4, from which $f(p,m)$ may be derived so that $S_x(p)$ is well defined (Hurwicz and Uzawa 1971).

1.5 Market Demand Functions

The market demand function is the sum of the individual demand functions over the set of consumers who are present in the market. Properly the individual demand function should be written $f^h(p,m)$ with a superscript to identify the consumer to whom it belongs. The superscript has been omitted in the previous discussion to lighten the notation. Suppose there are H consumers in the market indexed from 1 to H. Then the *market demand function* may be written $f(p,m^1,\cdots,m^H)$, where $f(p,m^1,\cdots,m^H) = \sum_{h=1}^{H} f^h(p,m^h)$. The properties we have found for demand functions apply to individual demand functions. It is important to ask to what extent these or similar properties may be found for market demand functions.

Let $\tilde{x} = (x^1,\cdots,x^H)$. If a *compensated market demand function* $f_{\tilde{x}}(p)$ is defined as the sum of the individual compensated demand functions $f_{\tilde{x}}^h(p)$, it will have the same properties that the individual compensated demand functions have. That is, the Jacobian, when it exists, will be symmetric and negative semidefinite, since the sum of matrices with these properties retain them. Similarly the Jacobian premultiplied or postmultiplied by the price vector gives 0. These results follow from our defining compensation for the market as compensation for each consumer in the market.

On the other hand, the properties of the Walrasian demand function for the market differ significantly from those for the individual consumer. The individual demand functions, if they are differentiable, must satisfy the Slutsky equation, that is, the equation of theorem 2, and this equation restricts the set of functions that may be individual demand functions.

Otherwise, the individual demand functions have been shown to be positive homogeneous of zero degree in lemma 10 and to satisfy Walras' law in lemma 6. It is clear that these properties will also hold of the sum of individual demand functions and therefore of the market demand function. However, we will see that the restrictions based on the Slutsky equation are removed as the number of consumers increases. That is, the dimensionality of the subspace on which the Jacobian of the Walrasian demand functions must be negative semidefinite is reduced.

Suppose there are N goods and H consumers where $N > H$. Assume $p > 0$ and that the individual demand functions are continuously differentiable. Then summing the Slutsky equations over the set of consumers gives

$$\frac{\partial f_i(p, m^1, \cdots, m^H)}{\partial p_j} = \sum_{h=1}^{H} \partial f_i^h(p, m^h) / \partial p_j$$

$$= \sum_{h=1}^{H} \partial f_i^h(p) / \partial p_j - \sum_{h=1}^{H} f_j^h(p, m^h) \cdot \partial f_i^h(p, m^h) / \partial m^h,$$

or

$$F(p, m^1, \cdots, m^H) = S(p, m^1, \cdots, m^H) - \left[\sum_{h=1}^{H} f_j^h f_{im}^h \right],$$

where $f_i^h(p)$ is the compensated demand function evaluated at $x^h = f^h(p, m^h)$. Consider an M-tuple of n-dimensional vectors $(v^1, \cdots, v^M)$ that are chosen to span the subspace orthogonal to the subspace spanned by the $f^h(p, m^h)$, $h = 1, \cdots, H$. M is greater than or equal to $N - H$, and $v^k f^h = 0$ for $k = 1, \cdots, M$ and all h. That is, income effects are 0 for price changes in this subspace. Let $A = [v^1, \cdots, v^M]$. A is a matrix of order $N \times M$. Then $[\sum_h f_j^h f_{im}^h] \cdot A = 0$ where the product matrix is $N \times M$. Let F and S now represent sums of the Jacobian matrices of the respective individual demand functions over the set of consumers. Thus over this subspace $A^T F A = A^T S A$, which is $M \times M$. Since S is symmetric, so is $A^T S A$. Thus $A^T F A$ is symmetric. Since S is negative semidefinite, $A^T F A$ is negative semidefinite. In other words, the Jacobian F of the Walrasian market demand functions, with prices as the independent variables and incomes fixed, is negative semidefinite on the subspace spanned by the v^k

which has dimension at least $N - H$. If the f^h are linearly independent, the dimension of the orthogonal subspace is exactly $N - H$. If there is only one consumer, the subspace has dimension $N - 1$. However, the requirement that F be negative semidefinite on a nontrivial subspace remains until the number of consumers with linearly independent demands is at least equal to N. We may state (Diewert 1977)

THEOREM 7 *Make assumptions 1 through 5 for individual demand functions. Let the distribution of income be given. When the Jacobian of the market demand functions with respect to prices exists, it is negative semidefinite on a subspace of dimension $N - \hat{H}$, where N is the number of goods and $\hat{H}$ is the number of consumers with linearly independent demands.*

Note that in the case of a single consumer, the price change leaves the consumer on his offer locus (curve in the case of two goods) which is tangent to the consumer's indifference locus at the vector of quantities demanded. For the case of many consumers, the price change leaves all consumers on their offer loci. Thus all changes in quantities demanded are substitution effects. If the loci are translated so that the vectors of quantities demanded are carried to the origin, we find that the quantity changes then lie in the intersection of the translated offer loci. Except for special cases, the dimensionality of this intersection will be $N - M$.

If additional assumptions are made on the variety of preference orders or on the distribution of income, it may be possible to restrict further the functions that may be market demand functions. A result of this type has been reached by Hildenbrand (1983). One of his goals is to discover conditions that imply that F is negative semidefinite for all positive price vectors. In particular, the diagonal elements of F will be negative, so demand for the ith good as a function of the price of the ith good will fall as the price rises. This is the condition that demand curves slope downward, which is a familiar assumption in partial equilibrium economic analysis. It is often referred to as the Law of Demand.

To simplify the mathematics and to reach an exact result, we will use a continuous distribution of income and demand rather than a discrete set of consumers. The distribution may be thought of as the limit of a histogram as the number of consumers increases without limit, or as the approximation of a histogram when the number of consumers is large. Also the consumers are assumed to have the same preference order. However, this is slightly less restrictive than it seems, since each set of consumers with a given preference order may be considered separately.

Let $P = \{p \in \mathbf{R}^n \mid p > 0\}$. Let $f(p,m)$ be a continuously differentiable demand function defined on $P \times R_+$. The conditions on preferences that lead to such a demand function will be examined more closely in chapter 2. However, the assumptions made for the classical theory in section 1.3 would be appropriate together with the assumption that $f(p,m)$ is regular for all $(p,m) \in P \times R_{++}$. Let ρ be the density of an income distribution with positive mean which is continuous and nonincreasing. The density ρ maps a closed interval $[0,b]$ into R_{++}. Also $\int_0^b \rho(m)\,dm = 1$ and $\int_0^b m\rho(m)\,dm > 0$. Since the income distribution is fixed, market demand depends only on prices. Define market demand $f(p)$ by $f(p) = \int_0^b f(p,m)\rho(m)\,dm$ for $p \in P$.

THEOREM 8   *With these assumptions*:

i. *For every $p \in P$ the Jacobian matrix $[f_{ij}(p)]$ is negative quasi-definite.*

ii. *For every p and q in P with $p \neq q$, $(p - q) \cdot (f(p) - f(q)) < 0$, which implies the weak axiom of revealed preference.*

Proof of (i)   Let $Sf(p,m)$ be the Jacobian of the compensated demand function at (p,m). Let $A(p,m)$ be $[a_{ij}] = [(\partial f_i(p,m)/\partial m) \cdot f_j(p,m)]$, the matrix of income effects at (p,m). Let $Jf(p,m) = [f_{ij}(p,m)]$ the gross substitution matrix. Then $Jf(p,m) = Sf(p,m) - A(p,m)$ by the Slutsky equation. By Leibniz's rule (Dieudonné 1960, p. 172) the Jacobian of the market demand function $f(p)$ is $Jf(p) = \int_0^b (Sf(p,m) - A(p,m)) \cdot \rho(m)\,dm$. But lemma 14 implies that $v^T(Sf(p,m))v < 0$ for $v \neq tp$ for any t by regularity of f. Therefore $v^T(\int_0^b Sf(p,m)\,dm)v < 0$ for $v \neq tp$.

To finish the proof, we must show that $A(p) = \int_0^b A(p,m)\rho(m)\,dm$ is positive quasi-semidefinite and that $v^T A(p)v > 0$ if $v = tp$ for some $t > 0$. But

$$v^T A(p)v = \sum_i \sum_j v_i v_j \int_0^b \left(\frac{\partial f_i(p,m)}{\partial m}\right) f_j(p,m)\rho(m)\,dm$$

$$= \int_0^b \left(\sum_i \left(\frac{\partial f_i(p,m)}{\partial m}\right) v_i\right) \left(\sum_j f_j(p,m)v_j\right) \rho(m)\,dm$$

$$= \int_0^b \left(\frac{\partial f(p,m)}{\partial m} \cdot v \right) (f(p,m) \cdot v) \rho(m) \, dm$$

$$= \frac{1}{2} \int_0^b \left(\frac{\partial (f(p,m) \cdot v)^2}{\partial m} \right) \rho(m) \, dm.$$

Since ρ is nonincreasing, the second mean value theorem (Dieudonné 1960, p. 169) implies that

$$v^T A(p)v = \frac{1}{2}\rho(0) \int_0^\xi \left(\frac{\partial (f(p,m) \cdot v)^2}{\partial m} \right) dm,$$

for some ξ, where $0 \le \xi \le b$. Therefore

$$v^T A(p)v = \tfrac{1}{2}\rho(0)[(f(p,m) \cdot v)^2]_0^\xi \ge 0.$$

If $v = tp$, then $f(p,m) \cdot v = tm$ by Walras' law. Therefore

$$v^T A(p)v = \tfrac{1}{2}\rho(0)[(tm)^2]_0^\xi > 0 \qquad \text{for } t > 0.$$

Therefore $JF(p)$ is negative quasi-definite.

Proof of (ii) Let

$$g(t) = (p - q)^T F(tp + (1 - t)q), \qquad 0 \le t \le 1.$$

Then

$$g'(t) = (p - q)^T [f_{ij}(tp + (1 - t)q)](p - q).$$

By the mean value theorem (Dieudonné 1960, p. 153) $g(1) - g(0) = g'(t')(1 - 0)$, some t', $0 \le t' \le 1$. That is, $g(1) - g(0) = (p - q)^T [f_{ij}(p')] \cdot (p - q)$, where $p' = t'p + (1 - t')q$. Since $[f_{ij}(p')]$ is negative definite, $p \ne q$ implies $g(1) - g(0) < 0$. In other words, $pf(p) - qf(p) < pf(q) - qf(q)$, or $pf(p) \ge pf(q)$ implies $qf(q) < qf(p)$ when $p \ne q$. This is the weak axiom. ∎

Since the market demand functions have been defined as the sum of individual demand functions, there is no problem of the existence of market demand functions so long as the individual demand functions do not depend on the consumptions of other individuals. However, it is not obvious that market demand functions exist when the choices of different consumers are interdependent. We will prove existence for the market demand correspondence where there is interdependence of choice and where the preference relations are not assumed to be transitive or complete. As for the market demand function the market demand correspondence is defined to be the sum of the individual demand correspondences given the distribution of incomes. Write $\tilde{x}$ as the H-tuple $(x^1, \cdots, x^H)$ and write $\tilde{x}_{(h)}$ as the corresponding $(H-1)$-tuple with the hth argument omitted. Let C^h be the set of commodity bundles $x^h \in \mathbf{R}^n$, which can be accepted by the hth consumer. P^h is now defined on $\tilde{C} = \prod_1^H C^h \subset \mathbf{R}^{nH}$. The strict preference correspondence with interdependence is written $P^h(x^h | \tilde{x}_{(h)})$ and refers to the set of commodity bundles strictly preferred to x^h by the hth consumer when other consumers are choosing $\tilde{x}_{(h)}$. Define

$$f^h(p, m^h | \tilde{x}_{(h)})$$

$$= \{y^h \in H(p, m^h) \mid y^h \in C^h$$

$$\text{and } y^h \in P^h(x^h | \tilde{x}_{(h)}) \text{ implies } y^h \notin H(p, m^h)\}.$$

Then $f(p, m^1, \cdots, m^H) = \sum_{h=1}^{H} f^h(p, m^h | \tilde{x}_{(h)})$, where the components x^k of the $x_{(h)}$ satisfy the relations $x^k \in f^k(p, m^k | \tilde{x}_{(k)})$, $k = 1, \cdots, H$. We must show that these relations can be satisfied for any $p > 0$. Then the correspondence f exists for $p > 0$. Since we will assume the distribution of incomes to be fixed, we may also write the market demand correspondence as $f(p)$.

The proof of existence for $f(p)$ will imply the existence of the individual demand function of section 1.2. Indeed the method of proof here is closely related to the proof of section 1.2, since the fixed point theorem which we will use may itself be proved by use of the KKM lemma. The lower section $L^h(x^h | \tilde{x}_{(h)}) = \{y^h | (x^h | \tilde{x}_{(h)}) \in P^h(y^h | \tilde{x}_{(h)})\}$. We will assume as in section 1.4 that the lower sections are open. A correspondence Φ is *lower semicontinuous* at a point z in its domain D if $z^s \to z$, $s = 1, 2, \cdots$, with $z^s \in D$ implies for any $y \in \Phi(z)$, there is $y^s \in \Phi(z^s)$ and $y^s \to y$. Equivalently Φ is *lower semicontinous* at z if for any $y \in \Phi(z)$ and neighborhood V of y there is a neighborhood U of z such that $z' \in U \cap D$ implies there is $y' \in V \cap D$ and $y' \in \Phi(z')$ (Berge 1963, p. 109). Φ is said to be *lower semicontinuous* if it is lower semicontinous at all points in its domain. We call $\{x \in X \mid y \in \Phi(x)\}$ a *lower section* of Φ at x.

LEMMA 17 *If the graph of a correspondence* $\Phi : X \to$ *subsets of* Y *has all lower sections open then* Φ *is lower semicontinuous.*

Proof Consider $y \in \Phi(x)$. By the assumption of open lower sections, there is a neighborhood U of x such that $x^s \in U$ implies $y \in \Phi(x^s)$. If $x^s \to x$, $s = 1, 2, \cdots$, for large s, $x^s \in U$. Therefore $y \in \Phi(x^s)$ for large s. In the definition of lower semicontinuity let $y^s = y$ for large s. ∎

The fixed point theorem that we need was proved by Gale and Mas-Colell (1975, 1979) and used to prove an existence theorem for competitive equilibrium. A correspondence $\Phi(x)$ is said to be *upper semicontinuous* if for any neighborhood W of $\Phi(x)$ there is a neighborhood V of x such that $y \in V$ implies $\Phi(y) \subset W$. However, if the range of Φ is contained in a compact set a correspondence is upper semicontinuous if and only if it has a closed graph, that is, if and only if $y^s \in \Phi(x^s)$, $y^s \to y$, and $x^s \to x$ imply $y \in \Phi(x)$ (Berge 1963, pp. 109, 112).

LEMMA 18 *Let* $X = \prod_{i=1}^m X_i$, *where* X_i *is a nonempty, compact, convex subset of* $\mathbf{R}^n$. *Let* Φ^i *map* $X \to$ *convex subsets of* X_i *(including* $\emptyset$*),* $i = 1, 2, \cdots, m$. *If the* Φ^i *are lower semicontinuous for all* i, *then there is* $x \in X$ *such that* $x^i \in \Phi^i(x)$ *or* $\Phi^i(x) = \emptyset$.

Proof Let $U_i = \{ x \in X \mid \Phi^i(x) \neq \emptyset \}$. Then Φ^i is a convex and non-empty-valued correspondence on the set U_i which is lower semicontinuous, and U_i is open relative to X. To see that U_i is open relative to X, consider a point x on the boundary of U_i that is not on the boundary of X, and suppose $x \in U_i$. In every neighborhood of x there is a point x' such that $\Phi^i(x')$ is empty. We will show that this contradicts the lower semicontinuity of Φ^i. We let y lie in $\Phi^i(x)$. Then we may choose a sequence x^s that converges to x but for which there is no corresponding sequence $y^s \to y$ with $y^s \in \Phi^i(x^s)$ since $\Phi^i(x^s)$ is empty. This is a contradiction. Therefore U_i is open.

Since Φ^i is lower semicontinous on U_i and convex valued, by Michael's selection theorem (Michael 1956, thm. 3.1''') there is a continuous function $f^i : U_i \to X^i$ such that $f^i(x) \in \Phi^i(x)$ for all $x \in U_i$. Define a correspondence $\Psi^i : X \to X^i$ by $\Psi^i(x) = \{ f^i(x) \}$ if $\Phi^i(x) \neq \emptyset$ and $\Psi^i(x) = X^i$ otherwise. Let $\Psi = \prod_{i=1}^m \Psi^i$. Then $\Psi : X \to$ nonempty convex subsets of X, and X is convex and compact. Moreover Ψ is upper semicontinuous. Therefore by Kakutani's fixed point theorem (Berge 1963, p. 174) there is $x \in X$ such that $x \in \Psi(x)$. Then for each i either $x^i \in \Phi^i(x)$ or $\Phi^i(x) = \emptyset$. ∎

Assume that the consumptions sets C^h are convex. Let $C = C^1 \times \cdots \times C^H$. We also make assumptions 7, 8, 9, and 10 for the consumption sets C^h and the relations $\mathscr{P}^h$ which now depend on the consumptions $x_{(h)}$ for other consumers. Then the correspondence P^h is defined on $\tilde{C}$ by means of the relation $\mathscr{P}^h$ of strict preference, and P^h maps $\tilde{C}$ into subsets of C^h. Interpret assumption 10 to mean that the correspondence P^h has open lower sections relative to $\tilde{C}$.

THEOREM 9   *Under the assumptions above, if $H(p, m^h) \neq \emptyset$ for all h and $p > 0$ then the market demand correspondence $f(p, m^1, \cdots, m^H)$ is well defined.*

Proof $P^h(x^h, \tilde{x}_{(h)})$ has open lower sections by assumption 10. Define $\bar{P}^h$ on C^h by $\bar{P}^h(x^h | \tilde{x}_{(h)}) = $ convex hull $P^h(x^h | \tilde{x}_{(h)})$. Given $(p, \tilde{m})$, let $B^h(x^h | \tilde{x}_{(h)})$ for $x^h \in C^h$ be $\bar{P}^h(x^h | \tilde{x}_{(h)}) \cap H(p, m^h)$. B^h maps $\prod_1^H H(p, m^h)$ into convex subsets of $H(p, m^h)$. Also $H(p, m^h)$ is compact by lemma 5 and not empty by the hypothesis. If we can show that $B^h(x^h | \tilde{x}_{(h)})$ also has open lower sections relative to $H(p, m^h)$, this will imply by lemma 17 that $B^h(x^h | \tilde{x}_{(h)})$ is lower semicontinuous. Then the B^h and the sets $H(p, m^h)$ will satisfy the conditions of lemma 18 for Φ^i and X^i. Therefore there is $\tilde{x} \in \prod_{h=1}^H H(p, m^h) = H(p, \tilde{m})$ such that $x^h \in B^h(x^h | \tilde{x}_{(h)})$ or $B^h(x^h | \tilde{x}_{(h)}) = \emptyset$, say $x^h = x^{*h}$. However $x^{*h} \in B^h(x^{*h} | \tilde{x}_{(h)})$ contradicts assumption 9. Therefore $B^h(x^{*h}, x^*_{(h)}) = \emptyset$ for all h. This implies that $x^{*h} \in f(p, m^h | x^*_{(h)})$ for all h. In other words, $f(p, m^1, \cdots, m^H)$ is well defined. Hence the proof of theorem 9 is completed when we have proved the next lemma.

LEMMA 19   *The correspondence B^h has open lower sections relative to $H(p, m^h)$.*

Proof Consider $(z^h, z_{(h)}) \in (B^h)^{-1}(x^h)$, which is equivalent to $x^h \in B^h(z^h, z_{(h)})$. By definition of B^h, x^h can be expressed as

$$x^h = \sum_{i=1}^{n+1} \lambda_i x_i^h, \qquad \text{where } \lambda_i \geq 0, \ \sum \lambda_i = 1, \ x_i^h \in P^h(z^h | z_{(h)}). \tag{16}$$

Then, by assumption 10, there is an open neighborhood U_h of $(z^h | z_{(h)})$ relative to C^h such that for any $y^h \in U_h$ we have $(y^h | z_{(h)}) \in (P^h)^{-1}(x_i^h)$.

Let $U = \bigcap_{h=1}^{H} U_h$. Then $(y^1, \cdots, y^H) \in U \cap H(p, m)$ implies $(y^h, y_{(h)}) \in (P^h)^{-1}(x_i^h)$. Thus $x_i^h \in P^h(y^h, y_{(h)})$. Finally (16) implies that $x^h \in \bar{P}^h(y^h, y_{(h)})$. Using the definition of B^h we find that $U \cap H(p, m) \subset (B^h)^{-1}(x^h)$ or $(B^h)^{-1}(x^h)$ is open relative to $H(p, m)$. ∎

Theorem 9 implies theorem 3 as the special case in which $H = 1$. Moreover the general method of proof will apply to the existence of a competitive equilibrium in chapter 6. This comes from the fact that both of these results involve maximization of preference, by one individual or many. If the demand is defined directly, and not derived from a system of preferences, even nontransitive preferences, so that maximization does not play the central role, a different approach to the existence of competitive equilibrium must be taken (see McKenzie 1954 and Debreu 1970, p. 183).

Appendix A: Continuity of $m_x(p)$

The concavity of $m_x(p)$ implies that it is continuous in the interior of its domain, that is, for $p > 0$. However, a general proof may be given that includes the boundary points and depends on the special properties of $m_x(p)$.

PROPOSITION $m_x(p)$ *is continuous for* $p \geq 0$.

Proof Suppose $m_x(p)$ is not continuous at some $p \geq 0$. Then there is $\varepsilon > 0$ and a sequence $p^s \geq 0$, $s = 1, 2, \cdots$, such that $p^s \to p$ and $|m_x(p^s) - m_x(p)| \geq \varepsilon$ for all s. Then there is a subsequence $p^s \to p$ (retain notation) and either

i. $m_x(p^s) \geq m_x(p) + \varepsilon$, or

ii. $m_x(p^s) \leq m_x(p) - \varepsilon$.

Consider case i. Let $w \in R(x)$ be a point such that

$$pw \leq m_x(p) + \frac{\varepsilon}{2}. \tag{A1}$$

According to case i and the definition of $m_x(p)$, there is $p^s \to p$ and $p^s w \geq m_x(p) + \varepsilon$. But by (A1) for large s we have $p^s \cdot w < m_x(p) + \varepsilon$. Therefore case i cannot arise.

Consider case ii. Let $w^s \in R(x)$ be a point where

$$p^s w^s \leq m_x(p^s) + \frac{\varepsilon}{4}. \tag{A2}$$

According to case ii, $p^s w^s \leq m_x(p) - 3\varepsilon/4$ for $s = 1, 2, \cdots$, and $p^s \to p$. Let $J = \{i \mid p_i > 0\}$ and $J' = \{i \mid p_i = 0\}$. For all i, w_i^s is bounded below. This implies

$$\sum_{i \in J'} p_i^s w_i^s \geq -\frac{\varepsilon}{4} \tag{A3}$$

for large s. If $J = \emptyset$, clearly, case ii is not possible. Suppose $J \neq \emptyset$. Note that w_i^s is bounded above for $i \in J$, since $p^s w^s \leq m_x(p) - \varepsilon < px$. Therefore

$$\sum_{i \in J} (p_i - p_i^s) w_i^s \to 0. \tag{A4}$$

For s large enough we have

$$m_x(p) \leq p w^s = \sum_{i \in J} p_i w_i^s \leq \sum_{i \in J} p_i^s w_i^s + \frac{\varepsilon}{4}$$

$$= p^s w^s - \sum_{i \in J'} p_i^s w_i^s + \frac{\varepsilon}{4} \leq p^s w^s + \frac{\varepsilon}{2} \leq m_x(p^s) + \frac{3\varepsilon}{4}. \tag{A5}$$

The second inequality is implied by (A4). The third inequality is implied by (A3). The fourth inequality is implied by (A2). However, (A5) contradicts case ii. Thus case ii cannot arise either. ∎

Appendix B: Negative Semidefiniteness of $[m_{ij}(p)]$

We will use this property for concave functions of one variable to prove the property for concave functions of many variables.

PROPOSITION $z^T[m_{ij}(p)]z$ *is negative semidefinite for* $p > 0$.

Proof   We have $d/dt \, m(tp + (1-t)p') = \sum_{i=1}^{n} m_i(tp + (1-t)p') \cdot (p_i - p_i')$, where p and p' are positive and $m_i(p) = \partial m(p)/\partial p_i$. Also we have $d^2/dt^2 \, m(tp + (1-t)p') = \sum_{i=1}^{n} \sum_{j=1}^{n} m_{ij}(tp + (1-t)p') \cdot (p_i - p_i')(p_j - p_j')$, where $m_{ij}(p) = \partial^2 m(p)/\partial p_i \partial p_j$. For t close to 1, p' may be chosen freely in a small neighborhood. Now $d^2/dt^2 \, m(tp + (1-t)p') \leq 0$ for t near 1 by concavity for functions of one variable. Therefore, evaluating the derivatives at $t = 1$, we have that $\sum_{i=1}^{n} \sum_{j=1}^{n} m_{ij}(p) z_i z_j$ is negative semidefinite. ∎

Appendix C: Euler's Theorem for $f(p)$

Euler's theorem on homogeneous functions is best known in economics for its application to the theory of production where it implies that in the absence of increasing returns and external economies all factors may be paid their marginal products and this will exactly exhaust the product when the production functions are homogeneous of the first degree. However, the theorem also applies to demand functions.

PROPOSITION *If the derivatives exist $\sum_{j=1}^{n} p_j \partial f_i(p)/\partial p_j = 0$.*

Proof By lemma 10, $f_i(tp) = f_i(p)$. Therefore taking derivatives with respect to t, we have $\sum_{j=1}^{n} p_j \partial f_i(tp)/\partial p_j = 0$. Take $t = 1$ to obtain the result. ∎

By the same method one may show that

$$g(tx) = t^r g(x) \quad \text{implies} \quad \sum_{j=1}^{n} \frac{x_j \partial g(x)}{\partial x_j} = r g(x).$$

In this case g is said to be homogeneous of degree r where r may be any real number.

Appendix D: Quasi-linear Preferences

A special type of preference order called *quasi-linear preferences* is sometimes assumed in order to eliminate the effect of income changes on demand for $n - 1$ of the goods. In a quasi-linear preferences order one good plays a special role. This good may be chosen as the numéraire. Let the numéraire have the index 1. Then the consumption set C is taken to be $\mathbf{R} \times \mathbf{R}_{+}^{n-1}$ where negative amounts of good 1 are allowed. Also good 1 is always desired; that is, $(x + (1, 0, \ldots, 0)) P x$ holds for any x. Finally the indifference sets are parallel displacements of each other along the first axis. Let $x_{(1)} = (x_2, \cdots, x_n)$.

THEOREM 10 *If the preferences are quasi-linear the utility function may be written $u(x) = x_1 + \phi(x_{(1)})$.*

Proof Choose an $\bar{x}_{(1)} > 0$, and for any x_1 define $u(x_1, \bar{x}_{(1)}) = x_1$. The line $L(x_{(1)})$ through $(0, \bar{x}_{(1)})$ parallel to the x_1 axis cuts every indifference set. Otherwise, by parallel displacement, it would cut no indifference set which is impossible. For any $x_{(1)}$ let $S(0, x_{(1)})$ be the indifference set containing $(0, x_{(1)})$. Define $\phi(x_{(1)}) = w_1$ where $S(0, x_{(1)}) \cap L(\bar{x}_{(1)}) = (y_1, \bar{x}_{(1)})$ Then for any $(0, x_{(1)})$, we set $u(0, x_{(1)}) = \phi(x_{(1)})$.

Now consider any point $(y_1, y_{(1)})$ and the indifference set $S(y_1, y_{(1)})$. Let $S(y_1, y_{(1)}) \cap L(\bar{x}_{(1)}) = (x_1', \bar{x}_{(1)})$. Then set $u(y_1, y_{(1)}) = x_1'$. Let $S(0, y_{(1)}) \cap L(\bar{x}_{(1)}) = (z_1, \bar{x}_{(1)})$. Then

$$u(y_1, y_{(1)}) - u(0, y_{(1)}) = u(x_1', \bar{x}_{(1)}) - u(x_1, \bar{x}_{(1)}) = x_1' - z_1.$$

However by parallel displacement $x_1' - z_1 = y_1 - 0 = y_1$. Therefore

$$u(y_1, y_{(1)}) = u(0, y_{(1)}) + y_1 = \phi(y_{(1)}) + y_1.$$

Since y_1 and $y_{(1)}$ are arbitrary this holds for any $y = (y_1, y_{(1)})$. In other words, $u(y) = y_1 + \phi(y_{(1)})$ for any $y \in C$. ∎

Appendix E: The Law of Demand and Risk Aversion

There is a remarkable relation, discovered by Mitiushin and Polterovich, between the Law of Demand and the coefficient of relative risk aversion (see Mas-Colell 1991). We consider the setting of the classical theory of section 1.3 except that assumption 13 is strengthened by replacing strict quasi-concavity by strict concavity for the utility function.

ASSUMPTION 13' The function u is continuous and strictly concave in C and with a nonzero second differential in the interior of C.

THEOREM 11 *Make assumptions 11, 12, and 13'. If*

$$-\frac{x^T[u_{ij}(x)]x}{xDu(x)} < 4$$

for all $x \in int\,C$*, where* $x = f(p, m)$*, then* $[\partial f_i(p, m)/\partial p_j]$ *is negative definite.*

Proof Since $u(x)$ is strictly quasi-concave the preferred set of x is convex and $P(x) \cap int\,C$ is strictly convex. Moreover, because u is differentiable in $int\,C$ by assumption 13' and monotone increasing by assumption 12, if $x \in int\,C$ the price vector $p \geq 0$ that supports $P(x)$ at x is unique up to multiplication by a positive constant (Rockafellar 1970, p. 242). If we set $px = 1$, then p is unique. Thus there is a function $g(x)$ mapping vectors $x \in \text{int } C$ into $\mathbf{R}_+^n$ such that $f(g(x), 1) = x$. The function g is called the inverse demand function. Taking the derivative with respect to x of the terms in the last equation gives $1 = [\partial f_i / \partial g_k] \cdot [\partial g_k / \partial x_j]$. This shows that $[\partial g_k / \partial x_j]$ is the inverse of $[\partial f_i / \partial g_k]$. Therefore, to prove the theorem, it is sufficient to prove that $Dg(x) = [\partial g_k(x)/\partial x_j]$ is negative definite under the hypothesis.

The Law of Demand is given by

$$(p' - p)(f(p', m) - f(p, m)) \leq 0$$

for any nonzero $p, p' \in \mathbf{R}_+^n$ and $m > 0$. It was shown in the proof of theorem 8 that the Law of Demand is implied if the Jacobian of the demand function $[\partial f_i(p, m)/\partial p_j]$ is negative definite for all $p > 0$. Since f is homogeneous of 0 degree in (p, m), we may set $m = 1$. We have by (5) that $x = f(p, 1)$ implies $Du(x) = \lambda p = \lambda g(x)$. Thus $x \cdot Du(x) = \lambda px = \lambda$. Therefore $g(x) = Du(x)/(x \cdot Du(x))$.

Differentiating this expression for $g(x)$ gives

$$Dg(x) = \frac{D^2 u(x)}{x \cdot Du(x)} - \frac{Du(x)(Du(x))^T}{(x \cdot Du(x))^2} + \frac{x^T D^2 u(x)}{(x \cdot Du(x))^2}.$$

Let $U = D^2 u(x)$ and $q = Du(x)$. Then $Dg(x) = (U/qx) - q(q^T + x^T U)/(qx)^2$. So

$$v^T Dg(x)v = \frac{v^T Uv}{qx} - \frac{(qv)^2}{(qx)^2} - \frac{qv(x^T Uv)}{(qx)^2}.$$

However, we may without loss of generality choose v so that $qv = qx$. Then we obtain

$$v^T Dg(x)v = \frac{v^T Uv}{qx} - 1 - \frac{x^T Uv}{qx}.$$

We have the identity

$$v^T Uv - x^T Uv \equiv (v - \tfrac{1}{2}x)^T U(v - \tfrac{1}{2}x) - \tfrac{1}{4}x^T Ux.$$

Therefore

$$v^T Dg(x)v = -1 + \left(\frac{(v - \tfrac{1}{2}x)^T U(v - \tfrac{1}{2}x)}{qx} - \frac{\tfrac{1}{4}(x^T Ux)}{qx} \right).$$

The hypothesis implies that the last term is less than 1. Also U is negative definite since by assumption 13' we have that $u(x)$ is strictly concave and twice differentiable. This implies that $v^T Dg(x)v$ is negative. ∎

Appendix F: The Strong Axiom of Revealed Preference

An axiom of revealed preference stronger than assumption 14 may be based on the relation $\mathscr{D}^*$ defined for $x, y \in C$ by $x\mathscr{D}^*y$ if and only if there is a sequence $x_1, x_2, \cdots, x_s$ for some $s \geq 1$ such that $x_i \mathscr{D} x_{i+1}$ for $i = 1$ to $s - 1$ and $x_1 = x$ and $x_s = y$. Then assumptions 14, 15, and 16 may be replaced by

ASSUMPTION 14' $\mathscr{D}^*$ is antisymmetric. That is, $x\mathscr{D}^*y$ and $y\mathscr{D}^*x$ implies $x = y$.

ASSUMPTION 15' The demand function $f(p,m)$ is continuous and satisfies a Lipschitz condition (Coddington and Levinson 1955, p. 8) with respect to m.

ASSUMPTION 16' If $x \in f(p,m)$ then $px = m$. For any $x \in C$ there is (p,m) with $p > 0$ and m a real number such that $x = f(p,m)$.

If $x \in C$ define $m_x^*(q)$ for any $q > 0$ by

$$m_x^*(q) \equiv \sup(m \mid x\mathscr{D}^*f(q,m)).$$

We will need

LEMMA 20 *Suppose that the demand function $f(p,m)$ satisfies assumptions 14', 15', and 16'. Let $x \in C$ and $(q,m) \in$ domain of f. Then $x\mathscr{D}^*f(q,m)$ for any $m < m_x^*(q)$ and $f(q,m)\mathscr{D}^*x$ for any $m > m_x^*(q)$.*

Proof See Uzawa (1971). ∎

Define $f_x^*(p)$ by

$$f_x^*(p) \equiv f(p, m_x^*(p)).$$

Also define $S_x^*(p)$ by $S_x^*(p) \equiv [\partial f_{x_i(p)}^* / \partial p_j]$. As in the case of $S_x(p)$ this definition is given for all $x \in C$ and $p > 0$. It is now possible to show that S^*, when it exists, is symmetric and therefore identical with S. We may prove the analog of lemma 8.

LEMMA 21 *Let $p > 0$. If the derivatives exist $p \cdot (\partial f_x^*(p)/\partial p_i) = 0$. Moreover $m_x^*(p)$ is a concave function.*

Proof We first prove that $p \cdot f_x^*(q) \geq p \cdot f_x^*(p)$ holds for all $p > 0$ and $q > 0$. Suppose not. Then there are $p > 0$ and $q > 0$ such that $p \cdot f_x^*(q) < p \cdot f_x^*(p)$. Recall that $f_x^*(p) = f(p, m_x^*(p))$ and $f_x^*(q) = f(q, m_x^*(q))$. Then continuity of f with respect to its second argument implies that there is $m < m_x^*(p)$ and $m' > m_x^*(q)$ such that $p \cdot f(q, m') < p \cdot f(p, m)$. Lemma 20 implies that $x \mathscr{D}^* f(p, m)$ and the definition of $\mathscr{D}^*$ implies that $f(p, m) \mathscr{D}^* f(q, m')$ so that $x \mathscr{D}^* f(q, m')$. Since $m' > m_x^*(q)$ this contradicts the definition of $m_x^*(q)$. Thus $p \cdot f_x^*(q) < p \cdot f_x^*(p)$ cannot hold.

Since $p \cdot f_x^*(q) \geq p \cdot f_x^*(p)$ for all $q > 0$, $p \cdot f_x^*(q)$ achieves a minimum at p. Then the first-order conditions for a minimum give $p \cdot (\partial f_x^*(p)/\partial p_i) = 0$. This proves the first proposition. By the preceding argument, $x = f(p, m)$ implies $p \cdot f_x^*(q) \geq p \cdot f_x^*(p)$ holds for all $p > 0$ and $q > 0$. Thus

$$m_x^*\left(\frac{p+q}{2}\right) = \left(\frac{p+q}{2}\right) \cdot f_x^*\left(\frac{p+q}{2}\right)$$

$$= \frac{p}{2} \cdot f_x^*\left(\frac{p+q}{2}\right) + \frac{q}{2} f_x^*\left(\frac{p+q}{2}\right)$$

$$\geq \frac{m_x^*(p)}{2} + \frac{m_x^*(q)}{2}.$$

This implies that m_x^* is a concave function. ∎

By use of lemma 21 we may prove the analogue of lemma 9.

LEMMA 22 *Let $p > 0$ hold. If the derivatives exist, $\partial m_x^*(p)/\partial p_i = f_{xi}^*(p)$, and $\partial f_{xi}^*(p)/\partial p_j = \partial^2 m_x^*(p)/\partial p_i \partial p_j$, $i, j = 1, \cdots, n$. Moreover the derivatives exist for almost all $p > 0$.*

Proof The first statement of the lemma is implied by the following series of equalities

$$\frac{\partial m_x^*(p)}{\partial p_i} = \frac{\partial(p \cdot f_x^*(p))}{\partial p_i} = f_x^*(p) + p \cdot \frac{\partial f_x^*(p)}{\partial p_i} = f_x^*(p).$$

The last equality is justified by use of lemma 21. The second statement of the lemma is implied by the concavity of $m_x^*(p)$ (Fenchel 1953, p. 142; Alexandroff 1939). ∎

Define $S_x^*(p) \equiv [\partial f_x^*(p)/\partial p]$. We may now prove

THEOREM 12   *Under assumptions 14' through 16', $S_x^*(p)$ exists for almost all $p > 0$. Moreover*

i. $S_x^*(p)$ *is symmetric.*

ii. $z^T S_x^*(p)z$ *is negative semidefinite.*

iii. $p^T S_x^*(p) = 0$ *and* $S_x^*(p)p = 0$.

Proof By lemma 22, $S_x^*(p)$ is the Hessian of the concave function $m_x^*(p)$. This implies that $S^*(p)$ is symmetric and negative semidefinite. From the definition of m_x^* it may be seen that the homogeneity of f of degree 0 implies that m_x^* is positive homogeneous of degree 1. This fact and homogeneity of f of degree 0 then implies from the definition of f_x^* that f_x^* is homogeneous of degree 0. Finally homogeneity of f_x^* of degree 0 and symmetry of S_x^* implies iii.   ■

Consider

$$\frac{\partial f_{xi}^*(p)}{\partial p_j} = \frac{\partial f_i(p,m)}{\partial p_j} + \frac{\partial f_i(p,m)}{\partial m} \cdot f_{xj}^*(p,m),$$

where $m = m_x^*(p)$. The equality follows from lemma 22 which allows $f_{xj}^*(p,m)$ to be substituted for $\partial m_x^*(p)/\partial p_j$. Comparing this formula with theorem 2 we observe that, when both $f_x(p,m)$ and $f_x^*(p,m)$ have well-defined derivatives, $S_x(p)$ and $S_x^*(p)$ are identical, but this is true almost everywhere by theorems 1 and 12 provided that the demand functions are the same. It has been shown by Uzawa (1971) that a relation $\mathscr{R}$ satisfying the assumptions 1, 2, 3, and 4 exists from which the demand functions which satisfy assumptions 14', 15', and 16' may be derived. Moreover $\mathscr{P}$ derived from $\mathscr{R}$ coincides with $\mathscr{D}^*$ for $p > 0$.

Appendix G: Group Demand Functions

The classical theory we described in section 1.3 is based on choices made by a single consumer to maximize a strictly quasiconcave utility function. However, many choices are made by groups of consumers, for example, families. Let the group have L members who are involved in decisions for group consumption and represent their utility levels over group consumption as vectors in $\mathbf{R}^L$. Let C be the possible consumption set for the group. Given $x \in C$, there are utility levels $u^l(x)$ for decision makers, which depend not only on the quantities of goods consumed by the group but on the way in which the consumption is managed. Let $u(x)$ represent the utility vector $(u^1(x), \cdots, u^L(x))$. We make assumptions 11, 12, and 13 for each u^l.

We may also consider a set $V(p,m)$ of utility vectors that are attainable given the income $m > 0$ of the group and the market prices $p > 0$, that is,

$$V(p,m) = \{u(x) \mid x \in C, px \le m\}.$$

Let $P(p,m) = \{u \in V(p,m) \mid u' \ge u, u' \in V(p,m) \text{ implies } u' = u\}$. $P(p,m)$ is the Pareto frontier of $V(p,m)$.

LEMMA 23 $V(p,m)$ *is a closed and strictly convex set.*

Proof   That $V(p,m)$ is closed follows from the fact that C is closed and $u(x)$ is continuous for all $x \in C$. The strict convexity of $V(p,m)$ follows from the convexity of C and the strict concavity of each $u^h(x)$.   ∎

We will assume that the decision makers achieve efficiency in their use of the group income. That is, they realize a point on the Pareto frontier $P(p,m)$. By the definition of $P(p,m)$, if $u \in P(p,m)$, then $V(p,m)$ and $u + \text{int } \mathbf{R}_+^L$ are disjoint. Therefore there is a vector γ that *separates* these sets in the sense that $v \in V(p,m)$ and $v' \in u + \text{int } \mathbf{R}_+^L$ implies $\gamma v < \gamma v'$ (see Fenchel 1953, p. 51; Rockafellar 1970, p. 97). Thus $\gamma u \ge \gamma v$ for any $v \in V(p,m)$. We say that γ *supports* $V(p,m)$ at u. If γ supported $v(p,m)$ at a second point v, it would also support points lying between u and v which contradicts lemma 23. Thus each point of the Pareto frontier $P(p,m)$ is associated with a unique supporting vector γ. The components of the vector γ may be thought of as relative weights given the utilities of the decision makers. It is harmless to normalize γ so that the components sum to 1. Define $U(x, \gamma) = \gamma \cdot u(x)$ where the utilization of x is such that $\gamma u(x)$ is maximized. If γ is constant, the theory of the group demand based on $U(x, \gamma)$ is the same as the theory of the single consumer described earlier. The interesting case arises if γ is a function such as $\gamma(p,m)$. Then the Slutsky relation of theorem 2 no longer holds. However, it is possible to derive a relation that is useful when the number of goods exceeds the number of members of the group (see Browning and Chiappori 1998).

The demand function may be written

$$f(p, m, \gamma(p,m)) = \{x \mid U(x, \gamma(p,m)) \geq U(z, \gamma(p,m))$$

$$\text{for } x \in C \text{ with } px \leq m, \text{ for all } z \in C \text{ with } pz \leq m\}.$$

Just as in the case of the demand of the individual consumer we may define $m_x(p|\gamma)$ as the minimum income sufficient to allow the utility level $U(x, \gamma)$ to be reached for fixed γ when the prices are given by p. Let $f_x(p, \gamma) = f(p, m_x(p|\gamma), \gamma)$. Then, if γ is constant, in complete analogy with the proof of theorem 2 we can derive

$$\frac{\partial f_i(p,m,\gamma)}{\partial p_j} = \frac{\partial f_{xi}(p,\gamma)}{\partial p_j} - f_j(p,m,\gamma)\left(\frac{\partial f_i(p,m,\gamma)}{\partial m}\right), \qquad (A6)$$

where f_{xi} is the compensated demand function for $f_i(x, \gamma)$ at $x = f(p, m, \gamma)$. If x is a regular value of $U(x, \gamma)$, it is implied by lemma 22 that the matrix $[\partial f_{xi}(p,\gamma)/\partial p_j]$ is symmetric. However, to obtain the full effect of the price change, we must differentiate the demand function with respect to γ, and γ with respect to p. If L is the number of consumers, this gives

$$\frac{\partial f_i(p,m,\tau)}{\partial p_j} = \frac{\partial f_{xi}(p,\gamma)}{\partial p_j} + \sum_{k=1}^{L-1}\left(\frac{\partial f_i(p,m,\gamma)}{\partial \gamma_k}\right)\left(\frac{\partial \gamma_k(p,m)}{\partial p_j}\right)$$

$$- \left(\frac{f_j(p,m,\gamma)\partial f_i(p,m,\gamma)}{\partial m}\right). \qquad (A7)$$

The sum is taken over only $L - 1$ weights, since the weights sum to one and thus they are not independent. The matrix $[\partial f_{xi}(p,\gamma)/\partial p_j] + \sum_{k=1}^{L-1} \partial f_i(p,m,\gamma)/\partial \gamma_k \cdot \partial \gamma_k(p,m)/\partial p_j$, which Browning and Chiappori call a pseudo-Slutsky matrix, is not symmetric but the sum of a symmetric matrix and a matrix of rank at most $L - 1$. This may be seen as follows: Let $A_k = \partial f_i(p,m,\gamma)/\partial \gamma_k \cdot \partial \gamma_k(p,m)/\partial p_j$, and let $A = \sum A_k$. The columns of A are indexed by j. Each column of A_k is a multiple of any column A_k^j. Assume that the number of goods exceeds the number of members of the group whose preferences matter. Suppose that the A_k^1 are linearly independent. Consider the subspace S of $\mathbf{R}^n$ spanned by the A_k^1. The dimension of S is $L - 1$. Thus the dimension of $S^{\perp}$, the orthogonal subspace to S, is $n - (L - 1)$. Since $S^{\perp}$ is the null space of A, the rank of

A cannot exceed $L - 1$. The rank of A should give some information about the number of independent decision makers in a consuming group. Browning and Chiappori (1998) apply this theory to an empirical study of the demand functions of households of two members using Canadian data.

We may state

THEOREM 13 *Let the demand of a group of L consumers maximize a weighted sum $U(x, \gamma) = \gamma \cdot u(x)$ of utilities of the members of the group for a group income m at prices p. Then, if the derivatives exist, the effect of price changes on group demand $x = f(p, m_x(p|\gamma), \gamma)$ may be expressed by the sum of a symmetric matrix $\partial f_{xi}(p, \gamma)/\partial p_j$, a matrix $-f_j \partial f_i/\partial m$ of rank one giving a group income effect, and a matrix $\sum_{k=1}^{L-1} \partial f_i/\partial \gamma_k \cdot \partial \gamma_k/\partial p_i$ of rank at most $L - 1$. The last matrix gives the effect of price changes on demand from affecting the relative weights of the members in decision making.*

2 Tâtonnement Stability of Equilibrium

In the theory of the exchange economy it is traditional to introduce an initial stock of goods from which the consumer trades. This procedure seems justified if the consumption set is assumed to lie in the positive orthant. Then the set of possible trades for the consumer is the consumption set less the initial stocks. However, quantities of personal services offered must be treated as negative numbers in the consumption bundles. So it is not possible to confine the consumption set to the positive orthant in general. Thus it might be reasonable to replace the consumption set by a trading set and dispense with the initial stocks. This is also recommended by the difficulty of determining what is consumed, even conceptually, as compared with what is traded. However, in this chapter we introduce the initial stocks, though this will not always be done in later chapters. The convention of initial stocks does have the advantage of allowing a well-defined displacement of the trading set as a consequence of the acquisition of additional goods by the consumer.

The exchange economy will be made up of a set of consumers or traders who have preferences over commodity bundles and who own certain initial stocks. Suppose that there are H consumers indexed by $h = 1, \cdots, H$. The hth consumer has initial stock $\omega^h \in \mathbf{R}^n$, where $\omega^h \geq 0$, and possible consumption set $C^h \subset \mathbf{R}^n$, where $C^h \neq \emptyset$. Let $\mathscr{R}^h$ denote the preference relation of the hth consumer. The economy E may be given by $(C^h, \mathscr{R}^h, \omega^h, h = 1, \cdots, H)$. A consumption bundle is $x \in C^h$, where x may contain negative elements as well as positive elements. The negative elements may represent labor services supplied by the consumer. If the sets C^h are considered as possible trading sets rather than as quantities consumed, it is possible to omit the initial stocks from explicit consideration. Then they appear implicitly as lower bounds on the trading sets C^h in certain directions. This is the convention we will follow in later chapters.

2.1 Excess Demand Functions

In this chapter the demand functions will be derived from preference orders $\mathscr{R}^h$ on the possible consumption sets $C^h \subset \mathbf{R}^n$. In order to facilitate the argument, stronger assumptions will be introduced than were used earlier. In addition to assumptions 1.1, 1.2, 1.3, and 1.4 of chapter 1, after replacing C by C^h, $h = 1, \cdots, H$, we now make

ASSUMPTION 1   If $x \in C^h$, there is $y \in C^h$ such that $y\mathscr{P}^h x$ (insatiability).

ASSUMPTION 2   There is $x < \omega^h$ such that $x \in C^h$ (interior point).

ASSUMPTION 3 C^h is convex and $x\mathscr{R}^h y$, $x \neq y$, implies $z\mathscr{P}^h y$ for $z = tx + (1 - t)y$, $0 < t < 1$ (strict convexity of preference).

These assumptions effectively place the argument in the context of the classical demand theory. In particular, goods are assumed to be divisible since C^h is convex. Furthermore we have

LEMMA 1   *(i) Assumptions 1 and 3 imply assumption 1.5 (local better point). (ii) Assumptions 2 and 3 imply assumption 1.6 (local cheaper point) for $M = p\omega^h$, $p \geq 0$, $p \neq 0$.*

Proof   (i) By 1 and 3, there is $z = ty + (1 - t)x$, and $z\mathscr{P}^h x$ for any t, $0 < t < 1$. (ii) This follows from $px < p\omega^h$.   ∎

Define the *individual excess demand correspondence* by

$$e^h(p) \equiv f^h(p, p\omega^h) - \{\omega^h\}, \qquad p \geq 0, p \neq 0.$$

Figure 2.1 illustrates the excess demand correspondence. Define the *market excess demand correspondence* $e(p)$ by

$$e(p) \equiv \sum_{h=1}^{H} e^h(p).$$

LEMMA 2   *Let $x \in e(p)$. Then (i) $px = 0$, (ii) $x \in e(tp)$, $p \geq 0$, $t > 0$.*

Proof   If $x \in e(p)$, there are $x^h \in e^h(p)$, $h = 1, \cdots, H$ such that $\sum x^h = x$. (i) By lemma 1.6, $z^h \in f^h(p, p\omega^h)$ implies $pz^h = p\omega^h$. Therefore $px^h = pz^h - p\omega^h = 0$. (ii) By lemma 1.10, $x^h \in e^h(p)$ implies $x^h \in f^h(p, p\omega^h) - \omega^h = f^h(tp, tp\omega^h) - \omega^h$. Thus $x^h \in e^h(tp)$ by the definition. The lemma follows from the definition of $e(p)$.   ∎

In the lemma (i) is known as Walras' Law, and (ii) defines homogeneity of 0 degree.

Define the *budget set* $H^h(p)$ of the hth consumer by

$$H^h(p) \equiv \{x \mid x \in C^h \text{ and } px \leq p\omega^h\}.$$

LEMMA 3   *$H^h(p)$ is lower semicontinuous for $p \geq 0$, $p \neq 0$.*

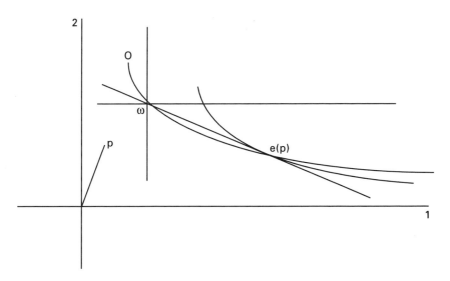

Figure 2.1
The initial stock is ω. The excess demand at prices p is $e(p)$ relative to the axes through ω. O is the offer curve.

Proof By assumption 2, there is $x \in C^h$ and $px < p\omega^h$. Then $p^s \to p$, $s = 1, 2, \cdots$, implies $p^s x < p^s \omega^h$ for s large. Let z be an arbitrary point of $H^h(p)$ not equal to x. Let $z^s = t^s z + (1 - t^s)x$, where t^s is maximal for $0 \le t^s \le 1$ and $z^s \in H^h(p^s)$. Then $z^s \to z$ if and only if $t^s \to 1$. Also $t^s < 1$ implies $p^s z^s = p^s \omega^h$, or else t^s would not be maximal.

Suppose $t^s \to 1$ does not hold. Then $t^s \to t < 1$ for a subsequence (retain notation). By continuity there is z' such that $z^s \to z'$. Then $pz' = p \cdot (tz + (1 - t)x) = p\omega^h$. But $px < p\omega^h$. So $pz > p\omega^h$ in contradiction to the fact that $z \in H^h(p)$. Therefore $t^s \to 1$ and $z^s \to z' = z$. This proves lower semicontinuity. ∎

The proof of lemma 3 is illustrated in figure 2.2.

LEMMA 4 *The market excess demand correspondence is single valued and continuous for $p > 0$.*

Proof It is sufficient to prove that $f^h(p, p\omega^h)$ is single valued and continuous. Suppose that $x \ne y$ and x and y are in $f^h(p, p\omega^h)$. By assumption 3, $z\mathscr{P}^h x$ and $z\mathscr{P}^h y$ where $z = (x + y)/2$. But $pz \le p\omega^h$. This contradicts the definition of $f^h(p, p\omega^h)$. Thus $e(p)$ is single valued and may be regarded as a function.

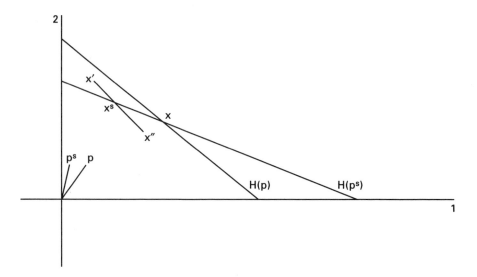

Figure 2.2
$x^s = t^s x' + (1 - t^s)x''$, where t^s is max for $x^s \in H(p^s)$. As p^s converges to p, x^s converges to x. Thus $H(p)$ is lower semicontinuous.

To prove continuity, assume there is a sequence of price vectors $p^s \to p$, $s = 1, 2, \cdots$, where $p > 0$ and $x^s = f^h(p^s, p^s\omega^h)$. We may suppose for $s > s'$ that $|p_i - p_i^s| < \varepsilon < \min p_i$ for $i = 1, \cdots, n$. By lemma 1.6 we have $p^s x^s = p^s \omega^h$. Thus $p^s x^s$ is bounded and p^s is bounded positive. Then $|x_i^s| \to \infty$ implies $x_j^s \to -\infty$ for some j, which is a contradiction of assumption 1.1. This implies that x^s is bounded as $s \to \infty$. Thus there is a point of accumulation. Let $x^s \to x$ along a subsequence (retain notation). By lemma 3, for any $z \in H^h(p)$ there is a sequence $z^s \to z$, $s = 1, 2, \cdots$, and $z^s \in H^h(p^s)$. Then $x^s \mathscr{R}^h z^s$, which implies $x \mathscr{R}^h z$ by assumption 1.4. Since it is also true that $px \leq p\omega^h$, we have that $x \in f^h(p, p\omega^h)$. Since f^h is single valued, $x = f^h(p, p\omega^h)$. This proves continuity of f^h and thus of $e(p)$. ∎

So that we may be able to use differential equation systems in discussing questions of stability of equilibrium for exchange economies, we will make a smoothness assumption on excess demand functions.

ASSUMPTION 4   The excess demand function $e^h(p)$ has continuous first-order partial derivatives for $p > 0$.

It may be shown that the assumptions 1.1 through 1.3 from chapter 1 and assumptions 1 through 4 above imply the existence of a utility function $u(x)$ on C^h that satisfies assumption 1.12 of the classical theory (Debreu 1954). Also assumption 1.13 is implied by regularity. Therefore from theorem 1.4 the condition of assumption 4 is implied for any $p > 0$ when $x = f(p, p\omega^h)$ is a regular value. As pointed out by Debreu (1972), the condition for regularity when $p > 0$ that the Hessian of u be negative definite on the budget hyperplane through $x = f(p, p\omega^h)$ is equivalent to a nonvanishing Gaussian curvature for the level set of u through x. Thus the assumption that all demand points are regular for $p > 0$, or equivalently the assumption that the level sets of u have nonvanishing Gaussian curvature, implies assumption 4.

Goods i and j are said to be *gross substitutes* if $\partial e_i(p)/\partial p_j \geq 0$ and $\partial e_j(p)/\partial p_i \geq 0$. When these inequalities are both strong, i and j are said to be *strong gross substitutes*. In this chapter we will sometimes (but only when explicitly mentioned) make

ASSUMPTION 5   All goods are (strong) gross substitutes for all $p > 0$.

This assumption will be referred to as the *gross substitute assumption* or, in the case of strong gross substitutes, as the *strong gross substitute assumption*.

Let $J(p) \equiv [e_{ij}(p)]$, $i, j = 1, \cdots, n$, represent the Jacobian, that is, the first derivative $De(p)$, of the excess demand functions $e(p)$. The gross substitute assumption is equivalent to requiring that J have off-diagonal terms nonnegative.

In order to exploit the gross substitute assumption, it is useful to prove

LEMMA 5   *The following relations hold for $J(p)$ with $p > 0$:*

i. $p^T J(p) = -e(p)$.

ii. $J(p)p = 0$.

Proof To obtain i, differentiate Walras' Law $pe(p) = 0$, which was proved in lemma 2. The relation ii is an immediate consequence of the homogeneity of $e(p)$ of degree 0. ∎

We may note that at equilibrium where $e(p) = 0$ relation i becomes $p^T J(p) = 0$, so the Jacobian matrix then satisfies part iii of theorem 1.1, which was proved for the net substitution matrix $S_x(p)$.

2.2   Market Equilibrium

In our discussion of the exchange economy we will follow tradition by assuming free disposal of goods implicitly. This avoids the necessity of introducing the disposal activities explicitly. The presence of disposal activities and no other production activities reduces the production set for the economy to the negative orthant. Then the only prices that are consistent with profit maximization are nonnegative. We will say that $p \geq 0$ is an *equilibrium price vector* for the exchange economy if $e(p) \leq 0$ and $p_i = 0$ for $e_i(p) < 0$. Thus, if $p > 0$ in equilibrium, it must be that $e(p) = 0$.

2.3   Matrices with Quasi-dominant Diagonals

In order to make use of the gross substitute assumption, we will prove some mathematical results in the form appropriate for our argument (McKenzie 1960a). Let A be a matrix $[a_{ij}]$, $i, j = 1, \cdots, n$, with $a_{ij} \in \mathbf{C}^n$, an n-dimensional vector space over the complex numbers. Let J be an arbitrary subset of $\{1, \cdots, n\}$. Let A_J be the principal submatrix with indexes in J. We say that A has a *quasi-dominant diagonal* (q.d.d.) if there are multipliers $d_i > 0$, $i = 1, \cdots, n$, such that for any principal submatrix A_J we have

$$d_j |a_{jj}| \geq \sum_{i \in J, i \neq j} d_i |a_{ij}| \qquad \text{for all } j \in J, \tag{1}$$

with strict inequality for some $j \in J$. If all the inequalities are strict A is said to have a *dominant diagonal*. We take the sum over the empty set to be 0. A first implication of q.d.d. is

LEMMA 6   *If a matrix A has* q.d.d., *then A is nonsingular.*

Proof   Suppose the $n \times n$ matrix A has q.d.d. with the multipliers d_i, $i = 1, \cdots, n$, and is singular. Let D be a diagonal matrix with the d_i on the diagonal. Consider the matrix $B = DA$. B is singular. Thus $q^T B = 0$ for some vector $q \neq 0$. Let $J = \{j \mid |q_j| \geq |q_i|, i = 1, \cdots, n\}$. Consider

$$q_j b_{jj} + \sum_{i \neq j} q_i b_{ij} = 0 \qquad \text{for } j \in J.$$

Then

$$|q_j b_{jj}| = \left| \sum_{i \neq j} q_i b_{ij} \right|, \qquad j \in J,$$

or

$$|q_j| |b_{jj}| \leq \sum_{i \neq j} |q_i| |b_{ij}| \leq \sum_{i \neq j} |q_j| |b_{ij}| \qquad \text{for } j \in J. \tag{2}$$

In other words, $|b_{jj}| \leq \sum_{i \neq j} |b_{ij}|$ for $j \in J$. But D may be chosen so that $|b_{jj}| \geq \sum_{i \neq j} |b_{ij}|$ for all j, since A has q.d.d. Therefore the inequalities in (2) are actually equalities. Since $|q_i| < |q_j|$ for $i \notin J$, $j \in J$, this implies that $b_{ij} = 0$ for $i \notin J$, $j \in J$. Thus $|b_{jj}| = \sum_{i \in J, i \neq j} |b_{ij}|$, $j \in J$. Since the principal submatrix A_J does not satisfy (1), this contradicts the definition of q.d.d. for A. We conclude that A cannot be singular. ∎

Let us say that a matrix A has a *nearly quasi-dominant diagonal* if it satisfies the condition described in (1) except that it is allowed that all inequalities are equalities. A first application of lemma 6, which is useful in arguments on global stability, is

LEMMA 7 *If a symmetric matrix A has a quasi-dominant diagonal which is negative, $z^T A z$ is negative definite. If A has a nearly quasi-dominant diagonal, $z^T A z$ is negative semidefinite.*

Proof Set $b_{ii}(t) = a_{ii}$, $b_{ij}(t) = t a_{ij}$, for $i \neq j$, $0 \leq t \leq 1$. Then

$$B(1) = A, B(0) = \begin{bmatrix} a_{11} \cdots \cdots 0 \\ 0 \cdots a_{ii} \cdots 0 \\ 0 \cdots \cdots a_{nn} \end{bmatrix}.$$

Since a_{ii} is negative, it is clear that $B(0)$ is negative definite. Also $B(t)$ has q.d.d. for all t. Thus by lemma 6 the principal minors of $B(t)$ do not change sign for t between 0 and 1. But for a symmetric matrix to define a negative definite quadratic form is equivalent to the condition that the principal minor of order k have the sign $(-1)^k$ (Debreu 1952). Since the signs of the principal minors of $B(0)$ satisfy this condition, so do those of $B(1)$. Thus $x^T B(1) x = x^T A x$ is negative definite. If nearly q.d.d. holds for A, q.d.d. holds for $B(t)$ when $0 \leq t < 1$. Thus $x^T A x$ is negative definite for $0 \leq t < 1$. Then the second statement of the theorem follows by continuity of $x^T B(t)x$ as a function of t. ∎

Lemma 7 requires that the matrix A be symmetric. However, for use in arguments on local stability, a stronger result is available.

LEMMA 8 *If a matrix A has a quasi-dominant diagonal that is negative, all its characteristic roots have negative real parts.*

Proof Consider $A - sI$. Let $\mathscr{R}(s)$ be the real part of s and $\mathscr{I}(s)$ the imaginary part. Suppose $\mathscr{R}(s) \geq 0$. Then

$$|a_{ii} - s| = |a_{ii} - \mathscr{R}(s) - i\mathscr{I}(s)| \geq |a_{ii} - \mathscr{R}(s)| \geq |a_{ii}|.$$

Thus $A - sI$ also has q.d.d. and it is nonsingular by lemma 6. Therefore s is not a characteristic root. ∎

2.4 The Process of Tâtonnement

The stability that we will first discuss may be described as the stability of a process of revision of the price vector in the light of excess demand. This process was referred to by its inventor as a tâtonnement (Walras 1874–77). It is intended to bear a significant relationship to the way in which prices might actually behave on competitive markets, at least on markets whose supplies from production have already been determined. When time is allowed for supplies of goods to be affected by new production, it might seem appropriate to introduce responses of production levels to profit opportunities in the manner of Marshall (1890) and indeed Walras. On exchange markets the supposition is that in the presence of excess demand, in the sense that maximization of preference leads to $e_i(p) > 0$, the ith price will rise. It is not clear why this price rise should occur in the presence of speculation, although in certain circumstances it may seem plausible. For example, the good is perishable like a fresh food so that speculation is restricted, or stocks are held by middlemen and excess demand is depleting the stocks. Similar arguments will apply to justify price decreases if a good is in excess supply. However, the application of these considerations to real markets where bargains are struck by individual traders at discrete moments of time and the only prices are those reached in these bargains is not obvious. In the process described by Walras, a market manager is postulated who calls out the prices and undertakes to revise the prices in the light of the value assumed by $e(p)$ at those prices, but this is not the process observed on most markets.

Perhaps the most fundamental fact about the price tâtonnement is that trading does not occur until the equilibrium has been reached. This means that it is a disequilibrium process whose precise course is not justified by economic considerations, that is, by the choices of economic agents who are maximizing preferences under constraints. We will consider another type of stability analysis where agents are assumed to correctly foresee future prices and prices are always equilibrium prices. Then it may occur that future prices asymptotically approach a path that is independent of initial conditions. This type of stability is sometimes referred to as a turnpike property. We will prove turnpike theorems in a later chapter. They concern capital accumulation, or the development of the economy over time along an equilibrium path.

Another possible interpretation of the tâtonnement is that it is a method for computing economic equilibrium given the excess demand functions. Then the search for conditions on the excess demand functions that will lead to a stable tâtonnement is a search for conditions that will lead to effective computation. It is known from counterexamples (Scarf 1960) that the simplest tâtonnement where the rate of price change is proportional to excess demand will not always lead to the equilibrium point. Locally any smooth tâtonnement will take this form when the goods are measured in appropriate units. On the other hand, other algorithms are known that are effective for computing equilibrium prices. The earliest example of an effective algorithm is that of Scarf (1973).

It has been left unclear in the discussion of tâtonnement precisely what is meant by the prices. Walras was very clear on this point. The essential thing about prices is that they determine the rates at which goods exchange. Since this is their only meaning, it is appropriate to select one commodity, which he termed the *numéraire* whose price is taken to be unity. Then the process of price revision only applies to $n - 1$ goods. Also Walras was always careful not to select money as the numéraire so that attention would not be distracted from the function of prices as simply representing the rates at which goods exchange. It is more appropriate to consider the role of money in models in which a sequence of markets is considered. There is little point in an attempt to give this degree of realism to the simple exchange market where the demand for goods is based on a static preference order.

2.5 Local Stability of the Tâtonnement

The tâtonnement was given its classic mathematical form by Samuelson
(1947). He represents the tâtonnement by a differential equation system
in which prices are functions of time with a rate of change for each good
which depends on the excess demand for that good. With the assumption
of a numéraire this system may be written

$$\frac{dp_i}{dt} = g_i(e_i(p)), \qquad i = 1, \cdots, n - 1. \tag{3}$$

The good with index n serves as numéraire and $p = (p_1, \cdots, p_{n-1})$. For
this role a good must be chosen whose exchange ratios with other goods
remains above 0 in the region over which the tâtonnement ranges. In these
equations g_i is a nonlinear function of a real variable which is differentiable
and sign preserving. That is, $g_i(s)$ has the sign of s.

Although the differential equation system (3) introduced by Samuelson
has been very popular for discussing tâtonnement stability it is not very
plausible. It is not reasonable that the rates of price revision should depend only on the excess demand for the good and not on its price level as
well. A more general representation of a process of price revision would be

$$\frac{dp_i}{dt} = h_i(p, 1), \qquad i = 1, \cdots, n - 1, \tag{4}$$

where $h_i(p, 1)$ is a real-valued function that is assumed to be differentiable
for $p > 0$ and to have the property that sign $h_i(p, 1) = $ sign $e_i(p, 1)$.

The assumption that h_i has the sign of e_i has far reaching implications.
We will need

PROPOSITION 1   *Let f and g be real-valued linear functions on R^n. If f and
g have the same null space $N \neq R^n$, it follows that $g = \alpha f$ for some real
number $\alpha \neq 0$.*

Proof Let x be any element of $\mathbf{R}^n$ which is not contained in N.
Then $f(x) \neq 0$. Let $y \in \mathbf{R}^n$ be arbitrary. Then $f(y - (f(y)/f(x))x) = 0$.
Therefore $y - (f(y)/f(x))x \in N$. Then $g(y - (f(y)/f(x))x) = 0$. There-
fore $g(y) = (g(x)/f(x))f(y)$, all y, or $g = \alpha f$ for $\alpha = g(x)/f(x)$. ∎

Let $Df_i(p) = (\partial f_i(p)/\partial p_1, \cdots, \partial f_i(p)/\partial p_{n-1})$ for any real-valued differentiable function f defined on $\mathbf{R}^{n-1}$ with $p \in \mathbf{R}^{n-1}$. We may prove

LEMMA 9   *Assume that $\bar{p}$ is an equilibrium price vector and $Dh_i(\bar{p}) \neq 0$,*
$i = 1, \cdots, n-1$. The linearization of the equation system (2) at $\bar{p}$ may be
written

$$\frac{dp_i}{dt} = \alpha_i \sum_{j=1}^{n-1} e_{ij}(\bar{p}, 1)(p_j - \bar{p}_j), \qquad i = 1, \cdots, n-1, \tag{5}$$

for some choice of the $\alpha_i > 0$.

Proof   The linearization of (4) is given by

$$\frac{dp_i}{dt} = \sum_{j=1}^{n-1} h_{ij}(\bar{p})(p_j - \bar{p}_j), \qquad i = 1, \cdots, n-1.$$

Consider the equation $[h_{ij}(\bar{p})]q = 0$ and the equation $[e_{ij}(\bar{p}, 1)]q = 0$.
Since e_i and h_i have the same signs in the neighborhood of $(\bar{p}, 1)$, it follows that Dh_i and De_i have the same null spaces. Therefore proposition 1
implies that $h_{ij} = \alpha_i e_{ij}$ for some choice of $\alpha_i > 0$. Moreover this argument
holds for all $i = 1, \cdots, n-1$. Thus the linearization of (4) at $\bar{p}$ may be
written in the form (5).   ∎

If the unit of measurement of the ith good is multiplied by the factor β_i,
the price is multiplied by the same factor and the quantity of the good in
the new units is multiplied by β_i^{-1}. Let the new prices be q and the new
excess demand function be g. Then $\bar{q} = \beta_i \bar{p}_i$ and

$$\frac{dq_i}{dt} = \frac{\beta_i dp_i}{dt} = \beta_i \alpha_i e_i(p, 1) = \beta_i \alpha_i \beta_i g_i(q, 1).$$

Then, if β_i is set equal to $\alpha_i^{-1/2}$ for $i = 1, \cdots, n-1$, $\beta_n = 1$, in the new
units the equation system (4) becomes

$$\frac{dq}{dt} = [g_{ij}(\bar{q}, 1)](q - \bar{q}) \tag{6}$$

for $i, j = 1, \cdots, n-1$. However, we will continue to use p for prices and
$e(p, 1)$ for excess demand in the normalized equation system. Thus for the
discussion of local stability, the simplest representation of tâtonnement by
a differential equation system is a general representation, so long as the
assumption is maintained that prices change in the direction of excess
demand. This has added significance when we recognize that conditions

for global stability are so severe that the subject of global stability has limited interest.

The differential systems above serve as continuous time representations of tâtonnement. Continuous revision of prices is not realistic for real markets or for markets with hypothetical managers. However, the discrete time models of tâtonnement are also not exact representations of real markets, and the continuous time models have some mathematical advantages. Let the reduced Jacobian $J_n(p, 1) \equiv [e_{ij}(p, 1)]_{n-1}^1$, where i and j range from 1 to $n - 1$. $J_n(p, 1)$ is the principal minor of $J(p, 1)$ which omits the numéraire. A square matrix A is said to be *decomposable* if it can be put into the form $\begin{bmatrix} A_{11} & A_{12} \\ 0 & A_{22} \end{bmatrix}$, where A_{11} and A_{22} are square by the same permutation of rows and columns. If this cannot be done A is said to be *indecomposable*. It is equivalent to say that a matrix $[a_{ij}]$, $i, j = 1, \cdots, n$, is indecomposable if $a_{ij} = 0$ for $i \in J$, $j \notin J$, implies $J = \emptyset$. In order to prove a result on local stability of the tâtonnement, it is helpful to have

LEMMA 10   *Make the gross substitute assumption. Then, if the Jacobian matrix $J(p, 1)$ is indecomposable and $p > 0$, the reduced Jacobian $J_n^T(p, 1)$ has a quasidominant diagonal.*

Proof I claim that $J_n^T(p, 1)$ has q.d.d. with the p_i as multipliers. Recall from lemma 5 that $J(p, 1)p = 0$. Suppose that there were a principal minor of J_n with indexes i and j in the set I and $\sum_{j \in I} e_{ij}p_j = 0$ for all $i \in I$. Since $\sum_{j=1}^n e_{ij}p_j = 0$ and $e_{ij} \geq 0$ for $i \in I$ and $j \notin I$, it follows that $e_{ij} = 0$ must hold for $i \in I$ and $j \notin I$. This is in contradiction to the assumption that J is indecomposable. So no such principal minor can exist and J_n^T satisfies the condition (1) for q.d.d.   ∎

We will say that an equilibrium of a differential equation system (that is, a constant solution of the system) is locally stable if every solution path starting in a sufficiently small neighborhood of the equilibrium point converges to it. There is a simple sufficient condition for the local stability of an autonomous nonlinear differential equation system such as (4).

LEMMA 11   *Let $dx/dt = Ax + f(x)$, where all the characteristic roots of A have negative real parts. Let f be continuous and of at least the second order in x. Then $x(t) = 0$ is a locally stable equilibrium solution.*

Proof See Coddington and Levinson (1955, p. 314).

It is now easy to prove

THEOREM 1   *Make the gross substitute assumption. Let $(\bar{p}, 1)$ be an equilibrium of the exchange economy whose excess demand functions are $e_i(p, p_n)$, $i = 1, \cdots, n$. Assume that $\bar{p} > 0$ and that the e_i as well as the h_i in the differential equation system (4) are continuously differentiable. If $J(\bar{p}, 1)$ is indecomposable, $(\bar{p}, 1)$ is a locally stable equilibrium of (4).*

Proof   By lemma 10, $J_n^T(\bar{p}, 1)$ has q.d.d. The gross substitute assumption implies that the diagonal terms are negative. Thus by lemma 8 all the characteristic roots of J_n^T, thus of J_n, have negative real parts. By lemma 11 this is a sufficient condition for the local stability of (4) if system (6) is a linear approximation to (4) at the equilibrium point. This is provided by lemma 9, since $e_{ij} = 0$ for $j = 1, \cdots, n - 1$ implies $e_{in} = 0$, and thus contradicts the assumption that $J(\bar{p})$ is indecomposable. Then the existence of continuous derivatives for the h_i and the e_i implies the condition of lemma 11.   ■

A square matrix A is said to be *negative quasi-definite* if $A + A^T$ is negative definite, or equivalently if the quadratic form $x^T A x$ is negative definite. We will see that a negative quasi-definite reduced Jacobian at equilibrium is implied by the gross substitute assumption and indecomposability at equilibrium and also by the weak axiom of revealed preference at equilibrium. We will need

PROPOSITION 2   *If a square matrix A is negative quasi-definite, the characteristic roots of A have negative real parts.*

Proof   Note that A is nonsingular. Let $\lambda + i\omega \neq 0$ be a characteristic value of A and let $x + iy$ be a corresponding characteristic vector. Then $(\lambda + i\omega)(x + iy) = A(x + iy)$. Expand and separate into real and imaginary parts.

$$\lambda x - \omega y = Ax, \tag{7}$$

$$\omega x + \lambda y = Ay. \tag{8}$$

Multiply (7) on the left by x^T and (8) on the left by y^T.

$$\lambda x^T x - \omega x^T y = x^T A x, \tag{7'}$$

$$\lambda \omega y^T x + \lambda y^T y = y^T A y. \tag{8'}$$

Add (7′) and (8′), and use $x^T y = y^T x$, to get

$$\lambda(x^T x + y^T y) = x^T A x + y^T A y. \tag{9}$$

Since the right hand side of (9) is negative by assumption and the left hand parenthesis is positive, it follows that λ is negative. ∎

LEMMA 12   *Let $(p, 1)$ be an equilibrium price vector. If the gross substitute assumption is satisfied and $J(p, 1)$ is indecomposable, $J_n(p, 1)$ is negative quasi-definite*

Proof   Let $A \equiv J_n(p, 1) + J_n^T(p, 1)$. We will show that A has a quasi-dominant diagonal at equilibrium. Consider $\sum_{j=1}^{n-1} p_j a_{ij} = \sum_{j=1}^{n-1} p_j(e_{ij} + e_{ji}) = (-e_{in} - e_i) + (-e_{ni}) \leq 0$ by lemma 5 and from the fact that $e_i = 0$ and $e_{ij} \geq 0$ for $i \neq j$. Since J is indecomposable, J_n^T has q.d.d. by lemma 10. It is shown in chapter 3, proof of theorem 3.1, that this implies that J_n has q.d.d. Since J_n^T has nonnegative off-diagonal elements A also has q.d.d. Then by lemma 7, A is negative definite, implying that J_n is negative quasi-definite. ∎

Another way to arrive at a reduced Jacobian that is negative quasi-definite is to assume that income effects of price change are small relative to substitution effects. By definition of the individual excess demand function

$$\frac{\partial e_i^h(p, 1)}{\partial p_j} \equiv \frac{\partial f_i^h(p, 1, m)}{\partial p_j} + \left(\frac{\partial f_i^h(p, 1, m)}{\partial m} \right) \cdot \omega_j^h,$$

where $m \equiv p\omega^h$. By theorem 1.2 this implies

$$\frac{\partial e_i^h(p, 1)}{\partial p_j} \equiv \frac{\partial f_{x_i}^h(p, 1)}{\partial p_j} - (f_j^h(p, 1, m) - \omega_j^h) \cdot \frac{\partial f_i^h(p, 1, m)}{\partial m}, \tag{10}$$

or

$$\frac{\partial e_i^h(p, 1)}{\partial p_j} \equiv \frac{\partial f_{x_i}^h(p, 1)}{\partial p_j} - e_j^h(p, 1) \cdot \frac{\partial f_i^h(p, 1, m)}{\partial m},$$

where $f_x^h(p, 1)$ is the compensated demand function relative to $x = f^h(p, 1, m)$. The first term on the right side of (10) is the substitution effect, and the second term is the income effect for the excess demand for the ith good when there is a change in the price of the jth good. Let $\bar{p}$ be an equilibrium of the nonlinear system (4), and choose units of measurement so that the linearization of (4) at $\bar{p}$ takes the form (6). We need a lemma that will be useful in other places.

LEMMA 13   *Let A be a square matrix of order n and rank $n - 1$. Suppose that $Aw = 0$ where $w_i \neq 0$ and $yA = 0$ where $y_i \neq 0$. Then A_{ii} is nonsingular, where A_{ii} is the principal submatrix that omits the ith row and column.*

Proof   Suppose that A_{ii} is singular and $A_{ii}x_{(i)} = 0$, where $x \neq 0$ is an n-vector, $x_{(i)}$ omits the ith component of x, and $x_i \neq 0$. Without loss of generality, let $i = n$. Consider $A \cdot (x_{(n)}, 0)^T = z$. Then $z_i = 0$ for $i = 1$ to $n - 1$. Now consider $yA = 0$, where y is an n-vector and $y_n \neq 0$ by hypothesis. This implies that the last row of A is a linear combination of the first $n - 1$ rows. Therefore $z_n = 0$ as well or $z = 0$. But $(x_{(n)}, 0) \neq \alpha w$ for any α, so A has rank no greater than $n - 2$. Since this contradicts the assumption, it must be that A_{ii} is nonsingular. ∎

Now we may prove

THEOREM 2   *Assume that equilibrium prices are positive and that the Jacobian matrix exists. If aggregate substitution effects are large relative to aggregate income effects at the equilibrium and the Jacobian of the excess demand functions at the equilibrium has rank equal to $n - 1$, the equilibrium is locally stable independently of the choice of numéraire.*

Proof   The result follows in the same way as in theorem 1. Let $f_x^h(\bar{p}, 1)$ be the compensated demand function where $x = e^h(\bar{p}, 1)$. Then by theorem 1.1, $S^h = [\partial f_{xi}^h(\bar{p}, 1)/\partial p_j]$, $i, j = 1, \cdots, n$, is negative semidefinite. Then $S = \sum_h S^h = [\partial f_{xi}(\bar{p}, 1)/\partial p_j]$, $i, j = 1, \cdots, n$, is negative semidefinite as a sum of negative semidefinite matrices. Let S_n be the principal submatrix of S which omits the nth row and column. Since $S(p, 1)^T = 0$ and $(p^T, 1)S = 0$ by theorem 1.1, it is implied by lemma 13 that S_n is nonsingular. Therefore S_n defines a negative definite quadratic form, and the characteristic roots of S_n are negative.

Let $J = [e_{ij}(\bar{p}, 1)]$, $i, j = 1, \cdots, n$, and J_n be its principal submatrix that omits the nth row and column. J differs from S by the sum of the income effects over the market. For small aggregate income effects the characteristic roots of J_n will be close to the characteristic roots of S_n. Thus the characteristic roots of the matrix $J_n(\bar{p}, 1) = [e_{ij}(\bar{p}, 1)]$, $i, j = 1, \cdots, n - 1$, have negative real parts for sufficiently small income effects. The argument holds for any assignment of indexes to the goods. Thus regardless of the choice of numéraire, the right-hand side of (6) has characteristic roots with negative real parts, and the corresponding nonlinear system is locally stable by lemma 11. ∎

Since the sum of the individual excess demands at equilibrium is zero, it is clear from the second term of (10) that aggregate income effects will be small if all consumers have marginal propensities to consume that are sufficiently similar, that is, terms $\partial f_i^h(\bar{p}, 1)/\partial m$ that are near to equality for all i and h. Similarly the aggregate income effects will be small if the individual excess demands are near enough to 0. Of course, these are sufficient conditions not necessary ones.

There is still a third assumption on the excess demand functions that leads to a negative quasi-definite reduced Jacobian at an equilibrium and therefore to local stability. This is the assumption that the weak axiom of revealed preference holds in some neighborhood of the equilibrium for the market excess demand functions. When applied to the market excess demand functions of an exchange economy in a neighborhood of equilibrium, the weak axiom takes the form:

Let $x = e(p)$ and $e(\bar{p}) = \bar{x} = 0$, where p and $\bar{p}$ are now vectors of dimension n. Then $x \neq \bar{x}$ and $p\bar{x} \leq px$ implies $\bar{p}\bar{x} < \bar{p}x$. In other words, $p\bar{x} \leq 0$ implies $0 < \bar{p}x = \bar{p} \cdot e(p)$.

However, $e(p) \cong J(\bar{p})(p - \bar{p})$ and $p \cdot e(p) = 0$ by Walras's Law. Thus, if the weak axiom holds between price vectors p near equilibrium and the equilibrium price vector $\bar{p}$, we have that $(p - \bar{p})^T J(\bar{p})(p - \bar{p}) < 0$, when $e(p) \neq 0$ and consequently $p \neq \alpha\bar{p}$. Thus $J(\bar{p})$ is negative quasi-semidefinite. By lemma 10 the excess demand functions are homogeneous of degree 0 and satisfy Walras' Law. Homogeneity implies $J(p)p = 0$ for any p and Walras' Law implies that at equilibrium $\bar{p}^T J(\bar{p}) = 0$. Let the nth good be numéraire. Then, if $J(\bar{p})$ has maximal permitted rank the reduced Jacobian $J_n(\bar{p})$ will be nonsingular by lemma 13. Since $J(\bar{p})$ is negative quasi-semidefinite, it follows that $J_n(\bar{p})$ is negative quasi-definite.

Let p once more represent the $n - 1$ vector of prices other than the numéraire. Then the discussion above justifies

THEOREM 3 *Assume that the functions h_i in (4) and e_i are continuously differentiable at an equilibrium $(\bar{p}, 1) > 0$. If the excess demand functions e_i*

satisfy the weak axiom of revealed preference in a neighborhood of $(\bar{p}, 1)$, *and the Jacobian has rank equal to* $n - 1$, *the equilibrium is locally stable.*

Proof By proposition 2 it is enough to show that under the conditions assumed the quadratic form defined by the reduced Jacobian is negative quasi-definite at equilibrium. But this is implied by the fact that the weak axiom holds for prices in a neighborhood of $(\bar{p}, 1)$ by the preceding discussion. ■

In the following argument p is again an n-vector. We proved in the discussion preceding theorem 3 that $J_n(\bar{p})$ is negative quasi-definite if $J(\bar{p})$ has maximal rank and the weak axiom holds near $\bar{p}$, an equilibrium price vector. The relationship among the three main conditions for local stability that we have found may be further clarified by use of the following lemma (see Hildenbrand and Jerison 1989 for a related result). If $x \in \mathbf{R}^n$, let $(x)^\perp = \{y \,|\, x \cdot y = 0\}$.

LEMMA 14 $J(p)$ *negative quasi-definite on the subspace* $(p)^\perp \cap (e(p))^\perp$ *for all* $p > 0$, *implies that the weak axiom holds over the set of positive prices.*

Proof For excess demand functions $e(p)$ we have $p \cdot e(p) = 0$ for any $p \geq 0$ by Walras' Law. The condition for the Weak Axiom to hold for excess demand functions is that $q \cdot e(p) \leq 0$ and $e(q) \neq e(p)$ imply $p \cdot e(q) > 0$. Consider the price vectors $p, q \geq 0$, $\neq 0$, where $q \cdot e(p) \leq 0$ and $e(p) \neq e(q)$. Define the price vector $q(t) = tq + (1 - t)p$ and the function $\Phi(t) = (q - p) \cdot e(q(t))$. By Walras' Law $\Phi(0) = (q - p) \cdot e(p) = q \cdot e(p)$. Also $\Phi(1) = (q - p) \cdot e(q) = -p \cdot e(q)$. Assume that $\Phi(0) = q \cdot e(p) \leq 0$. To show that the Weak Axiom holds, we must prove that $\Phi(1) = p \cdot -e(q) < 0$.

Since Φ is a continuously differentiable function of t and $\Phi(0) \leq 0$, we will establish the conclusion $\Phi(1) < 0$ if we can prove that $\Phi(t) = 0$ implies $\Phi'(t) < 0$. Since $q'(t) = (q - p)$, we must show that $(q - p) \cdot e(q(t)) = 0$ implies $\Phi'(t) = (q - p)^T J(q(t))(q - p) < 0$ By an appropriate choice of α and $w(t) \in (q(t))^\perp$, we may write $(q - p) = \alpha q(t) + w(t)$. With this expression we obtain $\Phi(t) = (q - p) \cdot e(q(t)) = (\alpha q(t) + w(t)) \cdot e(q(t))$. Thus using Walras' Law $\Phi(t) = 0$ implies that $w(t) \cdot e(q(t)) = 0$, that is to say, $w(t) \in e(q(t))^\perp$. Also we have

$$\Phi'(t) = (q - p)^T J(q(t))(q - p) = (\alpha q(t) + w(t))^T J(q(t))(\alpha q(t) + w(t)).$$

Differentiation of Walras' Law shows that $q(t)^T J(q(t)) = -e(q(t))$. Thus

$$\Phi'(t) = (-\alpha e(q(t)) \cdot (\alpha q(t) + w(t)) + w^T J(q(t))(\alpha q(t) + w(t))$$

$$= -\alpha e(q(t)) \cdot w(t) + w(t)^T J(q(t)w(t)).$$

However, we have seen that $\Phi(t) = 0$ implies $-\alpha e(q(t)) \cdot w(t) = 0$. Thus $\Phi'(t) = w(t)^T J(q(t))w(t)$, which is negative by the assumption that $J(q(t))$ is negative quasi-definite on the subspace $(q(t))^\perp \cap (e(q(t))^\perp$. Since $\Phi(0) \le 0$ and Φ is continuously differentiable, we have proved that $\Phi(1) < 0$ holds, establishing the Weak Axiom.   ∎

$J(p)$ negative quasi-definite on $(p)^\perp$ implies that $J(p)$ has rank $n - 1$, so by lemma 14, these conditions in a neighborhood of equilibrium are equivalent to the conditions of theorem 3. Also we have the

COROLLARY $J(p)$ *negative quasi-semidefinite and of rank $n - 1$ at p implies that the Weak Axiom holds in a neighborhood of p.*

Proof   Since homogeneity of zero degree of the excess demand function implies that $J(p)p = 0$, it follows that $J(p)$ of rank $n - 1$ implies that $J(p)$ is negative quasi-definite on the subspace orthogonal to p. Apply lemma 14 in a neighborhood of p.   ∎

Altogether the dominating condition for local stability seems to be that the Jacobian of the excess demand functions be negative quasi-semidefinite at equilibrium and of rank equal to $n - 1$. This condition is implied by theorem 3 if the weak axiom holds in a neighborhood of equilibrium and the Jacobian has rank equal to $n - 1$. It is also implied by small aggregate income effects at equilibrium by theorem 2 and by gross substitutes with indecomposibility at equilibrium by theorem 1.

Our models of tâtonnement involve the choice of a numéraire. This raises the question whether local stability depends on which good is chosen for this role. It has been shown by example that the choice of numéraire may determine whether a tâtonnement is stable (Mukherji 1973). On the other hand, as we showed explicitly in the proof of theorem 3, it may be seen that the proofs of theorems 1, 2, and 3 are not affected by the choice of numéraire. Thus gross substitutes with indecomposability of the Jacobian matrix, or small income effects with a Jacobian of rank equal to

$n-1$, or the Weak Axiom of Revealed Preference for market demand with a Jacobian of rank equal to $n-1$ is a sufficient condition for local stability independently of the numéraire. We may state

THEOREM 4 *Theorems 1, 2, and 3 are true independently of the choice of numéraire.*

Another question that may be raised is the severity of the assumption that equilibrium prices are positive. It will be shown in appendix B that it is sufficient to confine attention to positive prices in the case where the gross substitute assumption is made. However, in other cases the stability of equilibria with some zero prices may be considered. Suppose that $(\bar{p}, 1)$ is an equilibrium and $\bar{p}_i = 0$ for $i \in J \neq \emptyset$. If $e_i(\bar{p}, 1) < 0$ for all $i \in J$, the question of local stability may be answered in a reduced model of tâtonnement. Let I represent the set $\{1, \cdots, n\}$. We assume that $I \backslash J \neq \emptyset$. Consider

$$\frac{dp_i}{dt} = h_i(p, 1), \qquad i \in I \backslash J. \tag{11}$$

We assume that $h_i(p, 1)$ is well defined whenever $e_i(p, 1)$ is well defined, and in particular, they are both well defined and continuous for p in a neighborhood of $\bar{p}$ relative to R_+^n. Also h_i and e_i have the same signs in this neighborhood.

Consider the differential equation system

$$\frac{dp_i}{dt} = h_i(p, 1) \qquad \text{if } p_i > 0,$$

$$\frac{dp_i}{dt} = 0 \qquad \text{if } p_i = 0 \text{ and } e_i(p, 1) < 0. \tag{12}$$

By the continuity of the excess demand functions, there is a neighborhood V of $\bar{p}$ such that $p \in V$ implies $e_i(p, 1) < -\varepsilon$ for an $\varepsilon > 0$ for all $i \in J$ and consequently $h_i(p, 1) < -\delta$ for some $\delta > 0$ for $i \in J$. Thus, if p remains in V, the prices $p_i \to 0$ for $i \in J$ in finite time τ and thereafter they are constant. Thus the tâtonnement (12) is reduced to (11). If (11) is locally stable, there is a neighborhood W of $\bar{p}$ contained in V such that $p(0) \in W$ implies that $p(t) \in V$ for $t \geq 0$, so long as $p_i(t) = 0$ for $i \in J$ continues to hold, that is, so long as (10) remains valid (Coddington and Levinson 1955, p. 314). But $p_i(t) = 0$ does continue to hold for $p(t) \in V$.

The system (11) has as its linearization

$$\frac{dp_i}{dt} = [e_{ij}(\bar{p}, 1)]p, \qquad i, j \in I \backslash J, \tag{13}$$

where the matrix on the right-hand side is a principal submatrix of the matrix appearing on the right-hand side of (6). The conditions of the theorems 2 and 3 applied to the set of goods with positive prices imply that the matrix on the right-hand side of (9) is negative definite, which implies the local stability of (9). We have proved

THEOREM 5   *If the conditions of theorems 2 and 3 are applied to the subset of goods with positive prices local stability will hold for an equilibrium* $(\bar{p}, 1) \geq 0$ *if* $e_i(\bar{p}, 1) < 0$ *for all i such that* $\bar{p}_i = 0$.

The only case left is one where for some *i*th good $\bar{p}_i = 0$ and at the same time $e_i(\bar{p}, 1) = 0$. However, this case is on a razor's edge, and we will disregard it.

2.6   Tâtonnement with Expectations

In the discussion of the tâtonnement, no account has been taken of expectations about future prices. This procedure seemed to be justified by Walras through an assumption that future equilibrium prices are assumed to be equal to whatever prices are called in the course of the tâtonnement. It seems more reasonable to consider the possibility that the changing prices called on the current market may have varying effects on expectations of prices in future markets. We will introduce this consideration into the tâtonnement. Expected prices are likely to depend on the individual trader. However, it is often assumed that all traders agree on expectations or that an average expectation of the market may be used instead of individual expectations.

In *Value and Capital* Hicks considered a dynamic economic model with a succession of temporary equilibria. Each of these equilibria involves both current prices for trading in the current market and expected prices for trading in future markets. In the simplest case future prices could be taken to be the prices of the succeeding period. He defined the *elasticity of expectations* for the *i*th good as the ratio of the proportional change in the expected price of the *i*th good to the proportional change of its current price. Thus the expectations of the price of the ith good are made to depend only on its current price, and not on the current prices of other goods. A fundamental fact about expectations is that they are uncertain. Thus it would seem natural to suppose a distribution of future prices to be expected rather than a definite future price. However, Hicks chose a particular price to represent the probability distribution of future prices on the assumption that actions based on this price, assumed to be certain, would be the same as the actions based on the probability distribution of future prices. Such a price is referred to as a *certainty equivalent price*.

A formal model of a market in continuous time with current and expected prices was proposed by Arrow and Nerlove (1958). If the model were made a discrete time model, the results would not change significantly. The expected prices are not prices expected to be called as the tâtonnement proceeds but equilibrium prices expected to arise in future markets. Moreover, as we will interpret the model, the time that enters into the model is the time in which the tâtonnement takes place, not the time in which future equilibrium prices occur. The model is called *adaptive expectations*. Let p represent current (tâtonnement) prices, and let q represent expected future (equilibrium) prices, which may be taken to be certainty equivalent prices as assumed by Hicks (1939, p. 126). The certainty equivalent price may not exist. However, it was shown by Arrow (1990) that the certainty equivalent price will exist when all the uncertainty is concentrated on prices. Moreover the certainty equivalent price will be below the mean of the expected prices, as Hicks assumed, when the uncertainty is concentrated on prices and there is no uncertainty about technology. We will consider a continuous adjustment process rather than successive adjustments at discrete times, but this is not a matter of principle. Let the market excess demand function for current goods be $e(p, q)$, which is assumed to have continuous first-order partial derivatives. Consider the adjustment process

$$\frac{dp_i}{dt} = e_i(p, q),$$

$$\frac{dq_i}{dt} = k_i(p_i - q_i), \qquad k_i > 0, \; i = 1, \cdots, n-1, \tag{14}$$

$$p_n \equiv q_n \equiv 1,$$

Let $A = [\partial e_i(p,q)/\partial p_j]$, $B = [\partial e_i(p,q)/\partial q_j]$, $i,j = 1, \cdots, n-1$, where A and B are evaluated at equilibrium prices $\bar{p} = \bar{q}$ and $a_{ij} \geq 0$ for $i \neq j$, $b_{ij} \geq 0$ for all i, j. Let

$$C = \begin{bmatrix} A & B \\ K & -K \end{bmatrix},$$

where K is a diagonal matrix with $k_1 \cdots k_{n-1}$ on the diagonal. C is the Jacobian matrix of the right side of the differential equation system of (14). If C has no characteristic roots with real part equal to 0, then (14) is locally stable if and only if all characteristic roots of C have negative real parts.

Static expectations implies that $q \equiv p$. In this case $[\partial e_i(p,p)/\partial p_j] = A + B$. If C has no characteristic roots with real part 0, the corresponding tâtonnement is locally stable if and only if all characteristic roots of $A + B$ have negative real parts. The tâtonnement is described by the equation system

$$\frac{dp_i}{dt} = e_i(p,p), \qquad i = 1, \cdots, n-1,$$

$$p_n \equiv 1.$$

(15)

We will need (McKenzie 1960a).

LEMMA 15   *Let A be a square matrix $[a_{ij}]$ with $a_{ij} \geq 0$ for $i \neq j$. All the characteristic roots of A have negative real parts if and only if A has a dominant negative diagonal.*

Proof Sufficiency is provided by lemma 8. Necessity will be proved in appendix E of chapter 4.

THEOREM 6 (Arrow-Nerlove)   *Make the gross substitute assumption. Assume that neither C nor $A + B$ has a characteristic root with zero real part. Then the adaptive expectations process represented by (14) is locally stable if and only if static expectations represented by (15) is locally stable.*

Proof Sufficiency. By lemma 11, if (2) is locally stable then $A + B$ has all characteristic roots with negative real parts. By lemma 15, $A + B$ has $\mathscr{R}(\lambda) < 0$ for all roots λ if and only if there is $x > 0$ such that

$(A + B)x < 0$. Let $y = \begin{pmatrix} x \\ \beta x \end{pmatrix}$ for $\beta > 0$. There exists β such that $Cy < 0$, so once more by lemma 15, C has $\mathscr{R}(\lambda) < 0$ for every characteristic root λ.

Necessity. Similarly by lemma 11 if (14) is locally stable C has all characteristic roots with negative real parts. By lemma 15, $\mathscr{R}(\lambda) < 0$ for every characteristic root λ if and only if there is $\begin{pmatrix} v \\ w \end{pmatrix} > 0$ such that $C\begin{pmatrix} v \\ w \end{pmatrix} < 0$. Therefore $w > v$, which implies that $(A + B)v < 0$ also holds. Thus $A + B$ has $\mathscr{R}(\lambda) < 0$ for every root λ, and (15) is locally stable by lemma 11. ∎

COROLLARY   *Make the gross substitute assumption for $e(p,q)$ at equilibrium, and assume that $e(p,q)$ is homogeneous of zero degree in (p,q). If $[\partial e_i(p,q)/\partial p_j + \partial e_i(p,q)/\partial q_j]^1_n$ is indecomposable the adjustment process (14) is locally stable.*

Proof   Since $[\partial e_i(p,q)/\partial p_j + \partial e_i(p,q)/\partial q_j]^1_n$ is indecomposable, homogeneity of zero degree implies that $([\partial e_i(p,q)/\partial p_j + \partial e_i(p,q)/\partial q_j]^1_{n-1})^T$ has q.d.d. by the argument of lemma 10. Thus $(A + B)^T$ has q.d.d., and all its characteristic roots have negative real parts by lemma 8. However, $A + B$ has the same characteristic roots as $(A + B)^T$. Then the adjustment process (15) is locally stable by lemma 11. Therefore the adjustment process (14) is stable by theorem 6. ∎

If we think of the tâtonnement as a process occuping infinite (tâtonnement) time, the adjustment process for expected prices in (14) is equivalent to assuming that the expected price is a weighted average of all past current prices. This may be seen by differentiating the relation $q_i(t) = k_i \int_{-\infty}^{t} e^{-k_i(t-\tau)} p_i(\tau)\, d\tau$ with respect to t. If there is a limit L to the number of past prices that influence the current expected price, the expression for $q_i(t)$ may be written $k_i \int_{t-L}^{t} e^{-k_i(t-\tau)} p_i(\tau)\, d\tau + s^{-kL} p(t - L)$, and the formula $dq_i/dt = k_i(p_i - q_i)$ is still obtained by differentiation. The notion of adaptive expectations is somewhat reminiscent of the notion of normal prices, which was proposed as a stabilizing influence by Hicks (1946, p. 205).

We will consider another model of tâtonnement that allows for the influence of current (tâtonnement) prices on expected future (equilibrium) prices and therefore on the demand for current goods. It is similar to a model proposed by Arrow and Enthoven (1956). In this model price movements are projected into the future. This assumption tends to favor instability as compared with adaptive expectations. The model, which is called *extrapolative expectations*, is a variation on the Hicks theme of elasticity of expectations.

Consider the price adjustment without a numéraire

$$\frac{dp_i}{dt} = e_i(p, q),$$

$$\frac{dq_i}{dt} = \frac{\eta_i dp_i}{dt}, \qquad i = 1, \cdots, n. \tag{16}$$

We define the equilibrium set as $E = \{(p, q) \mid e(p, q) = 0\}$. E represents the set of prices, present and expected, which result in short-term equilibrium. The variation in p occurs in the course of the tâtonnement. These variations cause variations in the anticipated future equilibrium prices. Thus there is no reason why p need be equal to q in short term equilibrium. The tâtonnement is only on p.

THEOREM 7   *Assume that $0 \leq \eta_i < 1$ for all i and that e_i is homogeneous of zero degree in (p, q). Then if all goods are gross substitutes and $[e_{ij}(p, q)]_n^1$ is indecomposable, extrapolative expectations imply that (p, q) is locally stable with convergence to the equilibrium set E.*

Proof   Consider (p, q) where $e(p, q) = 0$. Let $[\eta_i]$ be the diagonal matrix with η_i, $i = 1, \cdots, n$, on the diagonal. Let $A = [\partial e_i / \partial p_j]$ and $B = [\partial e_i / \partial q_j]$ where $i, j = 1, \cdots, n$. By homogeneity $Ap + Bq = 0$. Thus $(A + [\eta_i]B)^T$ has q.d.d. which is negative since $\eta_i < 1$ for all i. Therefore $(A + [\eta_i]B)$ has roots with negative real parts by lemma 8.

Consider the linearization of (16) about an equilibrium price vector $(\bar{p}, \bar{q})$.

$$\frac{dp}{dt} = A(p - \bar{p}) + B(q - \bar{q}),$$

$$\frac{dq}{dt} = \frac{[\eta_i]dp}{dt} = [\eta_i](A(p - \bar{p}) + B(q - \bar{q})). \tag{17}$$

Let C be the coefficient matrix of the right side of (17). Consider

$$C - \lambda I = \begin{bmatrix} A - \lambda I & B \\ [\eta_i]A & [\eta_i]B - \lambda I \end{bmatrix}.$$

By subtracting $[\eta_i^{-1}]$ times the second row of blocks of $C - \lambda I$ from the first row of blocks and then adding $[\eta_i^{-1}]$ times the first column of blocks of the resulting matrix to its second column of blocks, we obtain

$$C' - \lambda I = \begin{bmatrix} -\lambda I & 0 \\ [\eta_i]A & A + [\eta_i]B - \lambda I \end{bmatrix}.$$

Now λ is a characteristic root of C if and only if the determinant of $C - \lambda I$ is 0, which is equivalent to having the determinant of $C' - \lambda I$ be 0. But the determinant of $C' - \lambda I$ is equal to $(-\lambda)^n |A + [\eta_i]B - \lambda I|$, which equals 0 if and only if $\lambda = 0$ or λ is a characteristic root of $A + [\eta_i]B - \lambda I$. If the initial prices are $(p(0), q(0))$ which lie in a small neighborhood of equilibrium prices $(\bar{p}, \bar{q})$, in the linear system $(p(t), q(t))$ converges to an equilibrium price vector (p^*, q^*) in a small neighborhood of $(\bar{p}, \bar{q})$. The difference between the initial price vector $(\bar{p}, \bar{q})$ and (p^*, q^*) is a linear combination of the characteristic vectors of the 0 roots of $C - \lambda I$. This difference lies in the tangent plane to the n-dimensional equilibrium manifold of the system (16) at $(\bar{p}, \bar{q})$ and differs from the manifold by a term of the second order. Thus the equilibrium manifold is stable although the equilibrium $(\bar{p}, \bar{q})$ is not. ∎

If the prices are normalized to equal 1, in equilibrium the numbers η_i are seen to be Hicks' elasticities of expectation. Then the stability result corresponds to the verbal arguments in *Value and Capital*. Elasticities of price expectations above unity may be destabilizing, while price expectations with elasticities less than unity are stabilizing.

2.7   An Economy of Firms

If we assume that the production side of the economy is composed of a finite number of firms each possessing a set of possible outputs, we may extend the stability results proved for the exchange economy to this production economy after making appropriate assumptions on the possible output sets. This is the economy studied by Hicks in *Value and Capital* (1939). It is also the economy used by Arrow and Debreu (1954) in their paper on existence of equilibrium. In the fully elaborated model of Debreu (1969), there is a single market in which both current and future goods, distinguished both by date and state of the world, are traded. The number of dates is finite as well as the number of states of the world, so formally speaking, the generalization amounts to an increase in the number of goods. However, the classification of goods by time and state of the world gives rise to new possibilities of analysing the development of the economy over time. We will explore some of these possibilities in chapter 7. We will now ignore the influence of price expectations and return to the static framework of earlier sections. This may be rationalized as before by making the Walras assumption that the future price is expected to equal the present price

In order to make the extension, we must define the supply of output from a firm. Let $Y^f \subset \mathbf{R}^n$ be the set of possible input–output combinations available to the fth firm. If $y \in Y^f$, then $y_i > 0$ means that the amount y_i of the ith good is an output when the production y is realized and $y_i < 0$ means that the amount y_i of the ith good is an input when the production y is realized. Assume with respect to Y^f

ASSUMPTION 6 Y^f is closed and convex.

ASSUMPTION 7 $Y^f \cap \mathbf{R}^n_+ = \{0\}$. Also Y^f is bounded from above.

ASSUMPTION 8 $Y^f \supset \mathbf{R}^n_-$.

Assumption 6 implies the neoclassical assumption that goods are divisible and that input–output combinations intermediate between producible input–output combinations are also producible. Assumption 7 says that inaction is possible and that there can be no outputs if there are no inputs. Also infinite outputs are not possible. Assumption 8 implies that any good can be disposed of freely, a neoclassical assumption.

Define the *efficiency frontier* of the production set for the fth firm by $E(Y^f) \equiv \{y \in Y^f \mid z \geq y \text{ and } z \in Y^f \text{ imply } z = y\}$. $E(Y^f)$ is also referred to in neoclassical discussions as the production possibility frontier. We make the further assumption

ASSUMPTION 9   Assume that $x \in E(Y^f)$, $y \in E(Y^f)$ and $x \neq y$. Then $z = \alpha x + (1 - \alpha)y \in E(Y^f)$ implies that $\alpha = 1$ or 0. Also $E(Y^f)$ is bounded.

The first part of assumption 9 says that the efficiency frontier does not contain flats. The second part adds boundedness below for $E(Y^f)$ to the boundedness above that follows from assumption 7.

For $p \geq 0$ define the *profit function* $\prod^f(p) = \sup py$ for $y \in Y^f$. $\prod^f(p)$ is the support function of the convex set Y^f (see Rockafellar 1970, sec.

13). It is quite analogous to the function $M_x(p)$ which was described in chapter 1. In analogy to lemma 1.3 we have

LEMMA 16 $\prod^f(p)$ *is positive homogeneous of degree 1, convex, and continuous.* $\prod^f(p)$ *is well defined for* $p \geq 0$.

Proof The properties listed in the first statement are true of support functions. The proof is entirely analogous to the proof of lemma 1.3 except that $\prod^f(p)$ is proved to be convex rather than concave. That is, we have for $p = tp' + (1-t)p''$,

$$\prod^f(p) \leq t \prod^f(p') + (1-t) \prod^f(p'').$$

This is convexity for $\prod^f(p)$.

The second statement follows from assumption 7 that Y^f is closed and bounded above.   ∎

The *supply correspondence* $s^f(p)$ of the fth firm is defined for $p \geq 0$ by

$$s^f(p) = \left\{ y \in Y^f \mid py = \prod^f(p) \right\}.$$

In other words, the principle of decision for the firm is to choose a profit-maximizing output given the market prices. Corresponding to lemmas 1.4 and 1.5, we have

LEMMA 17   *Make assumptions 6, 7, 8 and 9. Then the supply correspondence* $s^f(p)$ *is well defined for all* $p \geq 0$ *and homogeneous of degree 0. If* $p > 0$, *then* $s^f(p)$ *is a singleton. Also there is* $y \in s^f(p)$ *such that* $y \in E(Y^f)$. *For any* $y \in E(Y^f)$ *there is* $p \geq 0$ *and* $p \neq 0$ *such that* $y \in s^f(p)$.

Proof The fact that Y^f is closed means that if $s^f(p)$ is not well defined, it must be that any sequence $z^s \in Y^f$ with $pz^s \rightarrow \prod^f(p)$ is unbounded. But it is clear that such a sequence may be chosen to lie in $E(Y^f)$ which is a contradiction of assumption 9. Homogeneity is obvious.

Let $p > 0$ hold. Suppose that both x and y lie in $s^f(p)$. Then $z = tx + (1-t)y$, $t > 0$, is also profit maximizing and thus in $s^f(p)$. But this implies that $z \in E(Y^f)$ in contradiction to assumption 9. Thus $s^f(p)$ is a singleton.

Let $y \in E(Y^f)$. From the definition of efficiency $Y^f \cap (y + \operatorname{int} \mathbf{R}^n_+) = y$. By a separation theorem (Berge 1963, p. 163) there is $p \neq 0$ such that $pz \leq \mu$ for $z \in Y^f$ and $pz > \mu$ for $z \in y + \operatorname{int} \mathbf{R}^n_+$. Since y is a boundary point of $y + \operatorname{int} \mathbf{R}^n_+$ and lies in Y^f, $py = \mu$ holds. Also the second inequality implies that $p \geq 0$. Thus $y \in s^f(p)$. ∎

A further assumption must be made if $s^f(p)$ is to have properties like those that have been proved for the demand functions. We make the

ASSUMPTION 10 If $z \in \operatorname{int} E(Y^f)$ the price vector p such that $pz = \prod^f(p)$, that is, such that $z \in s^f(p)$, is unique except for multiplication by a positive constant.

The interior of $E(Y^f)$ is taken in the sense of Milnor (see Milnor 1965, p. 12). Assumption 10 means that the efficiency frontier is smooth. Indeed, $E(Y^f)$ is a smooth manifold with boundary. We may prove this in analogy to the results on minimum cost functions and compensated demand functions.

LEMMA 18 *Given assumptions 6 through 10, the first partial derivatives of $\prod^f(p)$ exist whenever $s^f(p) \in \operatorname{int} E(Y^f)$. They are continuous and $\partial \prod^f(p)/\partial p_j = s^f_j(p)$. Moreover for almost all $p > 0$ the second partial derivatives of $\prod^f(p)$ exist and $\partial \prod^f(p)/\partial p_j \partial p_i = \partial s^f_i(p)/\partial p_j$.*

Proof If $y = s^f(p) \in \operatorname{int} E(Y^f)$, it follows from lemma 17 that y has a neighborhood in $E(Y^f)$ where $s^f(p)$ is a well-defined function.

Let us say that y is a *subgradient* of a real-valued convex function g defined on an open region U of a finite-dimensional Euclidean space if $g(q) \geq g(p) + y \cdot (q - p)$ for all $q \in U$. It is easily verified that the elements of $s^f(p)$ are the subgradients of $\prod^f(p)$. Then it follows from lemma 17 that the subgradient of $\prod^f$ is unique at p. Therefore, by Rockafellar (1970, thm. 25.1), $\prod^f$ is differentiable at p. Indeed, by Rockafellar (cor. 25.5.1), $\prod^f$ is continuously differentiable at p. The proof that $\partial \prod^f(p)/\partial p = s^f(p)$ is entirely analogous to the proof in chapter 1 that $\partial M_x(p)/\partial p = f_x(p)$, replacing concave by convex and minimum by maximum. In analogy to lemma 1.8, it is shown that $p \cdot (\partial s(p)/\partial p_i) = 0$. Then the conclusion follows from the series of equalities

$$\frac{\partial \prod^f(p)}{\partial p_i} = \frac{\partial (p \cdot s^f(p))}{\partial p_i} = \frac{s^f_i(p) + p \cdot \partial s^f(p)}{\partial p_i} = s^f_i(p).$$

The second partial derivatives of a convex function exist almost every-where (Fenchel 1953, p. 142; Alexandroff 1939).   ∎

Corresponding to the matrix of partial derivatives of the household demand function $f^h(p,m)$ with respect to prices, there is the matrix $S^f(p) = [s_{ij}^f(p)]$, where $s_{ij}^f(p) = \partial s_i^f/\partial p_j$, $i,j = 1, \cdots, n$, the Jacobian of the supply functions of the fth firm. However, the properties of $S^f(p)$ are the analogues of the properties of the matrix $S_x^h(p)$ of partial derivatives of the compensated demand functions rather than those of the matrix $F^h(p,m)$ of partial derivatives of the Walrasian demand functions. In analogy with theorem 1.1, we have

THEOREM 8   *Given assumptions 6 through 10, $S^f(p)$ exists for almost all $p \geq 0$. Moreover,*

i. $S^f(p)$ *is symmetric.*

ii. $z^T S^f(p)z$ *is positive semidefinite.*

iii. $p^T S^f(p) = 0$ *and* $S^f(p)p = 0$.

Proof   From lemma 18, $S^f(p) = [\prod_{ij}^f(p)]$, where $\prod_{ij}(p) = \partial^2 \prod/\partial p_j \partial p_i$, $i,j = 1, \cdots, n$, when the derivatives exist. However, $[\prod_{ij}^f(p)] = D^2 \prod^f(p)$ the second differential of $\prod(p)$, which exists almost everywhere. As in the case of demand theory, this implies the symmetry of $[\prod_{ij}^f(p)]$. Since $\prod^f(p)$ is convex from lemma 16, it follows that $[\prod_{ij}^f(p)] = S^f(p)$ is positive semidefinite. Since $\prod^f(p)$ is homogeneous of degree 1, $\partial \prod^f(p)/\partial p$ is homogeneous of degree 0, and $p \cdot \partial \prod^f(p)/\partial p = 0$ by Euler's relation. This together with symmetry establishes (c).   ∎

With this preparation it is a small further step to make

ASSUMPTION 11   The derivatives $\partial s^f(p)/\partial p$ exist and are continuous for all $p > 0$.

In the economy where the production sector is composed of a finite number of firms whose production sets satisfy assumptions 6 through 11, we may consider the problem of local stability by methods closely allied to those used for the exchange economy. Define the market supply function as $s(p) = \sum_{f=1}^{F} s^f(p)$. In order to introduce the household side of the economy, it is necessary to recognize income from profit. Let α_h^f be the share of the fth firm owned by the hth consumer so that $\sum_{h=1}^{H} \alpha_h^f = 1$. Then income for the hth consumer is $m^h(p) = \sum_{f=1}^{F} \alpha_h^f \prod^f(p) + p w^h$ and $e^h(p) = f^h(p, m^h(p)) - w^h$. Now write $d(p) = \sum_{h=1}^{H} e^h(p)$. Then the market excess demand functions are defined by

$$e(p) = d(p) - s(p).$$

It is useful to establish Walras' Law for $e(p)$ in its new form.

LEMMA 19   *Market demand $d(p)$ is homogeneous of degree 0. Also Walras' Law holds for $e(p)$, or $pe(p) = 0$.*

Proof   The homogeneity of $d(p)$ of degree 0 follows from the homogeneity of $m^h(p)$ of degree 1 and the homogeneity of $f^h(p, m^h)$ of degree 0.

For Walras' Law we note that

$$pd^h(p) = pf^h(p, m^h(p)) - p w^h = m^h(p) - p w^h$$

$$= \sum_{f=1}^{F} \alpha_h^f \prod^f(p) + p w^h - p w^h,$$

so $pd(p) = \sum_{f=1}^{F} \sum_{h=1}^{H} \alpha_h^f \prod^f(p) = \sum_{f=1}^{F} \prod^f(p)$. On the other hand, $ps^f(p) = \prod^f(p)$ by definition, so $ps(p) = \sum_{f=1}^{F} \prod^f(p)$.   ∎

The tâtonnement process is defined by

$$\frac{dp_i}{dt} = d_i(p) - s_i(p), \qquad i = 1, \cdots, n-1, \tag{18}$$

where it is understood that the nth good is chosen as numéraire. We may now prove a theorem of Rader (1972) analogous to theorem 1.

THEOREM 9   *Let $e(\bar{p}) = 0$, where $\bar{p} > 0$. Assume that $d(p)$ satisfies the assumption of gross substitutes at $\bar{p}$. Make the assumptions of section 2.1 for consumer demand and assumptions 6 through 11 for supply from firms. Then, if $[\prod_{ij}]$ has rank $n-1$ or $[d_{ij}]$ is indecomposable, $\bar{p}$ is a locally stable equilibrium of the differential equation system (18).*

Proof   We use the second method of Liapounov (LaSalle and Lefshetz 1961). Let $V(p) = \sum_{i=1}^{n-1} e_i^2(p)$. It is clear that $V(\bar{p}) = 0$ and $V(p) > 0$ if p is not an equilibrium. Let $e_{ij}(p) = \partial e_i(p)/\partial p_j$. Then

$$\frac{dV}{dt} = 2\sum_i \sum_j e_{ij}(p)e_i(p)\frac{dp_j}{dt}$$

$$= 2\sum_i \sum_j e_{ij}(p)e_i(p)e_j(p), \tag{19}$$

where the summations are over $i, j = 1, \cdots, n - 1$. By Walras' Law $\sum_{i=1}^{n} p_i e_i(p) \equiv 0$. Differentiating Walras' Law gives

$$-\sum_{i=1}^{n} p_i s_{ij}(p) - s_j(p) + \sum_{i=1}^{n} p_i d_{ij}(p) + d_j(p) = 0. \tag{20}$$

Also theorem 8 implies that $\sum_{i=1}^{n} p_i s_{ij}^f(p) = 0$. Therefore

$$\sum_{i=1}^{n} p_i s_{ij}(p) = 0. \tag{21}$$

Then (20), (21), and $e(\bar{p}) = 0$ imply that $\sum_{i=1}^{n} \bar{p}_i d_{ij}(\bar{p}) = 0$. Thus $\sum_{i=1}^{n-1} \bar{p}_i d_{ij}(\bar{p}) \le 0$ for $j \ne n$.

By homogeneity from lemma 16, we also have that $\sum_{j=1}^{n} d_{ij}(\bar{p})\bar{p}_j = 0$. Thus by gross substitutes, $\sum_{j=1}^{n-1} d_{ij}(\bar{p})\bar{p}_j \le 0$ for $i \ne n$. Let $D_n = [d_{ij}]$, $i, j = 1, \cdots, n - 1$. Then $D_n + D_n^T$ has a nearly q.d.d. which is negative, so D_n defines a negative semidefinite quadratic form by lemma 7. On the other hand, if D is indecomposable so is $D + D^T$. Then $D_n + D_n^T$ is non-singular by lemma 6 and therefore defines a negative definite quadratic form.

Since $\prod^f(p)$ is convex the Hessian $[\prod_{ij}^f]$, $i, j = 1, \cdots, n$, is positive semidefinite. Let $\prod(p) = \sum_f \prod^f(p)$. Then $[\prod_{ij}]$ is also positive semi-definite. Since $p > 0$ and $[\prod_{ij}]p = 0$, if $[\prod_{ij}]$ has rank $n - 1$, its principal minors are nonsingular by lemma 13. Thus $[\prod_{ij}]_{n-1}^1$ is positive definite and $S_n = [s_{ij}]_{n-1}^1$ is positive definite by lemma 18.

From (19) $dV/dt = 2e_{(n)}^T[D_n - S_n]e_{(n)}$ where $e_{(n)} = (e_1, \cdots, e_{n-1})$. Therefore $dV/dt < 0$ for $e \ne 0$ if D_n is negative quasi-definite or S_n is positive definite, that is, if D is indecomposable or if S is of rank $n - 1$. If these conditions hold at $\bar{p}$, they also hold in a neighborhood of $\bar{p}$. Moreover the nonsingularity of $[e_{ij}(\bar{p})]_{n-1}^1$ implies that $\bar{p}$ is an isolated equilibrium. Since $V(p)$ is nonnegative and continuous, a small neighborhood of $\bar{p}$ may be defined by $U_\varepsilon = \{p \mid V(p) < \varepsilon\}$. Once p enters the neighborhood U_ε, it cannot leave, since $V(p)$ is decreasing in U_ε unless $p = \bar{p}$. Therefore, when either condition holds which implies that $[e_{ij}(\bar{p})]$ is negative quasi-definite, it must be that $p(t)$ converges to $\bar{p}$. Thus (18) is locally stable. ∎

Rader (1972) has an argument to indicate why one might wish to introduce firms into the tâtonnement in this way rather than assume simply that $[d_{ij} - s_{ij}]$ has the gross substitute property. For the sake of simplicity, we will suppose locally that only one good is an output, say the first, and there are n inputs. Also use the neoclassical model of production where output is a continuous function $g(x)$ of the inputs x, where g is strictly concave, and $x > 0$. Strict concavity of g implies that the Hessian $[g_{ij}(x)]$ is negative semidefinite. The firm's profit is $\prod(x) = qg(x) - wx$, where q is the price of the output and w is the vector of prices of the inputs. A necessary and sufficient condition for a maximum of $\prod$ at $x > 0$ is

$$qg_j(x) = w_j, \qquad j = 1, \cdots, n, \tag{22}$$

where $g_j(x)$ is $\partial g(x)/\partial x_j$. Differentiating (22) with respect to w gives

$$q[g_{ij}] \cdot \left[\frac{\partial x_i}{\partial w_j}\right] = I,$$

where I is the identity matrix. Suppose that $[g_{ij}]$ is nonsingular. Then

$$\left[\frac{\partial x_i}{\partial w_j}\right] = q^{-1}[g_{ij}]^{-1}. \tag{23}$$

The nonsingularity of g implies that $[g_{ij}]$ is negative definite. Also in neoclassical production it is normal to suppose that inputs are cooperative, that is, that $g_{ij} \geq 0$ holds for $i \neq j$. We will use two propositions from McKenzie (1960a). Proposition 3 has been introduced as lemma 15. Proposition 4 will be implied by theorem 3.1.

PROPOSITION 3   If $A = [a_{ij}]$ is a square matrix and $a_{ij} \geq 0$ for $i \neq j$, all characteristic roots λ of A have $\mathcal{R}(\lambda) < 0$ if and only if A has q.d.d. that is negative.

PROPOSITION 4   If $A = [a_{ij}]$ is a square matrix and $a_{ij} \geq 0$ for $i \neq j$, $A^{-1} \leq 0$ if and only if A has q.d.d. that is negative.

Since $[g_{ij}]$ is negative definite, its characteristic roots have negative real parts. The assumption that $g_{ij} \geq 0$ for $i \neq j$ together with proposition 3 implies that $[g_{ij}]$ has q.d.d. Then proposition 4 implies from (23) that $\partial x_i / \partial w_j \leq 0$. Thus, if x represents inputs of primary factors and the supplies of these factors from households are fixed, the gross substitute assumption cannot be made, since for these factors the entries in the Jacobian of excess demand are $e_{ij} = \partial x_i / \partial w_j$.

2.8 An Economy of Activities

Rader's theorem shows that the presence of production need not interfere with the stability of a tâtonnement, indeed may even promote it. However, the scope of theorem 8 is limited by the fact that it does not allow for the entry of new firms. This is the feature that justifies the assumption that production is subject to strictly decreasing returns, that is, the assumption that the aggregate production set is strictly convex. When entry of new firms is allowed, it is in the spirit of classical models to assume the aggregate production set to be linear, specifically to be a convex cone with vertex at the origin. This is the viewpoint of Walras. The production side of the economy is seen to be given by a technology that is freely available to the economic agents. The nonlinearities that may be expected from the organization of production in plants and firms may be regarded as indivisibilities from which we abstract as we abstract from the indivisibilities of many commodities. Approximate linearity of production follows from assuming that firms are small and entry is free, while convexity follows from assuming that the separate productive activities do not interfere with each other constructively or destructively.

We will set up the formal model by assuming that the activities are collected into linear processes characterized by production sets which are denoted by Y^a, $a = 1, \cdots, A$. The assumptions on the Y^a are analogous to those on the Y^f except for the differences that arise from the fact that the Y^a are assumed to be cones. Formally

ASSUMPTION 12 Y^a is a closed convex cone with vertex at the origin.

ASSUMPTION 13 $Y^a \cap \mathbf{R}^n_+ = \{0\}$.

ASSUMPTION 14 $Y^a \supset -\mathbf{R}^n$.

The efficiency frontier of the production set of the process is defined in the same way as for the firm, that is,

$E(Y^a) = \{y \in Y^a \mid z \geq y \text{ and } z \in Y^a \text{ implies } z = y\}$.

We then make

ASSUMPTION 15   If $x \in E(Y^a)$, $y \in E(Y^a)$, $x \neq 0$, and $y \neq \alpha x$ for any real α, then $z = \alpha x + (1 - \alpha)y \in E(Y^a)$ implies that $\alpha = 1$ or 0.

The effect of assumption 15 is that the only flats in $E(Y^a)$ are lines thorough the origin.

The *equilibrium profit functions* for the Y^a are defined by $\prod^a(p) = \sup py$ for $y \in Y^a$. It is defined for all p such that the supremum exists as a finite number. Thus $\prod^a(p)$ is the support function of the cone Y^a. Since $0 \in Y^a$, $\prod^a(p) \geq 0$ must hold. However, if $py > 0$ for some y, $\sup py = \infty$. Then p cannot be an equilibrium price.

In the activities model of production as in the firm model equilibrium is defined in terms of the maximization conditions for the consumer and the producer and the consistency of supply and demand when these conditions are satisfied. Let x^h, $h = 1, \cdots, H$, be the allocation of consumption to households, including their supplies of factors treated as negative quantities. Let y^a, $a = 1, \cdots, A$, represent the supplies from processes where inputs are entered as negative numbers. Let $p \in \mathbf{R}^n_+$, $p \neq 0$, be the price vector. Then $(x^1, \cdots, x^H, y^1, \cdots, y^A, p)$ is a competitive equilibrium of the economy of activities if the following conditions are met

i. $x^h \in C^h$ and, $px^h \leq pw^h$. Also, if $z \in C^h$, $zP^h x^h$ implies $pz > pw^h$, $h = 1, \cdots, H$.

ii. $y^a \in Y^a$ and $py^a = 0$, $a = 1, \cdots, A$. Also $z \in Y^a$ implies $pz \leq 0$.

iii. $\sum_{h=1}^{H} x^h = \sum_{a=1}^{A} y^a$.

It turns out that production in this type of model may also be consistent with a stable tâtonnement. Indeed, Walras was concerned with just such a model. However, the first rigorous example was provided by Morishima (1964, ch. 2). Also a simple example with a restricted list of goods and with no joint production is due to Mas-Colell (1983).

We will analyze a model that is an expanded version of that of Mas-Colell. Since Y^a is assumed to be a cone, the production set of a process will be made up of rays from the origin. It is convenient to take a normalized set of activities by intersecting the cone Y^a with the unit sphere. Let $S_1(0)$ denote the unit sphere. $\bar{Y}^a = Y^a \cap S_1(0)$ is the set of normalized activities. Given a price vector $p > 0$, we assume that the proportions in which inputs and outputs are combined is determined by selecting a normalized input–output vector $b^a \in \bar{Y}^a$ such that $pb^a \geq py$ for any $y \in \bar{Y}^a$. We will also refer to b^a as an activity vector of the ath process. The level of output in the ath process is given by $y^a = x_a b^a$ where x_a is a nonnegative real number representing the level of the activity b^a chosen from the process. In equilibrium $py^a = 0$ must hold. Otherwise, an incentive exists for either an expansion or a reduction of the level of the activity. The production set of the economy when the choice of activities has been made is given by the matrix $B = [b^a]$, $a = 1, \cdots, A$. B is an n by A matrix. The ith good is an input to the ath process if $b_i^a < 0$ and it is an output if $b_i^a > 0$. The net output from the production sector is given by $y = Bx$ where x is vector with A components. The dependence of the choice of activity on price may be represented explicitly by writing the functions $b^a(p)$ and $B(p)$.

In order to use the same methods for analyzing the tâtonnement as earlier an assumption of differentiability must be made.

ASSUMPTION 16   The functions $b^a(p)$ have continuous first order partial derivatives for all $p > 0$.

Assumption 16 implies that the efficiency frontier $E(Y^a)$ is smooth. It would be possible to give a background for assumption 16 analogous to lemma 18. Moreover the matrix of partial derivatives of $b^a(p)$ satisfies the conditions of theorem 8. The arguments are precisely the same and need not be repeated.

The profit of the ath process when the price vector is p is $\prod^a(p, x_a) = py^a = x_a pb^a$. Let α_h^a be the share of the ath process owned by the hth consumer so that $\sum_h \alpha_h^a = 1$. Then income for the hth consumer is $m^h(p, x) = \sum_a \alpha_h^a \prod^a(p, x_a) + pw^h$ and $e^h(p, x) = f^h(p, m^h(p, x)) - w^h$. Write $d(p, x) = \sum_h e^h(p, x)$ for $h = 1, \cdots, H$. We will continue the assumptions of section 2.1 for consumer demand, so the continuity of demand is not dependent on the level or distribution of profits, since a cheaper point is provided by initial stocks. Market excess demand is given by

$$e(p, x) = d(p, x) - B(p)x.$$

Let the nth good be numéraire. The tâtonnement is defined by the differential equation system

$$\frac{dp_i}{dt} = h_i \left(d_i(p,x) - \sum_a b_i^a(p)x_a \right),$$

$$\frac{dx_a}{dt} = q_a b^a(p) \cdot p,$$

(24)

where h_i and q_a are speeds of adjustment. However, the units of measurement for goods may be chosen so that $h_i = 1$ for all i. The linearization of (24) at equilibrium (of the market and of the differential equation system) is

$$\begin{bmatrix} dp_{(n)}/dt \\ dx/dt \end{bmatrix} = \begin{bmatrix} S_n(\bar{p}, \bar{x}) & -B_n \\ QB_n^T & 0 \end{bmatrix} \begin{bmatrix} (p_{(n)} - \bar{p}_{(n)}) \\ (x - \bar{x}) \end{bmatrix}$$

(25)

In (25) $p_{(n)} = (p_1, \cdots, p_{n-1})$. Also

$$Q = \begin{bmatrix} q_1 \cdots 0 \\ \cdots\cdots\cdots \\ 0 \cdots\cdots q_A \end{bmatrix}.$$

$S_n(p,x)$ is the sum of gross substitution matrices for consumers and processes omitting the nth good and the nth price. The typical element s_{ij} is given by

$$s_{ij}(p,x) = \left(\frac{\partial e_i(p,m)}{\partial p_j} + \sum_h \frac{\partial e_i^h(p,m)}{\partial m} \cdot \frac{\partial m^h}{\partial p_j} \right)$$

$$- \sum_a \bar{x}_a \frac{\partial b_i^a}{\partial p_j}, \qquad \text{where } i, j = 1, \cdots, n-1.$$

(26)

The partial derivative of $\sum_i b_i^a p_i$ with respect to p_j is $b_j^a + \sum_i p_i \partial b_i^a / p_j$. However, the second term is 0 so the partial derivative of $B^T p$ with respect to p is B^T. B_n is B omitting the nth row corresponding to the nth price, which is the numéraire and does not change.

It may be verified that should consumers have the same tastes, endowments, and shares in profits the consumer term of (26) would be the sum of derivatives of the compensated demand functions and therefore the matrix consisting of these terms would be negative semidefinite. Of course, it is possible that this term is negative quasi-definite if income effects almost cancel, even though consumers differ in all these respects. The industry term is positive semidefinite by the same arguments that led to the positive semidefiniteness of the Jacobian of the supply functions of firms. Thus it can happen that $S_n(\bar{p}, \bar{x})$ is negative quasi-definite.

The differential equation system (24) will be locally stable at $(\bar{p}_{(n)}, \bar{x})$ if the matrix on the right-hand side of (25) has characteristic roots all of whose real parts are negative. Write

$$J = \begin{bmatrix} S_n & -B_n \\ QB_n^T & 0 \end{bmatrix}.$$

It is sufficient to show that the roots of J have negative real parts. To this end, assume that S_n is negative quasi-definite and that B_n has rank equal to A, the number of processes. Note this implies that the number of activities in use is equal to $n - 1$. Consider $J\begin{pmatrix} w \\ z \end{pmatrix} = 0$. $B_n^T w = 0$ implies $w = 0$. Then $S_n \cdot 0 - B_n z = 0$ implies $z = 0$. Therefore J is nonsingular. Let $J\begin{pmatrix} p_{(n)} \\ x \end{pmatrix} = \lambda\begin{pmatrix} p_{(n)} \\ x \end{pmatrix}$, where λ and $(p_{(n)}, x)$ may be complex valued. This may be written

$$S_n p_{(n)} - B_n x = \lambda p_{(n)},$$
$$QB_n^T p_{(n)} = \lambda x. \tag{27}$$

Substituting for x in the first equation of (27) using the second equation, we obtain

$$S_n p_{(n)} - \lambda^{-1} B_n Q B_n^T p_{(n)} = \lambda p_{(n)}. \tag{28}$$

Multiplying (28) on the left by $\bar{p}_{(n)}^T$, the complex conjugate of $p_{(n)}^T$, gives

$$\bar{p}_{(n)}^T S_n p_{(n)} - \lambda^{-1} \bar{p}_{(n)}^T B_n Q B_n^T p_{(n)} = \lambda |p_{(n)}|^2. \tag{29}$$

Taking the real part of the terms of (29), we have

$$\bar{p}_{(n)}^T S_n p_{(n)} - \mathcal{R}(\lambda^{-1}) \bar{p}_{(n)}^T B_n Q B_n^T p_{(n)} = \mathcal{R}(\lambda) |p_{(n)}|^2. \tag{30}$$

Since the real parts of λ and λ^{-1} have the same sign, (30) is a contradiction unless $\mathcal{R}(\lambda)$ is negative or $p_{(n)} = 0$. However $p_{(n)} = 0$ implies by (27) that $x = 0$, since B_n is assumed to have rank A. This is inconsistent with the assumption that $(p_{(n)}, x)$ is a characteristic vector. Therefore we must conclude that $\mathscr{R}(\lambda)$ is negative. Thus the differential equation system (24) is locally stable at $(\bar{p}_{(n)}, \bar{x})$. We may state

THEOREM 10   *Suppose that assumptions 12 through 15 hold and assumption 16 holds in a neighborhood of the equilibrium $(\bar{p}, \bar{x})$ of the economy of processes. Then, if B_n is nonsingular and S_n is negative quasi-definite, the tâtonnement of prices and activity levels is locally stable at $(\bar{p}, \bar{x})$.*

Proof   The differential equation system (24) represents a tâtonnement of prices and activity levels which is thought to have some relation to the operation of actual markets with production, in the short run. It is clear that an equilibrium of the differential equation system (24) corresponds to an equilibrium of the economy of activities. The assumption that consumer demand functions $d(p, x)$ and process activity vectors $b^a(p)$ are continuously differentiable implies that (24) is locally stable if the linearization (25) is locally stable (Coddington and Levinson 1955, p. 314). However, (25) is locally stable if the characteristic roots of J have negative real parts. The preceding argument has shown that the characteristic roots of J do have negative real parts under assumptions 12 through 16. Therefore the system (24) and the tâtonnement it represents are stable at the equilibrium $(\bar{p}, \bar{x})$.   ∎

It may be shown that the assumption that B_n is of rank A is generic in the case of nonjoint production and one nonproduced good (Kehoe 1980). This means that the set of points in price space for which B_n is of rank A is open and dense.

2.9   Tâtonnement with Trading

The tâtonnement processes discussed so far do not allow for exchanges of goods while the processes are going on. The fundamental difficulty with introducing exchange is the possibility of speculation, that is, the exchange of goods with the expectation not of using the bundle that is held but of making further exchanges under more favorable conditions to arrive at the bundle that will be used. In other words, the consumers' demand function based on maximizing utility under budget constraints and the producers' supply function based on maximizing profit over a production set are not a valid basis for determining the exchanges that occur when there is speculation. Our earlier discussions, except for the consideration of price expectations in section 2.6, have proceeded as if only one market is to be held. Speculation arises when a succession of markets is expected. This is not a matter of the fact that both consumption and production take time. Time in this sense can be accommodated by the simple expedient of assigning dates to goods and services that represent the dates on which they are provided. This method was probably first used systematically by Hicks (1939) and the method was extended by Debreu (1959) to take account of uncertainty by also assigning states of the world to goods and services so that goods made available when it is raining are treated as different from goods made available when the weather is dry. These complications cause no problems for the case of time, and there is a certain plausibility to the treatment of uncertainty, although that case is less clear. However, the introduction of a succession of markets is a much more fundamental development. In the presence of such a prospect of future trading speculation cannot begin to be treated adequately unless there is an analysis of trading in assets whose values to current traders depend on the prices that prevail in future markets rather than on their utility for consumption or their use in production. A large literature has developed in the attempt to take account of the complications that arise from the introduction of all kinds of contracts involving the provision of goods in the future where the execution of the contracts may depend on various future events. See, for example, Radner (1972) and Magill and Quinzii (1996). However, these analyses have continued to employ a feature of the the single market; namely it is assumed that future prices are known for goods provided in given states of the world, although it is allowed that different traders may have different estimates of the probabilities that these states will be realized.

Unrealistic as it may be, we will simply banish speculation during the tâtonnement. We will assume that no utilization is occurring, speculation is absent, but the stocks of goods that the traders hold, and from which they trade, are changing as the result of exchanges that raise the utility value of the commodity bundles. However, the exchanges are only confirmed at equilibrium. We will present an analysis of the tâtonnement with trading under these conditions which was developed by Mukherji (1974).

We will give this setting a formal description. Let $\omega = \sum_h \omega^h$, for $h = 1, \cdots, H$, where ω^h is the hth trader's initial stock and $\omega^h \geq 0$. Assume that $\omega^h \in C^h$. Let $y^h(t)$ be the hth trader's stock at time t. Then $\sum_h y^h(t) = \omega$ and $y^h(0) = \omega^h$. Write $e^h(p, y^h) = f^h(p, py^h) - y^h$. Then

$e^h(p, y^h)$ is the hth trader's excess demand when holding $y^h \in C^h$. Let $Y = [y^1, \cdots, y^H]$ be the *allocation matrix*. Market excess demand is $e(p, Y) = \sum_h e^h(p, y^h)$.

The dynamic process is

$$\frac{dp_i}{dt} = e_i(p, Y), \qquad i = 1, \cdots, n. \tag{31}$$

$$\frac{dy^h}{dt} = v^h(p, Y), \qquad h = 1, \cdots, H. \tag{32}$$

The first equation describes the price tâtonnement, and the second equation describes the trading tâtonnement. From our previous remarks one would expect local stability to be discussed in the light of (24). However, we will conduct the argument formally as an exercise in global stability. We maintain assumptions 1.1 through 1.4 and assumptions 5, 6, 7, and 8. In particular recall assumption 8 that the excess demand functions $e^h(p)$ are continuously differentiable for $p > 0$. In addition we make

ASSUMPTION 17   Initial stocks are $w^h \geq 0$ and $w > 0$. For any allocation Y with $y^h \in C^h$, there is ε such that $p_i/|p| < \varepsilon$ implies $e_i(p) > 0$.

ASSUMPTION 18   For any allocation Y with $y^h \in C^h$ and $p > 0$ the stock adjustment $v^h(p, Y)$ is continuously differentiable and satisfies

i. $\sum_h v^h(p, Y) = 0$,

ii. $pv^h(p, Y) = 0$,

iii. $\sum_h |v^h(p, Y)| \neq 0$ holds if there is Y' such that $y'^h \mathcal{R}^h y^h$ for all h and $y'^h \mathcal{P}^h y^h$ for some h, where $py'^h = py^h$,

iv. $\sum_h |v^h(p, Y)| \neq 0$ implies, for some $\alpha > 0$, $(y^h + \alpha v^h(p, Y)) \mathcal{R}^h y^h$, for all h, and $(y^h + \alpha v^h(p, Y)) \mathcal{P}^h y^h$ for some h.

Assumption 17 ensures that prices remain positive so that the market excess demand function is always continuously differentiable. Assumption 18i requires that trading be efficient. Assumption 18ii requires that equal values be exchanged in trades. Assumptions 18iii and 18iv say that a trade occurs if and only if someone can benefit from the trade and no one is harmed.

Let the price vector π^h support the preferred set of y^h at y^h. That is, $\pi^h y > \pi^h y^h$ for $yP^h y^h$, for $y \neq y^h$. The existence of π^h is implied by the convexity of the preferred point set of y^h and the fact that y^h lies in the boundary of $P^h(y^h)$ by assumption 5. Uniqueness of π^h, up to multiplication by a positive number, follows from the existence of a smooth concave utility function whose graph has a unique normal at y^h (see Rockafellar 1970, p. 242). The support of the preferred set of y^h is the projection of the normal of the graph at y^h on the goods space.

LEMMA 20   Let $\pi = \sum_h \pi^h$. Then $\pi \cdot e(p, Y) > 0$ if no trade occurs and $e^h(p, y^h) \neq 0$ for some h.

Proof Let $e^{h_1}(p, y^{h_1}) = x^1 \neq 0$. Then $(y^{h_1} + x^1)\mathscr{P}^{h_1}y^{h_1}$ and therefore $\pi^{h_1}x^1 > 0$. Suppose that $\pi^{h_1}e^{h_2}(p, y^{h_2}) = \pi^{h_1}x^2 < 0$ for some h_2. Since the boundary of the preferred sets are smooth, it follows that $\lambda > 0$ and near 0 implies $(y^{h_1} - \lambda x^2)\mathscr{P}^{h_1}y^{h_1}$, while $(y^{h_2} + \lambda x^2)\mathscr{P}^{h_2}y^{h_2}$. But this implies trade is possible at the prices p which contradicts the hypothesis in the light of assumption 18iii. Therefore $\pi^{h_1}e^h(p, y^h) \geq 0$ for all h and >0 for $h = h_1$. On the other hand, if $e^{h_1}(p, y^{h_1}) = 0$, the same argument implies that $\pi^{h_1}e^h(p, y^h) \geq 0$ for all h. Thus $\pi e(p, Y) > 0$ if $e^h(p, y^h) \neq 0$ for some h. ∎

Lemma 20 allows the proof of a preliminary stability result.

LEMMA 21   If $p(t), Y(t)$ is a solution of the differential equation system (31) and (32) where $p(0) > 0$ and $Y(t) = Y$ for all t, then $p(t) \to p$ such that (p, Y) is an equilibrium of (31) and (32).

Proof Define π^h and π as before. Let $\|x\| = (\sum x_j^2)^{1/2}$. Define $V(p(t)) = \sum_h \|\pi^h - p(t)\|^2 \geq 0$. Then, by lemma 20,

$$\frac{dV}{dt} = -2\sum_h (\pi^h - p(t)) \cdot e(p(t), Y)$$

$$= -2\pi \cdot e(p(t), Y) < 0 \tag{33}$$

unless $e^h(p(t), Y) = 0$ for all h. The continuity of dV/dt follows from the continuity of $e(p(t), Y)$. Also $d\|p(t)\|^2/dt = 2p(t) \cdot e(p(t), Y) = 0$ by Walras' Law. Let $S = \{p > 0 \,|\, p_i/|p| \geq \delta > 0$ for all i, and $\|p\| = \|p(0)\|\}$. For $\varepsilon > 0$, let $U(\varepsilon) = \{p \,|\, p \in S$ and $V(p) < \varepsilon\}$. As a consequence of assumption 17 we may choose δ so that $p(t)$ remains in S for all $t \geq 0$. Suppose that $V(p(0)) \neq 0$. Then for $\varepsilon < V(p(0))$, $S - U(\varepsilon)$ is compact and nonempty. Then $dV/dt < 0$ and continuous for $p(t)$ in $S - U(\varepsilon)$ implies that there is ε' such that $dV/dt < -\varepsilon' < 0$ for $p(t)$ in $S - U(\varepsilon)$. Suppose that $p(t) \in S - U(\varepsilon)$ for all $t \geq 0$. Then

$$V(p(t)) = V(p(0)) + \int_0^t \frac{dV}{dt} \, d\tau \leq V(p(0)) - \varepsilon't.$$

Therefore $t > V(p(0))/\varepsilon'$ implies $V(p(t)) < 0$, which is impossible. Let $\varepsilon^t \to 0$ for $t = 1, 2, \cdots$. Then there is t^s such that $p(t) \in U(\varepsilon^s)$ for $t > t^s$. Let $W = \bigcap_{s=1}^{\infty}$ closure $U(\varepsilon^s)$. $W \neq \emptyset$ since the $U(\varepsilon^s)$ are nested sets. Thus $p(t) \to W$ as $t \to \infty$.

If $p \in W$ is a limit point of $\{p(t) \,|\, t \geq 0\}$, it follows by the definition of $U(\varepsilon)$ that $V(p) < \varepsilon$ for any $\varepsilon > 0$. Thus $V(p) = 0$ and $\pi^h = p$ for all h. Then $dV/dt = 0$ also holds which implies $\pi \cdot e(p, Y) = 0$ by (33). Since no trade occurs, by lemma 20 this implies $e^h(p, y^h) = 0$ for all h. It follows from the smoothness of the preferred sets that p is unique. Also, since no trade is occurring, $v^h(p(t), Y) = 0$ for all h. Then continuity of $v^h(p(t), Y)$ implies that $v^h(p, Y) = 0$. Since $e(p, Y) = 0$ as well, (p, Y) is an equilibrium of (31) and (32). $\blacksquare$

We say that Y is a Pareto optimal allocation or simply a *Pareto optimum* if there is no allocation matrix $\hat{Y}$ such that $\hat{y}^h \mathcal{R}^h y^h$ for all h and $\hat{y}^h \mathcal{P}^h y^h$ for some h. Supplementing the stability result for prices proved in lemma 21, there is a stability result for allocations.

LEMMA 22   *If $p(t), Y(t)$ is a solution of the system (31), (32) with $p(0) > 0$, $Y(t) \to Y^*$ as $t \to \infty$ where Y^* is a Pareto optimum.*

Proof $Y(t)$ is bounded since total stocks are fixed in amount. Thus there exists a sequence t_s, $s = 1, 2, \cdots$, with $t_s \to \infty$ such that $Y(t_s) \to Y'$ for some Y'. Suppose there is also a sequence $t_s' \to \infty$ where $Y(t_s') \to Y'' \neq Y'$. By assumption 18iv, $y^h(t) \mathcal{R}^h y^h(t')$ for all $t > t'$. Thus for any s, $y^h(t_{s'}') \mathcal{R}^h y^h(t_s)$ for some s' and for all $t_s' > t_{s'}'$. This argument may also be run in the opposite direction. Let $y^h(t) \to y$ and $y^{h'}(t) \to y'$. Then by continuity of the preference order, it follows that $y^{h'}$ is indifferent to y^h. Since this argument holds for all h, all limit points of $Y(t)$ are indifferent for all h.

Let $\bar{p}, Y^*$ be a limit point of $(p(t), Y(t))$. Consider a solution $(p'(t), Y'(t))$ with initial point $(p'(0), Y'(0)) = (\bar{p}, Y^*)$. Let $(p(t_v), Y(t_v)) \to$

$(\bar{p}, Y^*)$. By continuity of solutions with respect to initial conditions, $(p(t_v + t), Y(t_v + t)) \rightarrow (p'(t), Y'(t))$. Then $y'^h(t)$ is indifferent with y^{*h} by the argument above. Therefore there is no trade on the path $(p'(t), Y'(t))$ by (32) and assumption 18iv. By lemma 21, $p'(t) \rightarrow p^*$, where (p^*, Y^*) is an equilibrium of (31), (32). This implies that $e(p^*, Y^*) = 0$ and $v^h(p^*, Y^*) = 0$ for all h. Since $\pi \cdot e(p^*, Y^*) = 0$, it is implied by lemma 20 that $e^h(p^*, y^{*h}) = 0$ for all h.

Suppose that Y^* were not a Pareto optimum so that a Pareto superior allocation $\hat{Y}$ exists. By the definition of e^h and assumption 6, it must be that $p^*\hat{y}^h \geq p^*y^{*h}$ for all h and $>$ for some h. But this implies that $p^* \cdot \sum_h \hat{y}^h > p^* \cdot \sum_h y^{h*}$, so $\sum_h \hat{y} = \sum_h y^{*h}$ is impossible. Since this contradicts the assumptions, no such $\hat{Y}$ can exist and Y^* is a Pareto optimal allocation. The strict convexity of preferred point sets implies that the limit point is unique. Otherwise taking a convex combination of two limiting $Y's$ would produce an allocation superior for all h by the fact that limit $Y's$ are indifferent. ∎

We have now shown that $p(t)$ is stable given a fixed Y and that $Y(t)$ is stable along a solution path. However, this is not enough to prove stability for the solution path $p(t), Y(t)$. It is possible that $p(t)$ continues to move over a path whose length is unbounded, however close $Y(t)$ comes to Y^*. The stability of $p(t)$ that was shown in lemma 21 must be extended to a neighborhood of Y^* in order to complete the proof of stability for solution paths of the whole system (31), (32).

Define the Liapounov function $V(t) = V(p(t)) = \|p(t) - p^*\|^2$, where (p^*, Y^*) is an equilibrium of (31), (32) and therefore of the market. Then $e^h(p^*, Y^*) = 0$ for all h. Let $d/dt\, V(t)$ be the derivative along a solution path $p(t), Y(t)$ of (31), (32). Then Walras' Law implies

$$\frac{d}{dt} V(t) = \frac{d}{dt} V(p(t))$$

$$= 2(p(t) - p^*) \cdot \frac{dp}{dt}$$

$$= 2(p(t) - p^*) \cdot e(p(t), Y(t))$$

$$= -2p^* e(p(t), Y(t)). \tag{34}$$

LEMMA 23 $dV(t)/dt < 0$ *for* $p(t) \neq p^*$, $Y(t) = Y^*$. *Also* $dV(t)/dt$ *is continuous for* $p > 0$.

Proof $p(t) \cdot e^h(p(t), y^{h*}) = p(t) \cdot e^h(p^*, y^{h*}) = 0$ by Walras' Law and the conditions of equilibrium. Then the Weak Axiom implies

$$p^* e^h(p(t), y^{h*}) > p^* e^h(p^*, y^{h*}) = 0.$$

This implies $dV/dt < 0$ by (34). Continuity follows from the continuity of $e^h(p(t), y^{h*})$ for $p(t) > 0$ and assumption 8. ■

It is now possible to prove the full stability theorem.

THEOREM 11 (Mukherji 1971) *Let* $p(t), Y(t)$ *be a solution of (24), (25), where* $p(0), Y(0) > 0$. *Then* $p(t), Y(t) \rightarrow p^*, Y^*$ *as* $t \rightarrow \infty$, *where* p^*, Y^* *is an equilibrium.*

Proof By lemma 22, $Y(t) \rightarrow Y^*$, where Y^* is a Pareto optimal allocation. Let p^* satisfy $e(p^*, Y^*) = 0$. We will prove in chapter 5 that p^* exists since Y^* is Pareto optimal. Let $V(t)$ be defined relative to this p^*. As in the proof of lemma 21, $p(t)$ remains in the compact set $S = \{p \mid \|p\| = \|p(0)\|, \ p_i/\|p\| \geq \delta > 0\}$, where δ is chosen small enough. Also $V(t)$ is only zero at equilibrium prices. Therefore it suffices to prove that $V(t) \rightarrow 0$ as $t \rightarrow \infty$ along the solution path $p(t), Y(t)$ of (31), (32).

Suppose that $V(t) \geq \varepsilon > 0$ for $t \geq T$. Let $S'_\varepsilon = \{p \in S \mid \|p - p^*\|^2 < \varepsilon\}$. Let $S_\varepsilon = S - S'_\varepsilon$. Then $p(t) \in S_\varepsilon$ for $t > T$. Let $\mu = \max(-2p^* e(p(t), Y^*))$ for t such that $p(t) \in S_\varepsilon$. Then $\mu < 0$ by the proof of lemma 20. Let $\mathcal{Y} = \{Y \mid \sum_h y^h = \omega\}$. Since $dV/dt = -2p^* \cdot e(p(t), Y(t))$ is continuous it is uniformly continuous for all t such that $(p(t), Y(t)) \in S_\varepsilon \times \mathcal{Y}$, which is compact. Therefore there is $\delta > 0$ such that

$$\left| \frac{dV(t)}{dt} - (-2p^* \cdot e(p(t), Y^*)) \right| < -\frac{\mu}{2},$$

for $|Y(t) - Y^*| < \delta$ and $p(t) \in S_\varepsilon$.

This implies that eventually $dV/dt < \mu/2$ for $|Y(t) - Y^*| < \delta$ and $p(t) \in S_\varepsilon$.

By lemma 22 there is T_δ such that $|Y(t) - Y^*| < \delta$ for all $t > T_\delta$. Then by the choice of δ and T, it follows that $dV(t)/dt < \mu/2$ for $t > T' = \text{maximum}(T, T_\delta)$. This implies that $p(t) \in S'_\varepsilon$ for t large enough, which contradicts the assumption that $V(t) \geq \varepsilon$ for all $t > T$. Since $dV/dt < 0$, once $V(t) < \varepsilon$ holds, it continues to hold for all larger t. Since the choice of ε is arbitrary, it must be that $V(t) \to 0$ or equivalently $p(t) \to p^*$. Thus $p(t), Y(t) \to p^*, Y^*$ as $t \to \infty$, where (p^*, Y^*) has been chosen to be an equilibrium. ■

2.10 Global Stability with Gross Substitutes

In the subsequent discussion it is understood that the nth good is the numéraire whose price is always equal to 1 and $q = (q_1, \cdots, q_n)$. We will be concerned with the tâtonnement process

$$\frac{dq_i}{dt} = h_i(q), \qquad i = 1, \cdots, n,$$

$$\text{sign } h_i(q) = \text{sign } e_i(q), \qquad i = 1, \cdots, n, \tag{35}$$

$$h_n(q) \equiv 0.$$

This was our primary resource for the discussion of local stability in section 2.5. The local approximation of (35) in the neighborhood of equilibrium is the same as a local approximation of

$$\frac{dq_i}{dt} = e_i(q), \qquad i = 1, \cdots, n-1,$$

$$\frac{dq_n}{dt} \equiv 0. \tag{36}$$

after a change of units. However, for questions of global stability (35) and (36) are fundamentally different. In (36) the effects of price changes on the rate of price change for a good are proportional to their effects on the excess demand for that good regardless of the level of price. This specification seems entirely unreasonable from the standpoint of market behavior. However, the most meaningful economic condition leading to global stability, the gross substitute assumption, turns out to be effective for (35), so these difficulties are bypassed. See McKenzie (1960b). Of course, the gross substitute assumption is a particularly strong assumption especially if it is made globally. The other assumptions that we have used for local stability have been adapted to the global context, but only for systems similar to (36), not for very general systems like (35).

Economies where excess demand has the gross substitute property have very special characteristics, many of them first discovered and analyzed by Arrow and Hurwicz (1958, 1960, 1962) and Arrow, Block, and Hurwicz (1959). Given assumptions 1.1, 1.2, 1.3, 1.4, and 1, 2, and 3 above, the existence of an equilibrium follows from standard theorems. In particular, the proposition of Debreu (1970, p. 183) is well adapted to this case (also see appendix A of chapter 6 and McKenzie 1954). We make assumption 4 that excess demand functions are differentiable at positive prices and a weakened form of the gross substitution assumption 5. Initially we will assume that positive equilibrium price $\bar{q}$ exists.

ASSUMPTION 5′ $\partial e_i(q)/\partial q_j \geq 0$, for $i \neq j$ and $q > 0$.

The model of price tâtonnement that we will use is the general model given by the differential equation system (35). The first requirement is to bound the path of prices from initial prices $(\bar{q})$ that are positive. Choose units of measurement so that $\bar{q}$ is the unit vector $(1, \cdots, 1)$. Let i_0 be the index of a price for which $q_{i_0} \leq q_i$ for all i, and let i_1 be the index of a price for which $q_{i_1} \geq q_i$ for all i. We may prove

LEMMA 24   *A solution path $q(t)$ of (35) from $\bar{q}$ satisfies the condition $q_{i_0} \leq q_i(t) \leq q_{i_1}$ for all i and all $t \geq 0$.*

Proof We first show that at any disequilibrium price vector $q(t)$ a good with the lowest price relative to equilibrium has positive excess demand and a good with the highest price relative to equilibrium has negative excess demand. Consider $q_i' = q_i(t)/q_{i_0}(t)$ for $i = 1, \cdots, n$. Then $e(q') = e(q(t))$ by homogeneity. Consider a movement of prices along the line segment from the equilibrium price vector $\bar{q} = (1, \cdots, 1)$ to q' so that $q(\tau) = \bar{q} + \tau(q' - \bar{q})$ and $0 \leq \tau \leq 1$. Then we have $dq(\tau)/d\tau \geq 0$ and $dq_{i_0}(\tau)/d\tau = 0$. Thus by assumption 5′,

$$\frac{d}{d\tau}(e_{i_0}(q(\tau)) = \sum_{j=1}^{n} e_{i_0 j}(q(\tau))) \cdot \frac{dq_j(\tau)}{d\tau} \geq 0$$

for all τ between 0 and 1. Since $e_{i_0}(\bar{q}) = 0$, it follows that $e_{i_0}(q') = e_{i_0}(q(t)) \geq 0$. This implies that $dq_{i_0}(t)/dt \geq 0$ along the tâtonnement path. By an analogous argument it may be shown that $e_{i_1}(q(t)) \leq 0$ and $dq_{i_1}(t)/dt \leq 0$. Let $\mu_0(t) = \min q_i(t)$ for $i = 1, \cdots, n$, and let $\mu_1(t) = $ maximum $q_i(t)$ for $i = 1, \cdots, n$. From the definition of $\mu_0(\tau)$ it follows that the right-hand derivative $(d\mu_0(t)/dt)^+ = \min dq_i(t)/dt$ over the indexes i such that $q_i(t)$ is minimal, and the right-hand derivative $(d\mu_1(t)/dt)^+ = \text{maximum } dq_i(t)/dt$ over the indexes i such that $q_i(t)$ is maximal. Then $(d\mu_0(t)/dt)^+ \geq 0$ and $(d\mu_1(t)/dt)^+ \leq 0$ for all t, which implies that $\mu_0(0) \leq q_i(t) \leq \mu_1(0)$ for all t and all i or $q_{i_0} \leq q_i(t) \leq q_{i_1}$ for all t and all i. ∎

Let $I = \{1, \cdots, n\}$, $P = \{i \in I \,|\, h_i \geq 0\}$, and $N = \{i \in I \,|\, h_i < 0\}$. We take $h_n = 0$. Define $L(q) = \sum_{i \in P} q_i e_i(q) \geq 0$, and > 0, if q is not an equilibrium price. Also $dL/dt = dL(q(t))/dt$. We will use the function L, the value of excess demand to prove a global stability theorem in the manner of the second method of Liapounov (La Salle and Lefschetz 1961). Let W be the set of positive equilibria. We will prove that every path departing from positive initial prices converges asymptotically to W. Then if W is a singleton there is stability in the usual sense. It will also be shown that W is a convex set.

In preparation for the stability theorem some additional lemmas will be proved.

LEMMA 25 $L(q) = 0$ for $q > 0$ if and only if $q \in W$.

Proof The sufficiency of $q \in W$ is obvious, since then all $e_i(q) = 0$. Suppose that $e_i(q) \neq 0$ for some i so that $q \notin W$. Then $e_i(q) > 0$ for some i and q is not an equilibrium. Thus $q \in W$ is also necessary. ∎

LEMMA 26   *Let (E, F) be a nontrivial partition of I. Suppose that $\sum_{i \in E} q_i e_i(q) > 0$. Then, if e_{ij} exists for all $i, j \in I$, it follows that $e_{ij}(q) > 0$ for some $i \in E$, $j \in F$.*

Proof Differentiating Walras' Law with respect to q_j, $\sum_{i \in I} q_i e_{ij} = -e_j$. Thus

$$\sum_{i \in I} \sum_{j \in E} q_i e_{ij} q_j = -\sum_{j \in E} q_j e_j < 0. \tag{37}$$

But $e_{ij} \geq 0$ for $i \in F$, $j \in E$. Therefore from (30),

$$\sum_{i \in E} \sum_{j \in E} q_i e_{ij} q_j < 0. \tag{38}$$

By homogeneity $\sum_{j \in I} e_{ij} q_j = 0$, so

$$\sum_{i \in E} \sum_{j \in I} q_i e_{ij} q_j = 0. \tag{39}$$

Then (38) and (39) imply

$$\sum_{i \in E} \sum_{j \in F} q_i e_{ij} q_j > 0. \tag{40}$$

Since $q_i \geq 0$ there must be $e_{ij} > 0$ with $i \in E$, $j \in F$. ∎

With the help of lemma 26 it is possible to show that the derivative of L with respect to time is negative away from equilibrium.

LEMMA 27 *Suppose q is not an equilibrium. Then $dL/dt < 0$. Moreover dL/dt is continuous.*

Proof Using (35), we have

$$\frac{dL}{dt} = \frac{d(\sum_{i \in P} q_i e_i)}{dt} = \sum_{i \in P} h_i e_i + \sum_{i \in P} q_i \left(\frac{de_i}{dt} \right)$$

$$= \sum_{i \in P} h_i e_i + \sum_{i \in P} q_i \sum_{j \in I} e_{ij} h_j. \tag{41}$$

Substituting for e_i in (41), as in (37), we have

$$\frac{dL}{dt} = -\sum_{j \in P} h_j \sum_{i \in I} q_i e_{ij} + \sum_{i \in P} q_i \sum_{j \in I} e_{ij} h_j$$

by cancellation of terms

$$\frac{dL}{dt} = -\sum_{i \in N} \sum_{j \in P} q_i e_{ij} h_j + \sum_{i \in P} \sum_{j \in N} q_i e_{ij} h_j. \tag{42}$$

Note that for $i \in N$, $j \in P$, $e_{ij} \geq 0$, and that for $j \in P$, $h_j \geq 0$. Therefore the first term is less than or equal to 0. Also lemma 26 (with $E = P$) implies $e_{ij} > 0$ for some $i \in P$, $j \in N$. Also $h_j < 0$ for $j \in N$. Therefore the second term on the right in (42) is negative and $dL^+/dt < 0$.

Continuity of dL^+/dt follows from the continuity assumed for the e_{ij} and the h_j, together with the fact that when j moves between the sets P and N, the terms $q_i e_{ij} h_j$ change continuously between positive or negative values and 0. ∎

The first result on global stability for the gross substitute case (McKenzie 1960b) is

THEOREM 12 *Assume that a positive equilibrium price exists. If the gross substitute assumption holds, the differential equation system (35) has a unique solution $q(t; q^0)$ for any initial prices $q^0 > 0$. As t increases without limit, $q(t; q^0)$ approaches an equilibrium price $\bar{q} = \bar{q}(q^0)$. The set W of equilibria is compact and convex. If the full Jacobian $J(\bar{q}, 1)$ is indecomposable, W is a singleton.*

Proof Since $h(q)$ is continuously differentiable, the existence of a solution $q(t; q^0)$ for $q^0 > 0$ is provided by the Cauchy-Lipshitz theorem (Hartman 1967, pp. 8, 23). Normalize units of measurement for goods so that $\bar{q} = (1, \cdots, 1)$. By lemma 24 the solution path remains in the compact set $B = \{q \mid q_{i_0}^0 \le q \le q_{i_1}^0\}$, where $q_{i_0}^0$ is a minimal component of q^0 and $q_{i_1}^0$ is a maximal component of q^0. Thus the solution $q(t; q^0)$ can be continued for all $t \ge 0$. We will show that $L(t) = L(q(t; q^0))$ converges to 0 as $t \to \infty$.

Suppose that

$$L(q(t; q^0)) \ge \varepsilon > 0 \tag{43}$$

for all $t \ge 0$. Since $q(t; q^0)$ remains in B and B is compact, there is $q' \in B$ and a sequence t_s, $s = 1, 2, \cdots$, with $t_s \to \infty$ such that $q(t_s; q^0) \to q'$. It follows from lemma 27 that $L(q(t; q^0))$ is monotone decreasing. Therefore $L(q(t; q^0)) \to L(q')$. Suppose that q' is not an equilibrium. Then $dL(q')/dt < -\varepsilon$ for some $\varepsilon > 0$, again by lemma 27. Since $dL(q(t))/dt$ is continuous by lemma 27, $dL(q(t_s))/dt < -\varepsilon/2$ for all large s. Thus $L(q(t_s)) < 0$ must hold for sufficiently large s. This is a contradiction, so it must be that q' is an equilibrium $\bar{q}(q^0) \in W$. This argument may be made for any positive initial price vector q^0. Also $q(t; q^0)$, and thus $\bar{q}$ is a continuous function of the initial conditions q^0 (Coddington and Levinson 1955, p. 22).

Thus every limit point of a solution of (4) from positive initial prices is in W. Suppose there were two distinct limit points, q^1 and $q^2 \ne \alpha q^1$ for any α. Take the case of q^1, and choose the units so that $q^1 = (1, \cdots, 1)$. It is an immediate implication of lemma 24 that $q(t; q^0)$ in a close neighborhood of q^1 cannot leave a small neighborhood of q^1. Thus q^2 cannot be a distinct limit point and q' must be the unique limit point of the unique solution of (4) with the initial condition $q(0) = q^0$.

We next prove that W is convex. Suppose that q^1 and q^2 are distinct members of W. By homogeneity, $\alpha q^2 \in W$ for $\alpha > 0$. Let $q(s) = s\alpha q^2 + (1-s)q^1$, and let $dq_i/ds = \alpha q_i^2 - q_i^1$. Let E, F be a partition of I where $i \in E$ when $dq_i/ds \geq 0$, $i \in F$ when $dq_i/ds < 0$. If α is chosen large enough, $\alpha q_i^2 - q_i^1 > 0$ for all $i \in I$ and all prices are rising as t increases. If α is chosen small enough, all prices are falling as t increases. As α increases, the goods pass from F to E in the order of the ratios q_i^2/q_i^1, that is, in the order of the relative price increases from q^1 to q^2. With a proper choice of α the set E may be made to include any subset of goods whose ratios are larger than those of the complementary subset. Choose the indexes so that $i < j$ implies $q_i^2/q_i^1 > q_j^2/q_j^1$. Define $L_k(s) = \sum_1^k q_i(s) \cdot e_i(q(s))$. By an argument parallel to that above for $L(t)$, it follows that $dL(s)/ds < 0$. This implies that $L_k(1) < L_k(0) = 0$. Since this is a contradiction, it must be that $L_k(s) = 0$ for all s between 0 and 1. But this is not possible unless $e_i(q(s)) = 0$ for all s between 0 and 1, or $q(s) \in W$ for $0 < s < 1$. Thus W is convex.

If $\bar{q}$ is an equilibrium and the full Jacobian $J(\bar{q})$ is indecomposable, then $\bar{q}$ is a locally stable equilibrium by theorem 1. Since W is convex, this implies that W is a singleton. W is closed as a consequence of the continuity of $e(\bar{q})$. ∎

Theorem 12 uses the assumption that a positive equilibrium of (4) exists and that the initial price vector q^0 is positive. However, this theorem can be extended to other prices in a manner similar to the extension of the theorem on local stability to zero prices in theorem 5.

LEMMA 28 *Suppose that $e_i^h(\bar{q})$ is well defined and $\bar{q}_i = 0$ for some i. Under the gross substitute assumption there are constants $\bar{e}_i^h$ such that $e_i^h(q) = \bar{e}_i^h$ whenever $e_i^h(q)$ is well defined and $q_i = 0$.*

Proof We omit the superscript h on the excess demand function e^h of the hth consumer. First assume that all prices $\bar{q}_j \neq 0$ for $j \neq i$. Let $S_i = \{(q) \geq 0 \,|\, q_i = 0$ and $e(q)$ is well defined$\}$. Consider a function e_i^0 which is defined on S_i and equal to e_i there. Then it is implied by the homogeneity of e_i of degree zero that e_i^0 is homogeneous of degree 0. Since $\partial e_i^0/\partial p_j = \partial e_i/\partial p_j = e_{ij}$ it follows from Euler's relation that $\sum_{j \neq i} \bar{q}_j e_{ij}(\bar{q}) = 0$. But by the assumption of gross substitutes $e_{ij} \geq 0$ for $j \neq i$. Therefore $e_{ij}(\bar{q}) = 0$ must hold. But $\bar{q}$ is arbitrary in S_i except for points where $\bar{q}_j = 0$ for some $j \neq i$. Thus e_i is a constant e_i^0 over this subset of S_i. However, $e_i = e_i^0$ also holds at points where $p_j = 0$ for some $j \neq i$ if e_i is continuous there. To complete the proof, we need another lemma.

LEMMA 29   *If $e^h(\bar{q})$ is well defined and $q^s \to \bar{q}$, then $e^h(q^s) \to e^h(\bar{q})$ if $e^h(q^s)$ is well defined.*

Proof   Again we omit the superscript h on e^h. It is clear from the proof of lemma 4 that no difficulties arise so long as $e(q^s)$ is bounded. Therefore suppose that $e(q^s)$ is not bounded and take an unbounded subsequence, preserving notation. Let x^s be the intersection of the line segment from $e(q^s)$ to the commodity bundle z^s of the proof of lemma 4 with the ε-sphere about z^s. This intersection will exist for sufficiently large s. Let $z^s \to z = e(\bar{q})$. Then x^s is in the budget set for q^s. By the strict convexity of preferences, x^s is preferred to z^s. Since x^s is bounded, there is a point of accumulation x. Also x is in the budget set for $\bar{q}$. By continuity of preferences, x is at least as good as z. Then x is in the demand set for $\bar{q}$. This is a contradiction of strict convexity of preferences so $e(q^s)$ cannot be unbounded.   ∎

Lemma 29 establishes the continuity of e within the set S of prices for which e is well defined. Therefore within this set $e_i(q) = \bar{e}_i^0$ is valid.   ∎

The gross substitute assumption can only be applied where the excess demand function is well defined. Therefore, if we extend the gross substitute assumption to price vectors that contain some zero components, it must be assumed that excess demand is well defined at those price vectors. This not unreasonable to assume if the possible demand set for each consumer is bounded, or if the demand for any good reaches a saturation point whatever the consumption levels of other goods. However, with the gross substitute assumption it is implied by lemma 28 that if excess demand is negative at a zero price, it is always negative at a zero price regardless of the prices of other goods. On the other hand, with gross substitutes, raising the price of the zero priced good above zero cannot increase its demand. Thus a good that is ever in excess supply is always in excess supply when the excess supply is well defined, regardless of prices. Thus such a good is a free good not subject to economizing and should be ignored. This establishes

THEOREM 13   *If the gross substitution is made, it is sufficient to confine the tâtonnement process to goods that are not in excess supply at zero prices and to strictly positive prices.*

Theorem 11 seems to be the only global theorem on tâtonnement stability that uses meaningful assumptions from an economic viewpoint and uses a general adjustment process. It is possible to prove global stability under the other two assumptions used in the local theorems, that is, the assumption that the gross substitution matrix defines a negative definite quadratic form and the assumption that the Weak Axiom of Revealed Preference holds between an equilibrium price vector and any other price vector when these assumptions hold globally. However, to do so, we would have to use a variant of the adjustment process

$$\frac{dq_i}{dt} = e_i(q) \qquad \text{if } q_i > 0, \text{ and } i \neq n,$$

$$\frac{dp_i}{dt} = 0 \qquad \text{if } q_i = 0, \text{ or } i = n.$$

(44)

where it is understood that the $(n+1)$th good is numéraire. This adjustment process or its variants are only reasonable if the theorem is a local one.

Appendix A: Individual and Market Excess Demand Functions

We saw in chapter 1 that some of the restrictions on a Jacobian of individual demand functions also apply to a Jacobian of market demand functions when the number of consumers is smaller than the number of goods. Then it should not be surprising that having the number of consumers greater than or equal to the number of goods is necessary if homogeneity and Walras' Law are to characterize the continuous functions which may be market excess demand functions. Indeed, this is obvious from Diewirts' theorem 1.7. We will give a proof of this result, which is due to Debreu (1974). It is also true that having the number of consumers greater than or equal to the number of goods is a sufficient condition for homogeneity and Walras' Law to characterize market excess demand functions. This result was first proved by Sonnenschein (1972) and later refined by others, in particular, by Debreu (1974).

We will be concerned with an exchange economy with n goods. The consumers have preferences relations R^h satisfying the assumptions 1.2 through 1.4, 7, and also

ASSUMPTION 19 $C^h = \mathbf{R}^n_+$.

ASSUMPTION 20 For any $x \in C^h$, if $y \geq x$ and $y \neq x$, then $y \mathscr{P}^h x$. (Strict monotonicity)

The consumers own initial endowments ω^i. Because of strict monotonicity, assumption 20, the individual excess demand functions can be defined on the set of prices $R^n_{++} = \{p \in \mathbf{R}^n \mid p > 0\}$. However, since the individual excess demand functions e^h, $h = 1, \cdots, H$, are homogeneous of degree 0, it is sufficient to define them on $P = \{p \in \mathbf{R}^n_{++} \mid \sum_i p_i^2 = 1\}$. Since market excess demand functions are sums of the individual demand functions, they are also homogeneous and therefore fully specified when they are defined on P.

PROPOSITION (Debreu 1974) *For any ε with $0 < \varepsilon < 1/n$, there is a continuous function e that is defined on P such that e satisfies Walras' Law and homogeneity but e cannot be expressed on $P(\varepsilon) = \{p \in P \mid p_i \geq \varepsilon\}$ as a sum of fewer than n individual excess demand functions.*

Proof Select $p^0 \in P(\varepsilon)$ such that $p_i^0 > \varepsilon$ for all i. Define

$$e(p) = \left(\frac{pp^0}{pp}\right)p - p^0 = (pp^0)p - p^0.$$

Then $pe(p) = 0$ so $e(p)$ satisfies Walras' Law. Also

$$(p - p^0) \cdot e(p) = -p^0 \cdot e(p) = p^0 p^0 - (pp^0)^2 = 1 - (pp^0)^2 > 0. \qquad (A1)$$

Suppose that the number of consumers is $H < n$. Assume $e(p) = \sum_{h=1}^H e^h(p)$ for $p \in P(\varepsilon)$ for some choice of individual demand functions. Consider the matrix $[e_i^h(p^0)]$, $i = 1, \cdots, n$, $h = 1, \cdots, H$. Since $e(p^0) = 0$, $\sum_h e^h(p^0) = 0$. Thus the columns of $[e_i^h(p^0)]$ are linearly dependent. This implies that the square submatrix composed of the first H rows is singular. Therefore there exists $p' = (p_1', \cdots, p_H', 0, \cdots, 0)$ such that $p' \cdot e^h(p^0) = 0$ for all h. Choose $p^1 = (\alpha p^0 + (1 - \alpha)p')/|\alpha p^0 + (1 - \alpha)p'|$ for $\alpha > 0$ and α near 1. Then $p^1 \neq p^0$ and $p^1 \in P(\varepsilon)$.

Since $p^1 \cdot e^h(p^0) = 0$, the Weak Axiom of Revealed Preference implies that $p^0 \cdot e^h(p^1) \geq 0$. Therefore $(p^1 - p^0) \cdot e^h(p^1) \leq 0$. This contradicts (A1), so the assumption that $e(p)$ can be expressed in $P(\varepsilon)$ by $\sum_1^H e^h(p)$ is seen to be false. ∎

The close relation of this proposition to theorem 1.7 will be obvious. In theorem 1.7 it was shown for any differentiable demand functions where the number of consumers is less than the number of goods, given any prices and fixed incomes, that the Jacobian of the market demand function is negative semidefinite on the subspace of price changes that is orthogonal to the excess demands of all consumers. It is obvious that not all "market demand functions," as defined by Debreu, will satisfy this condition. What the proof does is to exhibit such a function that at equilibrium prices does not satisfy the Weak Axiom for a certain price change. On the other hand, the individual demand function must satisfy the Weak Axiom, and on the subspace of price changes that have no income effects for any consumer, this property is preserved when the individual demand functions are summed. Thus the putative market demand function cannot be expressed as a sum of individual demand functions when there are price changes that do not have income effects. But this is always true when the number of consumers is less than the number of goods. Therefore in this case the function considered cannot be a market demand function.

It is also intuitive that when no subspace exists that avoids income effects when prices change, any function satisfying homogeneity and Walras' Law can appear as a market demand function. In Diewert's case there is no subspace of price changes for which the Jacobian of excess demand is negative semidefinite, and in Debreu's case no subspace where the Weak Axiom holds for a sum of individual demand functions. However, making a rigorous argument for this result is a more complicated affair (see Debreu 1974).

Appendix B: The Gross Substitute Assumption

In this appendix we will prove some additional implications of the gross substitute assumption. We also make assumptions 1.1 through 1.4 and 1 through 4. Let $N = \{1, \cdots, n\}$. Recall that a Jacobian matrix J is decomposable if there is a subset of indexes $I \neq \emptyset$ and $N \backslash I \neq \emptyset$ such that $e_{ij} = 0$ for $i \in I$, $j \in N \backslash I$. In other words by identical permutations of rows and columns J can be put in the form $\begin{bmatrix} J_{11} & 0 \\ J_{21} & J_{22} \end{bmatrix}$ where J_{11} and J_{22} are square submatrices.

LEMMA 30   *Assume that the gross substitute assumption is satisfied by $e(p)$ for $p \geq 0$, $p \neq 0$. If $p_i = 0$ for $i \in I \neq \emptyset$, then $J(p)$ is decomposable. Indeed, $\partial e_i(p)/\partial p_j = 0$ when $i \in I$ and $j \in N \backslash I$.*

Proof Let $J(p)$ be the Jacobian matrix of $e(p)$. Let $p_i = 0$ for $i \in I$ and $p_i > 0$ for $i \in N\backslash I$. Consider $e(\alpha p)$ for $\alpha > 0$. By homogeneity of 0 degree of e, $\partial e(\alpha p)/\partial \alpha]_{\alpha=1} = 0$. Since all the prices with indexes in $N\backslash I$ rise with α but the demand for goods with indexes in I does not increase, it must be that $\partial e_i(q)/\partial q_j]_{q=p} = 0$ for all $i \in I$, $j \in N\backslash I$ and $J(p)$ is decomposable. ∎

LEMMA 31 *If $e(p)$ is not well defined at $p \geq 0$ and $p \neq 0$, where $p_i = 0$ for some i, then $p^v > 0$ and $p^v \to p$ implies that $|e(p^v)| \to \infty$.*

Proof $e(p)$ is well defined if and only if $e^h(p)$ is well defined for all h. Also since $e^h(p)$ is bounded below, $e(p)$ is bounded if and only if $e^h(p)$ is bounded for all h. Suppose that $e^h(p^v)$ is bounded. Then there is a subsequence and $x \in C^h$ such that $e^h(p^v) \to x$, where v now indexes the subsequence. Let x' satisfy $x'\mathcal{P}^h x$. Such an x' exists by assumption 1. Let $x'' \in C^h$ satisfy $x'' < \omega^h$. This is possible by assumption 2. Since the preference order is closed there is $\alpha < 1$ such that $(\alpha x'' + (1 - \alpha)x')\mathcal{P}^h x$. Again since the preference order is closed $(\alpha x'' + (1 - \alpha)x')\mathcal{P}^h e^h(p^v)$ for v large. By definition of e, it must hold that $p^v(\alpha x'' + (1 - \alpha)x') > p^v\omega^h$. Therefore in the limit $p(\alpha x'' + (1 - \alpha)x') \geq p\omega^h$. Since $px'' < p\omega^h$, it follows that $px' > p\omega^h$. Since this result holds for any x' with $x'\mathcal{P}^h x$, $x = e^h(p)$, or in other words, $e^h(p)$ is well defined. Thus, if $e^h(p)$ is not well defined, it is not bounded. However, if $e(p)$ is not well defined, some $e^h(p)$ is not well defined. Thus some $e^h(p)$ is unbounded, which means that $e(p)$ is unbounded. ∎

This lemma is complementary to the lemma on the continuity of the excess demand function lemma 4. Both results depend on the presence of cheaper points.

LEMMA 32 *Suppose that the gross substitute assumption holds over the domain D of the excess demand function e, where $D \subset R^n_+$ and $0 \notin D$. Assume that the Jacobian of e is indecomposable. Then, if $p^v \to p \neq 0$ where $p^v > 0$ and $p_i = 0$ for some i, $|e(p^v)| \to \infty$.*

Proof Since $J(p)$ is indecomposable lemma 30 implies that $p \notin D$, so $e(p)$ is not well defined. Then by lemma 31, $|e(p^v)| \to \infty$. ∎

With the help of Lemma 32, we may prove the main result.

THEOREM 14   *Consider an exchange economy. Assume that the gross sub-stitute assumption holds and the Jacobian matrix J is indecomposable over the domain D of the excess demand function e. Assume that $D \subset R_+^n$, $R_{++}^n \subset D$, and $0 \notin D$. Then the Weak Axiom of Revealed Preference holds between the equilibrium price $\bar{p}$ and any price vector $p \in D$.*

Proof   The Weak Axiom of Revealed Preference at an equilibrium price $\bar{p}$ relative to a price $p \neq \alpha\bar{p}$, for any α, is equivalent to

$$p \cdot e(p) \geq p \cdot e(\bar{p}) \text{ implies } \bar{p} \cdot e(p) > \bar{p} \cdot e(\bar{p}), \tag{A2}$$

that is,

$$p \cdot e(p) \geq 0 \text{ implies } \bar{p} \cdot e(p) > 0.$$

But $p \cdot e(p) = 0$ by Walras' Law. Therefore $\bar{p} \cdot e(p)$ attains its minimum value 0 at $\bar{p}$. Conversely, if $\bar{p} \cdot e(p)$ attains a minimum value at $\bar{p}$ and there is not a local minimum at any $p \neq \alpha\bar{p}$ for $\alpha > 0$, it follows that $\bar{p} \cdot e(p) > 0$ for any such p where $e(p)$ is well defined. In other words, by (A2) the Weak Axiom holds at $\bar{p}$.

It is necessary for an interior minimum that the first-order conditions hold. That is, $\sum_{i=1}^{n} \bar{p}_i e_{ij}(p) = 0$ for $j = 1, \cdots, n$, where $e_{ij} = \partial e_i(p)/\partial p_j$. Since $\bar{p} \cdot \partial e(p)/\partial p|_{\bar{p}} = 0$ by Walras' Law, $\bar{p}$ satisfies the necessary conditions. Since by lemma 32 an interior minimum must exist, the theorem is proved if we show that no $p > 0$ satisfies the necessary conditions for $p \neq \alpha\bar{p}$, $\alpha > 0$. Suppose, on the contrary, that p' is such a solution of the necessary conditions.

By lemma 32, $\bar{p} > 0$ must hold. Otherwise, by indecomposability of $J(\bar{p})$, it follows that $e(\bar{p})$ is not well defined. Let $k = p'_r/\bar{p}_r \geq p'_i/\bar{p}_i$ for all i. Then $k\bar{p}_i \geq p'_i$ for all i with equality for some i. Let I be the set of indexes for which the inequality is strict. Since $p' \neq \alpha\bar{p}$ for any $\alpha > 0$, I is not empty.

By homogeneity of zero degree $e(k\bar{p})$ is also an equilibrium. Suppose that $\sum_i \bar{p}_i \cdot e_{ij}(p') = 0$ for all j. That is, p' also satisfies the necessary conditions. Then

$$\sum_i k\bar{p}_i \cdot e_{ij}(p') = 0 \qquad \text{for } j \in N \backslash I, \tag{A3}$$

and Walras' Law implies

$$\sum_i p_i' \cdot e_{ij}(p') = -e_j(p') \qquad \text{for } j \in N\backslash I. \tag{A4}$$

Subtracting (A3) from (A4) gives

$$\sum_i (p_i' - k\bar{p}_i) \cdot e_{ij}(p') = -e_j(p') \qquad \text{for } j \in N\backslash I. \tag{A5}$$

The gross substitute assumption implies that $e_j(p') \leq 0$ for $j \in N\backslash I$, since $k\bar{p}_i = p_i'$ for $i \in N\backslash I$ while $k\bar{p}_i > p_i'$ for $i \in I$. This may be seen by allowing prices to move along the line segment from $k\bar{p}$ to p'. Along this path, prices are constant for $i \in N\backslash I$ and falling for $i \in I$. Therefore demand is either constant or falling for $j \in N\backslash I$.

All the terms on the left side of (A5) are less than or equal to 0. Moreover, by the condition of indecomposability for $J^h(p)$, at least one term with $i \in I$ and $j \in N\backslash I$ is negative. Thus for some $j \in N\backslash I$ the left side of an equation in (A5) is negative. This is a contradiction. Therefore no price vector $p' \neq \alpha\bar{p}$ satisfies the necessary conditions for an interior minimum, and $e(p)$ attains its minimum only on price vectors p such that $p = \alpha\bar{p}$ for $\alpha > 0$. Thus the Weak Axiom is satisfied. ■

It is not difficult to see from the proof that it would suffice to assume all consumers to have indecomposable Jacobians and only the total endowment to be positive, rather than each individual endowment. Then the consumer holding a nonzero stock of a good whose price is not zero would have unbounded demand if any price is zero. What is needed is to ensure that the cheaper point condition holds in order to prove lemma 31. It should also be noted that the argument does not imply that the gross substitute assumption in a neighborhood of an equilibrium is sufficient for the Weak Axiom to hold. This is because the proof uses the condition that a minimum exists in the price set over which the Weak Axiom is to be established. We showed that a minimum exists over the set of positive prices by appealing to the fact that excess demand is unbounded as the price vector approaches a point other than 0 in the boundary of the positive orthant.

Theorem 14 complements lemma 14 which assumes that the reduced Jacobian is negative definite rather than assuming gross substitutes. Also lemma 14 establishes the weak axiom without reference to the equilibrium prices and holds over any convex region of the price space where the negative definiteness assumption holds.

Appendix C: The Weak Axiom of Revealed Preference and Local Stability

We found in theorem 3 that the Weak Axiom of Revealed Preference implies local stability of the tâtonnement when the reduced Jacobian is nonsingular. However, Mukherji (1989) has shown that an implication also exists from stability to the Weak Axiom. The chosen consumption vectors can be subjected to a transformation such that the satisfaction of the Weak Axiom by the transformed vectors is necessary and sufficient for local stability under a nonsingularity condition.

Consider once more the adjustment process

$$\frac{dp_i}{dt} = \sum_{j=1}^{n-1} e_{ij}(\bar{p})(p_j - \bar{p}_j), \qquad j = 1, \cdots, n-1,$$

$$\tag{A6}$$

$$p_n \equiv 1.$$

In (A6) it is assumed that $\bar{p} > 0$ is an equilibrium and $e(\bar{p}) = 0$. This is the same process as (5) expressed in slightly different form. Write the full Jacobian as $J = [e_{ij}(\bar{p}, 1)]$, $i, j = 1, \cdots, n$, and the reduced Jacobian as J_n where the last column and row of J are omitted. From lemma 11 it is a sufficient condition for local stability of (A6) that the characteristic roots of J_n have negative real parts. However, if J_n is nonsingular this condition is also necessary (Coddington and Levinson 1955, p. 317). By a theorem of Liapounov (Bellman 1970, p. 254), J_n has all its characteristic roots with negative parts if and only if there exists a positive definite matrix B such that the matrix $BJ_n + J_n^T B$ is negative definite. We may prove

THEOREM 15 *Let $\bar{B} = \begin{bmatrix} B & 0 \\ 0 & 1 \end{bmatrix}$. If $J_n(\bar{p})$ is nonsingular, local stability of (A6) implies that there is a positive definite matrix B such that $(p - \bar{p})^T \bar{B} e(p) < 0$ for all p in a neighborhood U of $\bar{p}$, relative to the affine subspace $S = \{p \mid p_n \equiv 1\}$.*

Proof Nonsingularity of J_n and stability of (A6) imply by Liapounov's theorem that there exists a positive definite matrix B such that $BJ_n + J_n^T B$ is negative definite. Let $f(p) = (p - \bar{p})^T \bar{B} e(p)$. Then

$$\frac{\partial f(p)}{\partial p_k} = \sum_{i=1}^{n}\sum_{j=1}^{n}(p_i - \bar{p}_i)\bar{b}_{ij}e_{jk}(p) + \sum_{j=1}^{n}\bar{b}_{kj}e_j(p), \tag{A7}$$

where $\bar{B} = [\bar{b}_{ij}]$. Write $e_{jrk}(p)$ for $\partial^2 e_j(p)/\partial p_r \partial p_k$. Then differentiating (A7) with respect to p gives

$$\frac{\partial^2 f(p)}{\partial p_r \partial p_k} = \sum_{i=1}^{n}\sum_{j=1}^{n}(p_i - \bar{p}_i)\bar{b}_{ij}e_{jrk}(p) + \sum_{j=1}^{n}\bar{b}_{rj}e_{jk}(p) + \sum_{j=1}^{n}\bar{b}_{kj}e_{jr}(p). \tag{A8}$$

It is implied by (A7) that $\partial f(\bar{p})/\partial p_k = 0$ for all k since $e_j(\bar{p}) = 0$. Moreover (A8) gives

$$\left[\frac{\partial^2 f(p)}{\partial p_r \partial p_k}\right]_{p=\bar{p}} = \sum_{j=1}^{n}\bar{b}_{rj}e_{jk}(\bar{p}) + \sum_{j=1}^{n}\bar{b}_{kj}e_{jr}(\bar{p}). \tag{A9}$$

Note that the nth row and the nth column of $\bar{B}$ are composed of zeros except in the nth places. Then using the symmetry of $\bar{B}$ we have from (A9)

$$[\partial^2 f(p)/\partial p_r \partial p_k]_1^{n-1}]_{p=\bar{p}} = (BJ + J^T B). \tag{A10}$$

However, by Liapounov's theorem, the stability of (A6) implies that the right side of (A10) is negative definite. On the other hand, the left side of (A10) is the second derivative of $f(p)$ relative to S. Since the first derivative is zero by (A7), we conclude that $f(p)$ has a regular maximum at $\bar{p}$ over S. Therefore, for some neighborhood U of $\bar{p}$ relative to S, we have $f(p) < f(\bar{p})$ for all $p \neq \bar{p}$. ∎

COROLLARY   *If (A6) is locally stable with J_n nonsingular and $B = I$, then the Weak Axiom of Revealed Preference holds in the neighborhood U of $\bar{p}$ relative to S.*

Proof According to the Weak Axiom $p(e(p) - e(\bar{p})) = 0$ implies $(p - \bar{p})(e(p) - e(\bar{p})) < 0$ when $p \neq \alpha\bar{p}$ for any number $\alpha > 0$. However, the condition holds by Walras' Law and the fact that $e(\bar{p})$ is an equilibrium. Therefore $\bar{p}e(p) > 0$ is equivalent to the Weak Axiom for $p \in S$ relative to $\bar{p}$. However when J_n is nonsingular, according to theorem 14 stability of the adjustment process (A6) implies that $\bar{p}^T \bar{B} e(p) > 0$ holds. Since $\bar{B} = I$ the result follows. ∎

It is possible to prove a partial converse to theorem 14.

THEOREM 16   *Suppose that there is a positive definite matrix $\bar{B} = \begin{bmatrix} B & 0 \\ 0 & 1 \end{bmatrix}$*
such that $(p - \bar{p})^T \bar{B} e(p) < 0$ for all p in a neighborhood of $\bar{p}$ relative to S.
If $BJ_n + J_n^T B$ has rank $n - 1$, then (A6) is locally stable.

Proof Let $f(p)$ be as in the proof of theorem 15. By hypothesis $f(p)$
attains a local maximum at $\bar{p}$ relative to S. A necessary condition for the
maximum is that the second derivative of $f(p)$ relative to S be negative
semidefinite. It was shown in the proof of theorem 14 that this derivative
is equal to $(BJ_n + J_n^T B)$. Since $BJ_n + J_n^T B$ is nonsingular it is negative
definite. Then, by Liapounov's theorem, J_n is stable.   ∎

If $B = I$ the first condition of theorem 16 is implied by the Weak
Axiom of Revealed Preference. However, the second condition that $J_n + J_n^T$
be nonsingular is not implied by the condition of theorem 3 that J_n
be nonsingular. The converse implication is not true either.

Appendix D: Stability in a Temporary Equilibrium Model

The temporal structure of the models of price expectations which are
considered in theorems 6 and 7 are very simple. In theorem 6 the change
in the expected price comes from a comparison of the current tâtonnement price and the expected future equilibrium price. Also the tâtonnement price responds to excess demand, which in turn depends on the
tâtonnement price and the expected future price. If this rule has been followed over a period of (tâtonnement) time, the expected price may be
found by taking an average of previous prices with weights that vary with
the length of the lag and terminate at some finite lag L or extend to $-\infty$.
The formula for the expected price of the ith good is

$$q_{it} = q_{it-1} + \alpha_i(p_{it} - q_{it-1}).$$

In this formula q_{it} is the price at time $t + 1$ expected at time t, and a_{i1}
satisfies $0 \le a_i \le 1$. Note that the coefficients of p_{it} and q_{it-1} sum to 1.
Then, if the formula is iterated L times, the sum of the coefficients of the
equilibrium prices from p_{it-L} to p_{it} plus the coefficient of the expected
price q_{it-L} also equals 1. If L is allowed to grow without limit the coefficient of the term q_{it-L} approaches 0 and the sum of the coefficients of the

p_{it} is 1. Grandmont (1990, 1998) has presented a temporary equilibrium model for states of the economy which is reminiscent of the Arrow-Nerlove model. Grandmont allows the weights on states and expected states with different dates to vary arbitrarily, but the condition is retained that the coefficients on the right hand side of the formula for the expected state sum to 1. Then we have the useful property that if all past states equal $\bar{x}$ the expected state will equal $\bar{x}$.

The temporary equilibrium theory, as developed by Grandmont, refers to a sequence of equilibrium states, which might be regarded as corresponding to the Marshallian short period or to the Hicksian week. Of course, tâtonnement prices are not equilibrium prices. Thus the theories are distinct. The Arrow-Nerlove theory uses disequilibrium excess demand as the explanation for the movement of prices during the tâtonnement. On the other hand, the evolution of temporary equilibrium states, so far as it is analysed in the model, depends entirely on the movement of expectations, and the expectation function explains the expected equilibrium state in terms of the observation of earlier states and earlier expected states. To simplify the analysis, Grandmont represents the state of the economy by a single number.

A simplified model may be written

$$0 = \phi(x_t, x_t^e),$$
$$x_t^e = \psi(x_t, \cdots, x_{t-L}, x_{t-1}^e, \cdots, x_{t-L}^e). \tag{A11}$$

The linearization of the relations (A11) in the neighborhood of an equilibrium may be written, now using the letters x and x^e to represent deviations from equilibrium,

$$\begin{bmatrix} ax_t & cx_t^e \\ -\sum_{j=0}^{L-1} \alpha_j x_{t-j} & -x_t^e + \sum_{j=1}^{L} \beta_j x_{t-j}^e \end{bmatrix} = 0. \tag{A12}$$

Note that putting $L = 1$ the system (A12) is formally the same as that of Arrow-Nerlove. Grandmont also includes the economic state of the previous period as an argument of ϕ. However, it would seem appropriate to let last period's economic state be relevant to this period's equilibrium state only to the extent that it influences the expected economic state of next period. Indeed, if past states are relevant, why should not even earlier states be allowed an influence.

Suppose that (A12) has solutions which begin with deviations from stationary equilibrium values equal to x_0 and x_0^e and the solution exhibits a trend or cycle defined by powers of the complex number z, then it must be that

$$
\left[
\begin{matrix}
az^t & cz^{t-1} \\
-\sum_{j=0}^{L} \alpha_j z^{t-j} & -z^t + \sum_{j=1}^{L} \beta_j z^{t-j}
\end{matrix}
\right]
\begin{pmatrix} x_0 \\ x_0^e \end{pmatrix} = 0.
\tag{A13}
$$

However, for (A13) to have a solution, it is necessary that the matrix have a zero determinant. That is, it is necessary, after dividing z^t out of each column, that

$$
\left|
\begin{matrix}
a & cz^{-1} \\
-\sum_{j=0}^{L} \alpha_j z^{-j} & -1 + \sum_{j=1}^{L} \beta_j z^{-j}
\end{matrix}
\right| = 0
\tag{A14}
$$

Then it is implied by (A14) that

$$
a = \frac{c\sum_{j=0}^{L} \alpha_j z^{-j-1}}{(1 - \sum_{j=1}^{L} \beta_j z^{-j})} = 0.
$$

Therefore

$$
|a| \leq |c| \cdot \left| \frac{\sum_{j=0}^{L} \alpha_j z^{-j-1}}{(1 - \sum_{j=1}^{L} \beta_j z^{-j})} \right|.
\tag{A15}
$$

From (A15) it is clear that $|a| > |c| \cdot |\sum_{j=0}^{L} \alpha_j z^{-j-1}/(1 - \sum_{j=1}^{L} \beta_j z^{-j})|$ for all z with absolute value larger than or equal to 1 implies that any root λ of (A14) must have absolute value less than 1. It may be seen that the maximum value μ of $|\sum_{j=0}^{L} \alpha_j z^{-j-1}/(1 - \sum_{j=1}^{L} \beta_j z^{-j})|$ for $|z| \geq 1$ occurs when $|z| = 1$. Then $\mu = |\sum_{j=0}^{L} \alpha_j/(1 - \sum_{j=1}^{L} \beta_j)|$. Therefore we may state (following Grandmont except for the omission of the direct influence of the preceding state of the economy)

THEOREM 17   *The temporary equilibrium system (A11) is locally stable at an equilibrium if its linearization (A12) in the neighborhood of the equilibrium satisfies $|a| > |c|\mu$.*

This suggests that heavy dependence on the expected price, or a large $|c|$, leads to instability. Grandmont presents an extensive analysis of the implications of his model including particular models of learning such as recursive least squares and Bayesian learning.

Since future states are relevant it must be that present and future purchases are subject to a single budget constraint. This is the setting of some overlapping generations models where each generation works in the first period and retires in the second period. When durable goods are not present in such a model, the formation of expectations is the only dynamic feature. However, if durable goods are present, the course of capital accumulation has important dynamic features of its own which are hidden in this formulation. We will explore some of these features in chapter 7.

3 Leontief Models of Production

We have already met linear production models in section 2.8. The model described there had the special feature that in each process the only inputs were primary factors, that is, the services of labor or capital goods or inputs of natural resources. No flows of intermediate products between industries were included. The simple Leontief model has labor as the only primary factor, and each activity has only one output. On the other hand, the flow of intermediate products is recognized. Each industry, identified with its product, has a single output. The model will be generalized later in the chapter to include durable capital goods whose surviving stocks are treated as additional outputs. In subsequent chapters the linear production model will be generalized further to allow many primary inputs and joint outputs. In the von Neumann model, which is often used in the theory of capital accumulation, time is divided into periods of equal length, and a constant technology is assumed that describes the transformation of initial stocks of goods into terminal stocks of goods. Also the existence of equilibrium for a competitive economy will be established in a general activities model in which goods may be dated so that inputs and outputs of the same activities bear many different dates. Indeed, the number of dates will be infinite when the horizon is taken to lie at infinity.

3.1 The Simple Leontief Model

In the simple Leontief model (see Leontief 1941) each industry has a single output, and labor is the only unproduced factor of production. We normalize the basic input–output vectors of the industries so that a unit level of the process available to the industry uses one unit of labor. This is justified, since the processes are assumed to have the property that any nonnegative multiple of an input–output combination that is possible is also possible. This implies that goods are divisible. Also the fact that in describing the input–output combinations available to one industry no account is taken of the input–output combinations chosen by other industries means that the processes operate independently. No external economies impinge on other processes operating simultaneously. These two properties together, divisibility of processes and independence of processes, allow them to be multiplied and added. Suppose that the number of basic input–output vectors is finite. Then linearity has the consequence that the set of available input–output combinations from the economy as a whole, ignoring limits on the supply of primary resources, is a convex

polyhedral cone in the space of commodities, where the space of commodities is a real vector space.

We define a Leontief system by means of the coefficient matrix B.
Consider

$$Bx = y,$$

$$B = [b_{ij}], \qquad i, j = 1, \cdots, n, \tag{1}$$

$$b_{ij} \leq 0, \qquad i \neq j, \ b_{ii} > 0, \ x \geq 0.$$

By definition (1) is a *Leontief model* $\mathcal{L}$ with (square) coefficient matrix B.
An n-vector y is a possible net output of $\mathcal{L}$ if $Bx = y$, $x \geq 0$. The n-vector
x is the vector of activity levels. The coefficient b_{ij} is the input of the ith
good in the jth activity if $i \neq j$ and b_{ii} is the output of the ith good. The
set Y of possible net outputs of L is then given by

$$Y = \{ y \mid \text{there is } x \geq 0 \text{ and } Bx = y \}.$$

The simple Leontief model is illustrated in figure 3.1.

The first theorem (McKenzie 1960a) gives conditions under which the
set of possible net outputs of $\mathcal{L}$ contains output in all proportions.

THEOREM 1 *Suppose that B is the coefficient matrix of a Leontief model
$\mathcal{L}$. A necessary and sufficient condition for $Y \supset R^n_+$ is that B have q.d.d.*

Proof Sufficiency. Let B satisfy q.d.d. with d_i, $i = 1, \cdots, n$, as row multipliers for B. Lemma 2.6 implies that $Bx = y$ is solvable for arbitrary
$y \geq 0$. Suppose $Bx = y$, where $y \geq 0$ but not $x \geq 0$. Let $x_j < 0$ for $j \in N$,
$x_j \geq 0$ for $j \notin N$. Consider

$$\sum_{j \notin N} b_{ij} x_j + \sum_{j \in N} b_{ij} x_j = y_i \qquad \text{for } i \in N.$$

Multiplying by d_i and summing gives

$$\sum_{i \in N} \sum_{j \notin N} d_i b_{ij} x_j + \sum_{i \in N} \sum_{j \in N} d_i b_{ij} x_j = \sum_{i \in N} d_i y_i \geq 0.$$

By q.d.d., $\sum_{i \in N} d_i b_{ij} \geq 0$, all $j \in N$, and > 0, some $j \in N$. Therefore
$x_j < 0$ implies that the second term on the left is negative. However, the
first term is 0 or negative, since $b_{ij} \leq 0$, $i \neq j$. Thus the left-hand side is
negative, which is a contradiction, so $x_j \geq 0$, all j, and $N = \emptyset$.

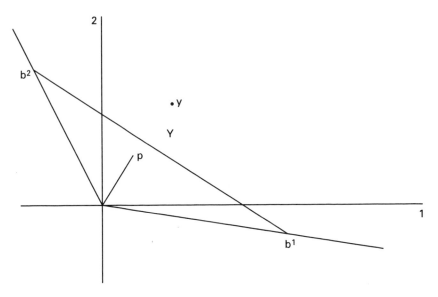

Figure 3.1
There is an output $y > 0$, so B has q.d.d. and Y contains R_+^n. Also there are prices $p > 0$, which satisfy $p^T B > 0$.

Necessity. Consider $Bx = y > 0$, or $x^T B^T = y^T > 0$. Then $x > 0$, and B^T has q.d.d. Therefore by the sufficiency argument $B^T p = \pi > 0$ may be solved for $p > 0$. Thus B also has q.d.d. with strict inequalities. ∎

Recall that a matrix B that has q.d.d. with strict inequalities has a dominant diagonal or d.d.

COROLLARY 1   *If B has q.d.d., it has d.d.*

Proof A matrix B has q.d.d. or d.d. if and only if the same is true for the matrix $\tilde{B}$ in which the elements have had their signs changed, if necessary, to give $\tilde{B}$ the sign distribution of a Leontief matrix, that is, the matrix of a Leontief system. But by the proof of theorem 1 the corollary holds for $\tilde{B}$, so it holds also for B. ∎

The utility of theorems on matrices with q.d.d. in economic theory comes from the fact that matrices naturally arise both in the theory of demand and in the theory of production where the prices serve as multipliers to establish the property of q.d.d. We saw an example from the theory of demand in the last chapter where the Jacobian of the market demand function had this property if it was indecomposable at equilibrium and all goods were gross substitutes. The matrix of a simple Leontief system $\mathcal{L}$ is an example from the theory of production. Let us define (p, y) as the equilibrium of a Leontief production sector $\mathcal{L}$ of an economy if $Bx = y \geq 0$ with $y \geq 0$ and there is $p \geq 0$ such that $p^T B = \pi^T \leq e^T = (1, \cdots, 1)^T$ and $\pi_i = 1$ if $x_i > 0$. We say that y is a *possible equilibrium output* if (p, y) is an equilibrium of the production sector for some p. Let Y_E be the set of possible equilibrium outputs. It follows that

COROLLARY 2   *If $y = Bx$ is a possible equilibrium output of $\mathcal{L}$ and $y > 0$, $Y_E \supset R_+^n$.*

Proof This follows immediately from the necessity part of the proof of theorem 1.   ∎

COROLLARY 3   *If B is the coefficient matrix of a Leontief model with q.d.d., then B^{-1} is nonnegative with a positive diagonal.*

Proof By corollary 2, if $y \geq 0$, there is $x \geq 0$ such that $y = Bx$. By lemma 2.6, B is nonsingular. Therefore $B^{-1}y = x \geq 0$. Consider $y = \delta^j$ where $\delta_i^j = 0$ for $i \neq j$ and $\delta_j^j = 1$. Let $B^{-1} = [\bar{b}_{ij}]$. If $\bar{b}_{ij} < 0$ for some i, then $x_i < 0$ in contradiction to corollary 2. On the other hand, if $\bar{b}_{jj} = 0$, it follows that $x_j = 0$, which implies by the sign distribution of B that $y_j = 0$, contradicting $y = \delta^j$.   ∎

The following result is sometimes useful.

LEMMA 1   *Let A be an $n \times n$ matrix $[a_{ij}]$, $a_{ij} \leq 0$, $i \neq j$, and $\sum_{i=1}^{n} d_i a_{ij} \geq 0$ for $j = 1, \cdots, n$, for some $d_i > 0$, $i = 1, \cdots, n$. A is nonsingular if and only if A has q.d.d. with these d_i as row multipliers.*

Proof Sufficiency. See lemma 2.6.

Necessity. Suppose that A does not have q.d.d. with these d_i as row multipliers but that A is nonsingular. By definition of q.d.d. there is $J \neq \emptyset$ and $a_{ij} = 0$, $j \in J$, $i \notin J$, and $\sum_{i \in J} d_i a_{ij} = 0$, all $j \in J$. Let $M = [a_{ij}]$, $i, j \in J$. M is singular, so there are x_j not all zero and $\sum_{j \in J} a_{ij} x_j = 0$. Put $x_j = 0$ for $j \notin J$. $Ax = 0$, $x \neq 0$, so A is singular. Since this is a contradiction, we conclude that A does have q.d.d. with these d_i as row multipliers.   ∎

A corollary to this lemma was proved and applied to the simple Leontief model by Solow (1952).

COROLLARY   *Under the conditions of lemma 1, $Y \supset R_+^n$ if and only if B has q.d.d. with these d_i as row multipliers.*

Proof Sufficiency. Apply theorem 1.

Necessity. If B does not have q.d.d. for these d_i, then B is singular by the lemma. Therefore B does not have q.d.d. by lemma 2.6. Then, by theorem 1, Y does not contain R_+^n.   ∎

Recall that the sufficiency part of lemma 1 was used in chapter 2 where it was applied to the Jacobian J of market excess demand. Walras' Law implies that $p^T J = 0$ at equilibrium. Let $p_{(n)} = (p_1, \cdots, p_{n-1})$. Then given gross substitutes $-p_{(n)}^T J_n \geq 0$ holds, so $-J_n$ is nonsingular if and only if it has a quasi-dominant diagonal with the components of $p_{(n)}$ as multipliers.

Consider an economy with $\mathscr{L}$ as the production sector. Suppose that p and x are vectors of prices and activity levels where $p > 0$, $x > 0$, $p^T B = \pi^T \geq 0$, and $Bx = y \geq 0$. π is the vector of value added. Let Π be the set of all possible π. The input–output vector of the jth industry for a unit level of activity is (b_{ij}), $i = 1, \cdots, n$.

THEOREM 2   *The following are equivalent:*

i. Every subset of industries with $b_{ij} = 0$ for $i \notin J$, $j \in J$, has $\pi_j > 0$, some $j \in J$.

ii. Every subset J of industries with $b_{ij} = 0$, for $i \in J$, $j \notin J$, has $y_i > 0$, some $i \in J$.

iii. $Y \supset R_+^n$, and $\Pi \supset R_+^n$.

Proof The result follows from theorem 1 and the corollary to lemma 1 together with the definition of q.d.d.   ∎

Condition i means that every subset of industries that makes no purchases from the complementary subset earns a return in some industry.

Condition ii means that every subset of industries that furnishes no output to the complementary subset has a positive net output of some good.

Condition iii means that net output can be produced in all proportions and value added may be realized in all proportions. Thus there is a choice of p that gives an equilibrium of the production sector for y in any proportions. Since output must be demanded in some proportions by consumers (whose only incomes are derived from wages), it is clear that some

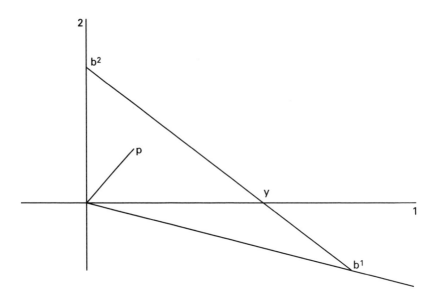

Figure 3.2
The simple Leontief model. Since $b_{12} = 0$ and $x > 0$, we have $\pi_2 = pb^2 > 0$ and $y_1 > 0$.

choice of y that will also equate supply to demand. Then the conditions for a competitive equilibrium, as we will later describe them, will be met. This can be termed a competitive equilibrium for the economy $\mathscr{L}$. Of course, this economy is not realistic since it ignores the role of time in production.

We allow the possibility that the complement of J is empty. Then conditions i and ii are trivially met. Figure 3.2 illustrates a case where one subset of industries receives no input from its complementary subset.

3.2   A Simple Leontief Model of Growth

In preparing for a Leontief model of growth, we will prove a mathematical result that is useful for this purpose and has many other applications as well. It is known in mathematical literature as a Frobenius theorem.

Let $S = \{x \mid \sum_{i=1}^{n} x_i = 1, x_i \geq 0\}$ be the unit simplex in R^n. Let the vector δ^i satisfy $\delta^i_j = 0$, for $j \neq i$, $\delta^i_j = 1$, for $j = i$. For an $n \times n$ nonnegative matrix $A = [a_{ij}]$, $a_{ij} \geq 0$, define the function $\mu_A(s) = \max_{x \in S} \min_j \sum_{i=1}^{n} x_i (s\delta^i_j - a_{ij})$. If s is large enough to give $[s\delta^i_j - a_{ij}]$ a positive diagonal, we may regard $(sI - A)^T$ as a Leontief matrix B, where units of commodities are chosen so that each activity produces s units of output. Recall that activities are normalized to use one unit of labor. Then $\mu_A(s)$ is the largest value that can be given the smallest net output over the industries of B when the labor supply is one unit. We will later find that the value of s that gives $\mu_A(s) = 0$ has a critical role to play in the simple Leontief growth model and its generalization has a similar role in the growth model due to von Neumann.

It is proved in the appendix that $\mu_A(s)$ is continuous. If A is indecomposable, it is clear that for sufficiently small $s_1 > 0$, $\mu_A(s_1) < 0$, and for sufficiently large s_2, $\mu_A(s_2) > 0$. Since μ_A is continuous, there is also $s^* > 0$ such that $\mu_A(s^*) = 0$. We will first prove a lemma.

LEMMA 2   *Suppose that an $n \times n$ matrix $A = [a_{ij}]$ is indecomposable with nonpositive off-diagonal entries, and there is $d > 0$ such that $d^T A \geq 0$. Then A has q.d.d. if and only if $\sum_{i=1}^n d_i a_{ij} > 0$ for some j.*

Proof   It is clear that the condition is necessary since otherwise A is singular and thus cannot have q.d.d. by lemma 2.6. For sufficiency, let $[a_{ij}]$, $i, j \in J$, be an arbitrary principal submatrix of A. If $\sum_{i \in J} d_i a_{ij} = 0$ for all $j \in J$ and $J \neq A$, it follows that $a_{ij} = 0$ for all $i \notin J$ and $j \in J$, so A is decomposable contradicting the hypothesis. On the other hand, if $J = A$, we have $\sum_{i=1}^n d_i a_{ij} = 0$ for all j, which again contradicts the hypothesis.   ∎

THEOREM 3 (McKenzie 1960a)   *Let $A = [a_{ij}]$ be an indecomposable square matrix with $a_{ij} \geq 0$, all i, j. Let $\mu_A(s^*) = 0$. Then $s^* > 0$ is a characteristic root of A, and there is $x^* > 0$ such that the corresponding characteristic vectors are multiples of x^*. Moreover $s^* \geq |\lambda|$, where λ is any characteristic root of A, and the inequality is strict if $a_{jj} > 0$ for some j. No other characteristic root has a nonnegative characteristic vector.*

Proof   Let x^* realize the maximum in $\mu_A(s^*)$. Suppose $x_j^* = 0$ for $j \in J \neq \emptyset$. Consider $\sum_{i=1}^n x_i^*(s^* \delta_j^i - a_{ij}) = \sum_{i \notin J} -x_i^* a_{ij}$, if $j \in J$. Since A is indecomposable, $\sum_{i \notin J} -x_i^* a_{ij} < 0$ for some $j \in J$. This contradicts the definition of s^*. Therefore $x^* > 0$.

Suppose $|\lambda| > s^*$ for some λ a characteristic root of A. Consider

$$|\lambda - a_{jj}| \geq |\lambda| - a_{jj} > s^* - a_{jj}. \tag{2}$$

But $\mu_A(s^*) = 0$ implies that $x_j^*(s^* - a_{jj}) \geq \sum_{i \neq j} x_i^* a_{ij}$, all j. Thus $\lambda I - A$ has a dominant diagonal. Therefore $\lambda I - A$ is nonsingular and λ cannot be a characteristic root. If $|\lambda| = s^*$, and $a_{jj} > 0$ for some j, $\lambda \neq s^*$ implies that the first inequality of (2) is strict for that j. Then the fact that A is indecomposable implies that $\lambda I - A$ has q.d.d. Thus λ is not a characteristic root in this case as well.

To show that s^* is a characteristic root, consider

$$s^* x_j^* - \sum_{i=1}^{n} x_i^* a_{ij} = y_j.$$

By definition of s^*, $y \geq 0$. If $y_j > 0$ for some j, $s^* I - A$ has q.d.d. by lemma 2, since $x^* > 0$ and $s^* I - A$ is indecomposable. Then, by corollary 1 to theorem 1, there is $x > 0$ and $x^T(s^* I - A) > 0$. Since x may be chosen in S, this contradicts $\mu_A(s^*) = 0$. Therefore $y = 0$ and s^* is a characteristic root with x^* as a characteristic vector.

Suppose that x^1 were also a characteristic vector for s^* with $x^1 \neq tx^*$ for any t. Consider $x^2 = x^* - rx^1$, r a real number. Let $r = x_{i_0}^* / x_{i_0}^1$ where $x_{i_0}^* / x_{i_0}^1 \leq x_i^* / x_i^1$ for all i. Then $x_{i_0}^2 = 0$ and $x^2 \geq 0$. Also $x^2 = 0$ implies that $x^1 = rx^*$, contradicting the hypothesis. Therefore x^2 is a characteristic vector and achieves the maximum in $\mu_A(s^*)$. This contradicts the positivity of the maximizing x for $\mu_A(s^*)$. Therefore, for s^*, there can be no characteristic vector $x^1 \neq tx^*$ for some real t.

Finally suppose that λ is a characteristic root with characteristic vector $x \geq 0$. Then $\lambda x = Ax \geq 0$, so $\lambda \geq 0$ holds. The same argument that gives $x^* > 0$ gives $x > 0$. Then by the previous argument $|\lambda'| > \lambda$ implies that $\lambda' I - A$ has a dominant diagonal. In other words, $\lambda \geq s^*$ and $s^* \geq \lambda$, or $s^* = \lambda$.   ∎

Theorem 3 is illustrated in figure 3.3.

In order to use the simple Leontief model as a model of growth of von Neumann type, we may interpret inputs as occurring at the beginning of a time period and outputs as occurring at the end of that time period. In effect all the goods explicitly represented are treated as circulating capital that is replenished at the beginning of the time period and entirely consumed during the time period, like seed in agriculture. Consider

$$y(t-1) = Ay(t), \qquad y(t-1) > 0,$$

$$p(t)^T = p(t-1)^T A, \qquad p(t-1) > 0, \tag{3}$$

$$A = [a_{ij}], \ a_{ij} \geq 0, \qquad i, j = 1, \cdots, n,$$

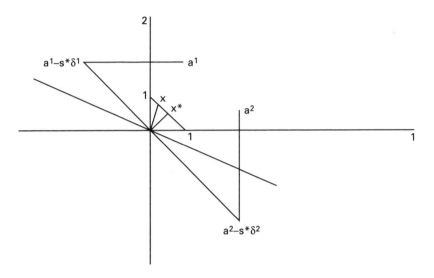

Figure 3.3
$A = (a^1 a^2)$. $x^*(A - s^*I) = 0$. For x not equal to x^*, min over j of $x(a^j - s^*\delta^j) < 0$. Thus $\mu_A(s^*) = 0$, and s^* is a characteristic root of A.

where $p(t)$ is the price vector at time t, $y(t)$ is the output at time t, a_{ij} is the input of the ith good needed per unit of output of the jth good. Equation system (3) is the simplest von Neumann growth model. The first equation says that the outputs at time $t - 1$ are just sufficient to supply the inputs required to produce the outputs at time t. This might be called the *balance condition*. The second equation says that the prices of goods at time t are just sufficient to cover the cost of production at the prices at time $t - 1$. This might be called the *profit condition*. Competitive equilibrium requires that both conditions be met in this model if all goods are produced. All goods must be produced if A is indecomposable and production is to continue indefinitely. We will discuss further the economic meaning of the von Neumann model in chapter 7, in particular, the absence of an explicit treatment of labor inputs and consumption.

The von Neumann theorem on maximal proportional growth for this model is

THEOREM 4   *If A is indecomposable, there is a unique r such that there is $y^* > 0$ and $p^* > 0$, and $y(t) = (1 + r)^t y^*$, $p(t) = (1 + r)^{-t} p^*$ is a solution of (3). Also $r > -1$ and r is the largest rate of proportional growth, as* *well as the smallest interest rate consistent with proportional price change.*

Proof For the first part of the theorem and the condition $r > -1$ apply theorem 3 to A and A^T. That r is the maximal proportional growth rate may be seen by choosing $s^* = (1 + r)^{-1}$ in the proof of theorem 3 and considering the condition $\mu_{A^T}((1 + r)^{-1}) = 0$. If there were an output y satisfying $(1 + r)^{-1}y \geq Ay$ and equality did not hold, then $\mu_{A^T}((1 + r)^{-1}) > 0$ would be implied by the argument used in the proof of theorem 3 to show that s^* is a characteristic root. A similar argument applies to $(1 + r)^{-1}p^T \leq p^T A$.   ∎

The prices $p(t)$ should be interpreted as discounted prices or present value prices at time 0. Then r is the minimum interest rate and also the maximal growth rate for balanced growth in the model (3).

3.3   The Simple Model with Variable Coefficients

The Leontief model has been described assuming fixed coefficients for each process. However, this assumption is less restrictive than it appears to be in the simple model. We will be able to show that even though coefficients are allowed to vary all efficient outputs may be produced without varying the coefficients. Consider the generalized model

$\mathscr{B}_j \subset \mathbf{R}^n$, $j = 1, \cdots, n$, where

$$b^j \in \mathscr{B}_j \text{ implies } b_j^j > 0, \; b_i^j \leq 0, \; i \neq j,$$

$$\tag{4}$$

$\mathscr{B}_j$ is closed and bounded from above.

Let $V = \{y \mid y \leq \sum_{j=1}^n x_j b^j, b^j \in \mathscr{B}_j, x_j \geq 0, y \geq 0, \sum_{j=1}^n x_j \leq 1\}$. We will say that (4) is the *generalized Leontief model* $\mathscr{L}_v$ with the set V of attainable outputs. Also B is said to be contained in $\mathscr{L}_v$ if $b^j \in \mathscr{B}_j$ for all j. As earlier the activities b_j are normalized on an input of one unit of labor and the unit of labor is chosen so that the total labor supply is one unit. The assumption that $\mathscr{B}_j$ is bounded above is equivalent to assuming that labor is an essential input for producing the jth good. We first prove

LEMMA 3   *V is compact and convex.*

Proof Let Y be the convex hull of the $\mathscr{B}_j$, $j = 1, \cdots, n$. Then $V = Y \cap \mathbf{R}_+^n$. Thus V is convex. For boundedness consider y^s, where $y^s \in V$,

$s = 1, 2, \cdots$. Let $y^s = \sum_{j=1}^n y^{js} = \sum_{j=1}^n x_j^s b^{js}$, $x_j^s \geq 0$, $\sum_{j=1}^n x_j^s \leq 1$. Suppose $|y^{js}| \to \infty$ for some j. Then $y_i^{js} \to -\infty$ for some $i \neq j$ since $\mathscr{B}_j$ is bounded above by (4). Therefore, if $y^s \geq 0$ is to hold so that $y^s \in V$, it must be that $\mathscr{B}_i$ is unbounded above, but this is forbidden by (4). Thus y^{js} must be bounded for each j. This implies that V is bounded.

To show that V is closed, let b_j be the upper bound on the $b^j \in \mathscr{B}_j$. Let $S = \{y \mid y_j \leq b_j, j = 1, \cdots, n\}$. Let $\overline{Y} = Y \cap S$. Then $\overline{Y}$ is closed and $V = \overline{Y} \cap \mathbf{R}_+^n$. V is closed as the intersection of closed sets. Since V is bounded and closed, it is compact in $\mathbf{R}^n$. ∎

Let $E = \{y \mid y \in V$, and $z - y \geq 0, z \in V$, implies $z = y\}$. E is the set of efficient outputs for $\mathscr{L}_v$. Let $B = [b_i^j]$ where $b^j \in \mathscr{B}_j$, $i, j = 1, \cdots, n$. Let $E(B) = \{y \mid Bx = y, x \geq 0, y \geq 0, \sum_{i=1}^n x_i = 1\}$. $E(B)$ is the set of efficient outputs of the simple model based on the activities in B.

LEMMA 4 $E(B)$ *is compact and convex.*

Proof $E(B)$ is the image of the unit simplex by a linear transformation. ∎

The next result is the famous nonsubstitution theorem of Samuelson (1951). The primal method of proof is due to McKenzie (1957). It shows that B may be chosen so that the Leontief models $\mathscr{L}$ and $\mathscr{L}_v$ are actually equivalent in the sense that substitution of inputs is not needed to achieve efficiency when there is only one unproduced input.

THEOREM 5   *If there is $y^* \in V$ and $y^* > 0$, then $E = E(B)$ for some B derived from $\mathscr{L}_v$.*

Primal Proof Let $\tau = \max t$ such that $ty^* \in V$. The existence of τ is guaranteed by the compactness of V according to lemma 3. Then $\tau y^* \leq B^* x^*$ for $\sum_{j=1}^n x_j^* \leq 1$, for some B^* in $\mathscr{L}_v$. For τ to be maximal both inequalities must be equalities. Using theorem 1 and the necessity part of its proof, we see that $Y(B^*) \supset \mathbf{R}_+^n$. Therefore there is $y^j \in E(B^*)$ such that $y_i^j = 0$, $i \neq j$, $y_j^j \neq 0$. Consider $\sigma y^* = \sum_{j=1}^n k_j y^j$, $\sum_{k=1}^n k_j = 1$, $k_j \geq 0$. By lemma 4, $E(B^*)$ is convex, so $\sigma y^* \in E(B^*)$. Therefore $\sigma = \tau$.

Suppose that there is $z \in V$ and $z \geq w$, $z \neq w$, where $w \in E(B^*)$. We may choose $z > 0$. Suppose that $z > 0$ does not hold. Consider $z' = tz + (1 - t)\tau y^*$ and $w' = tw + (1 - t)\tau y^*$, $0 < t < 1$. Then $z' > 0$ while $z' \geq w'$ and $z' \neq w'$, but convexity of V implies $z' \in V$, and convexity of $E(B^*)$ implies $w' \in E(B^*)$.

For some B in $\mathscr{L}_v$ it must be that $z = Bx$ where $\sum_{j=1}^n x_j = 1$, $x_j \geq 0$. Choose $z^j \in E(B)$ such that $z_i^j = 0$, $i \neq j$. Then for some k_j', $k_j'' \geq 0$, and $\sum_{j=1}^n k_j' = \sum_{j=1}^n k_j'' = 1$, we have $w = \sum_{j=1}^n k_j' y^j$ and $z = \sum_{j=1}^n k_j'' z^j$ using lemma 4 as before. Then either $k_j' = k_j''$ for all j or $k_{j_0}' > k_{j_0}''$ for some j_0. But $z_j = k_j'' z_j^j \geq k_j' y_j^j = w_j$, all j, with $>$ for some j_1. The first alternative implies that $y_{j_1}^{j_1} < z_{j_1}^{j_1}$. The second alternative implies that $y_{j_0}^{j_0} < z_{j_0}^{j_0}$.

Clearly, any choice of $v^j = y^j$ or z^j, $j = 1, \cdots, n$ will span $\mathbf{R}^n$. Let $\tau_0 y^* = \sum_{j=1}^n t_j v^j$ where $v^j = y^j$ if $y^j \geq z^j$, and $v^j = z^j$ if $y^j < z^j$ with $t_j \geq 0$, $\sum_{j=1}^n t_j = 1$. If $\tau \geq \tau_0$, then, from the choice of the v^j, $k_j \geq t_j$ must hold with $k_j > t_j$ for $z_j^j > y_j^j$. Thus $\sum_{j=1}^n t_j < 1$, which is a contradiction.

Therefore $\tau < \tau_0$, contradicting the choice of τ. Thus there cannot be $z \in V$ with $z \geq w$ and $z \neq w$. This means that $w \in E(B^*)$ implies that w is efficient. Then $E(B^*) \subset E$. Suppose $z \in E$ and $z \notin E(B^*)$. Then $\alpha z \in E(B^*)$ for $\alpha < 1$ and $\alpha z \notin E$, which contradicts $E(B^*) \subset E$. Therefore $E \subset E(B^*)$. In other words, $E = E(B^*)$. ∎

The primal proof is illustrated in figure 3.4.

As often happens in theories that use the properties of convex sets, there is also a proof of theorem 5 using the duality between convex sets

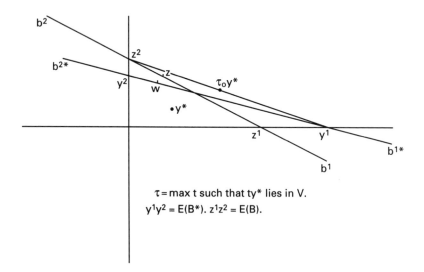

$\tau = \max t$ such that ty^* lies in V.

$y^1 y^2 = E(B^*)$. $z^1 z^2 = E(B)$.

Figure 3.4
$\tau_0 y^*$ lies in V, but $\tau_0 > \tau$, which is a contradiction. Therefore no such z exists or w is efficient in $\mathscr{L}$.

and their supports. Proofs by duality are often more elegant than the primal proofs—a fact that may be illustrated here.

A proof by duality was given by Stiglitz (1970). We approach the proof of the theorem by means of two lemmas.

LEMMA 5   *If $y \in E$, then there is $p \in R_+^n$ such that $py = 1$ and $py' \le 1$ for all $y' \in V$.*

Proof   By the definition, $y \in E$ implies that $y \in V$ and there is no $z > 0$ with $y + z \in V$. Thus $V \cap (y + \text{int } \mathbf{R}_+^n) = \emptyset$. By a separation theorem for disjoint convex sets (Berge 1963, p. 163), there is $p \in \mathbf{R}_+^n$, $p \ne 0$ such that $pz \le \pi$ for $z \in V$ and $pz \ge \pi$ for $z \in y + \text{int } \mathbf{R}_+^n$. Since $y + \text{int } \mathbf{R}_+^n$ is an open set, the second inequality is actually strict. Also by the second inequality $p \ge 0$ must hold. Since y lies in the closure of both sets, $py = \pi$. Finally $py^* > 0$ implies $\pi > 0$. Therefore we may choose p so that $\pi = 1$.   ∎

LEMMA 6   *Take $y > 0$ in lemma 5. Then p supports $\mathscr{B}_i$ at y^i, $i = 1, \cdots, n$, where $y = \sum \alpha_i y^i$ for $\alpha_i > 0$, and $\sum \alpha_i = 1$. Also $py^i = 1$, all i, so $p > 0$.*

Proof   By definition of V, $y \le \sum \alpha_i y^i$ for some $y^i \in \mathscr{B}_i$, $i = 1, \cdots, n$, $\alpha_i \ge 0$, $\sum \alpha_i \le 1$. If the first or third inequality were strict there would be $\alpha y \in V$ with $\alpha > 1$. Then $\alpha py > 1$ in contradiction to lemma 5. Also $y > 0$ implies $\alpha_i > 0$. Suppose $pz^i > 1$, $z^i \in \mathscr{B}_i$. Then $pz > 1$, where $z = \alpha y + \beta z^i$, $\alpha, \beta > 0$, $\alpha + \beta = 1$. Since $y > 0$, β small implies that $z > 0$, so $z \in V$. This is a contradiction of lemma 5, so $pz^i \le 1$, all $z^i \in \mathscr{B}_i$, all i. If $py^i < 1$ held, for some i, then $py < 1$ would hold, contradicting lemma 5. In other words, p supports $\mathscr{B}_i$ at y^i, all i, which implies $p > 0$.   ∎

With the aid of lemmas 5 and 6 the theorem may be proved. By the lemmas there is $p > 0$ such that $py = 1$, while $pz \le 1$ for all $z \in V$. Also $y = \sum_{i=1}^n \alpha_i y^i$, for $\sum \alpha_i = 1$, $\alpha_i \ge 0$, for some $y^i \in \mathscr{B}_i$, and $py^i = 1$, $i = 1, \cdots, n$.

Let $B = [y_j^i]$, $i, j = 1, \cdots, n$. Then $z \in E(B)$ implies $z = \sum_{i=1}^n \alpha_i y^i$, $\sum \alpha_i = 1$, $\alpha_i \ge 0$. Since $py^i = 1$, $pz = 1$. Suppose that there is $z' = z + w \in V$, $w \ge 0$, $w \ne 0$. Then $pz' > 1$, contradicting lemma 5. Therefore $z \in E$ or $E(B) \subset E$.

Consider $z \in E$, $pz \le 1$ by lemma 5. By theorem 1 and $y > 0$, there is α such that $\alpha z \in E(B)$, $\alpha \le 1$. Since $py^i = 1$ for all i and $\alpha z \in E(B)$, we have $p \cdot \alpha z = 1$. Thus $\alpha = 1$ and $z \in E(B)$. Therefore $E \subset E(B)$, so $E = E(B)$.

There may be many choices of the matrix B that give $E(B) = E$. Indeed, there may be an infinity of such choices. However, it is intuitive that the choice will be unique in almost all cases, and results of this type can be proved rigorously. Then no matter what output is required from the production sector, if the output is to be efficient, it must be produced with the technology represented by this B.

Unfortunately, as soon as there is more than one unproduced factor of production this result is lost. It should be noted that a produced factor must be currently produced to allow the theorem to be applied. If capital goods are treated as produced factors for the nonsubstitution theorem, it must be recognized that they were produced in the past. Then the labor inputs must be dated and inputs of different dates must be treated as different factors, so there are still many unproduced factors present after produced factors are reduced to labor inputs. However, if the supplies of all factors that save labor are changed to the quantities needed to hold their prices constant relative to labor, the theorem will remain valid. The domain in output space over which the nonsubstitution theorem holds may also be greatly restricted if processes have more than one output. The force of this consideration is strengthened by the fact that durable goods remaining at the end of the period must be treated as part of the output of a process. These topics are discussed in the next section.

3.4 Nonsubstitution with Capital Stocks

In the primary interpretation of the simple Leontief model, that is, apart from its interpretation as a von Neumann growth model, no initial stocks are required to support the production processes. Although there are intermediate products that are inputs derived from other industries, these are treated as continuous flows and do not require the maintenance of stocks. In the generalized model that will be discussed now the need for stocks of goods in addition to flows will be introduced (see Leontief 1953). It is immaterial whether the goods that are stocked are consumed in one or many uses. It is only relevant that the goods must be stocked if efficient production is to be achieved.

We will denote the models with capital stocks by $\mathscr{L}_c$. A model of this type was used for the proof of a turnpike theorem in McKenzie (1963) (see the appendix to chapter 7). Let a_j be the jth column of A and represent the flow of net inputs and outputs in an activity chosen from the jth process over one period. Let b_j be the jth column of B and represent the stocks of goods supporting production in the activity chosen from the jth process. Let $\mathcal{D}_j$ be the set of (a_j, b_j) which make up the jth process. Then $\begin{pmatrix} a_j + [\delta_i]b_j \\ -b_j \end{pmatrix}$ is a possible input–output vector using one unit of labor. Since the processes are assumed to be linear homogeneous, x units of labor can support an input–output vector x times this vector. The expression $[\delta_i]$ denotes a diagonal matrix with δ_i in the ith diagonal position, where δ_i is the *depreciation factor* for the ith good. δ_i represents the proportion of the ith stock that remains at the end of the period when an activity is used at unit level. Sometimes, for simplicity, we assume that δ_i is independent of the activity used.

Consider $\mathcal{D}_j \subset \mathbf{R}^{2n}$:

$$(a_j, b_j) \in \mathcal{D}_j \text{ implies } a_{jj} > 0, \ a_{ij} \leq 0 \text{ for } i \neq j, \ b_{ij} \geq 0.$$

$$\mathcal{D}_j \text{ is closed and } a_{jj} \text{ is bounded above over } \mathcal{D}_j. \tag{5}$$

Let $\mathcal{D}$ be the set of (A, B) whose jth columns belong to $\mathcal{D}_j$. Define $Y \subset \mathbf{R}^{2n}$ by

$$Y = \left\{ (y', -y)^T \ \middle| \ \begin{bmatrix} A + [\delta_i]B \\ -B \end{bmatrix} x \geq \begin{pmatrix} y' \\ -y \end{pmatrix} \right\}, \tag{6}$$

where $x_j \geq 0$ and $\sum_{j=1}^n x_j \leq 1$. We will say that (5) is a *Leontief model* $\mathcal{L}_c$ *with capital goods* and the set Y of attainable outputs. Activities have been normalized on one unit of labor. The inequalities imply free disposal of goods and labor.

Consider $(y', -y) \in Y$, where $y' = [\rho]y + c$. c is the consumption vector. $[\rho]$ is a diagonal matrix with diagonal elements equal to ρ. Then ρ is the growth factor for the capital stocks. Substituting for y, we obtain

$$(A + [\delta_i]B)x \geq [\rho]Bx + c, \quad \text{or}$$

$$(A - ([\rho - \delta_i])B)x \geq c, \tag{7}$$

where $x_j \geq 0$ and $\sum_{j=1}^h x_j \leq 1$.

The Leontief model with capital stocks is illustrated in figure 3.5.

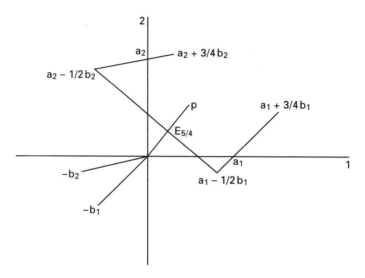

Figure 3.5
The Leontief model with capital goods. Here $\delta = 3/4$ and $\rho = 5/4$.

Let $V_\rho = \{c \mid c \geq 0 \text{ and } c \text{ is expressible by (7) for some } (A, B) \in \mathcal{D}\}$ with $\rho \geq 0$. Let R be the set of ρ satisfying the condition there is $c \in V_\rho$, $c > 0$, and c may be expressed by an $(A, B) \in \mathcal{D}$, where $(A - ([\rho - \delta_i])B)$ has off-diagonal elements that are nonpositive and positive diagonal elements. If some A has a dominant diagonal, then $\rho \in R$ if $\delta_i = \rho$ for all i. But this condition is not necessary. The necessary and sufficient condition for $\rho \in R$ when the sign conditions are met is, by theorem 1, that there is $(A, B) \in \mathcal{D}$ such that $(A - ([\rho - \delta_i])B)$ has a dominant diagonal. Let E_ρ be the efficient point set of V_ρ. For $\rho \in R$, E_ρ is the efficient point set of a Leontief model with variable coefficients $\mathcal{L}_{v\rho}$. $\mathcal{L}_{v\rho}$ has a set $\mathcal{A}_\rho$ of input–output matrices $\bar{A}_\rho$, where $\bar{A}_\rho \in \mathcal{A}_\rho$ implies that $\bar{A}_\rho = (A - [\rho - \delta_i]B)$ for $(A, B) \in \mathcal{D}$ and $\bar{A}_\rho$ has nonpositive off diagonal elements.

LEMMA 7 *If $\rho \in R$, there is (A_ρ, B_ρ) whose jth columns belong to $\mathcal{D}_j$ such that for any $c \in E_\rho$ there is $x \geq 0$, $\sum_{j=1}^n x_j = 1$, where $(A_\rho - [\rho - \delta_i]B_\rho)x = \bar{A}_\rho x = c$. Also there is $p > 0$ such that $p\bar{A}_\rho = \rho e$, and $p\bar{A}_\rho' \leq \rho e = (\rho, \cdots, \rho)$ for all $\bar{A}_\rho' \in \mathcal{A}_\rho$.*

Proof By theorem 5 there is a choice of $\bar{A}_\rho$ in $\mathcal{A}_\rho$ such that $E(\bar{A}_\rho) = E_\rho$. This gives the first statement of the lemma. Let $\mathcal{B}_{\rho j} \subset \mathbf{R}^n$ be the set of activities available in the jth process of $\mathscr{L}_{v\rho}$ to provide the jth column of $\bar{A}_\rho$. By lemma 6 the price vector p exists supporting the activity represented by the jth column of $\bar{A}_\rho$ over the set $\mathscr{B}_{\rho j}$ for each j. This implies the second statement of the lemma. We will say that p *supports* the production technology (A_ρ, B_ρ). ∎

We have the obvious

COROLLARY   *Under the conditions of lemma 7 there is a price vector $p > 0$*

such that

$$([\rho]^{-1}p^T, p^T)\begin{bmatrix} A_\rho + [\delta_i]B_\rho \\ -B_\rho \end{bmatrix} = e.$$

In the corollary we may interpret p as the price vector for goods exchanged at the beginning of a period and $[\rho]^{-1}p$ as the price vector for goods exchanged at the end of the period. The prices are present prices quoted at the beginning of the period and the price of labor at the start of the period has been set equal to 1. It is clear that this price sequence can be continued so that the price of labor at the beginning of the tth period quoted for trading at the beginning of the first period is ρ^{1-t} and the price vector for goods at the beginning of the tth period quoted for trading at the beginning of the first period would be $\rho^{1-t}p$. In other words, present prices are falling by the discount factor ρ^{-1}, assuming that ρ is larger than 1. As a consequence the value of the total capital stock at present prices is constant if ρ is the growth factor for capital. The sequence of outputs changing by the same factors period after period may be supported by a price sequence changing by the inverses of these factors. For the case where the capital stocks are growing by the same factors, that is, growth is proportional, the existence of sequences of proportional supporting prices has been shown by Malinvaud (1953) to be a general phenomenon, not confined to Leontief models. However, in the Leontief model a supporting price sequence for a proportional output sequence, growing by the factor ρ, is unique up to a positive factor independently of c. This has been called a nonsubstitution theorem for the Leontief model with capital stocks (Samuelson 1961; Mirrlees 1969), but it is important to notice that the meaning of nonsubstitution is not the same as before. In order to move from one proportional program to another, capital stocks must change. A traverse must be negotiated during which stocks are changing. Also, if net output is moved toward industries requiring larger capital stocks, net saving will be required. Thus there is no straightforward substitution of outputs, but intermediate periods of adjustment are needed in which prices and discount factors may be expected to change to accommodate demand conditions for an economic equilibrium over time. In the simple model no such traverse is needed and no price changes are required. We may prove

THEOREM 6   *Let the wage rate equal 1. Given a Leontief model $\mathscr{L}_\rho$ and any $\rho \in R$, there is a vector-valued function $f(\rho)$ for produced goods such that any price vector p that supports a production technology (A_ρ, B_ρ) in $\mathscr{L}_c$ satisfies the condition $p = f(\rho)$.*

Proof   Let $(p_t, p_{t+1}) = ([\rho^{-1}]p, p)$. By lemma 7 there is p such that

$$(p^T, [\rho^{-1}]p^T)\begin{bmatrix} A + [\delta_i]B \\ -B \end{bmatrix} \le e,$$

or equivalently $p^T(A - ([\rho - \delta_i])B) \le e$ for all $(A, B) \in \mathscr{D}$. Also $p^T(A_\rho - ([\rho - \delta_i])B_\rho) = e$ for some choice of (A_ρ, B_ρ). Let p' support a production technology (A'_ρ, B'_ρ) in $\mathscr{L}_c$. Let $\bar{A}_\rho(p) = A_\rho - ([\rho - \delta_i])B_\rho$ and $\bar{A}_\rho(p') = A'_\rho - ([\rho - \delta_i])B'_\rho$. Then

$$p^T \bar{A}_\rho(p') \le e, \quad p^T \bar{A}_\rho(p) = e,$$

and

$$p'^T \bar{A}_\rho(p) \le e, \quad p'^T \bar{A}_\rho(p') = e.$$

Also

$$[\bar{A}_\rho(p)]_{ij} \le 0, \text{ and } [\bar{A}_\rho(p')]_{ij} \le 0 \qquad \text{for } i \ne j.$$

By lemma 2.6 there are inverse matrices $[\bar{A}_\rho(p)]^{-1}$ and $[\bar{A}_\rho(p')]^{-1}$. Multiplying the inequalities on the right by the inverse matrices, we derive $(p - p') \le 0$ and $(p' - p) \le 0$, or $p - p' = 0$. Thus given $\rho \in R$, the supporting price vector p is unique, and we may write $p = f(\rho)$.   ∎

It is worth noting that in a proportional growth program the values of consumption and the total wage bill are equal. Consider $pc = p^T \bar{A}_\rho(p)x = ex = 1$ using lemma 7 and the definitions. This does not imply that all saving needs to be done out of income from the ownership of capital goods. It does imply that consumption out of income from capital must be balanced by saving out of wages.

The preceding discussion may give the impression that the support prices we have found that change over a period by factors inverse to the growth factor for stocks are not appropriate for other output sequences. However, this impression would be mistaken. Given any prices that satisfy the profit conditions, that is, that do not provide positive profits to any activity, any outputs that are feasible, using only the activities that show zero profits at these prices, are supported by these prices. However, proportional growth programs in which capital stocks grow by the same factors from period to period have special interest. This interest, in part, arises from considering economies in which the population, and consequently the labor supply, is growing by a constant factor γ so that per capita quantities remain constant if outputs also grow by the same factor γ. Alternatively, the population may be constant while the efficiency of labor increases by a factor γ each period. Then per capita quantities per unit of efficiency labor are constant.

On the other hand, there is a special interest in support prices that fall by a factor that is equal for all goods, say ρ^{-1}. This is because ρ^{-1} can be regarded as a discount factor, reducing future prices to present prices whatever objects are being valued. Then $r = (\rho - 1)$ is an interest rate. Thus theorem 6 may be interpreted as providing a price vector consistent with a discount factor ρ^{-1} or the corresponding interest rate r. Theorem 6 asserts that this price vector is independent of the composition of net output. In this sense theorem 6 is a nonsubstitution theorem for the Leontief model $\mathscr{L}_c$. Let t be the time at the end of the tth period. It is important to notice that the price sequences $\rho^{-t}p$ for produced goods and ρ^{-t} for labor provide support for a given technology (A_ρ, B_ρ) in a sequence of periods.

Suppose that population grows each period by a factor γ and the interest rate is r. Then the activities that meet the profit conditions are those supported by the price vector $(p, \rho p)$, where $p = f(\rho)$ with $\rho = 1 + r$. Consider $(A_\rho - [\gamma - \delta_i]B_\rho)x = c$. Let $\bar{A}_{\rho,\gamma} = A_\rho - [\gamma - \delta_i]B_\rho$. If $\gamma \geq 1$, then $\bar{A}_{\rho,\gamma}$ has off-diagonal elements nonpositive. Therefore $\bar{A}_{\rho,\gamma}^{-1}$ will exist and be nonnegative if and only if $\bar{A}_{\rho,\gamma}$ has a dominant diagonal. This will be true in particular if $\rho \in R$ and $1 \leq \gamma \leq \rho$, that is, if the growth factor for population is greater than or equal to one and less than or equal to the inverse of the discount factor, or what is the same thing, if the growth rate for population is greater than or equal to zero and less than or equal to the interest rate.

So far we have justified goods' prices that fall by the same factor ρ^{-1} each period by assuming that the price of labor falls by the factor ρ^{-1} each period. Thus the formula for the profit conditions in the first period is multiplied through by the factor ρ^{1-t} to give the profit conditions for the tth period, that is,

$$(\rho^{-t}p^T, \rho^{1-t}p^T)\begin{bmatrix} A + [\delta_i]B \\ -B \end{bmatrix} \le \rho^{1-t}e, \tag{8}$$

for all choices of (A, B) with equality for the choice (A_ρ, B_ρ). However, we could equally well have assumed that the efficiency of labor increases by the factor ρ each period so that the input of labor into each activity falls by the factor ρ^{-1} each period. Then an equilibrium path of growth with capital stocks increasing by the factor ρ each period would be consistent with a constant population provided that the utility functions are homothetic, that is, the surfaces of constant utility are projections of one such surface from the origin. Then with constant relative prices the consumption vectors lie on a line through the origin and expand by the factor ρ in each period. If the discount factor is ρ^{-1}, the present price of labor is constant over time at level 1.

The possibility that price changes for goods arise from changes in the productivity of labor suggests that we consider the case where productivity of labor changes by different factors in different industries; that is, the number ρ or the diagonal matrix $[\rho]$ is replaced by the diagonal matrix $[\rho_i]$ with ρ_i, $i = 1, \cdots, n$, on the diagonal. Then the conditions of equilibrium in the production sector are given by

$$([\rho_i]^{-1}p^T, p^T)\begin{bmatrix} A + [\delta_i]B \\ -B \end{bmatrix} \le e, \tag{9}$$

with equality for some choice $(A, B) = (A_{(\rho_i)}, B_{(\rho_i)})$. However, this construction is of doubtful utility since it cannot be continued for a sequence of periods. The wage of labor cannot differ between industries. Thus multiplication through by $[\rho_i]^{-1}$ in (9) does not satisfy the equilibrium conditions for the production sector unless $\rho_i = \rho$ for all i.

3.5   Current Prices and Interest Rates

The notion of an interest rate has been introduced in the context of a uniform decline in the prices of labor and commodities by a factor of p^{-1} each period. These prices are called present prices at $t = 0$ or prices discounted to the time $t = 0$. The interest rate was defined by $r = p - 1$. Then current prices are the prices p for commodities and 1 for labor as they appear in (7). However, this definition fails when prices are not falling by the same factors. The problem was first clarified by Malinvaud (1953). The present prices are the basic data, and the interest rates and current prices cannot be defined in general until a good is selected that is to have the current price 1 in each period. It may be thought of as a periodwise numéraire. (A numéraire in the original meaning of Walras would be a good whose present price at a specific time is chosen to be 1.) However, in the case represented by (7) all goods including labor are falling by the same factor, which is not affected by the choice of numéraire.

These relations are easily generalized so that they do not depend on the special features of the Leontief model. Let the present price vector in the tth period be $p^t = (p_1^t, \cdots, p_n^t)$ where there are n commodities all told. Let the jth commodity be a periodwise numéraire. Define $\beta_t = p_j^t/p_j^{t-1}$. Then $p_j^0 = \prod_{\tau=1}^{t} \beta_\tau^{-1} p_j^t$. If we define the current price vector P^t by $P^t = \prod_{\tau=1}^{t} \beta_\tau^{-1} p^t$, the jth current price will be constant at P_j^0. If all current prices are divided by P_j^0, the equilibrium conditions for the production sector are still satisfied after discounting, and in the new price system the current prices of the jth commodity are all equal to 1. With this choice of periodwise numéraire, the discount factor is β_τ and the interest rate is $\beta_\tau^{-1} - 1$. When the equilibrium conditions are considered, the present prices, that is, the discounted prices, must always be used. It makes no difference what time period is chosen to bear the time index 0.

Appendix: Continuity of $\mu_A(s)$

We will prove

LEMMA 8   *If A is a real square matrix, then $\mu_A(s)$ is a real-valued continuous function on the real line.*

Proof   Let $A = [a_{ij}]$, $i, j = 1, \cdots, n$, and let $S = \{x \in \mathbf{R}^n \mid x \geq 0$ and $\sum_i x_i = 1\}$. Let $\delta_{ij} = 1$ for $i = j$ and $\delta_{ij} = 0$ for $i \neq j$. Assume $s' > s$. Then

$\sum_i (s'\delta_{ij} - a_{ij})x_i - \sum_i (s\delta_{ij} - a_{ij})x_i = (s' - s)x_j$, for all j and all $x \in S$.
Therefore, since $(s' - s)x_j \leq s' - s$,

$$0 \leq \sum_i (s'\delta_{ij} - a_{ij})x_i - \sum_i (s\delta_{ij} - a_{ij})x_i \leq s' - s, \qquad \text{all } j, \text{ all } x \in S. \quad \text{(A1)}$$

Let $\min_j \sum_i (s'\delta_{ij} - a_{ij})x_i$ be achieved at j_1 for given $x \in S$. Then

$$\min_j \sum_i (s'\delta_{ij} - a_{ij})x_i = \sum_i (s'\delta_{ij_1} - a_{ij_1})x_i$$

$$\geq \sum_i (s\delta_{ij_1} - a_{ij_1})x_i \geq \min_j \sum_i (s\delta_{ij} - a_{ij})x_i. \quad \text{(A2)}$$

Let $\min_j \sum_i (s\delta_{ij} - a_{ij})x_i$ be achieved at j_2 for given $x \in S$. Then

$$s' - s + \min_j \sum_i (s\delta_{ij} - a_{ij})x_i = s' - s + \sum_i (s\delta_{ij_2} - a_{ij_2})x_i$$

$$\geq \sum_i (s'\delta_{ij_2} - a_{ij_2})x_i$$

$$\geq \min_j \sum_i (s'\delta_{ij} - a_{ij})x_i. \quad \text{(A3)}$$

The first inequality of (A2) and (A3) is implied by (A1). Then

$$0 \leq \min_j \sum_i (s'\delta_{ij} - a_{ij})x_i - \min_j \sum_i (s\delta_{ij} - a_{ij})x_i \leq s' - s \quad \text{(A4)}$$

for all $x \in S$. The first inequality is implied by (A2). The second inequality is implied by (A3).

Let $\max_{x \in S} \min_j \sum_i (s\delta_{ij} - a_{ij})x_i$ be achieved at x^1. Then

$$\mu_A(s) = \min_j \sum_i (s\delta_{ij} - a_{ij})x_i^1$$

$$\leq \min_j \sum_i (s'\delta_{ij} - a_{ij})x_i^1$$

$$\leq \max_{x \in S} \min_j \sum_i (s'\delta_{ij} - a_{ij})x_i$$

$$= \mu_A(s'). \quad \text{(A5)}$$

Let $\max_{x \in S} \min_j \sum_i (s'\delta_{ij} - a_{ij})x_i$ be achieved at x^2. Then

$$\mu_A(s') = \min_j \sum_i (s'\delta_{ij} - a_{ij})x_i^2 \leq \min_j \sum_i (s\delta_{ij} - a_{ij})x_i^2 + s' - s$$

$$\leq \max_{x \in S} \min_j \sum_i (s\delta_{ij} - a_{ij})x_i + s' - s = \mu_A(s) + s' - s. \tag{A6}$$

The first inequality of (A5) is implied by the first inequality of (A4). The first inequality of (A6) is implied by the second inequality of (A4). Then from (A5) and (A6) we have that $0 \leq \mu_A(s') - \mu_A(s) \leq s' - s$. This establishes the continuity of $\mu_A(s)$. The other properties are obvious. ∎

4 Comparative Statics

Probably the most frequent application of economic analysis is to the comparison of equilibrium positions of the consumer, the firm, the industry, or the economy when some parameter of the relevant model is changed. In this chapter we will chiefly be concerned with comparing the equilibria of the economy when the excess demand functions shift by small amounts. The questions of existence and uniqueness of equilibrium, although logically prior to comparative statics, will be dealt with in subsequent chapters. The mathematics used in their analysis is more advanced than the mathematics needed here. We will also consider the effects on the equilibrium of the firm or of the consumer when the number of constraints on their maximization problem is changed. This leads to the Le Chatelier theorems of Samuelson (1947).

4.1 The Local Theory of Comparative Statics

Many of the results on comparative statics for the economy as a whole consist in the application to comparative statics of the sufficient conditions for stability which were established in chapter 2. Some of these conditions were initially given as sufficient conditions for Hicksian stability. Hicksian stability is a generalization to economies with many goods of conditions known to be sufficient for tâtonnement stability of exchange economies where there are only two goods.

The Hicksian stability conditions were introduced in an economy of firms (Hicks 1939). It is assumed that the demand functions of consumers $d_i(p)$ and the supply functions of firms $s_i(p)$ are single valued, continuous, and differentiable in the neighborhood of equilibrium. Our assumptions of sections 2.1 and 2.7 suffice to establish these properties for supply and demand functions. The demand functions must allow for incomes which result from the distribution of the profits of firms. However, the profits of firms are determined by prices. Let $e_i(p) = d_i(p) - s_i(p)$, $i = 1, \cdots, n$, be the excess demand functions where $p \in R_+^n$ and the nth good is the numéraire. Introduce a set of $n - 1$ parameters $\alpha_1, \cdots, \alpha_{n-1}$, and write the excess demand functions as $e_i(p, \alpha)$ where $\partial e_i / \partial \alpha_j > 0$ for $i = j$, $\partial e_i / \partial \alpha_j < 0$ for $i = n$, and $\partial e_i / \partial \alpha_j = 0$ otherwise. The parameter α_j shifts excess demand from the nth good to the jth good. Shifts of demand between goods i and j can be represented by combining shifts between i and n with shifts between j and n. Let $p(\alpha)$ satisfy $e(p(\alpha), \alpha) = 0$ where $p(\alpha) > 0$. If the matrix $[\partial e_i / \partial p_j]$, $i, j = 1, \cdots, n - 1$, is nonsingular at $\bar{\alpha}$, the function $p(\alpha)$ exists in a neighborhood of $\bar{\alpha}$ and has continuous first derivatives by the implicit function theorem (Dieudonné 1960, p. 265). We say that $e(p(\alpha), \alpha)$ has *perfect Hicksian stability* at $(p(\bar{\alpha}), \bar{\alpha})$ if, for any j, $\partial p_j(\alpha)/\partial \alpha_j|_{\alpha=\bar{\alpha}} > 0$ when p_i is set equal to $p_i(\bar{\alpha})$ for $i \in I$, for any $I \subset$ complement $\{j, n\}$. Hicks' definition is slightly different from this one since he requires that excess demand decrease for a good if its price rises and certain other markets are equilibrated by their price changes. However, it seems more in accord with the spirit of comparative statics to refer to a change in the underlying conditions for equilibrium. The mathematical conditions are the same. Write $e_{ij}(p, \alpha) = \partial e_i(p, \alpha)/\partial p_j$. We may prove

LEMMA 1   *Let* $J_n = [e_{ij}(p(\alpha), \alpha)]_{n-1}^1$ *evaluated at* $\alpha = \bar{\alpha}$ *where* $p(\bar{\alpha}) > 0$ *and* $e(p(\bar{\alpha}), \bar{\alpha}) = 0$. *Then* $e(p(\alpha), \alpha)$ *has perfect Hicksian stability at* $\alpha = \bar{\alpha}$ *if and only if every principal minor of* J_n *of order* i *has* $\operatorname{sign}(-1)^i$.

Proof   Without loss of generality consider α_1, and let $I = \{i \mid 1 < i \leq s$ for $1 \leq s < n\}$. Then differentiating $e_i(p(\alpha), \alpha) = 0$ for $i \in I$ with respect to α_1 gives

$$[e_{ij}(p(\alpha), \alpha)]_s^1 \begin{pmatrix} dp_1 \\ \vdots \\ dp_s \end{pmatrix} = - \begin{pmatrix} e_{1\alpha_1} \, d\alpha_1 \\ 0 \\ \vdots \\ 0 \end{pmatrix}. \tag{1}$$

Therefore $\partial p_1/\partial \alpha_1 = -(|e_{ij}(p(\alpha), \alpha)|_s^2/|e_{ij}(p(\alpha), \alpha)|_s^1) \cdot e_{1\alpha_1}$ using Cramer's Rule. The conclusion of the lemma is immediate from this formula. Note that $s = 1$ implies $\partial p_1/\partial \alpha_1 = -e_{11}(p(\alpha), \alpha)^{-1} e_{1\alpha_1}$.   ∎

Let $[e_{i\alpha_i}]$ be the diagonal matrix with $e_{i\alpha_i}(p(\alpha), \alpha)$ on the diagonal. For any matrix $[a_{ij}]$ let $[a_{ij}]_J$ be the principal submatrix with $i, j \in J$. The implicit function theorem gives the general statement $[\partial p_i/\partial \alpha_i]_J = [e_{ij}]_J^{-1} [e_{i\alpha_i}]_J$. Note that Hicksian stability only considers the diagonal terms of $[\partial p_i/\partial \alpha_j]_J$.

Hicksian stability is defined in terms of comparative static properties of the equilibria, and lemma 1 gives sufficient conditions that these properties should hold. However, these conditions are not meaningful in economic terms. It is important to find conditions that imply them and appeal to economic intuition. There are two principal conditions of this type. One is the possibility that income effects from price changes are offsetting, since sellers gain from price changes when buyers lose, and vice versa. The other is a tendency for goods to be substitutes rather than complements (Hicks 1939, p. 47). Let $f^h(p, \alpha)$ be the compensated demand function of the hth consumer defined for the preference level of the commodity bundle $d^h(p, \alpha)$. Let $f(p, \alpha) = \sum_h f^h(p, \alpha)$ over the market. We are led to

THEOREM 1 *If income effects nearly cancel and* $|f_{ij}(p(\alpha), \alpha)|^1_{n-1} \neq 0$, *or if all goods are gross substitutes and* $[e_{ij}(p(\alpha), \alpha)]^1_n$ *is indecomposable, $e(p(\alpha), \alpha)$ has perfect Hicksian stability.*

Proof As income effects become small, $[e_{ij}(p(\alpha), \alpha)] \to [f_{ij}] - [s_{ij}]$ where the arguments $p(\alpha), \alpha$ are suppressed. But $[f_{ij} - s_{ij}]^1_{n-1}$ is negative definite, since $[f_{ij}]^1_{n-1}$ is negative definite from the assumption of nonsingularity and $[s_{ij}]$ is at least positive semidefinite. Therefore the principal minors of $[f_{ij} - s_{ij}]^1_{n-1}$ of order r have sign$(-1)^r$, and when there is near cancellation of income effects, $[e_{ij}(p(\alpha), \alpha)]$ also has this property.

On the other hand, if all goods are gross substitutes, $[e_{ij}(p(\alpha), \alpha)]^1_n$ indecomposable implies that proper principal minors have dominant negative diagonals as in the proof of lemma 2.10, using either Walras' Law or homogeneity of zero degree in p. Then by the proof of lemma 2.7 principal minors of order r have sign$(-1)^r$. ∎

Theorem 1 is a comparative static result since, by definition of Hicksian perfect stability, it implies that a shift of demand from the numéraire good to any other good will cause the price of that good to rise if its market is in equilibrium, even if some markets are not equilibrated. In the Hicks definitions the prices do not change for the goods whose markets are in disequilibrium. This failure of some markets to equilibrate might be explained by the presence of middlemen who are willing to adjust their stocks at the existing prices to absorb excess demand or supply.

Under the assumptions of theorem 1 it is also possible to show that increasing the number of markets that are equilibrated increases the response of the price of the good to which demand has shifted. Let $\partial p_1(\alpha)/ \partial \alpha_1]_s$ be the rate of change in the price of the first good when α_1 increases and prices are held constant for $i > s$. As we have seen, the derivatives $\partial p_i(\alpha)/\partial \alpha_i$, $i \in J$, are calculated from the relations $e_i(p, \alpha) = 0$ for $i \in J$ using the implicit function theorem with p_i, $i \in J$, as the dependent variables. Since the ordering of goods is arbitrary, we may concentrate on the case $i = 1$ and $J = \{1, \cdots, s\}$. We may prove

THEOREM 2 *If either income effects nearly cancel and principal minors of $|f_{ij}(p(\alpha), \alpha)|_{n-1}^1$ are nonzero, or if all goods are gross substitutes and $|e_{ij}(p(\alpha), \alpha)|_n^1$ is indecomposable, $\partial p_1 / \partial \alpha_1]_s < \partial p_1 / \partial \alpha_1]_{s+1}$ for $s \leq n - 2$.*

Proof Let $J_s^r = [e_{ij}(p(\alpha), \alpha)]_s^r$. Choose units for α_1 so that $e_{1\alpha_1}(p(\alpha), \alpha) = 1$. Then at $(p(\alpha), \alpha)$,

$$\frac{\partial p_1}{\partial \alpha_1}\bigg]_s = -\frac{|J_s^2|}{|J_s^1|} \quad and \quad \frac{\partial p_1}{\partial \alpha_1}\bigg]_{s+1} = -\frac{|J_{s+1}^2|}{|J_{s+1}^1|}.$$

Therefore the theorem holds if and only if

$$-\frac{|J_s^2|}{|J_s^1|} < -\frac{|J_{s+1}^2|}{|J_{s+1}^1|}. \tag{2}$$

Let $D = |J_{s+1}^1|$. Then $D_{11} = |J_{s+1}^2|$, $D_{s+1\,s+1} = |J_s^1|$, and $D_{11,s+1\,s+1} = |J_s^2|$. D and $D_{s+1\,s+1}$ have opposite signs under the hypothesis. Therefore the theorem holds if and only if

$$D_{11} D_{s+1\,s+1} < D D_{11,s+1\,s+1}. \tag{3}$$

By the proposition of appendix B, Jacobi's theorem,

$$\begin{vmatrix} D_{11} & (-1)^{s+2} D_{1\,s+1} \\ (-1)^{s+2} D_{s+1\,1} & D_{s+1\,s+1} \end{vmatrix} = D D_{11,s+1\,s+1} \tag{4}$$

or

$$D_{11} D_{s+1\,s+1} - D_{1\,s+1} D_{s+1\,1} = D D_{11,s+1\,s+1}.$$

However, if income effects cancel, the hypothesis implies $D_{1\,s+1} = D_{s+1\,1} \neq 0$. Thus $D_{1\,s+1} D_{s+1\,1} > 0$. By continuity the same is true for income effects small. Then (4) implies (3), and the conclusion of the theorem follows in the case of small income effects.

To give the proof in the case of gross substitutes we need

LEMMA 2 *Let A be an indecomposable square matrix with nonnegative off diagonal elements and a quasidominant negative diagonal. Then A has an inverse with all elements negative.*

Proof of the Lemma Since A is the negative of a Leontief matrix, it is implied by theorem 3.1 that its inverse has all elements nonpositive. Let $A^{-1} = [\bar{a}_{ij}]$, and without loss of generality, consider the first column of A^{-1}. Let $S = \{i \,|\, \bar{a}_{i1} = 0\} \neq \emptyset$. Let $\tilde{S}$ be the complement of S. Consider

$$\begin{bmatrix} A_{\tilde{S}\tilde{S}} & A_{\tilde{S}S} \\ A_{S\tilde{S}} & A_{SS} \end{bmatrix} \begin{pmatrix} \bar{a}_{\tilde{S}1} \\ \bar{a}_{S1} \end{pmatrix} = \begin{pmatrix} I_{\tilde{S}1} \\ I_{S1} \end{pmatrix}.$$

Since $1 \in \tilde{S}$, $I_{S1} = 0$. Then $A_{S\tilde{S}}\bar{a}_{\tilde{S}1} = 0$, which implies $A_{S\tilde{S}} = 0$, since $\bar{a}_{i1} \neq 0$ for $i \in \tilde{S}$ while $\bar{a}_{S1} = 0$. This contradicts the indecomposability of A. Therefore $\bar{a}_{i1} \neq 0$ for any i and $S = \emptyset$. ∎

We may now complete the proof of the theorem. If the assumption of gross substitutes holds, the hypothesis of the lemma is met for $A = J^1_{s+1}$. Thus J^1_{s+1} has a negative inverse. The elements of the inverse of J^1_{s+1} are $(-1)^{i+j}D_{ji}/D$, so D_{1s+1} and D_{s+11} have the same signs. This implies $D_{1s+1}D_{s+11} > 0$. Thus in the gross substitute case the conclusion of the theorem follows from (3) and (4) as before. ∎

The gross substitute case of theorem 2 is illustrated in figure 4.1.

If the reduced Jacobian at equilibrium, that is,

$$J_n = [e_{ij}(p(\alpha), \alpha)]^1_{n-1},$$

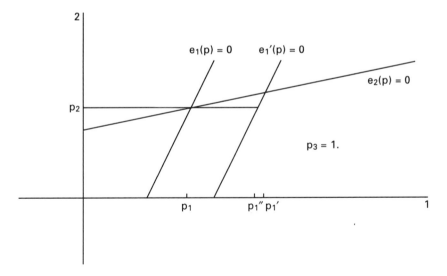

Figure 4.1
This illustrates the case of gross substitutes since e_{12} and e_{21} are both positive, and $e_{11}e_{22} > e_{12}e_{21}$. When demand shifts from good 3 to good 1, the excess demand function e_1 shifts to e'_1. The new equilibrium price p'_1 is greater than p''_1, which is the equilibrium price when p_2 is held constant.

has a dominant diagonal with $p_i(\alpha)$, $i = 1, \cdots, n - 1$, as multipliers, it has been shown by Mukherji (1975) that the relative price increase in the new equilibrium for the good to which demand has shifted is larger than the absolute value of the relative change in any other price. We will need

LEMMA 3   *If the transpose of the reduced Jacobian has a dominant negative diagonal with prices as multipliers with one set of units of measurement for goods, it has this property with any other set of units of measurement.*

Proof   Suppose $p_i e_{ii} + \sum_{j \neq i, 1} p_j |e_{ij}(p)| < 0$. For $i = 1, \cdots, n$, let β_j old units of the jth good equal 1 unit of the jth good with the new measurement. Denote the new prices by $\hat{p}$ and the new excess demand by $\hat{e}(\hat{p})$. Then $\hat{e}_i(\hat{p}) = \beta_i^{-1} e(p) = \beta_i^{-1} e_i(\beta_1^{-1}\hat{p}_1, \cdots, \beta_n^{-1}\hat{p}_n)$. Then $\hat{e}_{ij} = \beta_i^{-1} e_{ij}\beta_j^{-1}$. Therefore

$$\hat{p}_i \hat{e}_{ii} + \sum_{j \neq i, 1} \hat{p}_j |\hat{e}_{ij}| = \beta_i p_i \beta_i^{-1} e_{ii}\beta_i^{-1} + \sum_{j \neq i, 1} \beta_j p_j \beta_i^{-1} |e_{ij}|\beta_j^{-1}$$

$$= \beta_i^{-1}\left(p_i e_{ii} + \sum_{j \neq i, 1} p_j |e_{ij}|\right) < 0.$$

The inequality follows from the assumption.   ∎

THEOREM 3   *Assume $p(\alpha) > 0$. If $J_n^T(p(\alpha), \alpha)$ has a negative dominant diagonal with $p(\alpha)$ as multipliers, then $\partial p_i(\alpha)/\partial \alpha_i > 0$. Also $\partial p_i(\alpha)/\partial \alpha_i > |\partial p_j(\alpha)/\partial \alpha_i|$ for $j \neq i$ when units of measurement are chosen so that $p(\alpha) = (1, \cdots, 1)^T$. That is, the relative increase in $p_i(\alpha)$ is larger than the absolute value of the relative change in any other price.*

Proof   A square matrix of order n with a dominant negative diagonal has sign$(-1)^n$. This is seen by shrinking the offdiagonal elements and observing that the matrix does not change sign. Now applying Cramer's Rule as in the proof of theorem 1 shows that $\partial p_i(\alpha)/\partial \alpha_i > 0$. Choose units of measurement so that the equilibrium price vector is $\hat{p}(\alpha) = (1, \cdots, 1)$. By lemma 3, the reduced Jacobian in the new units of measurement satisfies $e_{ii} + \sum_{j \neq i, 1}^{n-1} |e_{ij}| < 0$. Without loss of generality, let $i = 1$. Write $[e_{ij}(\alpha)]^{-1} = [\bar{e}_{ij}]$, $i, j = 1, \cdots, n - 1$. It is clear from (2) that we must show $|\bar{e}_{11}| > |\bar{e}_{j1}|$ for all $j \neq 1$. If not, there is $k \neq 1$ such that $|\bar{e}_{k1}| \geq |\bar{e}_{j1}|$ for all j. For this k consider $\sum_{j=1}^{n-1} e_{kj}\bar{e}_{j1} = 0$, since $J_n J_n^{-1} = I$. Write $\sum_{j \neq k}$ for $\sum_{j=1, j \neq k}^{n-1}$. Then

$$|e_{kk}|\,|\bar{e}_{k1}| = |e_{kk}\bar{e}_{k1}| = \left|\sum_{j\neq k} e_{kj}\bar{e}_{j1}\right| \leq \sum_{j\neq k}|e_{kj}|\,|\bar{e}_{j1}| \leq \sum_{j\neq k}|e_{kj}|\,|\bar{e}_{k1}|.$$

This implies that $|e_{kk}| \leq \sum_{j\neq k}|e_{kj}|$. Applying the corollary to lemma 3.1 gives a contradiction of the assumption that J_n^T has dominant diagonal. Thus k does not exist, so $|e_{11}| > |\bar{e}_{j1}|$ for all $j \neq 1$. ∎

THEOREM 4 *Suppose that all goods are gross substitutes and $J = [e_{ij}(p(\alpha),\alpha)]$ is indecomposable. Then $e(p(\alpha),\alpha) = 0$ and $p(\alpha) > 0$ implies $\partial p_j(\alpha)/\partial\alpha_i \geq 0$ for all $i,j \neq n$. If J_n is indecomposable, $\partial p_j(\alpha)/\partial\alpha_i > 0$ holds for all $j \neq n$. Choose units of measurement so that $p(\alpha) = (1,\cdots,1)$. If $e_{nj} > 0$ for all $j \neq n$, $\partial p_i(\alpha)/\partial\alpha_i > \partial p_j(\alpha)/\partial\alpha_i$ for any $j \neq i$, for all i. That is, the relative increase in the ith price exceeds the relative increase in any other price.*

Proof Without loss of generality, put $i = 1$. Let $p_{(n)} = (p_1,\cdots,p_{n-1})^T$. As in the proof of lemma 1,

$$[e_{ij}(p(\alpha),\alpha)]_{n-1}^1\, dp_{(n)}(\alpha) = -(e_{1\alpha_1},0,\cdots,0)^T\, d\alpha_1.$$

$J_n = [e_{ij}]_{n-1}^1$ is nonsingular, since J indecomposable implies J_n has a quasidominant diagonal with prices as multipliers, so J_n is nonsingular. Then $\partial p_{(n)}(\alpha)/\partial\alpha_1 = -J_n^{-1}\cdot(e_{1\alpha_1},0,\cdots,0)^T$. But it is an immediate implication of theorem 3.1 that $-J_n^{-1}$ is nonnegative and has a positive diagonal. In other words, $\partial p_{(n)}(\alpha)/\partial\alpha_1 \geq 0$ and $\partial p_1(\alpha)/\partial\alpha_1 > 0$ hold.

On the other hand, J_n indecomposable implies, by lemma 2, that $-J_n^{-1}$ is positive, so in this case $\partial p_{(n)}(\alpha)/\partial\alpha_1 > 0$. It remains to prove that $\partial p_1(\alpha)/\partial\alpha_1 > \partial p_j(\alpha)/\partial\alpha_1$ for all $j \neq 1$ when $p(\alpha) = (1,\cdots,1)$. But this follows directly from theorem 3 and the fact that $-J_n^{-1}$ is positive. ∎

A final local result is found in Allingham (1975, p. 79). Let us say that an economy has *unit free stability* at an equilibrium if changing the units of measurement for goods while leaving the response of prices to a unit of excess demand the same does not affect the stability of equilibrium. This is equivalent to changing the rates of price response to excess demand while leaving the units unchanged. The result is

THEOREM 5 *If there is a demand increase for some good at an equilibrium with unit-free stability in an economy with a numéraire, the price of this good does not decrease.*

Proof The change of units replaces the reduced Jacobian J_n by DJ_nD, where D is a diagonal matrix with a positive diagonal. If A is a stable matrix, that is, has all characteristic roots with negative real parts, then A^{-1} is stable as well. Let $J_n^{-1} = ([e_{ij}]_{n-1}^1)^{-1} = [\bar{e}_{ij}]_{n-1}^1$. $DJ_n^{-1}D$ stable implies that $\sum_i d_{ii}\bar{e}_{ii}d_{ii} < 0$, since the trace is equal to the sum of the roots. If $\sum_i d_{ii}\bar{e}_{ii}d_{ii} < 0$ for all choices of positive d_{ii}, then $\bar{e}_{ii} < 0$ must hold. Therefore $J_n\, dp = -e_{i\alpha_i}\delta^i$, $\delta_i^i > 0$, $\delta_j^i = 0$, $j \neq i$, implies that $dp_i = -\bar{e}_{ii}e_{i\alpha_i}\delta_i^i \geq 0$. ∎

4.2 The Morishima Case

A pattern of substitution terms that is related to the gross substitute assumption was introduced by Morishima (1952). Local theorems may be proved for the Morishima case parallel to those proved for the gross substitute case both in the theory of stability of the tâtonnement, as we have seen, and in the theory of comparative statics (see Quirk and Saposnik 1968, pp. 213–15).

Let a square matrix $M = [m_{ij}]$, $i, j = 1, \cdots, n$, satisfy the conditions $m_{ii} < 0$, all i, and $I = (1, \cdots, n) = I_1 \cup I_2$, where $I_1 \neq \emptyset$, $I_2 \neq \emptyset$, $I_1 \cap I_2 = \emptyset$, and where $i \in I_k$, $j \in I_k$, $i \neq j$, implies $m_{ij} \geq 0$, while $i \in I_k$, $j \notin I_k$ implies $m_{ij} \leq 0$, and $m_{ij} < 0$ for some i, j, $i \neq j$. Then M is said to be a *Morishima matrix*.

If m_{ij}, m_{jk}, $m_{ik} \neq 0$, and i, j, k are all different, this definition implies that $\text{sign}(m_{ij}m_{jk}) = \text{sign}\, m_{ik}$. The intuitive interpretation of this rule of signs is that the substitute of a substitute is a substitute, the complement of a complement is a substitute, the substitute of a complement is a complement, and the complement of a substitute is a complement. We first prove a result that has stability implications.

LEMMA 4 *If M is a Morishima matrix, then the characteristic roots of M have negative real parts if and only if M has a dominant diagonal.*

Proof If M has a dominant diagonal, then the characteristic roots of M have negative real parts by lemma 2.8. Let D be the diagonal matrix with $d_{ii} = 1$ if $i \in I_1$ and $d_{ii} = -1$ if $i \in I_2$, where I_1 and I_2 form the partition of indexes in the definition of the Morishima matrix. Then $\bar{M} = DMD$ satisfies $\bar{m}_{ij} \geq 0$, $\bar{m}_{ii} = m_{ii}$. M and $\bar{M}$ have the same characteristic roots since they are similar. Also it is clear from the definition that M has a dominant diagonal if and only if $\overline{M}$ has a dominant diagonal. However, it is shown in theorem 21 of appendix E that if $\overline{M}$ has characteristic roots with negative real parts, then $\overline{M}$ has a dominant negative diagonal. Thus the dominant negative diagonal condition is both necessary and sufficient for the characteristic roots of M to have negative real parts. ∎

Lemma 4 allows us to prove a result on local stability of the tâtonnement for an exchange economy when the Jacobian of the excess demand functions at equilibrium is a Morishima matrix. This theorem is an analogue of theorem 2.1. There are, however, basic differences. In the case of the gross substitute assumption a dominant diagonal for the reduced Jacobian J_n is implied by the theory of consumer demand given indecomposability of the full Jacobian. But in the case where the reduced Jacobian J_n is a nontrivial Morishima matrix, it is necessary to assume directly that J_n has a dominant diagonal. Moreover this assumption implies that the substitution effects for the numéraire good $\partial e_i / \partial p_n$ are sufficiently large positive numbers.

Consider the differential equation system

$$\frac{dp_i}{dt} = h_i(p, 1), \qquad i = 1, \cdots, n-1. \tag{5}$$

THEOREM 6   *Let $(\bar{p}, 1)$ be an equilibrium of the exchange economy whose excess demand functions are $e_i(p, p_n)$, $i = 1, \cdots, n$. Assume that $J_n(\bar{p}, 1) = [e_{ij}(\bar{p}, 1)]_{n-1}^1$ is a Morishima matrix. Assume $\bar{p} > 0$ and that the e_i as well as the h_i in the differential equation system (5) are continuously differentiable. Then $(\bar{p}, 1)$ is a locally stable equilibrium of (5) if J_n has a dominant diagonal.*

Proof   By lemma 4, all the characteristic roots of the linear system approximating (5) have negative real parts if and only if J_n has a dominant diagonal. Since the diagonal terms of J_n are nonzero by assumption and the derivatives of h and e are continuous, $J_n(\bar{p}, 1) = [e_{ij}(\bar{p}, 1)]_{n-1}^1$ is a valid linear approximation of (5) by lemma 2.9, and local stability of the linear system implies local stability of the nonlinear system (5) by Coddington and Levinson (1955, p. 314). ∎

The first comparative static result is

THEOREM 7   *If J_n is a Morishima matrix, perfect Hicksian stability holds if and only if J_n has a dominant diagonal.*

Proof Since a Morishima matrix M has a negative diagonal, if it also has a dominant diagonal, the principal minors of order r have the sign $(-1)^r$. As we have seen, this follows from shrinking the off diagonal elements and observing that the principal minors have this property in the limit while their signs do not change. It is implied by corollary 2 to lemma 6.36 that any matrix with nonnegative off-diagonal elements whose principal minors have these signs has a dominant diagonal that is negative (also McKenzie 1960a, p. 60). Thus $\bar{M}$ has a negative dominant diagonal, which implies that M has one as well. ■

The assumption of a dominant diagonal allows the immediate application of Mukherji's result, theorem 3, to show that the price of a good to which demand has shifted from the numéraire increases and that its increase is larger than the absolute value of the change in any other price. As in the case of gross substitutes, what is added to Mukherji's result by using the sign distribution of the off-diagonal terms is the sign distribution of the price changes.

THEOREM 8 *Assume that the equilibrium price vector $p(\alpha) > 0$. Let $J_n = [e_{ij}(p(\alpha), \alpha)]_{n-1}^{1}$ be a Morishima matrix with a dominant diagonal and the nontrivial partition I_1, I_2. If $j \in I_1$, $\partial p_i(\alpha)/\partial \alpha_j > 0$ for $i = j$, and ≥ 0 for $i \in I_1$, $i \neq j$. On the other hand, $\partial p_i(\alpha)/\partial \alpha_j \leq 0$ for $i \in I_2$. The analogous result holds when i and j are exchanged. Choose units of measurement so that $p(\alpha) = (1, \cdots, 1)$. Then $|\partial p_i(\alpha)/\partial \alpha_i| > |\partial p_j(\alpha)/\partial \alpha_i|$, $j \neq i$. If J_n is indecomposable the weak inequalities are strong.*

Proof Define D as in the proof of lemma 4. Then consider $\bar{J}_n = DJ_nD$. The matrix $-\bar{J}_n$ has the sign distribution of a Leontief matrix and a dominant diagonal. Then corollary 3 to theorem 3.1 implies that the inverse of $-\bar{J}_n$ is nonnegative with a positive diagonal. By lemma 2 if $-\bar{J}_n$ is indecomposable $-\bar{J}_n^{-1}$ is positive. Now consider $\partial p(\alpha)/\partial \alpha_1 = -J_n^{-1}(e_{1\alpha_1}, 0, \cdots, 0)^T = -D\bar{J}_n^{-1}D(e_{1\alpha_1}, 0, \cdots, 0)^T$. This gives $D\partial p(\alpha)/\partial \alpha_1 = \bar{J}_n^{-1}(e_{1\alpha_1}, 0, \cdots, 0)^T$. Since $\bar{J}_n$ has a dominant diagonal, the result is implied by theorem 3. ■

It is an interesting fact that if J is a Morishima matrix, J_n can have neither perfect Hicksian stability nor characteristic roots, all of which have negative real parts. This is proved in

THEOREM 9 *Assume that the equilibrium price vector $p(\alpha) > 0$. If $J = [e_{ij}(p(\alpha), \alpha)]_n^{1}$ is a Morishima matrix, then J_n does not have all its charac-*

teristic roots with negative real parts, nor does it have Hicksian perfect stability.

Proof The theorem is proved once it is shown that J_n does not have a dominant diagonal. Let $J_n = \begin{bmatrix} M_{11} & M_{12} \\ M_{21} & M_{22} \end{bmatrix}$, where $M_{11} = [e_{ij}]$, $i, j \in I_1$, and similarly for M_{12}, M_{21}, and M_{22}. Let $p(\alpha) = \bar{p} = (\bar{p}_1, \bar{p}_2)^T$ where the partition corresponds to the partition of J_n. Without loss of generality, we may assume $n \in I_2$. Then $\bar{p}_1 M_{11} \geq 0$, since $(\bar{p}, 1)^T J = 0$, while $e_{ij} \leq 0$ for $e_{ij} \in M_{21}$, and for $i = n$ with $j \in I_1$. Suppose that J_n had a dominant diagonal. Let $\bar{J} = DJD$ as before. Then there is $x > 0$ such that $-\bar{J}_n x > 0$ by theorem 3.1. Therefore $\bar{p}_1 \bar{M}_{11} x_1 = \bar{p}_1 M_{11} x_1 < 0$. On the other hand, $\bar{p}_1 M_{11} \geq 0$ implies $\bar{p}_1 M_{11} x_1 \geq 0$, which is a contradiction. ∎

4.3 Global Comparative Statics

The global approach to comparative statics was introduced by Morishima (1964, ch. 1) in applying the gross substitute assumption. However, a particularly elegant statement of the theory when the assumption of strict gross substitutes is made may be found in Allingham (1975). He defines two sorts of economy, the revealed preference economy and the substitutive economy.

A *revealed preference economy* is an economy for which the weak axiom of revealed preference holds between an equilibrium price vector and any other price vector.

A *substitutive economy* is an economy for which $p_i' > p_i$ and $p_j' = p_j$ for all $j \neq i$ implies that $e_j(p') > e_j(p)$ for all $j \neq i$, whenever the excess demands are well defined.

In other words, in a substitutive economy the assumption of strict gross substitutes holds globally. For the differentiable case it is proved in appendix B of chapter 2 that the gross substitute assumption implies that the Weak Axiom of Revealed Preference holds between an equilibrium price vector and any other positive price vector. Thus at least in this case a substitutive economy must also be a revealed preference economy. However, the converse does not hold, so the revealed preference economy is a more general concept.

Let p be an equilibrium price. We will say that demand increases for the ith good at p when the excess demand functions e' replace the excess demand functions e if $e_i'(p) > 0$ and $e_j'(p) = 0$, for all $j \neq i, \neq n$, where n is the numéraire.

THEOREM 10 *Let demand increase for the ith good at an equilibrium price p in a revealed preference economy. If p' is the new equilibrium price, $p_i' > p_i$.*

Proof By the definition of a demand increase, $e_i'(p) > 0$, and $e_j'(p) = 0$ for $j \neq i, n$. Let $p_n \equiv 1$. Since $e'(p')$ is an equilibrium, $p \cdot e'(p') = 0$. Then, by the weak axiom, it follows that $p' \cdot e'(p) > 0$. Thus

$$p' \cdot e'(p) = p_i' e_i'(p) + e_n'(p) > 0.$$

Also

$$p \cdot e'(p) = p_i e_i'(p) + e_n'(p) = 0,$$

by Walras' Law. After subtracting, we have $(p_i' - p_i)e_i'(p) > 0$. Therefore $p_i' - p_i > 0$. ■

If the economy is substitutive, we may go further.

THEOREM 11 *Let demand increase for the ith good at equilibrium p in a substitutive economy. If p' is the new equilibrium price, $p_j' > p_j$ for all $j \neq n$.*

Proof Without loss of generality, we may let $i = 1$. Then

$$e_1'(p) > 0 \quad \text{and} \quad e_j'(p) = 0, \qquad j \neq 1, n, \tag{6}$$

since demand increases for good 1. Let $\alpha = \max_{j \neq n}(p_j/p_j') = p_k/p_k'$. If $p = p'$, it would follow that $e_1'(p') > 0$, so p' would not be an equilibrium. Therefore $p \neq p'$. If $\alpha \geq 1$, then $\alpha p_k' = p_k$ and $\alpha p_i' \geq p_i$ for all $i \neq k$. By the homogeneity of degree 0 of excess demand functions, $e'(\alpha p') = 0$. By the definition of a substitutive economy, $e_k'(\alpha p') > e_k'(p')$, since no price has fallen and a price other than k has risen. This contradicts (6). Therefore it must be that $\alpha < 1$, that is, $p_j' > p_j$ for all $j \neq n$. ■

Indeed, in a substitutive economy this result may be strengthened further.

THEOREM 12 *Let demand increase for the ith good at an equilibrium price p in a substitutive economy. If p' is the new equilibrium price, $p_j' > p_j$ for all $j \neq n$, and $p_i'/p_i > p_j'/p_j$ for all $j \neq i$.*

Proof Let α be chosen as in the proof of theorem 11. Without loss of generality, let demand increase for good 1. Define $\beta = \min_{j \neq n}(p_j/p_j') = p_h/p_h'$. Then $\beta \leq \alpha < 1$ must hold. Also $\beta p_h' = p_h$ and $\beta p_j' \leq p_j$, $j \neq h$. By homogeneity $e'(\beta p') = 0$. Since the economy is substitutive and no price has risen while some price other than h has fallen, $e_h'(\beta p') < e_h'(p)$. If $h \neq 1$, $e_h'(p) > 0$ in contradiction to (6). Therefore $h = 1$ must hold. ∎

4.4 Comparative Statics for the Individual Agent

Thus far the comparative statics results we have proved relate to the equilibrium of the market. There are also comparative static results for the individual economic agent. Whereas the comparative static results for the market were derived from sufficient conditions for stability of the market, the comparative static results for the individual agent are derived from the sufficient conditions for the maximization of the agent's objective function, that is, utility in the case of the consumer and profits in the case of the firm. The derivation of comparative static results from the sufficient conditions for maximization was a principal theme of Samuelson's *Foundations of Economic Analysis* (1947). He liked to refer to these results as applications of the Le Chatelier principle that plays a role in the theory of thermodynamics.

Let $x \in \mathbf{R}^n$, $x \geq 0$, be the vector of inputs, and let $w \in \mathbf{R}^n$, $w \geq 0$, be the vector of their prices. The price of the output is set equal to 1. The production function g maps $\mathbf{R}^n$ into $\mathbf{R}_+$. The production function gives the single output as a function of inputs. We may write a profit function for the firm before maximization as $\Pi(x, w) = g(x) - wx$. The assumption of a single output is not a restriction when output prices are given, and the analysis is on the effect of changes in the prices of inputs. Then the output can be regarded as the value at the given prices of whatever outputs are chosen. Of course, this neglects the choice of the output combination. The choice of the full input–output combination as it depends on varying input and output prices can be given the same type of analysis as the choice of inputs with varying input prices and fixed output prices. No new principles are introduced.

We assume that g is increasing, strictly concave, and twice continuously differentiable for $x > 0$. Then the profit function is also increasing, strictly concave, and twice continuously differentiable in x for given w. The necessary and sufficient conditions for a maximum of $\Pi(x, w)$ for given $w \geq 0$ at $\bar{x} > 0$ are

$$\Pi_{x_i}(\bar{x}, w) = g_i(\bar{x}) - w_i = 0, \qquad i = 1, \cdots, n, \tag{7}$$

where Π_{x_i} is the partial derivative of the profit function with respect to x_i, and g_i is the partial derivative of g with respect to x_i. Let $[g_{ij}(\bar{x})]$ be the Hessian matrix of g, or the $n \times n$ matrix of second partial derivatives of g. Differentiating (7) with respect to $\bar{x}$ and w gives $[g_{ij}(\bar{x})] \cdot d\bar{x} - dw = 0$. Let G_{ij} be the cofactor of $g_{ji}(\bar{x})$ in the determinant $G = |g_{ij}(\bar{x})|$. Assume that Π has a regular maximum at $\bar{x}$ so $|G| \neq 0$. Since by the strict concavity of g the maximum is unique, $\bar{x}$ is a function of w, and

$$D\bar{x}(w) = \frac{\partial \bar{x}}{\partial w} = [g_{ij}(\bar{x})]^{-1} = \left[\frac{G_{ij}}{G}\right]$$

by Cramer's rule. The existence of a differentiable function $\bar{x}$ that satisfies (7) in a neighborhood of w follows from the implicit function theorem (Dieudonné 1960, p. 265).

Now introduce constraints on the choice of x imposed by the supplies of capital goods, limits on factor supplies from the market, or other circumstances, and represented by functions $\gamma^k(x)$, $k = 1, \cdots, r$, $r < n$, where γ^k maps $x \in \mathbf{R}_+^n$ into $\mathbf{R}$. We assume γ^k to be a convex function, which is at least twice continuously differentiable, increasing in all arguments, and strictly increasing in at least one argument. Moreover there is $x > 0$ such that $\gamma^k(x) = 0$, for all k. The kth constraint imposes the condition that $\gamma^k(x) \leq 0$ must hold for x to be a feasible input vector. The set C_k of x that satisfy the kth constraint is called the kth constraint set. We will need

LEMMA 5   *The constraint set C_k is convex, closed, and has an interior.*

Proof   Let x and y lie in C_k. Then $\gamma^k(x) \leq 0$ and $\gamma^k(y) \leq 0$. Then since γ^k is convex and increasing, we have

$$\gamma^k(\alpha x + (1 - \alpha)y) \leq \alpha \gamma^k(x) + (1 - \alpha)\gamma^k(y) \leq 0, \qquad 0 \leq \alpha \leq 1.$$

Since γ^k is continuous, C_k is closed. Since γ^k is increasing and there is $x > 0$ with $\gamma(x) = 0$, in a small neighborhood of x any $x' < x$ satisfies $\gamma(x') \leq 0$. Thus C^k contains an open set.   ∎

A constraint is said to be *binding* if the achievement of the maximum of profit requires that $\gamma^k(x) = 0$ hold. When constraints 1 through r are binding, the maximum profit is achieved on the boundary of the general constraint set $C = \bigcap_{k=1}^{r} C^k$. Finally we assume that interior C is not empty.

By lemma 5, C_k and C are closed, convex sets. Given w, let $B(x, w) = \{y \mid \Pi(y, w) \geq \Pi(x, w)\}$. Since $\Pi(x, w)$ is strictly concave and continuous in x, $B(x, w)$ is closed and convex. The maximum profit under the constraint set C is achieved at $\bar{x}$ if $\bar{x} \in C \cap B(\bar{x}, w)$ and $C \cap \text{int } B(\bar{x}, w) = \emptyset$. By a separation theorem (Berge 1963), there is a vector $p \in \mathbf{R}_+^n$ such that $px \leq \mu$ for $x \in C$ and $px \geq \mu$ for $x \in \Pi(\bar{x}, w)$. Then since $\bar{x}$ belongs to both sets $p\bar{x} = \mu$.

LEMMA 6 *Differentiability of Π implies that p is unique. Moreover there is only one point $\bar{x}$ where separation of $B(\bar{x}, w)$ from the set C by a vector p can be achieved.*

Proof Differentiability implies that $p = \partial\Pi(x)/\partial x]_{x=\bar{x}}$ (see Rockafellar 1970, p. 242). Suppose there is a second point x' where $B(x', w)$ is separated from C by a vector p'. If $\Pi(x', w) > \Pi(\bar{x}, w)$ holds, then $\bar{p}x' > \mu$, so $x' \notin C$. Similarly, if $\Pi(\bar{x}, w) > \Pi(x', w)$ holds, $\bar{x} \notin C$. Therefore $\Pi(x', w) = \Pi(\bar{x}, w)$. By the strict concavity of Π, it follows that $x' = \bar{x}$. ∎

Since $\bar{x} \in$ boundary C^k for each $k = 1, \cdots, r$, there is $p^k \in \mathbf{R}^n$ such that $p^k x \leq 0$ for $x \in C^k$. Since γ^k is differentiable $p^k = \partial\gamma^k(x)/\partial x]_{x=\bar{x}}$ and p^k is also unique. A set of vectors are said to be *positively linearly independent* if no one of them is equal to a linear combination with positive coefficients of other vectors from the set. We say that the constraints are *independent* at x if the supporting vectors p^k at x are positively linearly independent.

LEMMA 7 *If all constraints are binding and the γ^k are independent, p supports C at x if and only if $p = \lambda_1 p^1 + \cdots + \lambda_r p^r$ for $\lambda_1, \cdots, \lambda_r \geq 0$, where p^k is a support of C_k at x and $p^k \geq 0, \neq 0$.*

Proof Since γ^k is increasing in each variable, it follows that $p^k \geq 0$ must hold. Move the origin of the space to x. Then each p^k satisfies $p^k x \leq 0$ for $x \in C$. Then any nonnegative linear combination p of the p^k satisfies $px \leq 0$ for $x \in C$, and p supports C at 0. On the other hand, if for some k' we have $\lambda_{k'} < 0$, consider the set of $x' \in C$ with $p^k x' \leq 0$ for all $k \neq k'$. If $p^{k'} x' \leq 0$ for all such $x' \in C$, the p^k are dependent contrary to assumption. Thus for some $x' \in C$ we have $px' > 0$, and p does not support C. ∎

Since we have $p^k = \gamma_x^k$, by lemmas 6 and 7 the following equations characterize the point of maximum profit.

$$\Pi_{x_i}(\bar{x}, w) - \sum_{k=1}^{r} \lambda_k \gamma_{x_i}^k(\bar{x}) = 0, \qquad \lambda_k \geq 0,$$

$$\gamma^k(\bar{x}) = 0, \qquad i = 1, \cdots, n, \quad k = 1, \cdots, r. \tag{8}$$

Write γ_{ij}^k for $\partial \gamma^k(x)/\partial x_j \partial x_i$ evaluated at $\bar{x}$. Differentiating (8) gives

$$\left[g_{ij} - \sum_k \lambda_k \gamma_{ij}^k \right] \cdot d\bar{x} - \sum_k \gamma_x^k \cdot d\lambda_k - dw = 0,$$

$$\sum_j \gamma_j^k \, d\bar{x}_j = 0, \qquad k = 1, \cdots, r.$$

Putting these relations in matrix form gives

$$\begin{bmatrix} [g_{ij} - \sum_k \lambda_k \gamma_{ij}^k] & [-\gamma_i^k] \\ [\gamma_j^k] & [0] \end{bmatrix} \begin{pmatrix} d\bar{x} \\ d\lambda \end{pmatrix} = \begin{pmatrix} dw \\ 0 \end{pmatrix}. \tag{9}$$

By the implicit function theorem (Dieudonné 1960, p. 267) if the matrix on the left of (9) is nonsingular (8) may be solved in a neighborhood of given initial values for $\bar{x}$ and λ as functions of w. Let ^rG be the determinant of the square matrix on the left-hand side of (9). It is of order $n + r$. Then $\partial(\bar{x}, \lambda)^T/\partial w = (^rG)^{-1}(I\,0)^T$.

Let $^rG_{ii}$ be the principal minor of ^rG that omits the ith row and column. The determinant of the left-hand side of (9) when the last constraint is omitted is $^{r-1}G = {}^rG_{n+rn+r}$. It is implied by the strict concavity of g and the convexity of the γ^k that $[g_{ij} - \sum_k \lambda_k \gamma_{ij}]$ is negative definite. Thus $[g_{ij} - \sum_k \lambda_k \gamma_{ij}]$ is also negative definite under constraint, since the terms of a quadratic form based on the matrix (9) arising from the terms $[\gamma_i^k]$ are zero when the constraints hold.

Consider a given maximum point under differing numbers, k and $k - 1$, of binding constraints. It is assumed when the kth constraint is added that the equilibrium has not changed but the new constraint is binding. That is, the new constraint is satisfied with equality. It is also assumed that the constraints continue to bind when the change is made in w. In particular, the maximum point $\bar{x}$ before the change in w satisfies $\gamma^k(\bar{x}) = 0$, while the maximum point $\bar{x}'$ after the change in w satisfies $\gamma^k(\bar{x}') = 0$. The first equation (8) and the monotonicity assumption imply that $\lambda_r = 0$. The original maximum point $\bar{x}$ will lie on a generalized corner of C of dimension $n - r$, which is the number of factors less the number of binding constraints. The corner represents the intersection of the binding constraints, and it is tangent to the profit function at $\bar{x}$. A change in the location and slope of the profit function that leaves all the constraints still binding will leave the maximum point on the same generalized corner, but it may be that $\bar{x}' \neq \bar{x}$. Also the new maximum in the absence of the kth constraint may lie at $\bar{x}'' \neq \bar{x}'$, $\neq \bar{x}$. The larger the number of independent binding constraints $r \leq n$, the smaller the generalized corner will be. This is the intuitive basis for the comparative static result.

THEOREM 13   *When the number of binding constraints γ_j, $j = 1, \cdots, r - 1$, is increased to r provided all constraints continue to bind, the response of the demand $x_i(w)$ for the ith factor by a profit-maximizing firm to a small increase of the ith factor price does not increase, that is, $|(\partial x_i(w)/\partial w_i)_r| \leq |(\partial x_i(w)/\partial w_i)_{r-1}|$ for $n \geq r \geq 1$.*

Proof If $n = r$, and all constraints continue to bind, the corner has dimension 0, so no change can occur. When there are r constraints with $r < n$, applying Cramer's rule gives $(\partial x_i(w)/\partial w_i)_r = {}^r G_{ii}/{}^r G$. By the conditions for maximization under constraints (see appendix D), ${}^r G_{ii}$ has the sign $(-1)^{n-1}$ while ${}^r G$ has the sign $(-1)^n$. Thus we have $(\partial x_i(w)/\partial w_i)_r < 0$. Since $\lambda_r = 0$ the submatrix in the upper left-hand corner of the matrix in (9) is not affected by the introduction of the new constraint (which if $r = 1$ is the only constraint). Therefore we have ${}^{r-1} G = {}^r G_{n+r n+r}$ and

$$\left(\frac{\partial x_i(w)}{\partial w_i}\right)_r - \left(\frac{\partial x_i(w)}{\partial w_i}\right)_{r-1} = \frac{{}^r G_{ii}}{{}^r G} - \frac{{}^r G_{n+r n+r, ii}}{{}^r G_{n+r n+r}}$$

$$= \frac{{}^r G_{ii}{}^r G_{n+r n+r} - {}^r G_{n+r n+r, ii}{}^r G}{{}^r G\, {}^r G_{n+r n+r}} \tag{10}$$

By Jacobi's theorem (see appendix B),

$${}^r G_{n+r n+r, ii}\, {}^r G = {}^r G_{ii}\, {}^r G_{n+r n+r} - ({}^r G_{i n+r})^2, \tag{11}$$

since the right-hand side is the value of the minor in the matrix of co-factors of ^rG complementary to the principal minor $^rG_{n+rn+r,\,ii}$ of ^rG. Substitute (11) in (10). This gives

$$\left(\frac{\partial x_i(w)}{\partial w_i}\right)_r - \left(\frac{\partial x_i(w)}{\partial w_i}\right)_{r-1} = \frac{(^rG_{in+r})^2}{^rG^rG_{n+rn+r}}. \tag{12}$$

As we noted above, as a consequence of maximization under constraint, both terms in parenthesis on the left are negative. Moreover, by the conditions for negative definiteness under constraint, the sign of the minors of the full-bordered matrix depends only on the number of variables, that is, the number of factors in this case, not on the number of constraints. Indeed, for the principal minors of size equal or larger than the number of constraints, the rule is the same whether the number of constraints is 0 or $n - 1$. See appendix C. Therefore ^rG and $^{r-1}G = {}^rG_{n+rn+r}$ both have the sign$(-1)^n$, and the right-hand side of (12) is nonnegative. Thus

$$\left|\left(\frac{\partial x_i(w)}{\partial w_i}\right)_{r-1}\right| \geq \left|\left(\frac{\partial x_i(w)}{\partial w_i}\right)_r\right|. \quad \blacksquare$$

Analogous results may be obtained in demand theory when the maximand is utility and the constraints include the monetary budget constraint and perhaps budgets of ration points or other restrictions. Also it is not necessary that the changes to which the equilibrium responds appear only in the maximand. They may also appear in the constraints. Indeed, a problem to consider would be where some rationing constraint is introduced and the price of some good is lowered. Of course, when the constraints are varied rather than the maximand the conditions of theorem 13 would not be met. On the other hand, a closer analogy to the problem of the profit-maximizing firm is that of compensated consumer demand under rationing constraints. Here the maximand is the negative of the expenditure function and the utility isoquant becomes a constraint along with the rationing constraints. Then theorem 13 will apply when a price is changed.

4.5   Comparative Statics and Supermodularity

The results of section 4.4 may be supplemented by use of the notion of supermodularity. (Milgrom and Roberts 1994). In this generalization the variables may be allowed to be discrete and differentiability need not be assumed. Define $z = x \vee y$, where x and y are vectors in $\mathscr{R}^n$ by $z_i = \max(x_i, y_i)$. Define $w = x \wedge y$ by $w_i = \min(x_i, y_i)$. Consider a set $S \subset \mathscr{R}^n$ that has the property that $x \in S$ and $y \in S$ implies that $x \vee y \in S$ and $x \wedge y \in S$. Such a set is said to be a *lattice*. A real-valued function f on a lattice $S \subset \mathscr{R}^n$ is said to be *supermodular* if $f(x \vee y) + f(x \wedge y) \geq f(x) + f(y)$. If the function f is differentiable, we may show that f is supermodular is equivalent to $\partial^2 f(x)/\partial x_i \partial x_j \geq 0$ for all $i \neq j$. It is sufficient to consider the two-dimensional case, which generalizes easily to n dimensions. Then $x = (x_1, x_2)$ and $y = (y_1, y_2)$.

THEOREM 14   *Let f map an open set S of $\mathscr{R}^2$ into $\mathscr{R}$. Assume that f is twice continuously differentiable. Then f is supermodular if and only if $\partial^2 f(x_1, x_2)/\partial x_2 \partial x_1 \geq 0$ for all $(x_1, x_2) \in S$.*

Proof Consider a point $x \in S$ and a point $y = (x_1 + \delta x_1, x_2 + \delta x_2)$, where $\delta x_1 > 0$, $\delta x_2 > 0$. Since S is open, for $\delta x_1, \delta x_2$ small enough y is also in S. Let $x' = (x_1 + \delta x_1, x_2)$ and $y' = (x_1, x_2 + \delta x_2)$. Then x is the infimum of (x', y') and y is the supremum of (x', y'). To show that supermodularity implies $\partial^2 f(x_1, x_2)/\partial x_1 \partial x_2 \geq 0$, consider

$$\frac{[f(x_1 + \delta x_1, x_2 + \delta x_2) - f(x_1 + \delta x_1, x_2)] - [f(x_1, x_2 + \delta_2 x_2) - f(x_1, x_2)]}{\delta x_1 \delta x_2},$$
(13)

where δx_1 and δx_2 are positive. By supermodularity, this expression is greater than or equal to 0. Let δx_2 converge to 0. Then expression (13) converges to

$$\frac{\partial f(x_1 + \delta x_1, x_2)/\partial x_2 - \partial f(x_1, x_2)/\partial x_2}{\delta x_1}.$$
(14)

Finally, as $\delta x_1 \to 0$, expression (14) converges to $\partial^2 f(x_1, x_2)/\partial x_1 \partial x_2 \geq 0$.

To show that $\partial^2 f(x_1, x_2)/\partial x_1 \partial x_2 \geq 0$ everywhere implies supermodularity, note that it follows from $\partial^2 f(x_1, x_2)/\partial x_1 \partial x_2 \geq 0$ that

$$\int_{x_1}^{x_1 + \delta x_1} \left(\frac{\partial^2 f(w, x_2)}{\partial w \partial x_2} \right) dw \geq 0,$$

or

$$\frac{\partial f(x_1 + \delta x_1, x_2)}{\partial z} - \frac{\partial f(x_1, x_2)}{\partial x_2} \geq 0.$$

Therefore

$$\int_{x_2}^{x_2+\delta x_2} \left(\frac{\partial f(x_1 + \delta x_1, z)}{\partial z} - \frac{\partial f(x_1, z)}{\partial z} \right) dz \geq 0. \tag{15}$$

Performing the integration in (15), we obtain

$$[f(x_1 + \delta x_1, x_2 + \delta x_2) - f(x_1 + \delta x_1, x_2)]$$
$$- [f(x_1, x_2 + \delta x_2) - f(x_1, x_2)] \geq 0,$$

which is supermodularity. ■

A generalization for comparative static results by use of super-modularity can be made most successfully with respect to section 4.4. Let S and S' be sets contained in $\mathbf{R}^n$. Assume that S and S' are lattices. We say that $S' \geq_s S$, or S' *majorizes* S, if $y \in S$ and $y' \in S'$ implies that $y \wedge y' \in S$ and $y \vee y' \in S'$. Denote the set of maximizers with respect to x of $f(x, z)$ for $x \in S$ by $M(S, z)$. We will prove a qualitative result that is global and parallels the result of section 4.4.

LEMMA 8   *If $f(x, z)$ is a real-valued supermodular function where $x \in S$ and $z \in \mathbf{R}^n$, then $z' \geq z$ and $S' \geq_s S$ implies that $M(S', z') \geq_s M(S, z)$. In this sense the set of maximizers with respect to x and S is monotone non-decreasing in x and S.*

Proof   Let $z' \geq z$ hold. Suppose $y \in M(S, z)$ and $y' \in M(S', z')$. Consider $y \vee y'$. Since $y \in M(S, z)$ and $y \wedge y' \in S$, we have $f(y, z) \geq f(y \wedge y', z)$. This together with $z' \geq z$ implies by supermodularity that

$$f(y \wedge y'), z) + f(y \vee y'), z') > f(y, z) + f(y', z').$$

Thus $f(y \vee y', z') > f(y', z')$. Therefore $y' \in M(S', z')$ implies $y \vee y' \in M(S', z')$.

Similarly consider $y \wedge y'$. Since $y \vee y' \in S'$ and $y' \in M(S', z')$, we have $f(y', z') \geq f(y \vee y', z')$, which implies, by supermodularity, that $f(y \wedge y', z) \geq f(y, z)$. Since $y \in M(S, y)$ and $y \wedge y' \in S$, this implies $y \wedge y' \in M(S, z)$. Therefore $M(S', z') \geq_s M(S, z)$. ■

It is convenient for the following discussion to define the profit function by $\Pi(x, w) = g(x) + wx$, where $x \in \Omega_x \subset \mathscr{R}_+^n$ is the vector of inputs and $w \in \Omega_w \subset \mathbf{R}_-^n$ is the vector of prices of inputs. Ω_x and Ω_w are the sets of possible values of x and w. They are assumed to be lattices. Also $g(x) \in \mathbf{R}$ is the quantity of output (which may be the value of the output of several goods at given prices). Let $S \subset \mathbf{R}^n$ denote the set of x that satisfy the constraints $\gamma^k(x) \leq 0$, $k = 1, \cdots, r$, and let S' correspond to the constraints $\gamma^k(x) \leq 0$, $k = 1, \cdots, r - 1$. We assume that these sets are lattices also. In our setting this virtually reduces the set of allowable constraints to those of the form $x_i - \omega_i \leq 0$ for $x \in \Omega_x$, where $\omega_i \geq 0$. In other words, the constraints are lower bounds on the allowable levels of some inputs. We will assume that the profit function $\Pi(x, w)$ is supermodular. If g is differentiable, it is clear that Π is supermodular if and only if $\partial^2 g(x, w)/\partial x_i \partial y_j \geq 0$ for all $i \neq j$, since $\partial^2 \Pi(x, w)/\partial x_i \partial w_j = 1$ for all i, j. This means that the inputs are complements.

THEOREM 15   *Let S and S' be as defined above. If $\Pi(x, w)$ is supermodular, then $w' \geq w$ and $S' \geq_s S$ implies that $\mu(S', W') = $ argument $\max_{x \in S'} \Pi(x, w') \geq_s \mu(S, W) = \arg\max_{x \in S} \Pi(x, w)$.*

Proof   Recall that $x < 0$. If $x \in S$, then $x' \in S$ for $x' \leq x$. Also $x \in S$ implies $x \in S'$. Then $x \in S$ and $y \in S'$ implies $x \wedge y \in S$, since $x \wedge y \leq x$. Also $x \vee y \in S'$, since both x and y lie in S'. This means that $S' \geq_s S$. The theorem is implied by lemma 8.   ∎

Theorem 15 implies that the increase in x_i from a decrease in the price w_i of an input is nondecreasing in S. This is clear if we first decrease w_i to w_i' so that x is replaced by x' and then remove a constraint so that S is replaced by S' where $S' \geq_s S$. Then x' is replaced by $x'' \geq x'$.

In one respect the supermodular theory is more special than the Samuelson theory. The Samuelson theory does not require that the cross derivatives of g be nonnegative, and it is not possible in general to remedy this situation by redefining variables to change their signs if the number of inputs exceeds two. In other words, the theory based on supermodularity requires that inputs be complements.

Appendix A: Local Uniqueness of Equilibrium

If the results of comparative statics for the economy are to be useful the equilibria must be locally unique and locally stable. Then, when some parameter changes and the equilibrium is displaced by a small amount, the economy will move to the new equilibrium position. If equilibrium is not locally unique it will in general not be possible to say to what new equilibrium the economy moves. Also, if the new equilibrium is not stable, the economy will not move to it even though it is locally unique. Thus theorems on tâtonnement stability of chapter 2 are relevant to the significance of the theorems on comparative statics found in this chapter. As it happens most of the results of comparative statics for the economy depend on the same sufficient conditions as the results on local stability of the tâtonnement and local stability provides local uniqueness. However, results on local uniqueness which do not depend on the sufficient conditions for local stability are of interest since the presence of local uniqueness leaves open the possibility of local stability.

A very general theorem on local uniqueness for exchange economies was proved by Debreu (1970). His theorem does not state conditions for local uniqueness but rather asserts that local uniqueness holds for almost all positive endowments in an exchange economy whose demand functions satisfy certain conditions. Theorems of this type are said to establish generic properties, and many have been proved in recent years.

Let the admissible set of wealth levels for the hth consumer be $M^h = \{m^h \in \mathbf{R} \mid m^h > 0\}$. Then the admissible set of wealth levels for the economy is $M = M^1 \times \cdots \times M^h$. Let the admissible set of endowments for the hth consumer be $\Omega^h = \{\omega \in \mathbf{R}^n \mid \omega > 0\}$. the admissible set of endowments for the economy is $\Omega = \Omega^1 \times \cdots \times \Omega^H$. Let the set of admissible prices be $P = \{p \in \mathbf{R}^{n-1} \mid p > 0 \text{ and } \sum_1^{n-1} p_i \leq 1\}$. The demand function of the hth consumer is $f^h(p, m^h)$ mapping $P \times M^h$ into $\mathbf{R}^{nh}$. The function f^h is assumed to be continuous and to satisfy Walras' Law, that is, $p \cdot f^h(p, m^h) = m^h$ for all $(p, m^h) \in P \times M^h$. Let $m^h = p\omega^h$. The excess demand vector of the economy with endowment vector ω is $e(p, \omega) = \sum_{h=1}^H f^h(p, m^h) - \sum \omega^h$.
Make

ASSUMPTION 1   *There is h such that* $(p^s, m^{hs}) \in P \times M^h$ *and* $(p^s, m^s) \to (p, m) \in (\bar{P} \backslash P) \times M^h$ *implies* $|f^h(p^s, m^{hs})| \to \infty$.

The assumption says that the norm of the hth consumer's demand function is unbounded as the price vector approaches the boundary of the normalized price set. If the admissible set of endowments has given bounds, this assumption can be relaxed to require that the consumer's demand exceed the bounds of the admissible endowment set.

Given $\omega \in \Omega^H$, p is an *equilibrium price vector* if

$$e(p,\omega) = \sum_1^H f^h(p, p\omega^h) - \sum_1^H \omega^h = 0.$$

Let $E(\omega)$ be the set of equilibrium price vectors. Suppose that the consumer with the index 1 satisfies assumption 1. Let $U = P \times M^1 \times \Omega^{H-1}$. U is contained in $\mathbf{R}^{nH}$ and U is open. For $e \in U$ write $e = (p, m^1, \omega^2, \cdots, \omega^H)$. Define the function F that maps U into $\bar{\Omega}$ by $F(e) = (x^1, \omega^2, \cdots, \omega^H)$ where

$$x^1 = f^1(p, m^1) + \sum_2^H f^h(p, p\omega^h) - \sum_2^H \omega^h. \tag{A1}$$

Since $p \cdot f^1(p, m^1) = m^1$ and $p \cdot f^h(p, p\omega^h) = p\omega^h$, if (A1) is multiplied by p, we obtain

$$px^1 = m^1. \tag{A2}$$

Substituting (A2) in (A1) shows that if $x^1 = \omega^1$, then p is an equilibrium. On the other hand, it is clear from (A2) that $x^1 \ne \omega^1$ implies that p is not an equilibrium. Thus $p \in E(\omega)$ is equivalent to $F(e) = \omega$.

LEMMA 9   *If $K \subset \Omega^H$ is compact, $F^{-1}(K)$ is compact.*

Proof Let e^s be a sequence in $F^{-1}(K)$, $e^s = (p^s, m^{1s}, \omega^{2s}, \cdots, \omega^{Hs})$. Then $F(e^s) = \omega^s \in K$. By (A2), $p^s \omega^{1s} = m^{1s}$, all s. Since $\omega^s \in K$, K is compact, and $p^s \in P$, m^{1s} is bounded. Then (p^s, m^{1s}, ω^s) has a subsequence converging to $(p, m^1, \omega) \in \bar{P} \times \bar{M}^1 \times K$. I claim that $p \in P$ and $m^1 \in M^1$. The second relation follows from (A2), since $p \ne 0$ and $\omega \in K$ implies that $\omega \in \Omega^H$, or $\omega > 0$. Suppose the first relation is false so $p \in \bar{P} \backslash P$. Then by assumption 1, $|f^1(p^s, m^{1s})| \to \infty$ along the subsequence. But $f^1(p^s, m^{1s}) \le \sum_{h=1}^H \omega^{hs}$. Otherwise, (A1) would imply $\sum_2^H f^h(p, p\omega^h) \ge 0$ does not hold, in contradiction to the definition of f^h. Therefore the first relation is true and $p \in P$.

Thus $e^s \to e \in U$ and $F(e) = \omega$ by continuity of F, that is, by continuity of the right side of (A1). Therefore $e \in F^{-1}(K)$, and $F^{-1}(K)$ is compact. ∎

LEMMA 10   *If $V \subset U$ is closed relative to U, then $F(V) \cap \Omega^H$ is closed relative to Ω^H.*

Proof Let $\omega^s \to \omega$ where $\omega^s \in F(V) \cap \Omega^H$ and $\omega \in \Omega^H$. We must show that $\omega \in F(V)$. Let $K = \{\omega^s\} \cup \{\omega\}$. K is compact and $K \subset \Omega^H$. But $\omega^s = f(e^s)$ for some $e^s \in V$ by assumption. Therefore $e^s \in F^{-1}(K)$. Since $F^{-1}(K)$ is compact by lemma 9, a subsequence $\{e^{s'}\}$ converges to $e \in F^{-1}(K)$. But $\{e^{s'}\} \subset V$ and V closed relative to U implies $e \in V$. Since F is continuous, $\omega \in F(V)$. ∎

Let $V = \{e \in U \mid \det(F'(e)) = 0\}$. Let $C = \{\omega \mid \omega = F(e) \text{ and } e \in V\} = F(V)$. $F'(e)$ is the Jacobian of F at e.

COROLLARY $C \cap \Omega^H$ *is closed relative to* Ω^H.

Proof Since F' is continuous, V is closed relative to U. Therefore, by lemma 10, $C \cap \Omega^H$ is closed relative to Ω^H. ∎

$\omega \in \Omega^H$ is said to be a *regular value* of F if $\omega = F(e)$ implies that $|F'(e)| \neq 0$. $\omega \in \Omega^H$ *is* said to be a *critical* value of F if it is not a regular value of F.

LEMMA 11 *If* $\omega \in \Omega^H$ *is a regular value of* F *then* $F^{-1}(\omega)$ *is finite.*

Proof By lemma 9, $F^{-1}(\omega)$ is compact. Let $e \in F^{-1}(\omega)$. Since $|F'(\omega)| \neq 0$, by the inverse function theorem (Dieudonné 1960, p. 268), there are neighborhoods U_e of e and V_e of ω that are homeomorphic under F where $e = F^{-1}(\omega)$. Since $F^{-1}(\omega)$ is compact, the cover $\{U_e\}$ of $F^{-1}(\omega)$ has a finite subcover. Since by the homeomorphism e is the only pre-image of ω in U_e, the number of elements of $F^{-1}(\omega)$ is finite. ∎

SARD'S THEOREM (Milnor 1965) *Let* M_1 *and* M_2 *be differentiable manifolds of dimensions* m_1 *and* m_2 *respectively,* $m_2 \geq m_1$. *Let* F *be a function mapping* M_1 *into* M_2. *If* F *is continuously differentiable, the set* C *of critical values of* F *has zero Lebesgue measure.*

We may now easily establish the theorem that provides a finite number of isolated equilibria for almost all endowments in the exchange economy.

THEOREM 16 *Given* H *continuously differentiable demand functions* $(f^1, \cdots, f^H)$, *if some* f^h *satisfies assumption 1, then the closure of the set of* $\omega \in \Omega^H$ *such that* $E(\omega)$ *is infinite has zero Lebesgue measure.*

Proof If $\omega \in \Omega^H$ and $E(\omega)$ is infinite then by lemma 11, $\omega \in C$. By Sard's theorem, $C \cap \Omega^H$ is of Lebesgue measure zero. By the corollary to lemma 10, $C \cap \Omega^H$ is closed relative to Ω^H. ∎

The theorem on the finiteness of the number of equilibria for an economy satisfying certain regularity conditions has been extended to economies with linear production sectors by Kehoe (1985). Note that the finiteness result does not depend on the existence of equilibria, and indeed, stronger assumptions are needed to prove that an equilibrium does exist, for example, assuming that all consumers satisfy assumption 1 (see Debreu 1970 for a proof).

Appendix B: Jacobi's Theorem

Consider the square matrix $A = [a_{ij}]$, $i, j = 1, \cdots, n$. The matrix of cofactors of A is $A^c = [A_{ij}]$, $i, j = 1, \cdots, n$, where A_{ij} is the cofactor of a_{ji} and equal to $(-1)^{i+j}$ times the minor of $|A|$ obtained by deleting the jth row and the ith column. Thus the inverse of A is $[A_{ij}/|A|]$ or $|A|^{-1}A^c$. Jacobi's theorem relates the minors of $|A|$ to the complementary minors of $|A^c|$. A complementary minor retains exactly the rows and columns which are deleted in the original minor.

PROPOSITION *Any mth order minor of $|A^c|$ is equal to the product of the complementary minor of $|A|$ and $|A|^{m-1}$.*

Proof It is sufficient to prove the proposition for principal minors. Also, without loss of generality, we may consider the minors lying in the upper left hand corner of $|A^c|$. Consider the mth-order principal minor of $|A^c| = |A_{ij}|_m^1$. It is easy to see that

$$|A_{ij}|_m^1 \cdot |A|$$

$$
= \begin{vmatrix} \begin{bmatrix} A_{11} \cdots A_{1m} \cdots A_{1n} \\ \cdots \cdots \cdots \\ A_{m1} \cdots A_{mm} \cdots A_{mn} \\ 0 \cdots 010 \cdots 0 \\ \cdots \cdots \cdots \\ 0 \cdots \cdots 01 \end{bmatrix} \cdot A \end{vmatrix} = \begin{vmatrix} |A|0 \cdots \cdots 0 \\ \cdots \cdots \cdots \\ 0 \cdots 0|A|0 \cdots 0 \\ a_{m+11} \cdots a_{m+1m} \cdots a_{m+1n} \\ \cdots \cdots \cdots \\ a_{n1} \cdots a_{nm} \cdots a_{nn} \end{vmatrix}
$$

$$= |A|^m \cdot |a_{ij}|_n^{m+1}.$$

Therefore $|A_{ij}|_m^1 = |A|^{m-1} \cdot |a_{ij}|_n^{m+1}$. ∎

Write $A^{-1} = [\bar{a}_{ij}]$. Since $\bar{a}_{ij} = A_{ij}/|A|$, the proposition implies that $|\bar{a}_{ij}|_m^1 = |A|^{-1} \cdot |a_{ij}|_n^{m+1}$.

Appendix C: Negative Definiteness under Constraint

Consider a quadratic form $x^T A x$ defined on $\mathscr{R}^n$ by a symmetric matrix A. We wish to determine conditions for $x^T A x$ to be negative definite on the subset of $\mathscr{R}^n$ that satisfy the r independent linear equalities $p_k \cdot x = 0$, $k = 1, \cdots, m$, with $m < n$. We may also refer to the matrix A as negative definite under constraint. We will complete the argument of Black and Morimoto (1968), which begins by arranging that the subspace spanned by the first m basis vectors is the subspace spanned by the vectors p_k. Also we will first derive conditions for A to be positive definite under constraint. Then conditions for negative definiteness and for semide-finiteness are immediate. Let $P = [p_{ik}]$, where $i = 1, \cdots, n$, and $k = 1, \cdots, m$, and the variables have been ordered so that the determinant of the first m rows is nonsingular. The matrix A will be expressed in terms of a new basis consisting of the m vectors p_k and $n - m$ of the original basis vectors, which are linearly independent of the p_i, reordered to be the last $n - m$ basis vectors. Then the first m original basis vectors (after reordering) are replaced by P. This is possible since the determinant of the first m rows of P is nonsingular.

Define the transformation $T = \begin{bmatrix} P^T & \\ 0 & I_{n-m} \end{bmatrix}$. Let $y = Tx$. Then expressed in the new basis the quadratic form, $x^T A x$ becomes $y^T B y$ where $B = T^{-1T} A T^{-1}$. Let B_4 be the matrix formed of the last $n - m$ rows and columns of B. When the constraints are imposed, the first m elements of $y = Tx$ will be zero, so $y^T = (0, \cdots, 0, x_{m+1}, \cdots, x_n)^T$. This implies that $x^T A x > 0$ under constraint if and only if $(x_{m+1}, \cdots, x_n)^T B (x_{m+1}, \cdots, x_n) > 0$. In other words, A is positive definite under constraint if and only if B_4 is positive definite without constraints. The necessary and sufficient condition for B_4 to be positive definite is that the increasing sequence of its principal minors be positive (for a very elegant proof, see Debreu 1952).

The conditions for A to be positive under the constraints $P^T x = 0$ are found in terms of the bordered matrix $D = \begin{bmatrix} A & P \\ P^T & 0 \end{bmatrix}$. Let

$$S = \begin{bmatrix} T & 0 \\ 0 & I_m \end{bmatrix}. \quad \text{Let} \quad E = S^{-1T}DS^{-1}. \quad \text{Then} \quad E = \begin{bmatrix} B & T^{-1T}P \\ P^T T^{-1} & 0 \end{bmatrix}.$$

However, it may be seen from $T^{-1T}T^T = I$ that $T^{-1T}P = \begin{bmatrix} I_m \\ 0 \end{bmatrix}$. Thus

$$E = \begin{bmatrix} B_1 & B_2 & I_m \\ B_3 & B_4 & 0 \\ I_m & 0 & 0 \end{bmatrix}, \quad \text{where} \quad B = \begin{bmatrix} B_1 B_2 \\ B_3 B_4 \end{bmatrix}. \quad \text{In the expansion of the}$$

determinant of E, the nonzero terms must only take elements from I_m when taking elements from the last m columns or the last m rows. This means that no element from B_1, B_2, or B_3 can be used in the expansion. Also to bring the I_m submatrices to diagonal positions requires exactly $2mn + m^2 - 2m$ exchanges of adjacent columns each of which multiplies the sign of the determinant of E by -1. Since $2mn + m^2 - 2m$ has the parity of m, we have $|E| = (-1)^m |B_4|$. From its definition $|E| = |D| \cdot |S^{-1}|^2$. Therefore $\text{sign}|D| = (-1)^m \text{sign}|B_4|$.

If M is a square $n + m$ matrix, let M_r denote the principal submatrix that omits the rows and columns with indexes $i, j = r + 1, \cdots, n$. To complete the proof, we must show that it is also true of the principal submatrices D_r of D for which $r > m$ that $D_r = S_r^T E_r S_r$ and that $|E_r| = (-1)^m |(B_4)_{r-m}|$. This would not be true in general for symmetric matrices related by an equivalence transformation. However, it is true in this case because of the particular form of S. We will show this explicitly for the simplest case where $n = 3$ and $m = 1$. Since there is only one constraint, we will write p_i in place of p_{i1}.

$$D = S^T E S$$

$$= \begin{bmatrix} p_1 & 0 & 0 & 0 \\ p_2 & 1 & 0 & 0 \\ p_3 & 0 & 1 & 0 \\ 0 & 0 & 0 & 1 \end{bmatrix} \begin{bmatrix} b_{11} & b_{12} & b_{13} & 1 \\ b_{21} & b_{22} & b_{23} & 0 \\ b_{31} & b_{32} & b_{33} & 0 \\ 1 & 0 & 0 & 0 \end{bmatrix} \begin{bmatrix} p_1 & p_2 & p_3 & 0 \\ 0 & 1 & 0 & 0 \\ 0 & 0 & 1 & 0 \\ 0 & 0 & 0 & 1 \end{bmatrix}$$

$$= \begin{bmatrix} p_1 b_{11} & p_1 b_{12} & p_1 b_{13} & p_1 \\ p_2 b_{11} + b_{21} & p_2 b_{12} + b_{22} & p_2 b_{13} + b_{23} & p_2 \\ p_3 b_{11} + b_{31} & p_3 b_{13} + b_{32} & p_3 b_{13} + b_{33} & p_3 \\ 1 & 0 & 0 & 0 \end{bmatrix} \cdot \begin{bmatrix} p_1 & p_2 & p_3 & 0 \\ 0 & 1 & 0 & 0 \\ 0 & 0 & 1 & 0 \\ 0 & 0 & 0 & 1 \end{bmatrix}$$

$$
= \begin{bmatrix}
p_1^2 b_{11} & p_1 p_2 b_{11} + p_1 b_{12} & p_1 p_3 b_{11} + p_1 b_{13} & p_1 \\
p_1 p_2 b_{11} + p_1 b_{21} & p_2^2 b_{11} + p_2 b_{21} & p_2 p_3 b_{11} + p_3 b_{21} & p_2 \\
 & + p_2 b_{12} + b_{22} & + p_2 b_{13} + b_{23} & \\
p_1 p_3 b_{11} + p_1 b_{31} & p_2 p_3 b_{11} + p_2 b_{31} & p_3^2 b_{11} + p_3 b_{31} & p_3 \\
 & + p_3 b_{12} + b_{32} & + p_3 b_{13} + b_{33} & \\
p_1 & p_2 & p_3 & 0
\end{bmatrix}.
$$

It is a consequence of the particular transformation chosen that the submatrix $D_2 = (S^T E S)_2$ contains no terms of B or p that have a subscript 3. If we now consider the problem with $A' = \begin{bmatrix} a_{11} & a_{12} \\ a_{21} & a_{22} \end{bmatrix}$ and $p' = (p_1, p_2)$, we find that $(S'^T E' S') = D'$ is identical to $D_2 = (S^T E S)_2$. But D' has the sign of $(-1)^1 |B_4'| = (-1)^1 |(B_4)_2|$ by the same argument that showed that $|D|$ has the sign of $|B_4|$. Thus the minors of B_4 are positive if and only if the submatrices $D_3 = D$ and D_2 have determinants with the signs $(-1)^m$.

This result generalizes to a problem with any values of m and n so long as $n > m$. Let $P_{(i)}$ be the matrix made up of the first i rows of P. Let A_i be the matrix made up of the first i rows and columns of A. We may state

THEOREM 17   *Let A be an $n \times n$ real symmetric matrix, and let p_j, $j = (1, \cdots, m)$, $m < n$, be linearly independent vectors in $\mathbf{R}^n$. Order the variables in x so that $|P_{(m)}|$ is not 0. Then $x^T A x > 0$ when $p_j^T x = 0$ for all j and $x \neq 0$, if and only if the determinant $\begin{vmatrix} A_i & P_{(i)} \\ P_{(i)}^T & 0 \end{vmatrix}$ has the sign $(-1)^m$ for all $i > m$.*

We may also prove

THEOREM 18   *Make the assumptions of theorem 17. Then $x^T A x \geq 0$ when $p_j^T x = 0$ for $j = 1, \cdots, m$, and $x \neq 0$, if and only if the determinant $\begin{vmatrix} A_i & P_{(i)} \\ P_{(i)}^T & 0 \end{vmatrix}$ has the sign $(-1)^m$ or 0 for all $i > m$.*

Proof   The condition for B_4 to be positive semidefinite is that an increasing sequence of the principal minors of B_4 be nonnegative (see Debreu 1952). (Since the order of the variables is irrelevant in the quadratic form $x^T B_4 x$, this result means that all principal minors are nonnegative.) Then the argument for theorem 17 shows that the necessary and sufficient condition for $x^T A x \geq 0$ is that the principal minors D_{jj} of D for $j > m$ have the sign of $(-1)^m$ or 0.   ∎

Finally we have

THEOREM 19 *Make the assumptions of theorem 17. Then $x^T A x < 0$ when $p_j^T x = 0$ for $j = 1, \cdots, m$, and $x \neq 0$, if and only if the determinant*
$$\begin{vmatrix} A_i & P_{(i)} \\ P_{(i)}^T & 0 \end{vmatrix} \text{ has the sign } (-1)^i \text{ for all } i > m.$$

Proof If the matrix M is negative definite, then $-M$ is positive definite. Then by the proof of theorem 17, $x^T A x$ is negative definite for $p_j^T x = 0$, $j = 1, \cdots, m$, and $x \neq 0$, if and only if the determinant $\begin{vmatrix} -A_i & P_{(i)} \\ P_{(i)}^T & 0 \end{vmatrix}$ has the sign $(-1)^m$ for all $i > m$. We can return to the matrix with A_i in the upper left corner by multiplying the first i rows by -1 then multiplying the last m columns by -1. The result is that for $x^T A x$ to be negative definite, $\begin{vmatrix} A_i & P_{(i)} \\ P_{(i)}^T & 0 \end{vmatrix}$ should have the sign $(-1)^{2m+i} = (-1)^i$ for all $i > m$.   ∎

Finally we have

THEOREM 20 *Make the assumptions of theorem 17. Then $x^T A x \leq 0$ when $p_j^T x = 0$ for $j = 1, \cdots, m$ and $x \neq 0$, if and only if the determinant*
$$\begin{vmatrix} A_i & P_{(i)} \\ P_{(i)}^T & 0 \end{vmatrix} \text{ has the sign } (-1)^i \text{ or } 0 \text{ for all } i > m.$$

Proof The theorem follows from the fact that a matrix M is negative semidefinite if and only if the principal minors M_i of M have the sign $(-1)^i$ or 0. The argument concludes as in the proof of theorem 19.   ∎

Appendix D: Maximization under Constraint

We seek conditions which characterize an argument of a local maximum of a function $f(x)$, where $f : \mathscr{R}^n \to \mathscr{R}$ when the argument x is constrained to satisfy conditions $g^k(x) = 0$, $k = 1, \cdots, r$. The functions f and g^k are assumed to be twice continuously differentiable and $r < n$. Also the vectors of partial derivatives of the g^k at x are assumed to be linearly independent. According to the *method of Lagrange*, it is sufficient to characterize the arguments of the maximum of the function $\phi(x, \lambda) = f(x) - \sum_k \lambda_k g^k(x)$ (see Courant 1936, p. 198). The first-order conditions for an argument that achieves an interior maximum are

$$\frac{\partial \phi(x)}{\partial x_i} = \frac{\partial f(x)}{\partial x_i} - \sum_k \frac{\lambda_k \partial g^k(x)}{\partial x_i} = 0, \qquad i = 1, \cdots, n.$$

$$\text{(A3)}$$

$$\frac{\partial \phi(x)}{\partial \lambda_k} = g^k(x) = 0, \qquad k = 1, \cdots, r.$$

These are conditions that lead to a stationary value for $\phi(x, \lambda)$. The second-order conditions, which are sufficient to imply that a local maximum has been reached, are found by differentiating (A3) and requiring that the differential be negative definite when the constraints are observed.

$$dx^T \left[f_{ij} - \sum_k \lambda_k g_{ij}^k \right] dx < 0,$$

$$\text{(A4)}$$

$$\sum_k \partial g^k \cdot dx = 0.$$

This is to say that the matrix in the first line of (A4) is negative definite under the constraints given in the second line. The conditions for this are given in terms of the principal minors of the matrix

$$D = \begin{bmatrix} f_{ij} - \sum_k \lambda_k g_{ij}^k & g_i^k \\ g_j^k & 0 \end{bmatrix}.$$

$$\text{(A5)}$$

In the matrix (A5) $i, j = (1, \cdots, n)$ and $k = 1, \cdots, r$. Thus (A5) has $n + r$ rows and columns. The necessary and sufficient condition for seminegative definiteness of $A = [f_{ij} - \sum_k \lambda_k g_{ij}^k]$ under the constraints $\partial g^k(x)/\partial x = 0$ are that the leading principal minors D_1^m of D have the sign $(-1)^r$ or 0 for $m > r$. For negative definiteness the sign should be $(-1)^r$. The proof for these conditions was given in appendix C.

Appendix E: Matrices Whose Roots Have Negative Real Parts

Matrices whose characteristic roots have negative real parts are of interest since the linear differential equations which are defined by them are stable and the nonlinear equations whose local approximations in the neighborhood of equilibrium give linear equations defined by them are locally stable.

We will say that the submatrix B is a component of $A = [a_{ij}]$ if $a_{ij} = 0$ when a_{ii} is an element of B, and $a_{jj} \notin B$. We first note

LEMMA 12   *If A_1 is a component of A, any characteristic root λ of the submatrix A_4 complementary to A_1 is a characteristic root of A.*

Proof   Let x be a characteristic vector for B corresponding to λ. Consider

$$A = \begin{bmatrix} A_1 & 0 \\ A_3 & A_4 \end{bmatrix} \begin{pmatrix} 0 \\ x \end{pmatrix} = \lambda \begin{pmatrix} 0 \\ x \end{pmatrix}.$$

Thus λ is a characteristic root for A.   ■

With the help of this lemma, we may prove

LEMMA 13   *Let B be a maximal proper component of $A = [a_{ij}]$, where $a_{ij} \geq 0$ for $i \neq j$. Let $\mu_A(s) = 0$. If $\mu_B(s) > 0$, then there is $s^* \geq s$ such that s^* is a characteristic root of A.*

Proof   Recall from section 3.2 that for a matrix A the definition of $\mu_A(s)$ is given by $\mu_A(s) = \max_{x \in S_n} \min_j \sum_{i=1}^n x_i(s\delta_j^i - a_{ij})$. Assume that $\mu_B(s) > 0$. Let P be the complementary submatrix of B. P is indecomposable since B is maximal. If $\mu_P(s) > 0$ held, then $\mu_A(s) > 0$ would hold contrary to the hypothesis. On the other hand, if $\mu_P(s) \leq 0$ holds, since μ is monotone and continuous (appendix A of chapter 3), there is $s^* \geq s$ where $\mu_P(s^*) = 0$. This implies that s^* is a characteristic root of P by theorem 3.3. Therefore, by lemma 12, s^* is also a characteristic root of A.   ■

With the help of this lemma we may prove

THEOREM 21   *Let A be a square matrix $[a_{ij}]$ with $a_{ij} \geq 0$ for $i \neq j$. All characteristic roots of A have negative real parts if and only if A has a quasidominant negative diagonal.*

Proof Sufficiency is implied by lemma 2.8. For necessity, assume that A does not have a quasidominant negative diagonal. Suppose that $a_{ii} \geq 0$ for $i = i_0$. Then, regardless of the choice of $x \in S_n$, if $y^T = x^T(-A)$, we have $y_{i_0} \leq 0$. This implies $\mu_A(0) \leq 0$. On the other hand, if $a_{ii} \leq 0$, since for all i, $x^T(-A) > 0$ cannot hold for $x > 0$, there would be a dominant (therefore a quasidominant) negative diagonal. This implies $\mu_A(0) \leq 0$ once more.

Let B be a minimal component of A under the condition that $\mu_B(0) \leq 0$. B must exist, although it may happen that $B = A$. Let P be a proper component of B. Then it must be that $\mu_P(0) > 0$. P may not exist in which case B is indecomposable. Consider $\mu_B(s) = 0$. Since μ is monotonic, we must have $s \geq 0$. If B is indecomposable, s is a characteristic root of B by theorem 3.3. On the other hand, if B is decomposable and P does exist, there is $s^* > s$ such that s^* is a characteristic root of P and therefore of B by lemma 12. In other words, if there is not a dominant negative diagonal, there must be a characteristic root that is nonnegative. ■

5 Pareto Optimality and the Core

At least from the time of the Physiocrats and Adam Smith (1776), most economists have believed that the equilibrium of the competitive market has desirable properties. Walras (1874–77) tried to define a notion of optimality for market equilibrium, but his proof seemed only to establish that each trader does as well as he can, given the prices he faces on the market. The modern idea was due to Francis Edgeworth (1881) and Vilfredo Pareto (1909) and is usually referred to as Pareto optimality. Loosely speaking, an economic situation is described as Pareto optimal if there is no feasible change in the situation that will benefit someone and injure no one. This definition does not depend on how the market operates. It is relative to the physical possibilities of production and distribution and the initial quantities of goods available. Thus it permits a comparison of the equilibrium of the competitive market with what is physically possible independently of the organization of the economy. We will give the analysis for an economy of firms, but the translation to an economy of activities should be obvious.

5.1 Pareto Optimum and Competitive Equilibrium

Let $C^h \subset \mathbf{R}^n$ represent the set of possible net trades for the hth consumer, $h = 1, \cdots, H$. Goods are perfectly divisible. Quantities of goods received are positive components of net trade vectors, and quantities of goods provided are negative components. An irreflexive binary relation $\mathscr{P}^h$ is defined on C^h for each h. $\mathscr{P}^h$ is a relation of strict preference, that is, $x\mathscr{P}^h y$ if and only if the hth consumer strictly prefers x to y.

Let $Y^f \subset \mathbf{R}^n$ be the set of possible input–output vectors for the fth firm, $f = 1, \cdots, F$, where quantities of outputs are positive components and quantities of inputs are negative components. We will usually refer to input–output vectors simply as outputs. The profit of the fth firm when output is y^f and prices are p is py^f. $Y = \sum_{f=1}^{F} Y^f$ is the set of possible outputs for the economy. Similarly $C = \sum_{h=1}^{H} C^h$ is the set of possible net trades for the economy.

The *budget set* for the hth consumer is defined as $H^h(p, m) = \{z \mid z \in C^h \text{ and } pz \le m^h\}$ where $m^h \in \mathbf{R}$ is the income of the consumer. The *preferred set* of the hth consumer at a commodity bundle x is defined as $R^h(x) = \{z \in C^h \mid \text{not } x\mathscr{P}^h z\}$. The *strictly preferred set* of the hth consumer at a commodity bundle x is defined as $P^h(x) = \{z \in C^h \mid z\mathscr{P}^h x\}$.

An *allocation of net trades* over consumers is represented by a list $(x^1, \cdots, x^H)$, also written $\tilde{x}$ or $\{x^h\}$, where $x^h \in C^h$, all h.

The *Pareto preferred set* for the economy for a given allocation $\tilde{x}$ to consumers is defined as

$$P(\tilde{x}) = \left\{ z \mid z = \sum_{h=1}^{H} z^h,\ z^h \in R^h(x^h),\ \text{all } h,\ \text{and } z^h \in P^h(x^h),\ \text{some } h \right\}.$$

The *Pareto weakly preferred set* for a given allocation $\tilde{x}$ is

$$R(\tilde{x}) = \left\{ z = \sum z^h \mid z^h \in R(x^h),\ \text{all } h \right\}.$$

A *competitive equilibrium with redistribution* is given by a list $(x^1, \cdots, x^H, y^1, \cdots, y^F, m^1, \cdots, m^H, p)$, also written $(\tilde{x}, \tilde{y}, \tilde{m}, p)$, which meets the conditions:

I. For all h, $x^h \in C^h$ and $px^h \le m^h$, and $z \in P^h(x^h)$ implies that $pz > m^h$.

II. For all f, $y^f \in Y^f$ and $py^f \ge pz$ for all $z \in Y^f$.

III. $\sum_{h=1}^{H} x^h = \sum_{f=1}^{F} y^f$.

I is the demand condition. II is the profit condition. III is the balance condition.

A *Pareto optimum* is given by a list $(x^1, \cdots, x^H, y^1, \cdots, y^F)$, abbreviated by $(\tilde{x}, \tilde{y})$, which meets the conditions:

I. $x^h \in C^h$ for all h, and $y^f \in Y^f$ for all f.

II. $z \in P(\tilde{x})$ implies $z \notin Y$.

III. $\sum_{h=1}^{H} x^h = \sum_{f=1}^{F} y^f$.

I is the possibility condition. II is the Pareto condition. III is the balance condition.

An allocation $\tilde{x}$ is *feasible* if $x^h \in C^h$ for all h and $\sum_h x^h \in Y$. We introduce

ASSUMPTION 1 Nonsatiation. If $\tilde{x}$ is feasible, the set $P^h(x^h)$ is not empty for any h.

ASSUMPTION 2 Continuity of preference. $R^h(x)$ is the closure of $P^h(x)$ relative to C^h if $P^h(x)$ is not empty.

LEMMA 1   *If the hth consumer is not satiated at x, then local nonsatiation assumption 1.5 holds for the hth consumer at x.*

Proof   Since $x \in R^h(x)$ and $x \notin P^h(x) \neq \emptyset$, assumption 2 implies that x is a boundary point of $P^h(x)$. Thus there is $z \in P^h(x)$ in every neighborhood of x. This is local nonsatiation.   ∎

We may now prove the First Theorem of Pareto Optimality.

THEOREM 1   *Assumptions 1 and 2 imply that the allocation $(x^1, \cdots, x^H, y^1, \cdots, y^F)$ of a competitive equilibrium with redistribution is a Pareto optimum.*

Proof   The intuitive meaning of the proof is very simple. Any consumption bundle equally good as the bundle that a consumer receives in a competitive equilibrium must cost at least as much. A better bundle must cost more, so the total consumption must cost more if it is Pareto preferred. But an alternative output must be worth the same or less for each firm, and thus an alternative total output must be worth the same or less for the whole economy. Then the bundle that costs more cannot be produced, and the Pareto preferred consumption is not feasible.

More formally, let $(\tilde{x}, \tilde{y}, \tilde{m}, p)$ be a competitive equilibrium with redistribution. Suppose $z \in R(x^h)$ and $pz < m^h$. For a sufficiently small neighborhood U of z, every point $w \in U$ satisfies $pw < m^h$. But, by assumption 1, $P^h(x^h) \neq \emptyset$. Then, by lemma 1, every neighborhood U contains a point $w \in P^h(x^h)$. This contradicts condition I of competitive equilibrium, so $pz \geq m^h$ must hold. Also condition I of competitive equilibrium requires $px^h \leq m^h$. Thus $px^h = m^h$. On the other hand, condition I of competitive equilibrium implies directly that $z \in P(x^h)$ implies $pz > m^h$. Suppose that there is $w \in P(x^1, \cdots, x^H) \cap Y$; that is, w is in the Pareto preferred set and w can be produced. Then, by definition of P, we have that $w = \sum_h w^h$, where $w^h \in R^h(x^h)$ for all h and $w^h \in P^h(x^h)$ for some h. This implies that $pw > \sum_{h=1}^H m^h = \sum_{h=1}^H px^h = \sum_{f=1}^F py^f$. The second equality follows from condition III of competitive equilibrium. But $py^f \geq pz$ for any $z \in Y^f$ for all f by the profit condition. Thus $w = \sum_f w^f$ with $w^f \in Y^f$, all f, implies that $pw \leq \sum_h py^f$. This is a contradiction. Therefore $P(x^1, \cdots, x^H) \cap Y = \emptyset$, and condition II of Pareto optimality is satisfied; conditions I and III of Pareto optimality are implied directly by the conditions of competitive equilibrium.   ∎

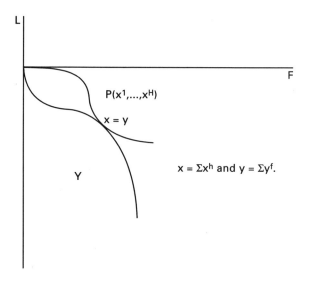

Figure 5.1
Illustrating the first theorem of welfare economics, the competitive equilibrium is x, which equals y. x is also a Pareto optimum.

Theorem 1 is illustrated in figure 5.1.

To prove that a Pareto optimal allocation can be realized as a competitive allocation with redistribution requires the introduction of convexity assumptions for consumers and producers. Consider the assumptions

ASSUMPTION 1′   Nonsatiation. If $\tilde{x}$ is feasible, the set $P^h(x^h)$ is not empty for *some h.*

ASSUMPTION 2′   Continuity of preference. *For all h, $P^h(x)$ is open relative to C^h and convex. Also $R^h(x)$ is the closure of $P^h(x)$ if $P^h(x)$ is not* empty.

ASSUMPTION 3   Consumer sets. C^h *is convex and bounded below for all h.*

ASSUMPTION 4   Production set. Y *is convex.*

The words in italics represent new assumptions.

LEMMA 2   *Under assumptions 1′, 2′, and 3, if x is feasible, $R(x)$ is the closure of $P(x)$.*

Proof From the definition it is clear that $R(x) = \sum_{h=1}^{H} R^h(x^h)$. Consider any feasible sequence $z^s \in P(x)$ where $z^s \to z$. Then for every z^s there is a choice of the z^{hs} such that every $z^{hs} \in R^h(x^h)$. The z^{hs} are bounded above, since z^s is feasible. Since the $z^s \to z$ and the z^s and the z^{hs} are bounded above, there is a subsequence (preserve notation) such that for each h we have that $z^{hs} \to z^h$ and $\sum_{h=1}^{H} z^h = z$. Since $R^h(x)$ is closed, $z^h \in R^h(x)$ for all h. Therefore $z \in R(x)$ and the limit of any convergent sequence in $P(x)$ lies in $R(x)$.

On the other hand, since x is feasible, by assumption 1′, there is k with $z^k \in P(x^k)$. Also, by assumption 2′, we have that $w^k \in R(x^k)$ is the limit of a sequence z^{ks} with $z^{ks} \in P^k(x^k)$. Then the sequence z^s with $z^{hs} = w^{hs}$ for $h \neq k$ lies in $P(x)$ and converges to w. Thus every $w \in R(x)$ is the limit of a sequence in $P(x)$. ∎

LEMMA 3 *Under assumptions 1′, 2′, and 3, if x is feasible, the Pareto preferred set $P(x)$ and the Pareto weakly preferred set $R(x)$ are convex.*

Proof Assumption 2′ implies that $P^h(x^h)$ is convex. Then $P(x)$ is convex as the sum of convex sets. Lemma 2 implies that $R(x)$ is convex as the closure of a convex set. ∎

It is useful to define a notion of quasi-equilibrium that relaxes the demand condition of competitive equilibrium. A *quasi-equilibrium with redistribution* is a list $(x^1, \cdots, x^H, y^1, \cdots, y^F, m^1, \cdots, m^H, p) = (\tilde{x}, \tilde{y}, \tilde{m}, p)$ that satisfies conditions II and III of competitive equilibrium but in place of condition I satisfies condition I′.

I′. For all h, $x^h \in C^h$ and $px^h \leq m^h$, and $px^h \leq pz$ for all $z \in R^h(x^h)$.

The meaning of condition I′ is that consumers are minimizing the costs, given prices p, of achieving bundles that are at least as good as the bundles x^h. However, they may not be maximizing their preference levels over the budget sets determined by p and $\tilde{m}$.

With the help of lemmas 2 and 3, we can show that a Pareto optimum can be realized as a quasi-equilibrium with redistribution. The Pareto optimum is not shown to realize a competitive equilibrium with redistribution on these assumptions. However, the quasi-equilibrium will be a competitive equilibrium if the cheaper point assumption holds, assumption 1.6. This observation was first made by Arrow (1951) in a fundamental paper for the modern approach to Pareto optimality.

The Second Theorem of Pareto Optimality is

THEOREM 2   If $(\tilde{x}, \tilde{y})$ is a Pareto optimum, under assumptions 1', 2', 3, and 4, there are $p \neq 0$ and $\tilde{m}$ such that $(\tilde{x}, \tilde{y}, \tilde{m}, p)$ is a quasi-equilibrium with redistribution.

Proof   By assumption 2', the Pareto preferred set $P(x)$ is convex. By the definition of a Pareto optimum, $z \in P(x)$ implies $z \notin Y$. Also Y is convex by assumption 4. Let $x = \sum_{h=1}^{H} x^h$. Let L be the smallest linear subspace containing $P(x)$ and Y. By a separation theorem (Berge 1963, p. 163) there is $p \in L$ with $p \neq 0$ and a real number κ such that $pz \leq \kappa$ for $z \in Y$, and $pz \geq \kappa$ for $z \in P(x)$. By lemma 2, $R(x)$ is the closure of $P(x)$. Therefore it is also true that $pz \geq \kappa$ for $z \in R(x)$. Since x lies in Y and $R(x)$, we have $\kappa = px$. Then we may choose $m^h = px^h$. If for some k there were $z^k \in R^k(x^k)$ such that $pz^k < m^k$, it would follow for $z \in R(x)$ where $z^h = x^h$ for $h \neq k$ that $pz < \kappa$. This is a contradiction, so p supports the weakly preferred sets $R^h(x^h)$ of each consumer. Thus condition I' of quasi-equilibrium is met.

But $x = \sum_1^F y^f$ and for any $z \in Y$, $z = \sum_1^F z^f$. Thus $\sum_1^F (pz^f - py^f) \leq 0$ for $z^f \in Y^f$, all f. Consider $z^f = y^f$ for $f \neq g$. Then $pz^g - py^g \leq 0$ for $z^g \in Y^g$. Since g is arbitrary, condition II of quasi-equilibrium is met. Condition III of quasi-equilibrium is met by the definition of a Pareto optimum.   ∎

We will show the quasi-equilibrium to be a competitive equilibrium when the cheaper point assumption is met.

A further lemma will prove useful.

LEMMA 4   If $pz \geq px$ for all $z \in P^h(x)$ where $x \in C^h$, and there is $w \in C^h$ such that $pw < px$, then $pz > px$ holds for all $z \in P^h(x)$.

Proof   Assume there is $z \in P^h(x)$ where $pz = px$. Since $P^h(x)$ is open in C^h and C^h is convex by assumption 3, there is $z' \neq z$ on the line segment from w to z and close to z such that $z' \in P^h(x)$. But $pz' < px$ in contradiction to the hypothesis. Thus $pz > px$ holds for all $z \in P^h(x)$.   ∎

COROLLARY   If $(\tilde{x}, \tilde{y}, \tilde{m}, p)$ is a quasi-equilibrium with redistribution where the cheaper point assumption is met for all h, then the quasi-equilibrium is a competitive equilibrium.

Proof   This follows directly from lemma 4 and the definitions.   ∎

It is intuitive that the convexity conditions can be relaxed and Theorem 2 may still hold in an approximate sense. Results of this type have been established by Starr (1969).

5.2 Competitive Equilibrium and the Core

An approach to competitive markets different from that of Walras was developed by Edgeworth (1881). Walras considered prices leading to offers to buy and sell which are aggregated over the market. Price lists are announced in sequence, and trades are carried out when demand and supply are in balance. On the other hand, Edgeworth considered bargaining among individual traders in which no bargains are final until a point is reached where no group of traders can conclude a new bargain that they prefer to their existing bargains. Edgeworth proved in the simplest case of trading in two goods that such a situation, in which no new bargains are possible that are preferred by some participants, will approach a competitive equilibrium as the number of traders increases indefinitely. This result has since been generalized to the case of many goods and to production economies. The path breaking paper was that of Debreu and Scarf (1963).

Consider an economy where the sets $C^h \subset \mathbf{R}^n$, $h = 1, \cdots, H$, represent the sets of possible net trades. $C = \sum_{h=1}^{H} C^h$ is the set of net trades possible for the set of all consumers. Recall that positive quantities represent amounts received by the consumer and negative quantities represent quantities provided by the consumer. The strictly preferred set $P^h(x)$ is defined as before. There is a production possibility set $Y \subset \mathbf{R}^n$. We will use the activities model of production, so Y will be a convex cone with vertex at the origin. These activities are available to all consumers. Recall that an *allocation of net trades* $\tilde{x}$ is a list $(x^1, \cdots, x^H)$ such that $x^h \in C^h$ for all h. We may also write $\{x^h\}$ for an allocation when no confusion will result. As before, a *feasible allocation* is an allocation that satisfies $\sum_{1}^{H} x^h \in Y$. Many of the results of this section may be found in McKenzie (1988, 1990) and McKenzie and Shinotsuka (1991).

A correspondence F is said to be *open valued* if $F(z)$ is an open set for every z in the domain of F. A set S' is open relative to a set S if S' is equal to the intersection of S with an open set. We make two assumptions on preferences.

ASSUMPTION 5 C^h is convex for all h.

ASSUMPTION 6   For all h, P^h is open valued relative to C^h. Let $\tilde{x} = (x^1, \cdots, x^H)$. If $\tilde{x}$ is feasible, then $P^h(x^h) \neq \emptyset$, and $R^h(x^h)$ is the closure of $P^h(x^h)$.

We also make two assumptions on production possibilities.

ASSUMPTION 7   The production set Y is a convex *cone with vertex at the origin*.

ASSUMPTION 8 $Y \cap \mathbf{R}_+^n = \{0\}$.

There are also two assumptions relating consumption sets and the production set.

Let $x_I = \sum_{h \in I} x^h$ and $C_I = \sum_{h \in I} C^h$ where I is a subset of consumers. An economy is said to be *irreducible* if for every nontrivial partition of the set of consumers into two subsets I_1 and I_2, the following condition holds. If $(x^1, \cdots, x^H)$ is a feasible allocation, then there are $w \in C_{I_2}$ and $y' \in Y$ such that $z_{I_1} = y' - x_{I_2} - \alpha w$ for some $\alpha > 0$ and $z^h \in P^h(x^h)$ for all $h \in I_1$. This idea is illustrated in figure 5.2.

ASSUMPTION 9 $Y \cap C^h \neq \emptyset$ *and relative interior* $Y \cap$ *relative interior* $C \neq \emptyset$.

ASSUMPTION 10   *The economy is irreducible.*

Assumption 7 implies that production processes are independent and divisible. Assumption 8 is only a convenience since goods produced out of nothing would be free. As before, italics indicate new assumptions.

Irreducibility means that given any feasible allocation of trades if the consumers are divided into two nonempty sets either set will have a possible trade some multiple of which, together with a possible output variation, improves the allocation to the members of the other set when added to the allocation they already receive. This idea and assumptions like 9 and 10 will play important roles whenever the existence of a competitive equilibrium is to be proved. Assumption 9 is called a social survival assumption. The role of the second part of assumption 9 is to guarantee that there is $z \in C^h$ with $pz < m^h$ for some h and the role of assumption 10 is to provide that if one consumer satisfies this condition, all do. Assumption 9 together with assumption 10 will allow prices that support preferred sets together with the production set to be realized as competi-

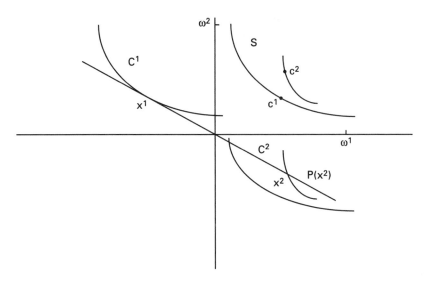

Figure 5.2
S is the possible consumption set for both traders. C^h is a possible trading set. ω^h is an endowment. c^h is a consumption for consumer h. x^h is a trade for consumer h. x^1 lies on the boundary of C^1. $P(x^2)$ is the preferred set of x^2. The economy is irreducible.

tive equilibrium prices. We will mean by the *relative interior* of a set S the interior of S relative to the smallest affine subspace containing S. We use this notion only with reference to convex sets. For convex sets that are not empty, the relative interior is not empty.

The central idea leading to the concept of the core is that of an improving coalition. Given an allocation $(x^1, \cdots, x^H)$, an *improving coalition B* is a subset of consumers such that for each $h \in B$ there is $z^h \in C^h$ with $\sum_{h \in B} z^h \in Y$ and $z^h \in P^h(x^h)$ for all $h \in B$. Then the *core* of the economy is defined as the set of all feasible allocations for which there is no improving coalition. This concept corresponds to Edgeworth's idea of equilibrium since, if an allocation is in the core, there will be no group of traders who can negotiate a new bargain among themselves, taking account of their production possibilities, that will improve the position of all the traders in the group. We will see that when the consumers are duplicated without limit, any allocation that remains in the core indefinitely can be realized as a competitive equilibrium. Also the subset of the core that assigns the same allocation to the replicas of each person will shrink to the set of competitive equilibria of the original economy.

Under the assumptions of this section, there is not a set of firms that exists independently of the choices of the agents. Rather there is a set of production possibilities, which are generated by activities available to any subset of agents that chooses to use them. For this reason the profit condition and the demand condition of competitive equilibrium will be stated differently from the condition given in section 5.1. The formulation used in section 2.8 is also inappropriate, since it is not useful in this context to collect the activities into processes. However, the conditions for competitive equilibrium will be equivalent under the present assumptions to those previously stated. We will say that $\{x^h\}$ is a *competitive allocation* if there is a price vector p and an output y such that

I. $px^h \leq 0$, and $z \in P^h(x^h)$ implies $pz > 0$ for all h.

II. $y \in Y$ and $py = 0$ while $z \in Y$ implies $pz \leq 0$.

III. $\sum_{h=1}^{H} x^h = y$.

Since an activity can operate at any positive level, a positive profit is inconsistent with profit maximization. Since an activity can operate at zero level a negative profit is also inconsistent with profit maximization. This leads to condition II. Thus in equilibrium profits are zero and $m^h = 0$ for all h. This leads to condition I. Condition III is unchanged.

It was shown in section 5.1 that local nonsatiation implies that a competitive equilibrium is a Pareto optimum. Local nonsatiation also implies that a competitive allocation lies in the core. In a Pareto improvement it is only required that some consumers benefit, not necessarily all consumers, while none suffers. The stronger criterion of improvement here may be defended as providing all members of an improving coalition with an incentive to act. Also the weaker definition is not sufficient for proving that the equal treatment core (defined below) converges to the set of competitive equilibria of the original economy as the economy is replicated.

THEOREM 3   *A competitive allocation is in the core.*

Proof Since $py = 0$, we have $p \cdot \sum_{h=1}^{H} x^h = 0$. Then $px^h \leq 0$ implies that $px^h = 0$ for all h. Suppose that B is an improving coalition by means of the allocation $\{z^h\}_{h \in B}$ where $\sum_{h \in B} z^h = z \in Y$. Then $z^h \in P^h(x^h)$ for all $h \in B$. However, $z^h \in P^h(x^h)$ implies that $pz^h > px^h$ from the demand condition of competitive equilibrium. Therefore $\sum_{h \in B} pz^h > \sum_{h \in B} px^h$

$= 0$. But $z \in Y$ and $pz \leq 0$ by condition II. Thus no such improving coalition B can exist, and $\{x^h\}$ lies in the core. ∎

For each h let the number of consumers identical to the consumer with index h be increased to r by adding new consumers and index the larger set by hs where $h = 1, \cdots, H$ and $s = 1, \cdots, r$. The economy that is replicated r times will be referred to as E_r. Allocations for E_r may be written $\{x^{hs}\}_r$. We will consider allocations $\{x^{hs}\}_r$ in the core in which $x^{h1} = x^{hs}$ for $s = 1$ to r. These allocations form the *equal treatment core*. That is, the replicas of a given consumer receive the same allocation. There will be no ambiguity if equal treatment allocations are indicated by the expression $\{x^h\}_r$. Thus an equal treatment allocation is given by the list $\{x^h\}$, $h = 1, \cdots, H$, whatever the number r of replications may be.

LEMMA 5   *As r increases, the allocations $\{x^h\}_r$ in the equal treatment core of E_r form a nonincreasing sequence of nested sets.*

Proof   If B is an improving coalition for the allocation $\{x^h\}_r$ when $r = s$, it is also an improving coalition when $r = s + 1$. Therefore, as r increases, no new allocations $\{x^h\}_r$ can appear in the equal treatment core. ∎

The basic result is

THEOREM 4   *Make assumptions 5 through 10. If $\{x^h\}_r$ is in the equal treatment core of E_r for all r, then $\{x^h\} = \{x^h\}_1$ is a competitive allocation for E_1.*

Proof   Assume that $\{x^h\}_r$ is an allocation in the equal treatment core for all values of r. For any $x \in C^h$ let $P^h(x)$ be the set of trades preferred to the trade x by consumers who are duplicates of the original consumer with index h. We may refer to them as consumers of the hth type. Since x is feasible, $P^h(x)$ is not empty, and $P^h(x)$ is open relative to C^h by assumption 6. Let $Q(x^1, \cdots, x^H)$ be the convex hull of the $P^h(x^h)$, $h = 1, \cdots, H$.

Suppose that $Y \cap Q(x^1, \cdots, x^H) \neq \emptyset$. Then there is a set of consumers B and weights α_i such that $\sum_{i \in B} \alpha_i z^i = y \in Y$, $\alpha_i > 0$, $\sum_{i \in B} \alpha_i = 1$, and there is $z^i \in P^{h(i)}(x^{h(i)})$ where the ith consumer of the set B is a replica of the $h(i)$th original consumer. The consumers may be chosen so that the number of consumers in B is less than or equal to $n + 1$, where n is the number of goods (Fenchel 1953, p. 37; Rockafellar 1970, p. 155). An equivalent condition for z^i is that $\sum_{i \in B} \alpha_i(z^i - y) = 0$. For any positive integer s let a_i^s be the smallest integer greater than or equal to $s\alpha_i$. By the first part of assumption 9, for each $i \in B$ there is $y^i \in C^{h(i)} \cap Y$. Let $w_s^i = (s\alpha_i/a_i^s)(z^i - y^i) + y^i$. Since w_s^i is a convex combination of z^i and y^i, it lies in $C^{h(i)}$ by assumption 5. Moreover, since $s\alpha_i/a_i^s \to 1$ as $s \to \infty$, we have $w_s^i \to z^i$ as $s \to \infty$.

Since the preferred sets are open relative to the C^i by assumption 6, we have $w_s^i \in P^{h(i)}(x^{h(i)})$ for all $i \in B$ for some number s which is large enough. Also

$$\sum_{i \in B} a_i^s w_s^i = \sum_{i \in B}(s\alpha_i z^i - s\alpha_i y^i + a_i^s y^i) = sy + \sum_{i \in B}(a_i^s - s\alpha_i)y^i.$$

As $0 \le a_i^s - s\alpha_i \le 1$ and $y^i \in Y$, $\sum_{i \in B} a_i^s w_s^i \in Y$, since Y is a convex cone by assumption 7. Let $K = \{h \mid h(i) = h \text{ for some } i \in B\}$, the set of all types present in coalition B. Let $B_h = \{i \in B \mid h(i) = h\}$, the set of individuals in coalition B of type h. Put $r = \max_{h \in K}(\sum_{i \in B_h} a_i^s)$, the largest number in B of any given type. If the economy has been replicated r times, there are enough traders of each type h in K to offer the net trade $\sum_{i \in B_h} a_i^s w_s^i$ needed from the hth type to achieve the improved allocation for all $i \in B$. Then the improving coalition can be formed if the original economy has been replicated r times. (See figure 5.3 for a simple case.) This contradicts the hypothesis. Therefore $Y \cap Q(x^1, \cdots, x^H) = \emptyset$. In other words, $\{x^h\}_r$ in the core for all r implies that the production set Y intersected with the convex hull of the $P^h(x^h)$, the sets of preferred trades of the original consumers, is empty.

Consider $Q(\tilde{x})$ and Y in the smallest linear subspace L that contains both C and Y. By a separation theorem for convex sets (Berge 1963, p. 162), there is a vector $p \in L$, $p \ne 0$, such that $pz \ge \mu$ for all $z \in Q(x^1, \cdots, x^H)$ and $pz \le \mu$ for all $z \in Y$. The fact that Y is a cone with vertex at the origin implies that $\mu = 0$. Since $P^h(x^h) \subset Q(x^1, \cdots, x^H)$, $pz \ge 0$ for all $z \in P^h(x^h)$. Since $x^h \in R^h(x^h)$, by assumption 6 there is a point $z \in P^h(x^h)$ in every neighborhood of x^h relative to L. Thus $px^h \ge 0$ must hold for all h. Since $(x^1, \cdots, x^H)$ is a feasible allocation, it is also true that $\sum_{h=1}^H x^h = y \in Y$. Therefore $p \cdot \sum_{h=1}^H x^h \le 0$. This implies that $px^h = 0$ must hold for all h.

To complete the proof, it is necessary to show that in fact $pz > 0$ for any $z \in P^h(x^h)$ for all h. We first prove a lemma.

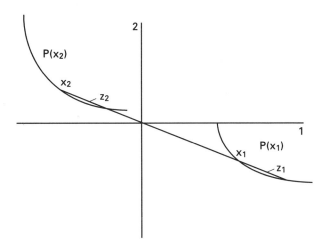

Figure 5.3
The trade x_1 for x_2 is not in the core for 5 replications, since 3 of z_2 equals 2 of z_1 and gives an improving coalition.

LEMMA 6   *Let sets A and B be convex sets in R^n. Suppose $0 \in A$. If relative interior $A \cap$ relative interior $B \neq \emptyset$ there is no hyperplane which separates A and B in the smallest linear subspace containing both.*

Proof   Let L be the smallest linear subspace containing A and B. If H is a hyperplane separating A and B in L, then there is $q \in L$, $q \neq 0$, such that $H = \{z \in L \mid qz = \mu\}$ and H separates A and B in L. However, q may be chosen so that $qz \leq \mu$ for all $z \in A$ and $qz \geq \mu$ for all $z \in B$. Then $y \in A \cap B$ implies $qy = \mu$. But $y \in$ relative interior A implies $qz = \mu$ for all $z \in A$. Similarly $qz = \mu$ for all $z \in B$. Then $0 \in A$ implies $\mu = 0$. Since A and B span L, this implies $qz = 0$ for all $z \in L$. Then $q \in L$ implies that $q = 0$. Since this is a contradiction of the choice of q, no such separation is possible.   ∎

The vector p supports Y. Thus $pz \leq 0$ for all $z \in Y$. Since relative interior $Y \cap$ relative interior C contains a point w by assumption 9, and since $0 \in Y$, it is implied by lemma 6 that $pw < 0$. Therefore $pw^h < 0$ for some $w^h \in C^h$ for some h. Let I be the set of consumers and $I_1 = \{h \in I \mid pw^h < 0 \text{ for some } w^h \in C^h\}$. That is, the members of I_1 have cheaper points. Let $I_2 = I - I_1$. Lemma 4 implies that $pz > 0$ holds for all $z \in P^h(x^h)$ for $h \in I_1$. However, by irreducibility, there is $v \in C_{I_2}$ and

$y' \in Y$ such that $z_{I_1} = y' - x_{I_2} - \alpha v$ for $\alpha > 0$ and $z^h \in P^h(x^h)$ for all $h \in I_1$. Since $py' \leq 0$, $px_{I_2} = 0$, and $pz_{I_1} > 0$, we have $pv < 0$. That is, some member of I_2 also has a cheaper point. This contradicts the definition of I_2. Therefore I_2 must be empty. Then $I_1 = \{1, \ldots, H\}$ and $pz > 0$ for $z \in P(x^h)$ for all h. Thus the demand condition of competitive equilibrium is met. Since $px^h = 0$ for all h and $y = \sum_{h=1}^{H} x^h$, we have $py = 0$. Also $pz \leq 0$ for all $z \in Y$ by the support property. Therefore the profit condition is met, and the balance condition is implied by the definition of a feasible allocation. Thus $\{x^h\}_1$ is a competitive allocation for E_1. ∎

Assume that the equal treatment core is not empty however many times the economy is replicated. Then with somewhat strengthened assumptions it is possible to go further and prove convergence of the set of allocations in the equal treatment core to the set of competitive allocations. Recall that the lower section of P is the set of z such that $x \in P(z)$. We replace assumptions 5, 6, and 7 with the stronger

ASSUMPTION 5′ $C^h \neq \emptyset$ is convex *and closed, and bounded from below*, for all h.

ASSUMPTION 6′   For all h, P^h is open valued relative to C^h *with open lower sections*. If $\tilde{x}$ is feasible, $P^h(x^h) \neq \emptyset$ and $R^h(x^h)$ is the closure of $P^h(x^h)$ for all h.

ASSUMPTION 7′ Y is a *closed* convex cone with vertex at the origin.

Let K_r be the set of allocations $\{x^h\}_r$ in the equal treatment core of E_r where there are r members of each type, and let W be the set of competitive allocations $\{x^h\}_1$ in E_1. Let the distance $d(K_r, W)$ of the equal treatment core to the set of competitive allocations in E_1 be given by

$$d(K_r, W) = \max_{x \in K_r} \min_{z \in W} |x - z| + \max_{z \in W} \min_{x \in K_r} |x - z|.$$

In this expression $x = (x^1, \cdots, x^H)$ is the list of allocations to the replicas of the initial set of consumers. Convergence of the equal treatment core to the set of competitive allocations of E_1 is defined by $d(K_r, W) \to 0$ as $r \to \infty$.

Let T_r be the set of equal treatment allocations which are feasible, that is,

$$T_r = \left\{ \{x^h\}_r \mid x^h \in C^h, \text{ all } h, \text{ and } \sum_{h=1}^{H} x^h \in Y \right\}.$$

Because of equal treatment and assumption 7' that Y is a cone, the index r is irrelevant to feasibility but not, of course, to the size of the core. We first prove

LEMMA 7 *Assumptions 5', 7', and 8 imply that T_r is compact.*

Proof To prove compactness, it suffices to show that every infinite sequence of allocations in T_r has a point of accumulation in T_r (Berge 1963, p. 90). Let $\tilde{x}^s = (x^{1s}, \cdots, x^{Hs})$, $s = 1, 2, \cdots$, be a sequence of allocations with $\sum_h x^{hs} = y^s \in Y$. I claim that $\tilde{x}^s$ is bounded. If not, since the C^h are bounded below, it must be that $x_i^{hs} \to \infty$ for some h and i. But for a subsequence (retain notation) $y^s/|y^s| \to y \ge 0$ and $\ne 0$. Y is closed by assumption 7'. Thus $y \in Y$, and assumption 8 is violated. This shows that x^{hs} is bounded for each h. Therefore there is a point of accumulation $(\bar{x}^1, \cdots, \bar{x}^H)$ for the sequence $(x^{1s}, \cdots, x^{Hs})$, $s = 1, 2, \cdots$. Then $\bar{x}^h \in C^h$ for all h, since C^h is closed by assumption 5'. The list $(\bar{x}^1, \cdots, \bar{x}^H)$ is a feasible allocation and lies in T_r. ∎

We may now prove

THEOREM 5 *Given assumptions 5', 6', 7', 8, 9, and 10, assume that the set of competitive allocations for E_1 and the equal treatment core for E_r as $r \to \infty$ are not empty. Then the equal treatment core converges to the set of competitive allocations of E_1.*

Proof From the definition of a competitive allocation, the competitive allocations of the original economy are the competitive allocations with equal treatment in the replicated economy. Since, by theorem 3, competitive allocations are always in the core, the second term of the distance formula is 0 for all r. Thus the theorem requires that the first term be shown to converge to 0. That is, the core shrinks down to the set of competitive equilibria. Suppose that $\{x^h\}_r$ is an allocation for which there is an improving coalition B. Recall that T_r is the set of equal treatment allocations that are feasible. Let the allocation to the replicas of the hth consumer be perturbed by Δx^h where $\sum_{h=1}^{H}(x^h + \Delta x^h) \in Y$, $|\Delta x^h| < \varepsilon >$ 0, and $x^h + \Delta x^h \in C^h$ for all h. By assumption 6' the preference correspondences P^h have open lower sections relative to C^h. Thus, if ε is sufficiently small, the new allocation $\{x^h + \Delta x^h\}_{h \in B}$ is still dominated by the same net trades achievable within B alone that dominated $\{x^h\}_{h \in B}$. Note that this argument critically used the fact that every member of B receives an improvement. Then the set of equal treatment allocations $T_r \backslash K_r$ for which there is an improving coalition is open relative to the set T_r of feasible equal treatment allocations. Therefore the set of allocations K_r is closed in T_r. Since K_r is contained in T_r and T_r is compact by lemma 7, K_r is compact (Berge 1963, p. 68).

By lemma 5, an allocation in the equal treatment core for the sth replica economy is in the equal treatment core for all $r < s$. Suppose there are allocations $\{w^h\}_r$ in K_r and at a distance of at least $\varepsilon > 0$ from any allocation in W for indefinitely large r. Since T_r is compact by lemma 7, there would be an accumulation point $\{z^h\}$ of the sequence $\{w^h\}_r$ where $\{z^h\}$ lies at least ε from any allocation in W. But lemma 5 implies that a sequence $\{w^h\}_r$ that converges to $\{z^h\}$ as $r \to \infty$ provides for any s a subsequence (save notation) along which $r > s$ holds, that converges to $\{z^h\}$ as $r \to \infty$, and is contained in K_s. Since K_s is closed, $\{z^h\}$ lies in K_s for all s. Therefore $\{z^h\}$ is a competitive allocation of E_1 by theorem 4, contradicting the inference from the definition of the sequence $\{w^h\}_r$ that $\{z^h\}$ lies at least ε from the set of competitive allocations of E_1. Thus no such sequence can exist, and it must be that K_r converges to W as $r \to \infty$. ∎

The Pareto optimum is an allocation for which the coalition of the whole is not an improving coalition, even in a weak sense. No other improving coalitions are considered, and in particular, not the coalitions composed of single consumers. On the other hand the competitive equilibrium does not allow any improving coalition. Moreover competitive equilibrium requires, for some price vector, that each consumer's allocation have zero value. In a sense the core is an intermediate notion, especially if we take a weaker definition of an improving coalition and thus a stronger definition of the core. This definition would serve for the proof of theorem 4 with no major change but not for the proof of theorem 5, which uses the fact that each consumer's allocation is dominated in an improvement. Let a *weakly improving coalition* B for an allocation $\{x^h\}$ be a coalition for which there is an allocation $\{z^h\}$ with $\sum_{h \in B} z^h = \sum_{h \in B} x^h$ such that $x^h \notin P^h(z^h)$ for any $h \in B$ and $z^h \in P^h(x^h)$ for some $h \in B$. Then the *strong core* is the set of allocations for which there is no weakly improving coalition. If an allocation is in the strong core, then for any coalition there is no allocation within its feasible set that is a Pareto improvement over its core allocation. The analogous relation holds between the ordinary core allocation and the *weak Pareto optimum*, defined as an allocation such that no reallocation can improve the position of every consumer. However, we will find that a slight strengthening of the irreducibility assumption, which we need for proving that the equal treatment core is not empty, will imply that the core and the strong core coincide. The set of competitive equilibrium allocations is the subset of the strong core in which the core allocations have zero value at a supporting price vector.

5.3   Nonemptiness of the Core

It has been proved that every competitive allocation is in the core. However, it may be of interest to show that the existence of an allocation in the core may be proved independently of the existence of equilibrium allocations. Indeed, we will find in the next section that the existence of a core allocation can be used together with the result of the last section to prove the existence of a competitive equilibrium. The economy is defined, as before, by means of consumption sets $C^h \subset \mathbf{R}^n$ and strict preference correspondences P^h, for $h = 1, \cdots, H$, and a production set Y. The graph of P^h is $G^h = \{(x, y) \mid y \in P^h(x)\}$. Compared with assumptions 5', 6', 7', 8, 9, and 10, the assumptions are strengthened in some respects and weakened in others. They are

ASSUMPTION 11 $C^h \neq \emptyset$ is convex, closed, and bounded below for all h.

ASSUMPTION 12   For all h, P^h is convex valued. *Also G^h is open relative to $C^h \times C^h$.*

ASSUMPTION 13 Y is a closed convex cone with vertex at the origin.

ASSUMPTION 14 $Y \cap \mathbf{R}^n_+ = \{0\}$.

ASSUMPTION 15 $Y \cap C^h$ is not empty for any h.

It will be noted that P^h is now assumed to be convex valued and to have an open graph. Assuming an open graph is slightly stronger than assuming P^h to be open valued and to have open lower sections. Note that P^h was not assumed to be convex valued in theorem 5 where convergence of the equal treatment core to the set of competitive equilibria for E_1 was proved. Convexity is also critical for the existence of competitive equilibrium, as we will find. On the other hand, irreducibility, interiority, and R^h the closure of P^h are not needed here. These assumptions are important for the existence of a competitive equilibrium but not for the existence of a point in the core.

We now establish some properties of the set of feasible allocations F_S, where $S \subset \{1, \cdots, H\}$. Let $x_S = (x_S^h)_{h \in S}$. $F_S = \{(x_S^h)_{h \in S} \mid x_S^h \in C^h$ for all $h \in S$ and $\sum_{h \in S} x_S^h \in Y\}$.

LEMMA 8 F_S is nonempty, compact, and convex.

Proof Assumption 15 and the fact that Y is a cone imply that F_S is not empty. F_S is compact by the argument of the proof of lemma 7. Convexity of F_S follows from the convexity of the C^h and Y.   ∎

Let $\mathscr{B}$ be a nonempty family of subsets of $\{1, \cdots, H\}$. Define $\mathscr{B}_h = \{S \in \mathscr{B} \mid h \in S\}$. A family $\mathscr{B}$ is *balanced* if there exist nonnegative weights $\{\lambda_S\}$ with $\sum_{S \in \mathscr{B}_h} \lambda_S = 1$ for all h. Let $I = \{1, \cdots, H\}$. The economy is said to be *0-balanced* if for any balanced family $\mathscr{B}$ with balancing weights $\{\lambda_S\}$, which satisfies $x_S \in F_S$ for all $S \in \mathscr{B}$, it follows that $x_I \in F_I$ where $x_I^h = \sum_{S \in \mathscr{B}_h} \lambda_S x_S^h$. It is as though λ_S were the proportion of each member's time devoted to the coalition S.

LEMMA 9   *The economy E_1 is 0-balanced.*

Proof To show that x_I is feasible, it is necessary and sufficient to show that $x_I^h \in C^h$ for all h and $\sum_{h \in S} x_I^h \in Y$. Since $x_S^h \in C^h$ for each $S \in \mathscr{B}_h$ by the feasibility of x_S and x_I^h is a convex combination of the x_S^h for $S \in \mathscr{B}_h$, x_I^h lies in C^h by the convexity of C^h. On the other hand, since Y is a cone with vertex at the origin, $\sum_{h \in S} x_S^h \in Y$ implies that $\sum_{h \in S} \lambda_S x_S^h \in Y$ and $\sum_{S \in \mathscr{B}} \sum_{h \in S} \lambda_S x_S^h \in Y$. But, since it is the same whether the sum proceeds first over the members of a coalition and then over coalitions, or over coalitions to which each person belongs and then over all persons, we have

$$\sum_{S \in \mathscr{B}} \sum_{h \in S} \lambda_S x_S^h = \sum_{h \in I} \sum_{S \in \mathscr{B}_h} \lambda_S x_S^h = \sum_{h \in I} x_I^h.$$

This completes the proof.   ∎

The following theorem is from Border (1985). It is rephrased to accord with our terminology

THEOREM (Border) *Let E be an economy given by the list $(C^1, \cdots, C^H, P^1, \cdots, P^H, Y)$ satisfying*

i. For each $h = 1, \cdots, H$, C^h is a nonempty convex subset of R^n.

ii. For any $S \subset I$, F_S is a nonempty compact subset of $\prod_{h \in S} C^h$.

iii. For each h, (a) P^h has an open graph relative to $C^h \times C^h$, (b) $x \notin P^h(x)$, (c) P^h is convex valued (but possibly empty).

iv. E is 0-balanced.

Then the core of E is not empty.

We may now assert

THEOREM 6   *Under assumptions 11 through 15 the economy E has a nonempty core.*

Proof Condition i in Border's theorem is contained in assumption 11. Lemma 8 implies condition ii. Condition iii is implied by assumption 12 and the definition of P^h. Condition iv is provided by lemma 9. Applying Border's theorem, the conclusion follows. ∎

5.4   The Existence of Competitive Equilibrium

We have proved the core not to be empty under assumptions that are weaker in some respects and stronger in other respects than the assumptions used to show that allocations that remain in the equal treatment cores of replicated economies are competitive allocations. We also found that the equal treatment core converges to the set of competitive allocations. This suggests that if the nonemptiness of the core can be extended to the equal treatment core, it will be possible to prove that a competitive equilibrium exists by using the strongest form of each assumption from earlier sections. However, to prove that the equal treatment core is not empty, it is necessary to strengthen the irreducibility assumption, although no irreducibility assumption was needed to prove the core nonempty.

A vector x^h is said to be a *worst element of C^h* if $y \in R^h(x^h)$ for all $y \in C^h$. We will say that the economy is *strongly irreducible* if it is irreducible, and whenever I_1, I_2 is a nontrivial partition of $\{1, \cdots, H\}$ and $x_{I_1} + x_{I_2} \in Y$ where x^h is not a worst element of C^h for any $h \in I_2$, there are $z_{I_1} + z_{I_2} \in Y$ with $z^h \mathscr{P}^h x^h$ for $h \in I_1$ and $z^h \in C^h$ for $h \in I_2$.

This concept differs from ordinary irreduciblility in that the net trade is required to be feasible. That is, z_{I_2} lies in C_{I_2} while previously $x_{I_2} + \alpha w$ need not lie in C_{I_2}. The assumptions of classical demand theory imply strong irreducibility. Another version of the irreducibility concept was introduced in Boyd and McKenzie (1993).

By theorem 5, we have found that under weak conditions the equal treatment core K_r converges to the set of competitive equilibria W of E_1. Bounding and closing C^h and closing Y, and introducing convexity of preferences with an open graph, it was possible to prove that the core of E_r is not empty. This result did not require irreducibility. However, in order to obtain the existence of competitive equilibrium, we will require stronger forms of assumptions 12 and 10.

ASSUMPTION $12'$ For all h, P^h is convex valued *and transitive. For all* $x \in C^h$, $P^h(x) \neq \emptyset$ *and $R^h(x)$ is the closure of $P^h(x)$. G^h is open* relative to $C^h \times C^h$.

ASSUMPTION $10'$ The economy is *strongly irreducible.*

Recall that x is *indifferent* with y, $x \mathscr{I}^h y$, if $x \mathscr{R}^h y$ and $y \mathscr{R}^h x$ where $z \mathscr{R}^h w$ means not $w \mathscr{P}^h z$. We also define $I^h(x) = \{y \mid y \mathscr{I}^h x\}$. Then $y \in I^h(x)$ means $x \notin P^h(y)$ and $y \notin P^h(x)$. Strong irreducibility and transitivity of preference are used to imply that replicates of a given consumer receive allocations which are indifferent. This result is needed to show that K_r is not empty if the core of E_r is not empty.

In order to prove K_r not empty we will need a further lemma.

LEMMA 10   *Under assumptions 11, $12'$, 13, and $10'$, suppose that $\{x^{hk}\}_r$, $h = 1, \cdots, H$, and $k = 1, \cdots, r$, is an allocation in the core of E_r. Then for any h, $x^{hk} \mathscr{I}^h x^{hk'}$ holds for all k and k'.*

Proof   Let the allocation $\{x^{hs}\}_r$ where $h = 1, \cdots, H$ and $s = 1, \cdots, r$ lie in the core for the economy E_r. I claim that $x^{hs} \mathscr{I}^h x^{ht}$ for all h, s, t. Suppose not. Consider a replica with index $ht(h)$, for each original consumer with index h, where $ht(h)$ satisfies $x^{hs} \mathscr{R}^h x^{ht(h)}$ for all $ks = 1, \cdots, r$. That is, $ht(h)$ has an allocation that is no better, and perhaps is poorer, than the allocation of any other of the r replicas of h. The existence of $ht(h)$ is guaranteed by assumption $12'$ the transitivity of preference, and it is for this reason that transitivity is introduced. Consider the coalition $B = \{1t(1), \cdots, Ht(H)\}$ and the allocation to the member of B with index $ht(h)$ of $(1/r)\sum_{h=1}^{r} x^{hs} = x^{h}$. Since $R^{h}(x)$ is the closure of $P^{h}(x)$ by assumption 12', R^{h} is convex valued. Therefore for each h we have $x^{h}\mathscr{R}^{h}x^{ht(h)}$. Also, if $x^{ih}\mathscr{P}^{i}x^{it(i)}$ for some i, s, then x^{i} is a convex combination involving a relative interior point of $R^{i}(x^{it(i)})$, which is interior relative to C^{h}, so x^{i} cannot lie on the boundary of $R^{i}(x^{it(i)})$ relative to C^{h}. Therefore $x^{i}\mathscr{P}^{i}x^{it(i)}$ holds.

Now $\sum_{h=1}^{H} x^{h} = (1/r)\sum_{s=1}^{r}\sum_{h=1}^{H} x^{hs}$ and $(1/r)\sum_{s=1}^{r}\sum_{h=1}^{H} x^{hs} \in Y$ since $\{x^{hs}\}_{r}$ is feasible and Y is a cone. Thus $\{x^{h}\}_{1}$ is a feasible allocation. By strong irreducibility and convexity we will see that it is possible to spread the gain received by i from the allocation $\{x^{h}\}_{1}$ to all h. Let $S_{1} = \{h \mid h \neq i\}$ and $S_{2} = \{i\}$. Since x^{i} is not a worst element of C^{i}, strong irreducibility implies that there is a feasible allocation $\{z^{h}\}$ with $z^{h}\mathscr{P}^{h}x^{h}$ for $h \in S_{1}$. Take the convex combination $\{\lambda x^{h} + (1 - \lambda)z^{h}\}$ for $0 \leq \lambda < 1$. This is a feasible allocation, preferred by all $h \in S_{1}$ to $\{x^{h}\}$ and, since $x^{i}\mathscr{P}^{i}x^{it(i)}$, for λ sufficiently close to 1, also preferred by i. Thus B is an improving coalition, and $\{x^{hs}\}_{r}$ is not an allocation in the core of E_{r} contrary to the assumption. Therefore $x^{hs}\mathscr{I}^{h}x^{hs'}$ must hold for all s, s'. ∎

Note that lemma 10 implies that the weak and strong cores coincide under strong irreducibility.

LEMMA 11   *Under the assumptions of lemma 10 the equal treatment core K_{r} of E_{r} is nonempty if the core of E_{r} is nonempty.*

Proof According to lemma 10, for any allocation in the core the allocations received by the replicas of a given h in the original economy are indifferent. Then, by the convex valuedness of the relation $\mathscr{R}^{h}$, the equal treatment allocation in which each replica of h receives x^{h}, as defined in the proof of lemma 10, satisfies $x^{h}R^{h}x^{hs}$ for all h, s. Thus, if there is no improving coalition for the allocation $\{x^{hs}\}_{r}$, there is also no improving coalition for the allocation $\{y^{hs}\}_{r}$ in which $y^{hs} = x^{h}$ for all h, s. Therefore $\{y^{hs}\}_{r}$ is in the core of E_{r}. ∎

LEMMA 12   *Under assumptions 11, 13, 14, 15, 10', and 12', the equal treatment core K_{r} of E_{r} is not empty.*

Proof By theorem 6, the core of E_{r} is not empty. By lemma 11, this implies that the equal treatment core K_{r} of E_{r} is not empty. ∎

We may now prove

THEOREM 7   *Under assumptions 9, 11, 13, 14, 10', and 12' the economy E_1 has a competitive equilibrium, and $K = W$.*

Proof   The assumptions imply the assumptions of section 5.3, so by theorem 6, the core of E_r is not empty for any r. Since the assumptions also imply the assumptions of lemma 12, the set of equal treatment allocations in the core is not empty for any E_r. From the proof of theorem 5 the set K_r is closed. Also the K_r are nested by lemma 5. Therefore $K = \bigcap_{r=1}^{\infty} K_r$ is not empty. But the assumptions imply the assumptions of section 5.2, so by theorem 4, K is included in the set of competitive allocations for E_1. Indeed, by theorem 5, the equal treatment core of E_r converges to the set of competitive allocations of E_1 as $r \to \infty$, so K is precisely the set of competitive allocations. Finally the proof of theorem 4 provides a price vector p that supports any allocations $\tilde{x} \in K$ in a competitive equilibrium given by $(p, y, \tilde{x})$ where $y = \sum_{h=1}^{H} x^h$.   ∎

Once transitivity is introduced, the Scarf theorem (1967) becomes available for proving that the core is not empty, so it would be enough to stay with open lower sections and open values. On the other hand, it is use of the weak core that requires strong irreducibility and convexity of $R^h(x)$. The weak core is needed in the proof that the equal treatment core K_r is closed so that K is not empty. However, we know from the theorem of Gale and Mas-Colell (1975) that existence of competitive equilibrium can be proved without these assumptions and without transitivity. Indeed, we know from Moore (1975) and McKenzie (1981) that individual survival in assumption 15 is also not needed for proving the existence of competitive equilibrium. The assumption of an open graph for the preference correspondence can be further weakened to lower semicontinuity of the preference correspondence (see McKenzie 1981). The line of proof that we have followed is that used by Boyd and McKenzie (1993) to prove a theorem for the case of an infinite number of goods, except that they need to assume transitivity at the earlier stage where it is proved that the core is not empty. This is to allow the use of the Scarf theorem for a nonempty core, which is proved in the utility space, rather than the Border theorem, which is proved in the goods space. The Border proof makes essential use of the finite dimensionality of the goods space. On the other hand, his assumption that P^h has an open graph can be relaxed to lower semicontinuity of P^h. Whether the line of proof we have used here for the finite case can be improved to match the results of Gale and Mas-Colell, and McKenzie, is an open question so far as I know.

A further strengthening of the assumptions can reduce the core of E_r to the equal treatment core. Assume that preferences are strictly convex in the sense that $x \mathscr{I}^h y$ and $z = \alpha x + (1 - \alpha)y$, for $x, y \in C^h$ and $0 < \alpha < 1$ implies $z \mathscr{P}^h x$. Then we may prove a result used by Debreu and Scarf (1963).

LEMMA 13 *Assume that $\mathscr{P}^h$ is strictly convex, $R^h(x^h)$ is the closure of $P^h(x^h)$ when $\tilde{x}$ is feasible, and E_1 is strongly irreducible. Then all allocations in the core of E_r are equal treatment allocations.*

Proof The conclusion of the lemma is equivalent to the statement that an allocation in the core of E_r has $x^{hs} = x^{hs'}$ for all $s, s' = 1, \cdots, r$. Suppose not. For any h, let $\bar{x}^h = x^{ht(h)}$ where $x^{hs} \mathscr{R}^h x^{ht(h)}$ for all s. Then by strict convexity of preference $(1/r) \sum_{s=1}^{r} x^{hs} \mathscr{R}^h \bar{x}^h$ for $h = 1, \cdots, H$ with $\mathscr{P}^h$ in place of $\mathscr{R}^h$ for at least one h. Strong irreducibility implies that $\mathscr{P}^h$ can be realized for all h. But $\sum_{h=1}^{H} (1/r) \sum_{s=1}^{r} x^{hs} \in Y$. Thus $B = \{t(1), \cdots, t(H)\}$ is an improving coalition, and $\{x^{hs}\}_r$ is not in the core of E_r contrary to assumption. This implies that $x^{hs} = x^{hs'}$ for all $s, s' = 1, \cdots, r$, holds, and all allocations in the core of E_r are equal treatment allocations. ∎

6 Existence and Uniqueness of Competitive Equilibrium

The idea of a competitive equilibrium was introduced in chapter 2 on stability. A natural question is whether an equilibrium can be expected to exist under reasonable assumptions. The global stability theorems of chapter 2 imply the existence and uniqueness of equilibrium in the context of an exchange economy under assumptions that include differentiability and gross substitutes. This is a rather narrow setting for existence and, as the appendix at the end of the chapter will show, existence in the presence of differentiability and a boundary condition can be proved more easily without establishing global stability. Existence is also implicit in chapter 3 for linear economies with a single nonproduced factor. The assumptions used in chapter 4 to derive comparative static results imply existence and local uniqueness. However, we are able to obtain local uniqueness in a generic sense under much more general conditions. Also, in the discussion of Pareto optimality in chapter 5, a type of existence result is contained in the second welfare theorem. That is, under certain assumptions rather similar to the ones that will be used in this chapter, there is a competitive equilibrium corresponding to an arbitrary Pareto optimum. Then, when Pareto optima exist for every distribution of welfare, a way is provided for the proof that an equilibrium exists for an arbitrary distribution of initial wealth. Such an approach was used by Negishi (1960) and was developed further by Arrow and Hahn (1971). Moreover in the setting of chapter 5 assumptions were given under which the equal treatment core was found not to be empty. Since points that remain in the equal treatment cores of replicated economies converge to competitive equilibria, this provides another route to a proof of existence.

A proof of existence of equilibrium is useful for showing that the model may be capable of application. An existence proof also forces the theorist to examine his assumptions and thus recognize ways in which the assumptions are unrealistic. Then he may seek weaker assumptions in the hope of achieving a model that is more relevant to the problems addressed by empirical workers and policy makers. Finally the existence proofs have promoted the attainment of consistency in economic theory by the use of the axiomatic method.

6.1 Existence in an Economy of Activities

An economy of activities was described in section 2.8. The salient feature of that model is that the production side is described by closed convex cones $Y^a \subset \mathbf{R}^n$, $a = 1, \cdots, A$, each providing the basis for an industry. In the discussion of existence we will drop the assumption that $Y^a \supset R_-^n$. We need not assume free disposal in order to establish the existence of competitive equilibrium. However, we retain the assumption that $Y^a \cap \mathbf{R}_+^n = \{0\}$. That is, production of something from nothing is not permitted. Let $Y = \sum_{a=1}^A Y^a$. An economy may be given by a list $(Y, C^1, \cdots, C^H, P^1, \cdots, P^H)$ in which Y is the aggregate production set, $C^h \subset \mathbf{R}^n$ is the set of possible net trades of the hth consumer, and P^h is the strict preference correspondence of the hth consumer over this set. We also refer to the sets of possible net trades as the trading sets. The positive components of a trade represent quantities of goods received, and the negative components represent quantities of goods provided. Initial stocks are not introduced explicitly, but notice that the addition of stocks ω to the holdings of the hth consumer shifts his net trading set C^h by $-\omega$.

The assumptions on the production sector are

ASSUMPTION 1 $Y \subset \mathbf{R}^n$ is a closed, convex cone with vertex at the origin.

ASSUMPTION 2 $Y \cap \mathbf{R}_+^n = \{0\}$. int $Y \neq \emptyset$.

Neither of these assumptions is implied by the conditions imposed on the production sets for processes in chapter 2. In the case of assumption 1 this is because the sum of closed convex cones need not be closed. In three dimensions consider adding a half line L from the origin to a smooth pointed cone with vertex at the origin that has a nonempty interior and contains $-L$ in its boundary. The sum will be an open half space together with the line $L \cup -L$. Notice that the first part of assumption 2 is not a substantive assumption, since any goods producible from nothing in unlimited amounts would be free and could be ignored. The second part is quite strong, but it will be possible to relax the interiority assumption.

On the side of consumers the assumptions are extensions of those of chapters 1 and 5 with a few important differences. In chapter 1, convexity assumptions on the consumer sets C^h and on the preference correspondences were not needed for the direct approach to demand theory, but they will be needed for existence. In chapter 5, convexity assumptions were needed, but closedness was not assumed either for production or consumer sets until we addressed the question of the convergence of the core to the set of competitive equilibria. However, these properties are crucial for the proof of existence of competitive equilibrium. The assumptions on trading sets are

ASSUMPTION 3   The sets C^h of possible net trades, $h = 1, \cdots, H$, are convex, closed, and bounded below.

A binary *strict preference relation* $\mathscr{P}^h$ is defined on C^h. Intuitively $x\mathscr{P}^hy$ means x is strictly preferred to y by the hth consumer. The *preference relation* $\mathscr{R}^h$ is defined by $x\mathscr{R}^hy$ if not $y\mathscr{P}^hx$. The correspondences R^h and P^h are defined in terms of $\mathscr{R}^h$ and $\mathscr{P}^h$ as in chapter 1. The graph of the correspondence P^h is the set of elements (x, y) in $C^h \times C^h$ such that $y \in P^h(x)$.

ASSUMPTION 4   For all h the correspondence P^h is convex and open valued relative to C^h with open lower sections. P^h is irreflexive and transitive, and $R^h(x)$ is the closure of $P^h(x)$ for all $x \in C^h$ for which $P^h(x) \neq \emptyset$.

In addition assumptions are made on relations between the aggregate production set Y and the consumer sets C^h. Let $C = \sum_{h=1}^{H} C^h$. The *feasible set* is $F = C \cap Y$.

ASSUMPTION 5   If $x \in F$, there is $z^h \in C^h$ for each h such that $z^h\mathscr{P}^hx^h$.

ASSUMPTION 6 $C^h \cap \operatorname{int} Y \neq \emptyset$ for any h.

Assumption 5 implies insatiability within the feasible set. This assumption was also used for the first theorem on Pareto optimality. Assumption 6 is a stronger version of assumption 5.9, which was used for the proof that an allocation in the core of an economy, replicated indefinitely often, is a competitive equilibrium. It will be possible to weaken this assumption using the concept of an irreducible economy.

LEMMA 1   *F is bounded.*

Proof   Suppose that there is $x^s \in F$ and that $|x^s| \to \infty$, $s = 1, 2, \cdots$. Consider $y^s = x^s/|x^s|$. Since y^s belongs to the unit sphere which is compact, there is a point of accumulation y. Since C^h is bounded below by assumption 3, so is C and thus F. Therefore $y \geq 0$ and $\neq 0$. But Y closed implies $y \in Y$, contradicting assumption 2. Thus no such sequence x^s exists.   ∎

Lemma 1 has the following

COROLLARY   *Over the set of feasible x the consumer trade x^h remains in a bounded region for all h.*

Proof It follows from lemma 1 that $\sum_{h=1}^{H} x^h = x \in F$ implies that $|x| < \xi$ for some real number ξ. Let $\xi' < 0$ be a lower bound on x_i^h for $x^h \in C^h$ for all h and i. Then $\xi' \le x_i^h \le \xi - (H-1)\xi'$ for all h. ∎

LEMMA 2 *Let x satisfy $px \le 0$ and $|x| < \xi$. If there is $z \in P^h(x)$ with $pz \le 0$, there is $w \in P^h(x)$ where $|w| < \xi$ and $pw \le 0$.*

Proof Consider $w = \alpha x + (1 - \alpha)z$, $0 \le \alpha \le 1$. We have $pw \le 0$ and, for α near 1, $|w| < \xi$. Since, by assumption 4, $P^h(x)$ is an open convex set relative to C^h, and $z \in P^h(x)$ while x lies in the boundary of $P^h(x)$, it follows that $w \in P^h(x)$ (see Fenchel 1953, p. 40; Rockafellar 1970, p. 155). ∎

Lemma 2 implies that the demand condition is not affected by sufficiently large bounds on the sets of possible net trades. Therefore we may impose bounds on the sets of possible net trades without affecting the set of competitive equilibria. We introduce the

AUXILIARY ASSUMPTION The sets of possible net trades C^h are bounded.

Let $Y^* = \{p \mid p \in \mathbf{R}^n$ and $py \le 0$ for all $y \in Y\}$. Y^* is the dual cone of Y. The *individual demand correspondence* $f^h(p)$ is defined for $p \in Y^*$, $p \ne 0$, by

$$f^h(p) = \{x \mid x \in C^h, px \le 0, \text{ and } z\mathscr{P}^h x \text{ implies } pz > 0\}.$$

This definition is equivalent to the definition given in section 1 of chapter 1 in the case where $m = 0$. The *market demand correspondence* is $f(p) = \sum_{h=1}^{H} f^h(p)$.

In this setting a *competitive equilibrium* is a list $(p, y, x^1, \cdots, x^H)$ which satisfies the following conditions

I. $x^h \in f^h(p)$ for all h.

II. $y \in Y$ and $pz > py = 0$ implies $z \notin Y$.

III. $y = \sum_{h=1}^{H} x^h$.

The price vector is p. The output of the production sector is y. And x^h is the net trade of the hth consumer. The first condition is the demand condition that every consumer receives a commodity bundle that he chooses from the budget set given by p. The second condition is the profit condition that no process can earn positive profit and processes in use earn 0 profit. The third condition is the balance condition that demand equals supply.

Let $\bar{y}$ be an interior point of Y. An interior point exists by assumption 6. Define $S = \{p \mid p \in Y^* \text{ and } p\bar{y} = -1\}$.

LEMMA 3   *S is convex and compact.*

Proof   Convexity and closedness are obvious. To show that S is bounded, suppose, on the contrary, that there is an unbounded sequence p^s, $s = 1, 2, \cdots$, contained in S. Consider the sequence $q^s = p^s/|p^s|$. The sequence q^s lies on the unit sphere, which is a compact set. Therefore there is a point of accumulation $q \in Y^*$, $q \neq 0$. We may assume that $q^s \to q$. But $q^s\bar{y} = -1/|p^s| \to 0$ as $s \to \infty$, so $q\bar{y} = 0$. This contradicts $\bar{y} \in \text{int } Y$. Thus no such sequence p^s can exist in S and S is bounded.   ∎

LEMMA 4   *The individual demand correspondence $f^h(p)$ is upper semicontinuous and convex valued. Moreover $px \leq 0$ for $x \in f(p)$, and if $f(p) \cap Y \neq \emptyset$, $px = 0$.*

Proof   Since the range of f^h is contained in a compact set by the Auxiliary Assumption, upper semicontinuity means that $p^s \to p$ and $x^s \to x$, where $x^s \in f^h(p^s)$, $s = 1, 2, \cdots$, implies $x \in f^h(p)$ (Berge 1963, p. 112). Suppose that such a sequence is given. Let z be an arbitrary element of $H^h(p) = \{z \in C^h \mid pz \leq 0\}$. Assumption 6 provides a cheaper point. Then lemma 2.3 implies that the budget set $H^h(p)$ is lower semicontinuous. Thus there is a sequence $z^s \to z$ with $p^s z^s \leq 0$. It follows from the definition of $f^h(p^s)$ that $z^s \mathscr{P}^h x^s$ does not hold. That is, $x^s \mathscr{R}^h z^s$ holds for all s. Suppose $z \mathscr{P}^h x$ held. Then since, by assumption 4, $P^h(x)$ is open and $x \in$ boundary $P^h(x)$, any $y = \alpha x + (1 - \alpha)z$, $0 < \alpha \leq 1$, is preferred to x. Moreover, since the lower set of z under P^h is open, for α near 1, $z \in P^h(y)$. Then we have for large s and α near 1 that $y \mathscr{P}^h x^s$ and $z^s \mathscr{P}^h y$, so by transitivity $z^s \mathscr{P}^h x^s$. This is a contradiction. Thus we conclude that $z \mathscr{P}^h x$ cannot hold. Since z is an arbitrary element of the budget set, it follows that $x \in f^h(p)$ by definition of f^h. Therefore $f^h(p)$ is upper semicontinuous.

Convexity follows immediately from the fact that $\mathscr{R}^h$ and $\mathscr{P}^h$ are convex valued. It is clear from the definition of f that $px \leq 0$ for $x \in f(p)$. If $f(p) \cap Y \neq \emptyset$, there is $y \in P^h(x)$ for all $x \in f^h(p)$ by assumption 5. Since $P^h(x)$ is the interior of $R^h(x)$ relative to C^h by assumption 4, there is $z \in P^h(x)$ in every neighborhood of $x \in f^h(p)$. From the definition of $f^h(p)$ this implies that $px = 0$ for $x \in f(p)$ which is Walras' Law.   ∎

The proof that a competitive equilibrium exists will be made by showing that a mapping F of $S \times C$ into the set of convex subsets of $S \times C$ has a fixed point that is an equilibrium. Let $\pi(x)$ be the maximum nonnegative number π such that $\pi x + (1 - \pi)\bar{y} \in Y$, where $x \in C$ and $\bar{y} \in$ int Y. Define the map $h : C \to$ boundary Y by $h(x) = \pi(x)x + (1 - \pi(x))\bar{y}$. We must show that $\bar{y}$ can be chosen so that the number $\pi(x)$ exists for all $x \in C$ and $h(x)$ is well defined.

LEMMA 5   *It is possible to choose $\bar{y}$ so that the function $h(x)$ is well defined for all $x \in C$.*

Proof   Let $\bar{y} = \alpha z$ for $z \in$ int Y. Suppose that $x \in C$ is given, and no matter how large α is chosen, the number π is unbounded. Then $(\alpha(1 - \pi)/\pi)z + x \in Y$ for all large π. Let $w(\alpha, \pi) = (\alpha(1 - \pi)/\pi)z + x$. As $\pi \to \infty$, $w(\alpha, \pi) \to w(\alpha) = -\alpha z + x$, which lies in Y since Y is closed. Also $w(\alpha)/\alpha = -z + (x/\alpha) \in Y$, and as $\alpha \to \infty$, $-z + (x/\alpha) \to -z$, which also lies in Y since Y is closed. Thus z and $-z$ are in Y, and since z is interior to Y, $Y = \mathbf{R}^n$ in contradiction to assumption 2. This shows that α may be chosen so that h is well defined for any given $x \in C$.

Suppose $w(\alpha, \pi) \notin Y$. Since Y is closed, $(\alpha(1 - \pi)/\pi)z + x' \notin Y$ will hold for any x' near enough to x. In other words $\pi(\alpha)$ exists for any x in a sufficiently small open neighborhood $U(x)$ of x, relative to C. Since C is compact by the Auxiliary Assumption, there is a finite set $\{x_i\}$, $i = 1, \cdots, N$, such that $\bigcup_{i=1}^{N} U(x_i) = C$. Therefore we may choose $\alpha = \max \alpha_i$, where $\pi(x)$ exists for $x \in U(x_i)$. For this α, $\pi(x)$ exists for all $x \in C$ and $h(x)$ is well defined.   ■

We will also need to establish the continuity of h over $x \in C$.

LEMMA 6   *h is continuous at x for $x \in C$.*

Proof   Consider $z^s \to z$, $s = 1, 2, \cdots$, and $y^s = h(z^s)$ where $z^s \in C$. Since C is closed $z \in C$. Suppose that y^s does not converge to $y = h(z)$. Let $y = \pi z + (1 - \pi)\bar{y}$. Let $y^s = \pi^s z^s + (1 - \pi^s)\bar{y}$. By the proof of lemma 5, for any $\varepsilon > 0$ we have $(\pi + \varepsilon)z^s + (1 - (\pi + \varepsilon))\bar{y} \notin Y$ for large s. Thus $\pi^s \le \pi + \varepsilon$ for large s. By compactness of the interval $[0, \pi + \varepsilon]$, there is a subsequence $\{\pi^s\}$ (retain notation) such that $\pi^s \to \pi'$. Let $y' = \pi'z + (1 - \pi')\bar{y}$. Since $\bar{y} \in$ int Y, π^s, π', and π are all greater than 0. Since π is maximal, $\pi' \le \pi$. Suppose $\pi' < \pi$. Solve the relation $y = \pi z + (1 - \pi)\bar{y}$ for z. Then substitute in the expression for y' to obtain $y' = \alpha y + (1 - \alpha)\bar{y}$,

$\alpha = \pi'/\pi$, $0 < \alpha < 1$. Since $\bar{y} \in \text{int } Y$, there is a neighborhood V of 0 such that $w \in \bar{y} + V$ implies that $w \in \text{int } Y$. Since $y \in Y$, all w' such that $w' \in \alpha y + (1 - \alpha)(\bar{y} + V)$ lie in Y. These are all w' such that $w' \in y' + (1 - \alpha)V$. Then $y' \in \text{int } Y$, and $y^s \in \text{int } Y$ for large s. This contradicts the definition of $y^s = h(z^s)$. Thus $\pi' = \pi$ and $y' = y$. ∎

Next define the correspondence g : boundary $Y \to$ subsets of S by

$$g(y) = \{p \mid p \in S \text{ and } py = 0\}.$$

LEMMA 7   *The correspondence g is upper semicontinuous.*

Proof Let y^s, $s = 1, 2, \cdots$, be a sequence lying in the boundary of Y and converging to $y \in$ boundary Y. Let $p^s \in g(y^s)$ and $p^s \to p$. Then $p^s \cdot y^s = 0$ and $p^s \in S$. Also $p \in S$, since S is closed. Since the inner product is continuous, $py = 0$. Thus $p \in g(y)$. Since S is compact by lemma 3, g is upper semicontinuous (Berge 1963, p. 112). ∎

We define the correspondence $F : S \times C \to$ subsets of $S \times C$ by

$$F(p, x) = ((g \circ h)(x), f(p)).$$

LEMMA 8   *The correspondence F is upper semicontinuous and convex valued.*

Proof The function h is continuous by lemma 6. The correspondence g is upper semicontinuous by lemma 7. Therefore $g \circ h$ is upper semicontinuous (Berge 1963, p. 113). The upper semicontinuity of the market demand correspondence f is given by lemma 4. Then F is upper semicontinuous, since both its components are upper semicontinuous (Berge 1963, p. 114).

To see that the correspondence $g \circ h$ is convex valued, first note that h is single valued. Also g is the intersection of the set of normals to a boundary point of Y, which is convex, and the set S, which is convex. Thus g is convex valued, and $g \circ h$ is convex valued. Lemma 4 implies that the demand function f is convex valued. Therefore F is convex valued. ∎

We may now prove the existence theorem (McKenzie 1959).

THEOREM 1   *Under the assumptions 1 through 6, the economy $\mathcal{E}_a = (Y, C^1, \cdots, C^H, P^1, \cdots, P^H)$ has a competitive equilibrium.*

Proof By lemma 8, the correspondence F is upper semicontinuous and convex valued. Moreover F maps the compact convex set $S \times C$ into the collection of convex subsets of $S \times C$. By the Kakutani fixed point theorem (Berge 1963, p. 174), there is a point $(p^*, x^*) \in F(p^*, x^*)$. Let $y^* = h(x^*)$. It will be shown that (p^*, x^*) corresponds to a competitive equilibrium $(p^*, y^*, x^{*1}, \cdots, x^{*H})$.

By the definition of $f(p^*)$, $x^* \in f(p^*)$ implies there is $x^{h*} \in f^h(p^*)$ such that $\sum_{h=1}^{H} x^{*H} = x^*$. Thus the demand condition, or condition I of competitive equilibrium, is met by this choice of x^{*h} for $h = 1, \cdots, H$. Moreover the definition of F implies $p^* \in (g \circ h)(x^*) = g(y^*)$. Therefore $p^*z > p^*y^* = 0$ implies $z \notin Y$ by definition of g. In other words, the profit condition, condition II of competitive equilibrium, is met.

The balance condition, condition III, remains to be proved. Consider

$$y^* = h(x^*) = \pi x^* + (1 - \pi)\bar{y}. \tag{1}$$

Multiplying by p^* gives $p^*y^* = \pi p^*x^* + (1 - \pi)p^*\bar{y}$. But $p^*y^* = 0$, so

$$\pi p^*x^* = (\pi - 1)p^*\bar{y}. \tag{2}$$

Suppose $\pi > 1$. Then (1) implies $x^* \in Y$. Therefore, by assumption 5, no consumer is satiated. Then $p^*x^* = 0$, which contradicts (2), since $\bar{y} \in \text{int } Y$. Then it must be that $\pi \leq 1$. This implies $p^*x^* \geq 0$. Since $x^* \in f(p^*)$, it follows from lemma 4 that $p^*x^* \leq 0$. Therefore $p^*x^* = 0$ and $\pi = 1$. From (1) it follows that $x^* = y^*$, and the balance condition, condition III of competitive equilibrium, is met. This completes the proof that $(p^*, y^*, x^{*1}, \cdots, x^{*H})$ is a competitive equilibrium for the economy $(Y, C^1, \cdots, C^H, P^1, \cdots, P^H)$ when the auxiliary assumption is made.

We must show that the equilibrium is preserved when the bounds on the sets C^h are removed. This will be true if $x^{*h} \in f^h(p^*)$ continues to hold. However, since the fixed point x^* is feasible, by the corollary to lemma 1 the bounds may be chosen large enough to insure that x^{*h} lies in C^h for each h. Suppose there is a point outside the bounds that is preferred to x^{*h}. Then it is implied by lemma 2 that there is a point within the bounds that is also preferred to x^{*h}. Since this contradicts the fact that $x^{*h} \in f^h(p^*)$ when the bounds are imposed, no such preferred point can exist. ∎

Figure 6.1 illustrates theorem 1.

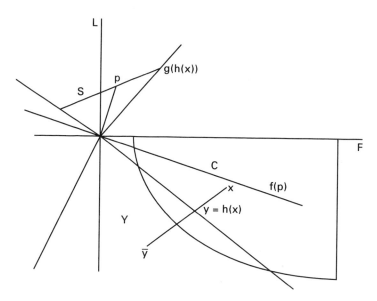

Figure 6.1
$F(p, x) = (f(p), g(h(x)))$, where f is the market demand function, h is a projection of x on the boundary of Y, and g is the set of prices normal to Y at y. F maps $S \times C$ into convex subsets. A fixed point of F is a competitive equilibrium.

6.2 Existence in an Economy of Firms

In the economy of activities the individual firms are suppressed. In effect the view is taken that the way in which ownership of the industrial processes and plants is organized is not important. Only the processes and plants themselves matter, and these are treated as sufficiently divisible relative to the scale of the market that the industrial activities may be regarded as divisible. In the present discussion we will take the diametrically opposed view that the firms are fundamental to production and each firm owns a technology or a possible production set Y^f that is given. The firm trades in the goods that are used in production or that issue from production but not in the things that determine the possible production set which it owns. The set of firms, $f = 1, \cdots, F$, is also given. This approach to the competitive economy was taken by Arrow and Debreu in their classic article (1954). It was adopted by them from Hicks' book *Value and Capital* (1939). Hicks justifies the approach by concentrating his attention on the single proprietorship. Arrow and Debreu, on the other hand, allow corporations which are held through stock ownership. However, they cannot allow the reorganization of ownership into a different set of corporations.

The method of proof of the existence of a competitive equilibrium, which extends the proof of Gale and Mas-Colell (1975), will also be different from the method of the last section. In proving existence for an economy of activities, a critical role was played by the demand correspondences. Their properties of upper semicontinuity and convex valuedness allow the application of the fixed point theorem. These properties were deduced from assumptions made on the individual preference orders such as transitivity. However, such a dependence on transitive preference orders is not essential. The demand correspondences themselves could be taken as basic without reference to the preference apparatus (McKenzie 1954). On the other hand, in the order of proof that we will now use, there is no explicit reference to demand correspondences. The proof depends directly on the preference correspondences. This facilitates the use of weaker assumptions on the preference relations, which are not assumed to be transitive. The method of proof requires the use of well-defined preference correspondences.

In the economy with firms there is a set of firms owning production sets $Y^f \subset \mathbf{R}^n$. The social production set is $Y = \sum_{f=1}^{F} Y^f$. The *asymptotic cone* of B is the cone $A(B)$ spanned by the set $\{y \mid y = \text{limit } x^s/|x^s|, s = 1, 2, \cdots$, where $x^s \in B$ and $|x^s| \to \infty\}$. If B is convex, then $A(B)$ is convex. Also, if B is a closed convex set that contains 0, $A(B) \subset B$. (See Fenchel 1953, p. 42; Rockafellar 1970, p. 61.) An equivalent definition may be found in Debreu (1959, p. 22.)

The assumptions for the production sector are

ASSUMPTION 7 $Y^f \subset \mathbf{R}^n$ is a closed convex set. Also $0 \in Y^f$.

ASSUMPTION 8 $Y \cap \mathbf{R}_+^n = \{0\}$, $\text{int } A(Y) \neq \emptyset$, and $A(Y) \cap -A(Y) = \{0\}$.

Let $A(Y)$ be the asymptotic cone of Y. $A(Y)^*$ is the dual cone of $A(Y)$. Since Y is closed, convex and contains 0, we have that $A(Y) \subset Y$. This follows from the fact that the set of points spanning $A(Y)$ is the closure of a convex set of points contained in Y. Therefore supremum $py < \infty$ for $y \in Y$ implies $p \in A(Y)^*$. However, the converse is not true.

For p on the boundary of $A(Y)^*$, it is possible that py is unbounded on Y. This is most easily seen by considering $Y \subset \mathbf{R}^2$ with $Y = \{y \mid y \le (l, \log(-l))\}$, where $l < 0$ is the input of labor. The asymptotic cone $A(Y)$ is the third quadrant and its dual cone is the first quadrant. Then $p = (0, 1) \in A(Y)^*$, but $py \to \infty$ along the efficiency frontier $y = (l, \log(-l))$ as $l \to -\infty$.

These assumptions for the production sector differ from those for the production sector of the economy of activities in several respects. Y is a sum of sets Y^j, and Y need not be a cone. Also Y does not contain an entire line. However, Y has an asymptotic cone with an interior, so there is still an analogy with the previous model. It may be that the asymptotic cone is the negative orthant, which recognizes the presence of free disposal, but free disposal is not assumed. Interiority assumptions are removed in the next section. Mathematically speaking, allowing Y^f to be a more general convex set is not a significant difference, since we do not prevent Y^f in the economy of firms from being a cone. Also by introducing an entrepreneurial factor for each firm, Y for the economy with firms can be converted into a cone without affecting the implications of the model (see McKenzie 1959, 1981). However, in economic terms, the viewpoints expressed by the models are quite different and may fairly be said to represent the divergence between the approaches to economics of Marshall and Walras. Marshall emphasized the role of the firm and Walras that of the industrial process.

LEMMA 9   *Y is closed.*

Proof   It is sufficient to prove that the sum of two production sets Y^1 and Y^2 is closed. Consider a sequence y^s, $s = 1, 2, \cdots$, such that $y^s = y^{1s} + y^{2s}$, where $y^{1s} \in Y^1$ and $y^{2s} \in Y^2$, and $y^s \to y$. Suppose that $y \notin Y$. If y^{1s} and y^{2s} are bounded, then a subsequence converges to $y^1 + y^2 = y \in Y$, since Y^1 and Y^2 are closed. Therefore y^{1s} or y^{2s} is unbounded. Since y^s converges, if one of y^{1s} and y^{2s} is unbounded, so is the other. Let $\bar{y}^{1s} = y^{1s}/|y^{2s}|$ and $\bar{y}^{2s} = y^{2s}/|y^{2s}|$. Along a subsequence (retain notation) $y^{2s} \to \infty$. Along a further subsequence (retain notation) $\bar{y}^{2s} \to \bar{y}^2 \in A(Y^2)$. Since $\bar{y}^2 \ne 0$ and $y/|y^{2s}| \to 0$, it follows that $\bar{y}^{1s} \to \bar{y}^1 \in A(Y^1)$, and $\bar{y}^1 + \bar{y}^2 = 0$. Since $0 \in Y^f$ by assumption 7, it follows that Y contains Y^1 and Y^2. Then $A(Y)$ contains $A(Y^1)$ and $A(Y^2)$, so the implication that $\bar{y}^1 + \bar{y}^2 = 0$ contradicts assumption 8. Therefore $y \in Y$ must hold and Y is closed. ∎

On the consumption side, as before, there are trading units called consumers who possess possible net trading sets C^h. They also have preference relations, which will be given by correspondences P^h representing
relations of strict preference. The assumptions made on the trading sets
are

ASSUMPTION 9   The sets of possible net trades $C^h \neq \emptyset$, $h = 1, \cdots, H$, are
convex and closed. Also for all h there is b^h such that $b^h < x^h$.

ASSUMPTION 10   The correspondence P^h maps C^h into the set of subsets
of C^h that are open relative to C^h. Also P^h has open lower sections relative to C^h and satisfies the condition $x \notin$ convex hull $P^h(x)$.

Assumption 9 is unchanged from assumption 3. However assumption
10 is weaker than assumption 4. In particular, the role of convexity is
weakened and transitivity of preference is dropped.

It is convenient to define an extension of the preference correspondence.
Define the correspondence $\hat{P}^h$ by

$$\hat{P}^h(x) = (\text{convex hull } (x, P^h(x)) \backslash \{x\}).$$

LEMMA 10   *The correspondence $\hat{P}^h$ is convex and open valued relative to
C^h, and lower semicontinous.*

Proof   Convex valuedness is obvious from the definition.

Since P^h has open lower sections relative to C^h by assumption 10, it is
lower semicontinous by lemma 1.17. Let $z = \lambda w + (1 - \lambda)x$, $0 < \lambda \leq 1$,
where $w \in P^h(x)$. Then $z \in \hat{P}^h(x)$. If $x^s \to x$ with $x^s \in C^h$, $s = 1, 2, \cdots$,
there is $w^s \to w$ with $w^s \in P^h(x^s)$ by lower semicontinuity of P^h. Then
$z^s \to z$ where $z^s = \lambda w^s + (1 - \lambda)x^s$ and $z^s \in \hat{P}^h(x^s)$. Thus $\hat{P}^h$ is lower
semicontinuous.   ∎

The definition of $\hat{P}^h$ implies that x lies in the boundary of $\hat{P}^h(x)$ if
$\hat{P}^h(x)$ is not empty. Let $z = \lambda w + (1 - \lambda)x$, $0 \leq \lambda \leq 1$. Then $pz > px$
implies that $pw > px$. Therefore, if x is among the points chosen from the
budget set by a consumer with the preference correspondence $\hat{P}^h$, then it
is among the points chosen from the same budget set by a consumer with
the preference correspondence P^h. This means that a competitive equilibrium found while using $\hat{P}^h$ is also valid for the original preferences given
by P^h.

Let $\bar{y}$ be a point interior to $A(Y)$. It exists by assumption 8. Define a normalized price set $S = \{p \mid p \in A(Y)^* \text{ and } p\bar{y} = -1\}$. The argument of lemma 3 applies, and S is convex and compact. For $p \in S$ the maximum profit of the fth firm, when it exists, is $\pi^f(p) = \max py$ for $y \in Y^f$. The hth consumer is paid the fraction α_h^f of the profit of the fth firm. The feasible set $F = C \cap Y$. Assumptions on the relations between the production and trading sectors are

ASSUMPTION 11   If $x \in F$, $x = \sum_{h=1}^{H} x^h$, $x^h \in C^h$, then $P^h(x^h) \neq \emptyset$ for any h.

ASSUMPTION 12 $C^h \cap \operatorname{int} A(Y) \neq \emptyset$ for any h.

Assumption 11 is the same as assumption 5 made for the economy of activities. Assumption 12 is quite strong as was assumption 6 used in the model of the economy of activities. It will be weakened in the next section when the notion of an irreducible economy is used.

LEMMA 11 F is nonempty, convex, and compact.

Proof $F = Y \cap C$ is not empty by assumption 12, since $x^h \in A(Y) \cap C^h$ for all h, and $A(Y)$ a cone implies that $\sum_{h=1}^{H} x^h \in C \cap Y$. F is convex, since Y and the C^h are convex. Also $|x^h| \to \infty$ for some h implies that $|\sum_{h=1}^{H} x^h| \to \infty$ by C^h bounded below, so the argument of lemma 1 applies and F is bounded. Y is closed by lemma 9. Then C^h closed for all h implies that F is compact.   ∎

Let $F^f = \{y^f \in Y^f \mid \text{there is } \bar{y} = \sum_{g \neq f} y^g \text{ and } \bar{y} + y^f \in F\}$. F^f is the set of feasible outputs for the fth firm. We prove

LEMMA 12 F^f is compact.

Proof   Suppose that F^f contains an unbounded sequence y^{fs}, $s = 1, 2, \cdots$. Let $y^s = y^{fs} + \bar{y}^s$. Since F is compact a subsequence (retain notation) $y^s \to y \in F$. Thus the sequence $\bar{y}^s$ provided by consumers and other firms is also unbounded. However $\bar{y}^s$ is bounded by the argument of lemma 11. This is a contradiction, so the sequence y^{fs} does not exist, or F^f is bounded. Since Y^f is closed, F^f is compact.   ∎

We introduce bounded production sets $\hat{Y}^f$ and $\hat{Y}$. By lemma 11, F is bounded above by a vector f. Since $0 \in Y^f$, it follows that f is also an upper bound on the feasible output of any subset of firms taken in isolation. Let $b = \sum_{h=1}^{H} b^h$. Then no single firm has a feasible output less than $b - f$. We define $\hat{Y}^f = \{y \mid y \in Y^f \text{ and } y > b - f\}$. By the argument of lemma 1, $\hat{Y}^f$ is also bounded above and thus compact, since it is closed. Also $\hat{Y}$ is defined by $\hat{Y} = \{y \mid y \in \sum_{f=1}^{F} \hat{Y}^f \text{ and } y > b\}$. Since $\hat{Y}^f \subset Y^f$ and $Y = \sum_{f=1}^{F} Y^f$, we have $\hat{Y} \subset Y$. Moreover $y^g \in Y^f$ and $y^g < b - f$ for some g implies $y = \sum_{f=1}^{F} y^f < b$, so $y \notin \hat{Y}$. Thus $y \in Y^f$ and $y > b$ if and only if $y \in \hat{Y}$. The upper bound on total production and the lower bounds on consumption sets allow us to introduce upper bounds $f - b$ on the consumption sets $\hat{C}^h$, that is, $\hat{C}^h = \{x \mid x \in C^h \text{ and } x < f - b\}$.

Let the income function $m^h(p) = \sum_{f=1}^{F} \alpha_h^f \pi^f(p)$, where $\sum_{h=1}^{H} \alpha_h^f = 1$, $\alpha_h^f \geq 0$. The number α_h^f represents the ownership share of household h in firm f. Let $m(p) = \sum_{h=1}^{H} m^h(p)$, and $\pi(p) = \sum_{f=1}^{F} \pi^f(p)$. Then it is clear that $m(p) = \pi(p)$.

LEMMA 13   *Consider the economy with production sets $\hat{Y}^f$ and $\hat{Y}$. The profit function π^f is continuous over S for all f, and thus the income function m^h is continuous over S for all h.*

Proof   Since π^f is a support function for $\hat{Y}^f$, it is convex and thus continuous over the interior of its domain. However, the compactness of $\hat{Y}^f$ implies that the domain of π^f is $\mathbf{R}^n$, which contains S in its interior. Since m^h is a linear combination of the π^f, it is also continuous over $\mathbf{R}^n$ and thus over S.   ∎

For $p \in S$ we define the *open budget correspondence* Γ^h by

$$\Gamma^h(p) = \{x \mid x \in \hat{C}^h \text{ and } px < m^h(p)\}.$$

The open budget correspondence Γ^h replaces the weak inequality in the definition of H^h in chapter 2 with a strict inequality.

LEMMA 14   *The budget correspondence Γ^h is open valued on S relative to $\hat{C}_h$, convex valued and lower semicontinuous. Moreover H^h is lower semicontinuous.*

Proof   That $\Gamma^h(p)$ is open in $\hat{C}^h$ and convex valued is clear from the definition. Assumption 12 guarantees that $\Gamma^h(p) \neq \emptyset$ for any $p \in S$. The proof of lower semicontinuity for H^h is virtually identical to the proof of lemma 2.3. The income function $m^h(p)$ is substituted for the wealth function $p\omega^h$. Since the income function m^h is continuous by lemma 13, the argument goes through as before.

To see that Γ^h is lower semicontinous, take an arbitrary point y in $\Gamma^h(p)$, and hence in interior $H^h(p)$ relative to $\hat{C}^h$. Let U be any open neighborhood of y relative to $\hat{C}^h$. Then, by lower semicontinuity of H^h, there is a neighborhood V of p relative to S such that $p' \in V$ implies $H^h(p') \cap U \neq \emptyset$ (Berge 1963, p. 109). $H^h(p')$ has an interior relative to $\hat{C}^h$ since assumption 12 provides a cheaper point. Let $y' \in \text{int } H^h(p')$. Then $y' \in \Gamma^h(p')$. Also U is open relative to $\hat{C}^h$. Therefore $H^h(p') \cap U \neq \emptyset$ implies $\Gamma^h(p') \cap U \neq \emptyset$, or $p' \in V$ implies $\Gamma^h(p') \cap U \neq \emptyset$. Since y and p are arbitrarily chosen Γ^h is lower semicontinuous. ∎

In the present setting a *competitive equilibrium* $(p, y^1, \cdots, y^F x^1, \cdots, x^H)$ may be characterized by the conditions

I. $px^h \leq m^h(p)$, and $z \in P^h(x^h)$ implies $pz > m^h(p)$ for all h.

II. $y^f \in Y^f$ and $pz > py^f$ implies $z \notin Y^f$ for all f.

III. $y = \sum_{f=1}^{F} y^f = x = \sum_{h=1}^{H} x^h$.

I is the demand condition. II is the profit condition. III is the balance condition. They are equivalent in the new setting to the corresponding conditions in the economy of activities. The major differences are that formerly the profit condition asserted that no profitable activities exist and the activities in use do not make losses, while now the profit condition asserts that each firm is maximizing profit over its set of possible outputs. However, the formal statement of condition II can be brought close to the earlier condition if we observe that $py^f \geq pz$ for all $z \in Y^f$ and for all f is equivalent to $py \geq pz$ for all $z \in Y$.

II'. $y \in Y$ and $pz > py$ imply that $z \notin Y$.

The equivalence is a consequence of the independence of the outputs of different firms. That is, there are no external economies of production and $Y = \sum_{f=1}^{F} Y^f$ (see Koopmans 1957, p. 12).

The proof of existence makes use of a fixed point theorem found in Gale and Mas-Colell (1975).

LEMMA 15   *Let* $X = \prod_{i=1}^{m} X_i$, *where* $X_i \subset R^n$ *is compact, convex, and not empty. Let* φ_i *map* X *into the set of convex subsets (including $\emptyset$) of* X_i,

$i = 1, \cdots, m$. *If the* φ_i *are lower semicontinuous, there is* x *in* X *such that, for all* i, $x^i \in \varphi_i(x)$ *or* $\varphi_i(x) = \emptyset$.

Proof   See the proof of lemma 1.18.   ∎

We will now define the mapping whose fixed points will be equilibria. Let $\pi(p) = \sum_{f=1}^{F} \pi^f(p)$. For $p \in S$, $\tilde{x} = (x^1, \cdots, x^H) \in \prod_{h=1}^{H} \hat{C}^h$, and $x = \sum_{h=1}^{H} x^h$, define

$$g_h(p, \tilde{x}) = \begin{cases} \Gamma^h(p) & \text{if } px^h > m^h(p), \\ \Gamma^h(p) \cap \hat{P}^h(x^h) & \text{if } px^h \leq m^h(p) \text{ for } h = 1, \cdots, H, \end{cases}$$

$$g_0(p, \tilde{x}) = \{q \mid qx > \pi(q) \text{ and } q \in S\}.$$

In these definitions for the income functions $m^h(p)$, we assume productions sets $\hat{Y}^f$. Note, however, that $q \in g_0(p, \tilde{x})$ implies that q separates x and $A(Y)$, since $\pi(q) \geq 0$ is implied by the assumption that $0 \in Y$. Also $g_h(p, \tilde{x})$ is either the open budget set or the intersection of the open budget set with the preferred set of the hth consumer.

LEMMA 16   *The correspondences* g_0 *and* g_h, $h = 1, \cdots, H$, *are open valued relative to* S *and* C^h, *respectively, convex valued, and lower semicontinuous.*

Proof   The g_h are open valued and convex valued since Γ^h has these properties by lemma 14, and $\hat{P}^h$ is open valued relative to $\hat{C}^h$ and convex valued by lemma 10. If $px^h > m^h(p)$, lower semicontinuity of g_h follows by lemma 14 from the lower semicontinuity of $\Gamma^h(p)$ and the continuity of $m_x(p)$.

It remains to show that $g_h = \hat{P}^h \cap \Gamma^h$ is lower semicontinuous at (p, x^h) when $px^h \leq m^h(p)$ holds. Let y^h be an arbitrary element of $g_h(p, \tilde{x})$. Then $py^h < m^h(p)$. Let U be an arbitrary neighborhood of y^h relative to $\hat{C}^h$. We will show that there is a neighborhood V of $(p, \tilde{x})$ relative to $S \times \prod_{k=1}^{H} \hat{C}^k$ such that $g_h(p', \tilde{x}')$ intersects U for any $(p', \tilde{x}')$ in V. We have that $\hat{P}^h$ is lower semicontinuous by lemma 10. Thus there is a neighborhood V' of $(p, \tilde{x})$ such that $(p', \tilde{x}') \in V'$ implies that $\hat{P}^h(x'^h)$ intersects U. Since $m^h(p)$ is continuous by lemma 13 and $py^h < m^h(p)$ there is a neighborhood V'' of $(p, \tilde{x})$ such that $(p', \tilde{x}') \in V''$ implies for $z = g_h(p', \tilde{x}')$ that $p'z < m^h(p')$. Then $g^h(p', \tilde{x}')$ intersects U for any $(p', \tilde{x}') \in V = V' \cap V''$. This establishes lower semicontinuity of g^h for all $h = 1, \cdots, H$.

Let $q \in g_0(p, \tilde{x})$, so $qx > \pi(q)$ holds. The profit function is continuous from lemma 13. Then $q'x' > \pi(q')$ holds for all (q', x') in a sufficiently small neighborhood of (q, x), or $q' \in g_0(q', x')$. This means that $(p^s, \tilde{x}^s) \to (p, \tilde{x})$ implies that there is $q^s \in g_0(p^s, \tilde{x}^s)$ and $q^s \to q \in g_0(p, \tilde{x})$, or $g_0(p, \tilde{x})$ is lower semicontinuous. Convex and open valuedness of g_0 is clear. ∎

The first proof of existence without transitive preferences was given by Mas-Colell (1974). The order of proof to be used here is a modification of that of Gale and Mas-Colell (1975).

THEOREM 2   *Under assumptions 7 through 12 the economy $\hat{\mathscr{E}} = (\hat{Y}^1, \cdots,$ $\hat{Y}^H, \hat{C}^1, \cdots, \hat{C}^H, \hat{P}^1, \cdots, \hat{P}^H)$ has a competitive equilibrium $(\hat{p}, \hat{y}^1, \cdots,$ $\hat{y}^F, \hat{x}^1, \cdots, \hat{x}^H)$.*

Proof   Let $X = S \times \prod_{h=1}^{H} \hat{C}^h$. The set X is convex and compact. Then g_0 maps X into the set of convex subsets of S (including $\emptyset$) and g^h maps X into the set of convex subsets of $\hat{C}^h$ (including $\emptyset$), which is compact. Also the g^h and g_0 are lower semicontinuous and open valued from lemma 16. Therefore the assumptions of lemma 15 are satisfied, and there is a point $(p, x^1, \cdots, x^h)$ or $(p, \tilde{x})$ that satisfies the conditions:

i. If $px^h > m^h(p)$, either $x^h \in \Gamma^h(p)$ or $\Gamma^h(p) = \emptyset$.

ii. If $px^h \leq m^h(p)$, either $x^h \in \Gamma^h(p) \cap \hat{P}^h(x^h)$ or $\Gamma^h(p) \cap \hat{P}(x^h) = \emptyset$.

iii. Either $px > \pi(p)$, or the set $\{q \mid qx > \pi(q) \text{ and } q \in S\} = \emptyset$.

If $px^h > m^h(p)$, then $x^h \notin \Gamma^h(p)$ by definition of $\Gamma^h(p)$. Also, by assumption 12, $\Gamma^h(p)$ is never empty. Thus, by condition i, $px^h > m^h(p)$ cannot hold. On the other hand, if $px^h \leq m^h(p)$, the definition of $\hat{P}^h$ implies that $x^h \notin \hat{P}^h(x^h)$. Therefore we must conclude that $\Gamma^h(p) \cap \hat{P}^h(x^h) = \emptyset$ by condition ii. Note that this implies that $\Gamma^h(p) \cap P^h(x^h) = \emptyset$, since $P^h(x^h) \subset \hat{P}^h(x^h)$.

To establish the demand condition, condition I of competitive equilibrium, we need only show that there is no point $z \in \hat{P}^h(x^h)$ where $pz = m^h(p)$. Suppose there is such a point z. As we noted above there is a point $w \in \hat{C}^h$ with $pw < 0 \leq m^h(p)$. Consider a point z' on the line segment from w to z and very close to z. Then z' satisfies $pz' < m^h(p)$, and since $\hat{P}^h(x^h)$ is open relative to $\hat{C}^h$, we may choose $z' \in \hat{P}^h(x^h)$. This contradicts $\Gamma^h(p) \cap \hat{P}^h(x^h) = \emptyset$. Therefore no such point z can exist and condition I of competitive equilibrium is met.

Let $x = \sum_{h=1}^{H} x^h$. Since we have shown that $px^h \le m^h(p)$, it follows that $px = \sum_{h=1}^{H} px^h \le \sum_{h=1}^{H} m^h(p) = \sum_{f=1}^{F} \pi^f(p) = \pi(p)$. Thus $px > \pi(p)$ is false, and the set $\{q \mid qx > \pi(q) \text{ for } q \in S\}$ is empty. Suppose $x \notin \hat{Y}$. Let $\bar{y}$ be an interior point of $A(Y)$. Such a point exists by assumption 8. Since $A(Y)$ is a cone, $\bar{y}$ may be chosen so that $\bar{y} > b$ and $\bar{y} \in \hat{Y}$. Since $x \in \sum_{h=1}^{H} \hat{C}^h$, we have $x > b$. Suppose $x \notin \hat{Y}$. Consider $y' = \alpha \bar{y} + (1 - \alpha)x$ where α, $0 \le \alpha \le 1$, is minimal for $y' \in \hat{Y}$. Then y' lies in the boundary of $\hat{Y}$ and, since $y' > b$, also on the boundary of Y. By a separation theorem (Berge 1963, p. 163), there is q such that $qx > \mu$ and $qy' = \mu$ and $qz \le \mu$ for all $z \in Y$ and some real number μ. However, by its definition $\pi(q) = \mu$. Therefore we conclude that that $qx > \pi(q)$. Since $0 \in Y$, it must be that $\mu \ge 0$. Since $z \in A(Y)$ implies $z \in Y$, $qz \le \mu$ for all $z \in A(Y)$. Therefore $q \in S$. However, as we have seen, condition iii implies that $qx \le \pi(q)$ for all $q \in S$. This is a contradiction, so it must be that $x \in \hat{Y}$. Thus condition III, the balance condition of competitive equilibrium is met.

Since x is feasible, by assumption 11 for each h there is $z \in P^h(x^h)$. Suppose that $px^h < m^h(p)$ held for some h. Then there is $z' \in \hat{P}^h(x^h)$ in every neighborhood of x^h, and in particular, z' may be chosen so that $pz' < m^h(p)$, which contradicts $\hat{P}^h(x^h) \cap \Gamma^h(p) = \emptyset$. Therefore $px^h = m^h(p)$ holds for all h and $px = \sum_{h=1}^{H} m^h(p) = \pi(p)$. Since $x \in Y$ and $px = \pi(p)$, if we set $x = y$, then $py \ge pz$ for any $z \in Y$, and condition II$'$ of competitive equilibrium, the profit condition, is met. Thus we have proved that there is a competitive equilibrium for the economy $\hat{\mathscr{E}}$. ∎

We may now prove the

COROLLARY *Under assumptions 7 through 12 there is a competitive equilibrium for the economy* $\mathscr{E}_f \equiv (Y^1, \cdots, Y^F, C^1, \cdots, C^H, P^1, \cdots, P^H)$.

Proof Since the F^f are bounded, the Y^f may be bounded without affecting the equilibria provided that a maximum of py^f within bounds implies that py^f is maximal when the bounds are removed. It follows from the linearity of py^f and the convexity of Y^f that a local maximum of py^f is also a global maximum. However, the maximum over $\hat{Y}$ is a local maximum for Y, since $\hat{Y}$ and Y coincide in the region $B = \{y \mid y > b\}$ where the equilibrium output $\hat{y}$ must lie. Thus maximum profits for $\hat{Y}$ are also maximum profits for Y.

When the extended preference correspondences are introduced, local nonsatiation holds and the preference correspondences $\hat{P}^h$ are convex valued. Thus lemma 1 applies, and we are also able to bound the consumption sets above without affecting the set of equilibria. Introducing bounded consumption sets does not change the implications of the demand condition of competitive equilibrium when the extended preferences $\hat{P}^h$ are used, since a point that exceeds the upper bound and is strictly preferred to x^h according to $\hat{P}^h$ gives rise to a strictly preferred point within the bounds according to $\hat{P}^h$. But the choices under $\hat{P}^h$ are the same as the choices under P^h. Thus, if the demand condition is met for $\hat{P}^h$ and $\hat{C}^h$, it is also met for P^h and C^h.

Thus the profit condition and the demand condition are met for $\mathscr{E}_f$ when they are met for $\hat{\mathscr{E}}$. On the other hand, the balance condition is the same for these economies. Therefore an equilibrium for $\hat{\mathscr{E}}$ is also an equilibrium for $\mathscr{E}$. ∎

6.3 Interiority and Irreducibility

Most of the interiority assumptions that were made in the last two sections can be removed without prejudice to the existence of equilibrium. They were used in two ways, to allow the application of the fixed point theorems and to ensure that the fixed point is a competitive equilibrium. For example, in section 6.1 an interior point of Y is used to provide a convex set of normalized prices and to define the projection mapping whose fixed points are equilibria. On the other hand, the presence of a point of C^h in the interior of Y is used to provide a cheaper point so that the demand functions are upper semicontinuous. In section 6.2 the interior of $A(Y)$ is also used in the definition of the normalized set of prices. The role of the point of C^h that lies in int $A(Y)$ is the same as the role of the point in $C^h \cap$ int Y in the proof of section 6.1, that is, to provide a cheaper point, which implies that the demand condition is met. The first of these functions of interiority is replaced by introducing a temporary interior which is gradually eliminated, giving rise to a sequence of equilibria whose points of accumulation are equilibria for the original model. The second function is replaced by an assumption that the economy is irreducible in the sense that however the economy is split into two parts, each part has something that is useful to the other.

Our model of an economy of firms has greater generality in one respect than our model of an economy of activities, since consumers are not required to observe transitivity in their choices. Of course, the activities model can also dispense with transitivity (McKenzie 1981). On the other hand, even though a given population of firms is assumed, the survival assumption is more effectively modeled in the activities model, once entrepreneurial factors are introduced. Moreover it has been shown in the activities model (McKenzie 1981) that the survival assumption can be dropped when irreducibility is assumed. However, the argument is too involved to be introduced here. Also the firms model is easily modeled as an activities model (McKenzie 1959). Entrepreneurial factors may be introduced, one for each firm. The ownership of these factors are distributed in the same pattern as the ownership of the firm. Also the production set of the firm is then a convex cone that is the projection from the origin of the set $(-\delta^f, Y^f) \subset \mathbf{R}^F \times \mathbf{R}^n$, where δ^f is a vector in $\mathbf{R}^F$ with 1 in the fth place and 0 elsewhere. Figure 6.2 illustrates a simple case with one firm. After this transformation, assuming Y is closed, we see that the asymptotic cone of Y is equal to Y. Now a survival assumption can take account of the distribution of profits. To accommodate the activities model in the model with firms, one can simply assume that there is only one firm and it owns the activities production set. However, this does not make good economic sense. Formally we will use the firms model in this section while recalling that the production set Y and its asymptotic cone $A(Y)$ can be identified by the means described. The full program of proof along the lines of theorem 1 without transitivity of preference and without the survival assumption may be found in McKenzie (1981).

Recall the definition of an irreducible economy in section 5.2. Assumption 11 may be replaced by

ASSUMPTION 13   The economy is irreducible.

Finally most of the interiority required by assumptions 8 and 12 may be removed by use of assumption 13 and a change in the order of proof. It is enough to introduce

ASSUMPTION 14 $Y \cap \mathbf{R}^n_+ = \{0\}$. Also $A(Y) \cap -A(Y) = \{0\}$.

ASSUMPTION 15 $C^h \cap A(Y) \neq \emptyset$ for all h. Relative interior $C \cap$ relative interior $Y \neq \emptyset$.

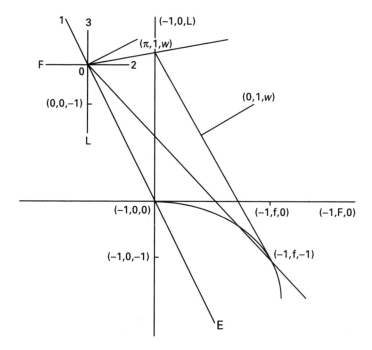

Figure 6.2
Introducing an entrepreneurial factor E whose axis is perpendicular to the paper. Food production is a function ϕ of e and labor l. The wage $w = \phi'_l(e, l)$. Profit $\pi = \phi'_e(e, l)$. Also $(\pi, 1, w) \cdot (-1, f, -l) = 0$, since $\phi(e, l) = \phi'_e \cdot e + \phi'_l \cdot l$.

Recall that the relative interior is the interior relative to the smallest affine subspace (or flat) containing the set. The first part of assumption 15 ensures that each consumer has available some bundle in his net trading set at any prices that are consistent with the profit conditions, that is, at any price vectors that lie in the dual cone of the asymptotic cone of the production set for which supremum py for $y \in Y$ is finite. This will imply that his demand correspondence is well defined. The second part of assumption 15 will be used to guarantee that some consumer has a cheaper point in his budget set, and then assumption 13 together with the first part of assumption 15 will be used to extend this condition to all consumers. This is sufficient to permit the proof of existence along the same lines as before.

Let L be the smallest affine subspace of $\mathbf{R}^n$ that contains $Y \cup C$. Since Y contains the origin, L is a linear subspace.

LEMMA 17 $Y \neq L$.

Proof If $Y = L$ then $Y \supset C$. If C is bounded consider the dense denu-
merable subset of C with rational coefficients. Arrange this subset in a
sequence, and choose a subsequence x^s, $s = 1, 2, \cdots$, such that $s > t$
implies $x^s \in P(x^t)$ unless $P(x^t)$ is empty. In the latter case set $x^s = x^t$ for
all $s > t$. Since there is a point of accumulation, we may assume the subsequence converges to a limit x. Then x is a point of satiation, since $x \in$
$R^h(y)$ for all y with rational coefficients and thus for all $y \in C$ since
$R^h(y)$ is closed. Consequently the complement of h among consumers
cannot improve on an allocation of x to the hth consumer. Since all
points in C are feasible, this contradicts irreducibility.

If C is unbounded select a sequence x^s such that $|x^s| \to \infty$. Consider
the sequence $x^s/|x^s| = \bar{x}^s$. Since $\bar{x}^s$ lies in a compact set contained in
$L = Y$, there is a point of accumulation $\bar{x} \in Y$. However, $\bar{x} \geq 0$, since C
is bounded below. This contradicts assumption 14.   ∎

Let r be the dimension of L. Y may not have an interior relative to L.
However, we will extend L to a space of dimension $r + 1$ by introducing
an $(n + 1)$th pseudogood and taking the Cartesian product $L \times \mathbf{R}$. Consider a new process of production $A(\varepsilon) = \{(y, -\delta) \mid (y, -\delta) = \delta(z, -1)$ for
$z \in L$, $\|z\| \leq \varepsilon \geq 0$, and $\delta \geq 0\}$. $\|\cdot\|$ is the Euclidean norm. Note that
the new good is a universal productive factor that can produce a joint
product consisting of all goods. Let $Y' = \{(y, 0) \mid y \in Y\}$. Define $Y(\varepsilon) =$
$\{(y, -\delta) \mid (y, -\delta) = z + w$ with $z \in Y'$, $w \in A(\varepsilon)\}$. The new technology
$A(\varepsilon)$ is a closed convex cone and may be incorporated into the production
set of every firm. For $\varepsilon > 0$ the social production set $Y(\varepsilon)$ now has an interior in $L \times \mathbf{R}$. The asymptotic cone $A(Y(\varepsilon))$ contains $A(\varepsilon)$ and thus has
an interior in $L \times \mathbf{R}$ for $\varepsilon > 0$ as well. In particular, the point $(0, -1)$
corresponding to the origin of L is interior to $A(Y(\varepsilon))$. Next the net
trading sets C^h are expanded to allow the offer of $1/H$ units of the
$(n + 1)$th good. $C'^h = \{(x, -\delta) \mid x \in C^h$ and $0 \leq \delta \leq 1/H\}$. Finally new
preference correspondences are defined by $(x, -\delta) \in P'^h(z, -\gamma)$ if and only
if $(z, -\gamma) \in C'^h$ and $x \in P^h(z)$ with $(x, -\delta) \in C'^h$.

We will show when assumptions 7, 9, 10, 13, 14, and 15 are met by the
economy $\mathscr{E}$, the proof of theorem 1 may be applied to establish the existence of a competitive equilibrium for the economy $\mathscr{E}(\varepsilon)$ with the production set $Y(\varepsilon)$, the trading sets C'^h, and the preference correspondences
P'^h. Then the strategy of proof of existence for the economy with the

social production set Y is to let $\varepsilon = \varepsilon^s \to 0$ for $s = 1, 2, \cdots$, and observe that an accumulation point exists for the series of equilibria and that it is an equilibrium for $\mathscr{E}(0)$. Finally we observe that equilibrium for the economy $\mathscr{E}(0)$ with social production set $Y(0)$ and the trading sets C'^h and preference correspondences P'^h implies an equilibrium for the economy $\mathscr{E}$ with social production set Y, the trading sets C^h, and the preference correspondences P^h.

LEMMA 18 *The economy $\mathscr{E}(\varepsilon) = (Y(\varepsilon), C'^1, \cdots, C'^H, P'^1, \cdots, P'^H)$ has a competitive equilibrium if the economy $\mathscr{E}$ satisfies assumptions 7, 9, 10, 13, 14, and 15.*

Proof To see that $Y(\varepsilon)$ is closed, let $(z^s, -\delta^s) = (y^s, 0) + \delta^s(w^s, -1)$ where $(y^s, 0) \in Y'$, and $(w^s, -1) \in A(\varepsilon)$. Suppose that $(z^s, -\delta^s) \to (z, -\delta)$, $s = 1, 2, \cdots$. Since $\|w^s\| \le \varepsilon$, there is a point of accumulation and for a subsequence (retain notation) $w^s \to w$. Therefore $y^s \to y = z - \delta w$ along the same subsequence. Moreover $y \in Y$ since Y is closed. Then $(z, -\delta) \in Y(\varepsilon)$ and $Y(\varepsilon)$ is closed. Thus assumption 7 is met by $Y(\varepsilon)$.

To see that $Y(\varepsilon) \cap (\mathbf{R}_+^n \times \mathbf{R}_+) = \{0\}$, note that the component $-\delta$ of $(z, -\delta) \in Y(\varepsilon)$ is negative or 0. Then $\delta = 0$ implies that $z = y \in Y$ while $Y \cap \mathbf{R}_+^n = \{0\}$ by assumption 14. Also it is clear that $A(Y') \cap -A(Y') = \{0\}$, since $\delta \ge 0$ and $A(Y) \cap -A(Y) = \{0\}$ by assumption 14. Finally $Y(\varepsilon)$ has an interior in $L \times \mathbf{R}$ since $A(\varepsilon)$ has an interior from its construction. $A(Y(\varepsilon))$ has an interior in $L \times \mathbf{R}$ since it contains $A(\varepsilon)$. Thus assumption 8 is met.

The new trading sets C'^h are the old trading sets expanded to include the added good. They are bounded below in the new good by $1/H$. Thus they satisfy assumption 9. The new preference correspondences are seen to be convex. It is also easy to see that $P'^h(x, -\delta)$ is open relative to C'^h, since $P^h(x)$ is open relative to C^h and the $(n+1)$th good does not affect preferences. Lower semicontinuity and the condition that $(x, -\delta) \notin P'^h(x, -\delta)$ follow from these properties for $P^h(x)$. Thus assumption 10 is met by the P'^h.

Irreducibility implies assumption 11, since a single consumer can be taken to be one element of the partition, and whatever the allocation may be within the feasible set, it must be possible to make that consumer better off. This leaves assumption 12 to be accounted for. Let $(\bar{y}, -1)$ be a point in the interior of $Y(\varepsilon)$ relative to $L \times \mathbf{R}$. Let $S(\varepsilon) = \{(p, \pi) \in A(Y(\varepsilon))^* \cap (L \times \mathbf{R}) \mid (p, \pi) \cdot (\bar{y}, -1) = -1\}$. The only use of assumption 12 is to ensure that every consumer always has income in the sense that at any price vector (p, π) in $S(\varepsilon)$ his budget set contains a point (z, ζ) such that $(p, \pi) \cdot (z, \zeta) < m^h(p, \pi)$. That is, the set $\Gamma^h(p, \pi) \neq \emptyset$. This will eliminate the possibility that for some h there is a vector (z, ζ) with $(p, \pi) \cdot (z, \zeta) = m^h(p, \pi)$, where $(z, \zeta) \in P^h(x, \xi)$ at a fixed point $((p, \pi), (\tilde{x}, \tilde{\xi}))$.

However assumption 15 and the possibility that consumers have, with the trading sets C'^h, of supplying the $(n + 1)$th good implies that $C'^h \cap$ interior $A(Y(\varepsilon))$ relative to $L \times \mathbf{R}$ is not empty for $\varepsilon > 0$. Thus assumption 12 is satisfied as well. Therefore the economy $E(\varepsilon) = (Y(\varepsilon), C'^1, \cdots, C'^H, P'^1, \cdots, P'^H)$ has a competitive equilibrium for $\varepsilon > 0$ by theorem 2. ∎

With the help of lemma 18 it is possible to prove

THEOREM 3   *Under assumptions 7, 9, 10, 13, 14, and 15 the economy $\mathscr{E} = (Y, C^1, \cdots, C^H, P^1, \cdots, P^H)$ has a competitive equilibrium.*

Proof It has been established in lemma 18 that the economy $\mathscr{E}(\varepsilon) = (Y(\varepsilon), C'^1, \cdots, C'^H, P'^1, \cdots, P'^H)$ has a competitive equilibrium for $\varepsilon > 0$. Let $\varepsilon^s \to 0$ as $s \to \infty$, $s = 1, 2, \cdots$. Since the interior of $A(Y(\varepsilon))$ relative to $L \times \mathbf{R}$ vanishes along the sequence, the set $S(\varepsilon)$ becomes unbounded. Therefore the price vectors must be given a further normalization. Consider the price and goods vectors such as p and y now to lie in $L \times \mathbf{R}$. If $(p^s, y^s, \tilde{x}^s)$ is the corresponding sequence of equilibria, let $p'^s = p^s / \|p^s\|$. Since the feasible sets $F(\varepsilon^s)$ and $F^f(\varepsilon^s)$, and the set $S(\varepsilon)$ are bounded by the arguments of lemmas 3, 11, and 12, this sequence has a point of accumulation $(p, y, \tilde{x})$. I claim that $(p, y, \tilde{x})$ is a competitive equilibrium for the economy $E(0)$. The balance condition is obvious. If the profit condition did not hold, then $py < pz$ for some $z \in Y(0)$. But, since $z \in Y(0) \subset Y(\varepsilon^s)$, for large s we have $p'^s y^s < p'^s z^s$ for a sequence z^s converging to z in contradiction to the profit condition for $E(\varepsilon^s)$. Only the demand condition needs to be established.

If some consumer has a cheaper point in the limit economy $E(0)$, the irreducibility condition will be found to imply that all consumers have cheaper points. We will show that assumption 13 implies that p may be chosen so that $pz < m(p) = \pi(p)$ holds for some $z \in C$.

In $L \times \mathbf{R} \subset \mathbf{R}^{n+1}$ consider the limit price vector $(p_1, \cdots, p_n, p_{n+1})$ in $\mathbf{R}^{n+1}$. Note that $p_{n+1} = 0$, since there is free disposal of the pseudogood in $Y(0)$ while $A(0)$ is not productive. Also the new good has no effect on consumer preferences. Thus we may pay attention to $p' = (p_1, \cdots, p_n, 0)$. Since $p' \cdot z \leq \pi(p') = m(p')$ for all $z \in Y(0)$, it is sufficient to show that p' cannot separate $Y(0)$ and C'. But $p'_{n+1} = 0$ implies that it is sufficient to show that no vector $q \in L$ separates Y and C. However, Y and C have a relative interior point in common by assumption 15. Also $0 \in Y$. This implies by lemma 5.6 that Y and C cannot be separated in L. Therefore p' cannot separate Y and C, so $p' \cdot z < m(p')$ holds for some $z \in C$. Then some consumer has a cheaper point in the limit. Since $p'_{n+1} = 0$, y^h_{n+1} is irrelevant to producer profits. Also x^h_{n+1} is irrelevant to consumer choices. Therefore the added dimension may be eliminated without affecting the conditions for competitive equilibrium. Thus an equilibrium for $\mathscr{E}(0)$ implies an equilibrium for $\mathscr{E}$.

Let I_1 be the set of h for whom $\Gamma^h(p) \neq \emptyset$. Let I_2 be the complementary subset of consumers for whom $\Gamma^h(p) = \emptyset$. For any vector $z = \sum_{h=1}^H z^h$ and subset I of consumers, let $z_I = \sum_{h \in I} z^h$. Also let $C_I = \sum_{h \in I} C^h$. Suppose that $I_2 \neq \emptyset$. By assumption 13, there are $w \in C_{I_2}$ and $y' \in Y$ such that $z_{I_1} = y' - x_{I_2} - \alpha w$, for $\alpha \geq 0$, where $z^h \in P^h(x^h)$ for all $h \in I_1$. Taking the inner product of both sides with p gives

$$py' = pz_{I_1} + px_{I_2} + \alpha pw. \tag{3}$$

Let $I = I_1 + I_2$. The left-hand side of (3) is $py' \leq m_I(p)$, since $m_I(p) = \max pz$ for $z \in Y$. Also $px_{I_2} = m_{I_2}(p)$ by continuity of the function m_{I_2}. Then $pw \geq m_{I_2}(p) \geq 0$ follows since, from the definition of I_2, $\Gamma^h(p) = \emptyset$ for $h \in I_2$. Finally $pz^h > m^h(p)$ holds for all $h \in I_1$, since for $h \in I_1$, $\Gamma^h(p) \neq \emptyset$. Otherwise, since P^h is open in C^h relative to $L \times \mathbf{R}$, there would be a convex combination z' of z^h and a point $z \in C^h$ with $pz < m^h(p)$ such that $z' \in P^h(x^h)$ in contradiction to $\Gamma^h(p) \cap P^h(x^h) = \emptyset$ for all ε such that $0 < \varepsilon < 1$. These values imply that the right-hand side of (3) is greater than $m_I(p)$. Since this is a contradiction, the set I_2 must be empty.

Thus all the conditions for equilibrium in $\mathscr{E}(0)$ are satisfied. Consequently $\mathscr{E}$ has an equilibrium. ∎

The first proof of existence of an equilibrium using irreducibility to weaken the interiority assumptions was given by McKenzie (1959). Moore (1975) showed that irreducibility could also replace the survival assumption, that is, the assumption that $C^h \cap Y \neq \emptyset$ holds for all h. McKenzie (1981) combined these generalizations with the absence of transitivity of preference in a theorem on the existence of competitive equilibrium for the economy of activities.

6.4   Existence of Competitive Equilibrium with an Infinite Commodity Space

The economies for which the existence question has been addressed in the preceding sections have the feature that only a finite number of goods appear. It may be reasonable to suppose that an infinity of goods for delivery on one date belong to a compact space which can be adequately approximated by a finite subset of goods. However, if we wish to deal with an economy that has an indefinite or infinite horizon, this approximation is not available. Goods for delivery at different dates must be regarded as different goods. It was a major contribution of *Value and Capital* (Hicks 1939) to provide a full-scale analysis of an economy in which this fact is properly recognized. Then, if the horizon is infinite, the number of goods must be infinite even when deliveries are scheduled at discrete intervals. The infinity of goods must be dealt with together, since the market is analyzed as though all trades occur simultaneously. This is a limiting form of the futures economy of Hicks. When uncertainty is introduced in the manner of Debreu (1959) by also distinguishing goods by the states of the world in which they are delivered, the sets of possible future states in each period must be foreseen. It may be acceptable to assume a finite number of states of the world in each period, but to give an infinite horizon, a finite approximation requires an arbitrary truncation of time. Then goods of the terminal period must be valued in an arbitrary way.

We will prove a theorem which generalizes a theorem of Peleg and Yaari (1970) for an exchange economy with the positive orthants as the consumption sets. Then the trading sets are positive orthants displaced by subtracting the initial stocks. In the theorem to be proved the trading sets are convex but are not required to be displaced positive orthants. Also production is allowed. The method of proof is parallel to the proof of existence in the finite case presented in chapter 5. A similar proof was given by Peleg and Yaari for the infinite case. The proof is based on the theorem of Scarf on the nonemptiness of the core. Scarf assumes that the traders have continuous and quasiconcave utility functions over their possible trading sets C^h. Peleg and Yaari make this assumption and also assume strict quasiconcavity. Our assumptions will imply that continuous utility functions exist that are quasiconcave but not necessarily strictly quasiconcave.

The commodity space s^n is the Cartesian product $\prod_{t=0}^{\infty} \mathbf{R}^n(t)$, endowed with the product topology where $\mathbf{R}^n(t)$ has the norm topology. If $z \in s^n$, then $z = (z_0, z_1, \cdots)$, and $z_t \in \mathbf{R}^n(t)$ represents quantities of goods in period t. There are a finite number of traders, 1 to H. The set of possible net trades for the hth trader is $C^h \subset s^n$. We do not place additional restrictions on the growth of conceivable trading sequences, although the production sequences may be unbounded. In a decentralized economy the consumer does not take into account production possibilities when choosing a trading sequence, but rather looks at what is affordable. Any bound on the growth of the optimal trading path must come from the budget constraint. Let C_t^h be the projection of C^h into $\mathbf{R}^n(t)$. If $w_t \in C_t^h$, then $w_{it} < 0$ implies that the quantity w_{it} of the ith good is provided by the hth consumer and $w_{it} > 0$ implies that the quantity w_{it} of the ith good is received by the hth consumer at time t. The trading set C_0^h includes the initial stocks of goods that the consumer may be able to provide, including produced goods. However, for C_t^h with $t > 0$, the hth consumer provides only labor services and other unproduced goods.

A binary relation $\mathscr{Q}$ is said to be *irreflexive* if $z\mathscr{Q}z$ does not hold for any z. There is an irreflexive relation $\mathscr{P}^h$ of *strict preference* defined on C^h and a correspondence P^h defined on C^h by $P^h(z) = \{w \mid w \in C^h \text{ and } w\mathscr{P}^h z\}$.

The production set is Y. Inputs are negative numbers and outputs are positive numbers. The inputs and outputs of the production sector include the capital stocks. That is, the initial capital stocks in a period are inputs and the terminal capital stocks are outputs. These do not appear in the consumer net trading sets C_t^h except for C_0^h. In an economy with certainty the ownership of capital stocks is inessential. Only the value of investment is significant for the consumer, and the sequence of investment values over time is implicit in his pattern of consumption.

The assumptions have been strengthened from those used in section 6.1 to allow the proof that the core of the economy with an infinity of commodities is not empty and to obtain a compact set of prices. The economy $\mathscr{E}$ is given by the list $(Y, C^1, \cdots, C^H, P^1, \cdots, P^H)$. P^h is a correspondence from C^h to the set of subsets of C^h and $P^h(w)$ is the strictly preferred set of w. If $z \in P^h(w)$, the trade w is less desirable to the trader than the trade z. The *preference correspondence* R^h is defined in terms of P^h by $z \in R^h(w)$ if and only if $w \in P^h(z)$ is not the case. Recall that a *lower section* of the correspondence $f : X \rightarrow \{\text{subsets of } X\}$, at a point $y \in X$, is the set $\{z \mid y \in f(z)\}$. The *graph* of f is the set $\{(y,z) \mid z \in f(y)\}$. We define $C = \sum_{h=1}^{H} C^h$. The *norm* of $z_t \in \mathbf{R}^n$ is $|z_t| = \sum_{i=1}^{n} |z_{it}|$. Let $l_{\infty}^n = \{z \in s^n \mid z_t \text{ is bounded in norm uniformly over } t\}$. Let $l_1^n = \{z \in s^n \mid \sum_{t=0}^{\infty} |z_t| < \infty\}$. Let $e_t = (1, \cdots, 1)$. For any vector z let $z^+ = \max(z, 0)$, and let $z^- = z^+ - z$. In the assumptions the terms open and closed will refer to the topology of s^n. The assumptions are

ASSUMPTION 16 Y is a closed convex cone with vertex at the origin that contains no straight lines.

ASSUMPTION 17   Given any t and $\delta > 0$ there is $\varepsilon > 0$ such that $y \in Y$ and $|y_t^+| > \delta$ implies $|y_s^-| > \varepsilon$ for some $s \leq t$.

ASSUMPTION 18 C^h is convex, closed, and bounded below by $\bar{z} \in l_{\infty}^n$.

ASSUMPTION 19   For all h the correspondence P^h is convex and open valued relative to C^h with open lower sections. P^h is transitive and $R^h(x)$ is the closure of $P^h(x)$ for all $x \in C^h$ for which $P^h(x) \neq \emptyset$. Also $x \in C^h$ with $z \geq x$, and $z_t > x_t$ for some t, implies that $z \in P^h(x)$.

ASSUMPTION 20   The economy $\mathscr{E}$ is strongly irreducible.

ASSUMPTION 21   There is $\bar{x}^h \in C^h - Y$ with $\bar{x}^h \leq 0$ for all h and $\sum_{h=1}^{H} \bar{x}^h = \bar{x} < 0$, with $\bar{x}_s = \bar{x}_t$ for all s and t. For any $x^h \in C^h$ let $z^h \in R^h(x^h) - Y$ and $\delta > 0$. Then there is τ_0 and for each $\tau > \tau_0$ there is $\alpha > 0$ with $(z_0^h + \delta e_0, \cdots, z_\tau^h, \alpha \bar{x}_{\tau+1}^h, \alpha \bar{x}_{\tau+2}^h, \cdots) \in R_t^h(z^h) - Y$.

These assumptions are similar to the assumptions used in sections 6.1 and 6.2, modified to take account of the presence of an infinite number of goods. The technology exhibits constant returns to scale by assumption 16. However, diminishing returns are realized to variable factors when some factors are held constant. Diminishing returns to firms may be represented in this way by introducing entrepreneurial factors (McKenzie 1959). Assumption 17 is needed to establish compactness of the feasible set, since s^n is not a Banach space, and the argument based on $Y \cap s_+^n = \{0\}$ does not work. Assumption 19 implies that a continuous utility function exists on the feasible trading set. Strong irreducibility is defined in chapter 5. The last part of assumption 19 says that an increase in the quantity of all goods for some period with no losses in other periods leads to a preferred stream. The first part of assumption 21 provides for a constant path of production and trading for the economy as a whole in which all goods are in excess supply in every period. This may be thought of as a kind of Slater Condition (see Uzawa 1958, p. 34). The second part of assumption 21 provides that additional initial stocks make it possible to replace the tail of a path of net supply that is sufficiently distant by this constant path.

It is implied by continuity of preferences in the product topology and the second part of assumption 21 that for any consumer a late tail of his stream of net trades after production may be replaced with 0's without leaving $R^h(x^h) - Y$, provided that inputs are increased in the first period. Let $e \in s^n$, where $e = (e_0, e_1, \cdots)$ and $e_t = (1, \cdots, 1)$. In the exchange economy, with a consumption set equal to s_+^n, and endowment $(\omega^1, \cdots, \omega^H)$ such that $\omega^h \in s_+^n$ for all h and $\omega_t^h > \delta e_t$ for all t, assumption 21 is implied. The trading set C^h is $s_+^n - \omega^h$. Choose $\bar{x}^h > -\omega^h$ to satisfy the first part of assumption 21. Then the second part of assumption 21 follows for any $\alpha < 1$, since the net trading vector with a tail from $\alpha \bar{x}^h$ lies in C^h for any τ.

In an exchange economy a lower bound b^h for C^h has often been taken to be the negative of a vector of endowments held by the hth trader, which lies in C^h. In a production economy where productive services are traded, the requirement that b^h lie in C^h would be very restrictive. Even in a trading economy it is not satisfactory, since it implies that the subsistence level for consumers allows no substitution between goods. Also it would mean that consumption in an earlier period had no effect on the possible consumption set of later periods.

We mean by an *allocation* of net trades an H-tuple $\tilde{x} = (x^1, \cdots, x^H)$ such that $x^h \in C^h$ for all h. A *feasible allocation* must also satisfy the condition $\sum_{h=1}^{H} x^h \in Y$. Then the set of feasible allocations for the economy is $F = \{(x^1, \cdots, x^H) \mid x^h \in C^h, \text{ all } h, \text{ and } \sum_{h=1}^{H} x^h \in Y\}$. The set of feasible allocations F^h for the hth consumer is the projection of F into the hth consumer's net trading set. The proof that the core is not empty will closely follow the proof of theorem 5.6, which is the analogous result for economies with a finite set of commodities. A set $S \subset s^n$ is *bounded* if its projection into each coordinate subspace is bounded.

LEMMA 19 *For any $\bar{y} \in s^n$ the set $B = \{y \in Y \mid y \geq \bar{y}\}$ is bounded.*

Proof Suppose not. Then there is a sequence $y^s \in Y$ with $|y_t^s| \to \infty$ for some t. Since y^s is bounded below by $\bar{y}$, this implies for some t and some i that we have $y_{it}^s \to \infty$. Consider $z^s = y^s/|y_{it}^s|$. $z^s \in Y$ since Y is a cone. However, for all $\tau \le t$ it must eventually hold for all i and any $\varepsilon > 0$ that $z_{i\tau}^s > -\varepsilon$, while for some i we have $|z_{it}^s| = 1$. Then $z \notin Y$ by assumption 17. Since this is a contradiction, no such sequence z^s can exist or B is bounded. ∎

We may now prove feasible allocations to be compact.

LEMMA 20   *F and F^h are nonempty, compact, and convex.*

Proof By assumption 21, there is $\bar{x} \in C - Y$ with $\bar{x} < 0$. Then $0 \in C - Y$ by monotonicity, assumption 19. Thus there are $x^h \in C^h$ with $\sum_{h=1}^{H} x^h \in Y$. This means that $(x^1, \cdots, x^H) \in F$, or F is not empty. F is convex by the convexity of Y and of C^h for each h. F is closed since Y is closed, and C^h is closed for each h. To prove compactness, it is sufficient by Tychonoff's theorem (Berge 1963, p. 79) to prove that the projection of F into each factor F^h of the product is compact. Similarly F^h is compact if the projection of F^h into each factor F_t^h is compact. Since F_t^h is closed and lies in $\mathbf{R}^n$, it is compact if it is bounded. However, $C \cap Y$ is bounded since C is bounded below by $H\bar{z}$ by assumption 18, and the set $\{y \in Y \mid y \ge H\bar{z}\}$ is bounded by lemma 19. Let $\bar{w}$ be an upper bound for $C \cap Y$, and let $(x^1, \cdots, x^H) \in F$. Then $\bar{z} \le x^h \le \bar{w} - (H - 1)\bar{z}$. Therefore F^h and F are compact. ∎

The Border theorem that we used in chapter 5 to obtain a nonempty core does not apply to the model with an infinity of goods. Therefore in this section we will have to appeal to the Scarf theorem (1967). Since the proof of the Scarf theorem makes use of utilities, we need to prove that our assumptions imply that utility functions exist.

First we will show that assumption 19 implies that R^h is transitive, which implies that indifference I^h is transitive. I^h is defined by $y \in I^h(x)$ if and only if $y \in R^h(x)$ and $x \in R^h(y)$.

LEMMA 21   *$\mathscr{R}^h$ is transitive. Also $x \in P^h(y)$, and $y \in R^h(z)$ implies $x \in P^h(z)$. Similarly $x \in R^h(y)$, and $y \in P^h(z)$ implies $x \in P^h(z)$.*

Proof Assume that $x\mathscr{R}^h z$ and $z\mathscr{R}^h y$. Since $R^h(z)$ is the closure of $P^h(z)$, in every neighborhood U of x, there is a point $x' \in P^h(z)$. Also for any z' sufficiently close to z, we have $x' \in P^h(z')$ since lower sections are open.

As before, for any neighborhood V of z there is a point $z'' \in P^h(y)$. By choosing V small enough, we may take $z' = z''$ to get $x'\mathscr{P}^h z''\mathscr{P}^h y$ so that $x'\mathscr{P}^h y$ by transitivity of strict preference. Since x' may be chosen in an arbitrary neighborhood U of x, it follows that $x \in$ closure $P^h(y)$ or $x \in R^h(y)$. In other words, $\mathscr{R}^h$ is transitive. For the first part of the second proposition, suppose that $z \in R^h(x)$ held. Then, by transitivity of $\mathscr{R}^h$, we have $y \in R^h(x)$, which is a contradiction of $x \in P^h(y)$. The second part is proved in the same way. ∎

In order to apply the theorem of Scarf on nonemptiness of the core, we need to show that the preference order $\mathscr{P}^h$ may be represented by a utility function, that is, a numerical function on the commodity bundles in C^h.

With the help of lemmas 20 and 21, we may prove that a utility function exists.

LEMMA 22   *There is a continuous function $u^h : F^h \to R$ such that $x^h P^h z^h$ if and only if $u^h(x^h) > u^h(z^h)$.*

Proof I claim that there is a worst and a best element of F^h. Suppose there is not a worst element in F^h. For each $y \in F^h$ there is some $x \in F^h$ with $y \in P^h(x)$. It follows that $\{P^h(x) \mid x \in F^h\}$ is an open cover of F^h. By lemma 20, F^h is compact. Therefore it has a finite subcover $\{P^h(x_n)_{n=1}^N\}$. Take a worst element x^* of $\{x_1, \cdots, x_N\}$. By transitivity and irreflexivity x^* cannot be in any of the $P^h(x_n)$. This contradicts the fact that the $P^h(x_n)$ cover F. It follows that a worst element of F^h exists. An analogous argument using open lower sections shows that a best element exists.

Let a be a best element and b a worst element of F^h. Let $J = \{(1-\theta)a + \theta b \mid 0 \le \theta \le 1\}$ and define $u^h((1-\theta)a + \theta b) = 1 - \theta$. For arbitrary $x \in F^h$, consider $J \cap P^h(x)$ and $J \cap P_-^h(x)$ where $P_-^h(x) = \{y \mid x\mathscr{P}^h y\}$ is the lower section of P^h at x. Both of these sets are open in J. Since $P^h(x)$ is convex by assumption 19, $J \cap P^h(x)$ is an interval unless it is empty. If $J \cap P^h(x) = \emptyset$, put $u^h(x) = 1$. Otherwise by assumption 19, $J \cap R^h(x)$ is the closure of $J \cap P^h(x)$, and we may put $u^h(x) = 1 - \theta$. Then x is indifferent to $(1-\theta)a + \theta b$ which lies in the boundary of $J \cap P^h(x)$ and is not equal to a. Since $R^h(x)$ is the closure of $P^h(x)$, θ is unique. If $J \cap P_-^h(x)$ is empty, x must be indifferent to the worst point of F^h, and we set $u^h(x) = 0$.

It is implied by the transitivity of indifference that the set $\{y \in F^h \mid u^h(y) > u^h(x)\} = P^h(x)$ and $\{y \in F^h \mid u^h(y) < u^h(x)\} = P_-^h(x)$ for any

$x \in F^h$. These sets are open. Also they are pre-images of open sets that generate the relative topology of $[0, 1]$. Therefore the pre-image of any open set of $[0, 1]$ is open, and u^h is continuous (Berge 1963, p. 56).   ■

Let u^h be a continuous utility function representing P^h on F^h. Recall that $\tilde{x} = (x^1, \cdots, x^H)$. Let $U(\tilde{x})$ be the vector of utilities $(u^h(x^h))$ and $\tilde{F} = U(F)$. The set $\tilde{F}$ is the utility possibility set of the economy. Note $\tilde{F}$ is compact, hence bounded. For any coalition S define

$$V(S) = \left\{ \zeta \in \mathbf{R}^H \mid \zeta_h \le u^h(x^h) \text{ for all } h \in S \text{ with } x^h \in C^h \text{ and } \sum_{h \in S} x^h \in Y \right\}.$$

$V(S)$ is the set of utility vectors whose projection on the utility subspace of the coalition S lies in or below the utility possibility set of S. A set W is *comprehensive* if $\zeta \in W$ and $\eta \le \zeta$ implies $\eta \in W$. Note that $V(S)$ is closed, nonempty, comprehensive, and bounded above in $\mathbf{R}^H$. Moreover, if $\xi \in V(S)$ and $\xi_h \ge \eta_h$ for all $h \in S$, then $\eta \in V(S)$.

Let $\mathscr{B}$ be a nonempty family of subsets of $\{1, \cdots, H\}$. Define $\mathscr{B}_h = \{S \in \mathscr{B} \mid h \in S\}$. A family $\mathscr{B}$ is balanced if there exist nonnegative weights w_S with $\sum_{S \in \mathscr{B}_h} w_S = 1$ for all h. A *V-allocation* is an element of $V(\{1, \cdots, H\})$. A coalition S can *improve* on a V-allocation ξ if there is a $\eta \in V(S)$ with $\eta_h > \xi_h$ for all $h \in S$. The *core* of V is the set of V-allocations that cannot be improved upon by any coalition. The following theorem is from Scarf (1967).

THEOREM (Scarf) *Suppose* $\bigcap_{S \in \mathscr{B}} V(S) \subset V(1, \cdots, H)$ *whenever B is a balanced family. Then V has a nonempty core.*

LEMMA 23   *Under assumptions 16 through 19 and 21 the economy $\mathscr{E}$ has a nonempty core.*

Proof Let $\mathscr{B}$ be a balanced family of sets with balancing weights w_S and let $(\zeta_1, \cdots, \zeta_H) \in \bigcap_{S \in \mathscr{B}} V(S)$. By lemma 19, the feasible set of a coalition is not empty. Therefore for each coalition S there are $x_S^h \in C^h$ for $h \in S$ with $\sum_{h \in S} x_S^h = y^S \in Y$ and $u^h(x_S^h) \ge \zeta_h$ for all $h \in S$. Now consider $x^h = \sum_{S \in \mathscr{B}_h} w_S x_S^h$. Note that $u^h(x^h) \ge \zeta_h$ by convexity of preferences. Also

$$\sum_{h=1}^H x^h = \sum_{h=1}^H \sum_{S \in \mathscr{B}_h} w_S x_S^h = \sum_{S \in \mathscr{B}} w_S \left(\sum_{h \in S} x_S^h \right) = \sum_{S \in \mathscr{B}} w_S y^S \in Y.$$

That $(\zeta^1, \cdots, \zeta^H)$ is feasible for the entire economy is implied by the feasibility of $(x^1, \cdots, x^H)$. Therefore $(\zeta^1, \cdots, \zeta^H) \in V(1, \cdots, H)$. Scarf's theorem now shows that the core of V is nonempty.

Now let $\tilde{\zeta} = (\zeta^1, \cdots, \zeta^H)$ be in the core of V, and take $\tilde{x} \in F$ with $U(\tilde{x}) \geq \tilde{\zeta}$. It is clear that $\tilde{x}$ is a core allocation. Therefore the core of the economy is not empty. ∎

We may now begin the main body of the proof. We consider the set $C^h - Y$ of possible trades with production for the hth consumer. The *set of admissible price vectors* is taken to be s_+^n. Unlike the admissible price vectors in our earlier models of the competitive economy, the price vectors in s_+^n are not all contained in the dual space of the commodity space. The dual space s^{n*} contains only those $p \in s_+^n$ that have a finite number of nonzero components. For $p \in s_+^n$ the *budget set* of the hth trader is $H^h(p) = \{x \mid x \in C^h \text{ and } px \leq 0\}$. A *competitive equilibrium* for the economy $\mathscr{E} = \{Y, C^1, \cdots, C^h, P^1, \cdots, P^h\}$ is a list $(p, y, x^1, \cdots, x^H)$ such that p is admissible and the following conditions are met.

I. $px^h \leq 0$ and $z \in P^h(x^h)$ implies $pz > 0$.

II. $y \in Y$ and $py = 0$ and $\limsup_{\tau \to \infty} pz(\tau) \leq 0$ for any $z \in Y$, where $z(\tau) = (z_1, \cdots, z_\tau, 0, \cdots)$.

III. $\sum_{h \in I} x^h = y$.

The first condition is the usual demand condition. The second condition is the profit condition. The limit superior handles cases where the limit may not exist. In these cases such paths cannot permanently increase profits over the equilibrium path. It should be recalled that all paths are infinite paths. If a path can be "terminated," this means that it has a zero tail after termination. Then, by condition II, the "terminated" path cannot make a profit. The third condition is the balance condition. Our objective is to prove

THEOREM 4   *The economy $\mathscr{E}$ has a competitive equilibrium under assumptions 16 through 21.*

The proof of theorem 4 will begin with a series of lemmas. Consider the replication of the economy $\mathscr{E}$. In the economy $\mathscr{E}_r$ where $\mathscr{E}$ has been replicated r times there are r copies of each trader who appears in $\mathscr{E}$. Each copy has the same trading set and preference correspondence as the original trader. We will use the idea of the equal treatment core introduced in chapter 5. The *equal treatment core* is equal to the set of allocations in the core of the replicated economy $\mathscr{E}_r$ such that each trader in $\mathscr{E}_r$ who is a replica of a given trader in E_1 undertakes the same net trade. Then an allocation in the equal treatment core K_r of $\mathscr{E}_r$ may be represented by $\{x^h\}_r$, where $\{x^h\}$ is the allocation of net trades to the original traders and r is the number of replications. Let K_1 be the core of the economy $\mathscr{E}_1$. We must first show that the equal treatment core is not empty for any r. Recall that x is indifferent with y, $x\mathscr{I}^h y$, if $x\mathscr{R}^h y$ and $y\mathscr{R}^h x$ where $x\mathscr{R}^h y$ means not $y\mathscr{P}^h x$.

LEMMA 24　*If $\{x^{hk}\}_r$, $h = 1, \cdots, H$, and $k = 1, \cdots, r$, is an allocation in the core of $\mathscr{E}_r$ then, for h given, $x^{hk} I^h x^{hk'}$ holds for all k and k'.*

Proof The proof of lemma 5.10, which depends on strong irreducibility, applies here. ∎

LEMMA 25　*The equal treatment core K_r of $\mathscr{E}_r$ is not empty if the core of E_r is not empty.*

Proof The proof of lemma 5.11 which follows directly from the previous lemma also applies here. ∎

LEMMA 26　$K_r \neq \emptyset$ *for any $r \geq 1$.*

Proof By lemma 23, the core of $\mathscr{E}_r$ is not empty. By lemma 25, this implies that the equal treatment core K_r of $\mathscr{E}_r$ is not empty. ∎

It is not enough that the equal treatment core be nonempty. We must also prove that it is closed.

LEMMA 27　*The equal treatment core K_r is compact.*

Proof Suppose that the allocations $\{x^{h^s}\}_r$, $s = 1, 2, \cdots$, lie in K_r and converge to $\{x^h\}_r$. Suppose that $\{x^h\}_r$ is not in K_r. Let w^{hi} be a net trade for the ith copy of the hth original trader. Then there is an improving coalition B such that $w^{hi} \in P^h(x^h)$ for $hi \in B$ and $\sum_{hi \in B} w^{hi} \in Y$. By the fact that $P^h(x^h)$ has open lower sections $w^{hi} \in P^h(x^{h^s})$ will hold when s is large. This implies that B is improving for $\{x^{h^s}\}_r$ for large s, and thus $\{x^{h^s}\}_r$ is not in K_r, contrary to the assumption. Therefore $\{x^h\}_r \in K_r$ must hold and K_r is closed. Since K_r is closed and lies in a compact feasible set by lemma 20, it is compact (Berge 1963, p. 68). ∎

Let $K = \bigcap_{r=1}^{\infty} K_r$. That is, $\{x^h\} \in K$ if $\{x^h\}_r \in K_r$ for all r.

LEMMA 28   *K is not empty.*

Proof If B is an improving coalition for an allocation $\{x^h\}_r$ in $\mathscr{E}_r$ it is also an improving coalition for the allocation $\{x^h\}_{r+1}$ in E_{r+1}. Thus $K_{r+1} \subset K_r$ and the K_r, $r = 1, 2, \cdots$, form a nested sequence of sets which are nonempty by lemma 22 and compact by lemma 27. Therefore the limit point $\{x^h\}$ of a convergent sequence $\{x^h\}_r$ as $r \to \infty$ lies in every K_r. Then $\{x^h\}$ lies in K. ∎

To prove theorem 4, we will show that $(x^1, \cdots, x^H) \in K$ implies that there is p and y such that $(p, y, x^1, \cdots, x^H)$ is a competitive equilibrium for $\mathscr{E}$. Let $G = $ convex hull $(\bigcup_{h=1}^{H} R^h(x^h))$.

LEMMA 29   *G is closed in s^n.*

Proof C^h is bounded below by assumption 18, and therefore G is bounded below. Let $z^s \in G$, $s = 1, 2, \cdots$, and $z^s \to z$. We must show that $z \in G$. Since G is the convex hull of $\bigcup_{h=1}^{H} R^h(x^h)$ and since $R^h(x^h)$ is convex, for each s it is possible to choose $\alpha_{hs} z^{hs} = w^{hs}$, $z^{hs} \in R^h(x^h)$, $\sum_{h \in I} \alpha_{hs} = 1$, $\alpha_{hs} \geq 0$, such that $z^s = \sum w^{hs}$. Suppose there is w^{hs} that is unbounded as $s \to \infty$. Since z^{hs} is bounded below by assumption 18 and $0 \leq \alpha_{hs} \leq 1$, this implies that z^s is unbounded above in contradiction to $z^s \to z$. Therefore w^{hs} is bounded, and there is a subsequence z^s (retain notation) such that w^{hs} converges to a point w^h. By choosing further subsequences, one finds a subsequence z^s such that w^{hs} converges to w^h for all h, and moreover $\alpha_{hs} \to \alpha_h$.

Let $I = \{h \mid \alpha_h > 0\}$. For $h \in I$, $w^{hs}/\alpha_{hs} = z^{hs} \to w^h/\alpha_h \in C^h$. For $h \notin I$, $\alpha_{hs} \bar{z} \leq w^{hs} = \alpha_{hs} z^{hs}$ where $\bar{z}$ is the lower bound on C^h from assumption 18. Taking the limit shows $0 \leq w^h$ for $h \notin I$. Now consider $w^h/\alpha_h + \sum_{i \notin I} w^i$, which is in $R^h(x^h)$ for $h \in I$ by periodwise monotonicity. Moreover, since $\sum_{h \in I} \alpha_h = 1$, we have

$$\sum_{h \in I} \alpha_h \left(\frac{w^h}{\alpha_h} + \sum_{i \notin I} w^i \right) = \sum_{h=1}^{H} w^h = z.$$

Then $z \in G$ by its definition so G is closed. ∎

We will need the following theorem adapted from Choquet (1962).

THEOREM (Choquet) *Let Z be a convex set in s^n closed in the product topology. If Z contains no straight lines, then for any two subsets X and Y of Z closed in the product topology the sum $X + Y$ is closed.*

LEMMA 30 $G - Y$ *is closed in s^n.*

Proof From assumption 18 we have $G - Y \subset \bar{z} + s_+^n - Y$. Both $G - \bar{z}$ and $-Y$ are closed and contained in $s_+^n - Y$. Now suppose that $s_+^n - Y$ contains a straight line. Then there is z such that z and $-z$ are contained in $s_+^n - Y$, so there are y, $y' \in Y$ with $z \geq -y$, $-z \geq -y'$. This implies that $y + y' \geq 0$. Since Y is a cone $\lambda(y + y') \in Y$ for every $\lambda \geq 0$. However, by lemma 19, $\{y \in Y \mid y \geq 0\}$ is bounded. Thus it must be that $y + y' = 0$. But then $y = -y'$. Since Y contains no straight lines by assumption 16, $y = -y' = 0$, so $z = 0$ as well. It follows that $s_+^n - Y$ contains no straight lines. Thus we need only show that $s_+^n - Y$ is closed and apply Choquet's theorem.

Let $z^n \to z$ with $z^n \in s_+^n - Y$. Then there are $y^n \in Y$ with $-z^n \leq y^n$. Since z^n converges, the y^n are bounded below. By lemma 19, this implies that y^n is bounded. Thus y^n has a convergent subsequence with limit $y \in Y$. Since $-z^n \leq y^n$, $-z \leq y$ and $z \in s_+^n - Y$. Thus $s_+^n - Y$ is closed. ∎

LEMMA 31 $K \neq \emptyset$ *implies that there is no $z \in G$ and $y \in Y$ such that $z - y \leq 0$ and $z_t - y_t < 0$ for some t.*

Proof Recall that $Q(\tilde{x})$ is the convex hull of the $P^h(x^h)$. It was proved in establishing theorem 5.4 that $0 \notin Q(\tilde{x}) - Y$ when K is not empty. The argument is not changed in the infinite-dimensional case. Thus it cannot hold that there are

$$w^h \in P^h(x^h) \quad \text{such that} \quad \sum_{h=1}^{H} \alpha_h w^h = y \in Y, \tag{4}$$

where $\alpha^h \geq 0$, $\sum \alpha_h = 1$.

Let $z \in G$, $y \in Y$, with $z \leq y$ and $z_t < y_t$ for some t. We have $z = \sum_h \alpha_h z^h$ for some $z^h \in R^h(x^h)$, $\alpha_h \geq 0$, $\sum \alpha_h = 1$. Therefore $\sum_h \alpha_h(z^h + (y - z)) = y \in Y$. But $z^h \in R^h(x^h)$ implies $z^h + (y - z) \in P^h(x^h)$ by periodwise monotonicity. Letting $w^h = z^h + (y - z)$ gives an instance of (4), since $\sum_{h=1}^{H} \alpha_h w^h = y \in Y$. Thus no such z can exist. ∎

LEMMA 32 *For any $\varepsilon > 0$ there is $p \in s^{n*}$ such that $pz > -\varepsilon|p_0|$ for all $z \in G - Y$. Also $p \geq 0$, $|p_0| > 0$.*

Proof For $\varepsilon > 0$ let $a(\varepsilon) = (-\varepsilon e_0, 0, 0, \cdots)$ where $e_0 = (1, \cdots, 1)$. By lemma 31, $a(\varepsilon) \notin G - Y$. By lemma 30, $G - Y$ is closed. Also $\{a(\varepsilon)\}$ is compact. By a separation theorem (Berge 1963, p. 251), there is a continuous linear functional $f \in s^{n*}$ with $f \neq 0$ such that $f(z) > f(a(\varepsilon)) + \delta$ for any $z \in G - Y$ and some $\delta > 0$. However, any such f may be represented by a vector $p \in s^n$ with $p \neq 0$ but $p_t = 0$ for all but finitely many t, where

$$f(z) = pz = \sum_{t=0}^{\infty} p_t z_t \geq -\varepsilon|p_0| + \delta$$

for any $z \in G - Y$ and some $\delta > 0$. Periodwise monotonicity and the separation condition imply that $p \geq 0$. Thus we have for some $p \geq 0$, $p \neq 0$,

$$pz > -\varepsilon|p_0| \qquad \text{for all } z \in G - Y. \tag{5}$$

However, $x^h \in R^h(x^h)$ for all h and $\sum_{h=1}^{H} x^h = y$ for some $y \in Y$, since $\{x^h\}$ is an allocation. Therefore $0 \in G - Y$. Since $Y = Y + Y$ and $0 \in G - Y$, it follows that $-Y \subset G - Y$. Substituting $-y$ for z in (5), we find that $py < \varepsilon|p_0|$ for all $y \in Y$, and $|p_0| \neq 0$. ∎

Define d^h by $d_0^h = x_0^h + e_0$, $d_t^h = x_t^h$ for $t = 1, \cdots, \tau$, and $d_t^h = \alpha \bar{x}_t^h$ for $t > \tau$. By assumption 21, we may choose α and τ so that $d^h \in R^h(x^h) - Y$. By periodwise monotonicity, $d^h \in P^h(x^h)$ if $\tau = \infty$. Using the assumption that P^h is open valued relative to C^h, we may choose $\tau < \infty$ so that $d^h \in P^h(x^h)$ still holds. Also τ and α may be chosen uniformly for all h. Then $d^h \in G - Y$, and we have $pd^h > -\varepsilon|p_0|$ by lemma 32 Let $d_0^{h\prime} = d_0^h + e_0$ and $d_t^{h\prime} = d_t^h$ for $t > 0$. By monotonicity, $d^{h\prime}$ is also in $P^h(x^h)$. Define $\bar{c}^h$ by $\bar{c}^h = d^{h\prime} - \alpha \bar{x}^h$. Then $\bar{c}_t^h = 0$ for $t > \tau$. Since $p\bar{x}^h \leq 0$, we have $p\bar{c}^h > p_0 e_0 = |p_0|$ whenever $\varepsilon < 1$ from (5) and the definition of $d^{h\prime}$. Let $\bar{c} = (1/H) \sum_{h=1}^{H} \bar{c}^h$.

For $\varepsilon < 1$ we define the *price set*

$$S(\varepsilon) = \{p \in ba_+ \mid pw \geq -\varepsilon \text{ for all } w \in (G - Y) \cap l_\infty^n \text{ and } p\bar{c} = 1\}.$$

In the definition of $S(\varepsilon)$ we allow the possibility that $pw = \sum_{t=0}^{\infty} p_t w_t = \infty$. The space ba is the dual space of l_∞^n (Dunford and Schwartz 1957, pp. 240, 296). The space ba may be decomposed into l_1^n and purely finitely additive measures, which are 0 on vectors in l_∞^n that have a finite number of nonzero components (Dunford and Schwartz 1957, p. 163). We will be able to find prices in l_1^n.

LEMMA 33 $S(\varepsilon)$ *is not empty for* $1 > \varepsilon > 0$. *Moreover, when* $p \in S(\varepsilon)$, $pz \leq 0$ *for all* $z \in Y \cap l_\infty^n$.

Proof By lemma 32, there is $p \geq 0$ such that $pz \geq -\varepsilon|p_0|$ for all $z \in G - Y$. Since $p \in s^{n*}$, it has only a finite number of nonzero components, so $p \in l_1^n \subset ba$. Also $(1/|p_0|)pz \geq -\varepsilon$. Let αp satisfy $\alpha p\bar{c} = 1$. As we have seen, from the definition of $\bar{c}$ we have $p\bar{c} \geq |p_0|$. Therefore α is well defined and positive. To show that $\alpha p \in S(\varepsilon)$, we must show that $\alpha pz \geq -\varepsilon$ holds for all $z \in G - Y$. Since $pz < 0$ is possible and $\alpha > 0$ holds, we require $\alpha < 1/|p_0|$. However, the definition of α implies $\alpha = 1/p\bar{c}$, and $p\bar{c} \geq |p_0|$ by the definition of $\bar{c}$. Thus $\alpha p \in S(\varepsilon)$ and $S(\varepsilon)$ is not empty for any ε with $1 > \varepsilon > 0$.

Now let $p \in S(\varepsilon)$. Since $Y = Y + Y$ and $0 \in G - Y$, we find by adding $-Y$ to both sides that $-Y \cap l_\infty^n \subset (G - Y) \cap l_\infty^n$. Therefore $pz \leq \varepsilon$ for all $z \in Y \cap l_\infty^n$ by the definition of $S(\varepsilon)$. Since $\alpha z \in Y$ for any $\alpha > 0$, it follows that $pz \leq 0$ for all $z \in Y \cap l_\infty^n$. ∎

We will use the weak topology for ba as the dual space of l_∞^n (Berge 1963, p. 236). In the weak topology for a dual space, convex sets that are closed and bounded in the norm topology (equivalent in this case to closed and bounded in the weak topology; Kelley and Namioka 1963, pp. 154–55) are compact by the theorem of Alaoglu (Berge 1963, p. 262).

LEMMA 34 $S(\varepsilon)$ *is weakly compact when* $\varepsilon < 1$.

Proof Let p be an arbitrary element of $S(\varepsilon)$. Let $\bar{x} = \sum_1^H \bar{x}^h$. Consider the point w of $G - Y$ where $w = \bar{c} + \alpha\bar{x}/H$. See assumption 20 for the definition of $\alpha\bar{x}^h$. By definition of $S(\varepsilon)$, we have $pw = p(\bar{c} + \alpha\bar{x}/H) \geq -\varepsilon$, or

$$-p\bar{x} \leq \frac{H(1+\varepsilon)}{\alpha}. \tag{6}$$

$S(\varepsilon)$ is closed by continuity of the inner product since it is defined by weak inequalities. Since $p \geq 0$, $p \neq 0$, and $\bar{x}$ is constant and strictly negative, $S(\varepsilon)$ is bounded by (6). Consequently, by Alaoglu's theorem, $S(\varepsilon)$ is weakly compact. ∎

LEMMA 35 $S = \bigcap_{0<\varepsilon<1} S(\varepsilon)$ is not empty. Also $\bar{p} \in S$ implies $\bar{p}z \geq 0$ for all $z \in (G - Y) \cap l_\infty^n$.

Proof $S(\varepsilon)$ is not empty by lemma 33 and weakly compact by lemma 34. Since the sets $S(\varepsilon)$ are nested, their intersection S is not empty by the finite intersection property (Dunford and Schwartz 1957, p. 17). The last statement of the lemma follows from the fact that $\bar{p} \in S(\varepsilon)$ for all small ε and $pz \geq -\varepsilon$. ∎

THEOREM (Yosida-Hewitt)   *If λ is in ba and $\lambda \geq 0$, then there is a unique decomposition $\lambda = \lambda_1 + \lambda_2$, $\lambda_1, \lambda_2 \geq 0$, where λ_1 is countably additive and λ_2 is a purely finitely additive set function* (Dunford and Schwartz 1957, p. 163).

It is easily seen that λ_1 lies in l_1^n in our case. We consider the decomposition of $\bar{p} \in S$ into $p^* \in l_1^n$ and p_f, which is purely finitely additive. Since $\bar{c}$ has only a finite number of nonzero components, we have $p_f\bar{c} = 0$ and $p^*\bar{c} = \bar{p}\bar{c} = 1$. Thus $p^* \neq 0$. For an elementary proof of these facts, see Prescott and Lucas (1972).

LEMMA 36   *The price vector p^* satisfies $p^*w = \lim_{\tau\to\infty} p^*w(\tau) \geq 0$ for all $w \in G$ and $\limsup_{\tau\to\infty} p^*y(\tau) \leq 0$ for all $y \in Y$.*

Proof Let $z = w - y$ with $w \in G$ and $y \in Y$. Define $w_{it}^- = 0$ for $w_{it} \geq 0$ and $w_{it}^- = w_{it}$ for $w_{it} < 0$. For $w \in C^h$, $\bar{z}^- \leq w^-$ by assumption 18. Since G is a convex hull of sets that lie in the C^h, this implies that $w^- \in l_\infty^n$. On the other hand, $p^*w = p^*(w - w^-) + p^*w^-$. The first term is finite or $+\infty$, while the second term is finite, since $p^* \in l_1^n$. Thus p^*w is either finite or $+\infty$.

Take $z \in G - Y$. Recall that $G = \text{convex hull } (\bigcup_{h=1}^{H} R^h(x^h))$ where $(x^1, \cdots, x^H) \in K$. Let $\varepsilon > 0$. Write $z = \sum_{h=1}^{H} \alpha_h z^h$ with $z^h \in R^h(x^h) - Y$. For τ large, $\bar{z}^h(\tau) = (\varepsilon e_0 + z_0^h, z_1^h, \cdots, z_\tau^h, 0, \cdots) \in R^h(x^h) - Y$ by assumption 21 and monotonicity. Thus

$$\bar{z}(\tau) = \sum_{h=1}^{H} \alpha_h \hat{z}^h(\tau) \in (G - Y) \cap l_\infty^n. \tag{7}$$

Apply $\bar{p} \in S$ to (7) to see $\varepsilon|p_0^*| + \sum_{h=1}^{H} \alpha_h p^* z^h(\tau) = \bar{p}\hat{z}(\tau) \geq 0$ for τ large. Letting $\tau \to \infty$, we find that $\varepsilon|p_0^*| + \liminf_{\tau\to\infty} p^* z(\tau) \geq 0$. Since ε was arbitrary, $\liminf_{\tau\to\infty} p^* z(\tau) \geq 0$. On the other hand, we have $-Y \subset G - Y$. Therefore $\liminf_{\tau\to\infty} p^*(-y(\tau)) \geq 0$, or equivalently $\limsup_{\tau\to\infty} p^* y(\tau) \leq 0$ for any $y \in Y$. ∎

Proof of Theorem 4 I claim that $(p^*, y, x^1, \cdots, x^H)$ where $y = \sum_{h=1}^{H} x^h$ and $(x^1, \cdots, x^H) \in K$ is a competitive equilibrium for $\mathcal{E}$. Since C^h is bounded below by $\bar{z}$, and $p^* \geq 0$, either $\sum_0^T p_t^* x_t^h$ converges to a finite limit $p^* x^h$, as $T \to \infty$, or $p^* x^h = +\infty$. In any case $p^* x^h \geq 0$ for all h, since $x^h \in G \subset G - Y$. Also, by lemma 36, we have $\limsup_{\tau\to\infty} p^* z(\tau) \leq 0$ for $z \in Y$. But then $0 \leq \sum_{h=1}^{H} p^* x^h = p^* y \leq 0$. Therefore $p^* x^h$ for all h and $p^* y = 0$. Note that for this y the limit superior is the limit as $\tau \to \infty$. Therefore the profit condition, condition II of competitive equilibrium, is met. Condition III is an immediate consequence of the fact that $(x^1, \cdots, x^H)$ is an allocation and $y = \sum_{h=1}^{H} x^h$.

The first part of condition I follows from the support of G by p^*. To complete the proof of theorem 4, we must show that $w^h \in P^h(x^h)$ implies that $w^h \notin H^h(p^*) = \{z^h \mid p^* z^h \leq 0\}$. That is any point preferred by the hth consumer must lie outside his budget set. By lemma 5.4, which is valid for the infinite case by the same argument used in chapter 5, this will hold if every consumer has a point w in his trading set which satisfies $pw < 0$. Consider $\bar{x}^h \in C^h - Y$. Then $\bar{x}^h = w^h - y'$ for some $w^h \in C^h$ and $y' \in Y$. So

$$p^* w^h = p^* \bar{x}^h + p^* y' \leq p^* \bar{x}^h,$$

where $\bar{x}^h$ is from assumption 21. Note that $p^* w^h$ is well defined since $w^h \in C^h$, and $p^* \bar{x}^h$ is well defined since $0 \geq \bar{x}_t^h \geq \bar{x}_t$ and $\bar{x}_t$ is constant over t. Thus $p^* y'$ is also well defined as $\lim_{\tau\to\infty} p^* y'(\tau)$. Since $\bar{x} = \sum_h \bar{x}^h < 0$, at least one consumer has $p^* \bar{x}^h < 0$ and thus $p^* w^h < 0$.

Let I_1 be the set of indexes h such that there is $w \in C^h$ with $p^* w < 0$. Let I_2 be the complementary subset of indexes. We have just shown that I_1 is not empty. Suppose that $I_2 = \emptyset$. By strong irreducibility, assumption 20, there is a feasible allocation $\{z^h\}$ with $z^h \mathscr{P}^h x^h$ for all $h \in I_1$. Then $p^* z^h > 0$ for $h \in I_1$ must hold. However, $p^* z^h \geq 0$ for $h \in I_2$ by assumption. Thus $p^*(z_{I_1} + z_{I_2}) = p^* y' > 0$. But $y' \in Y$ by feasibility, so $p^* y' \leq 0$. This is a contradiction, so I_2 must be empty. Then by lemma 5.4, $z^h \in P^h(x^h)$ implies $p^* z^h > 0$ for all h. This establishes the second part of condition I for competitive equilibrium. Therefore $(p^*, y, x^1, \cdots, x^h)$, where $y = \sum_{h=1}^{H} x^h$, is a competitive equilibrium of $\mathscr{E}$. ∎

Let us say that an allocation in K is an *Edgeworth equilibrium*. We have shown that any Edgeworth equilibrium is a competitive equilibrium. It follows from theorem 5.4, whose proof is valid for the infinite case, with trivial changes to take account of the new profit conditions, that any competitive equilibrium is an Edgeworth equilibrium. Thus we have the

COROLLARY *An allocation is an Edgeworth equilibrium of the economy $\mathscr{E}$ if and only if there is a price vector p for which it is a competitive equilibrium.*

6.5 Uniqueness of Equilibrium

It is implied by global stability that equilibrium is unique. Thus the first uniqueness theorems for competitive equilibrium were the theorems on global stability given gross substitutes. However, the assumption of gross substitutes for the entire price domain is very restrictive. An important generalization of this assumption was obtained by Gale and Nikaido (1965) who took one of the implications of gross substitutes for the Jacobian of the excess demand functions and showed that the implication is a sufficient condition for uniqueness. The assumption of gross substitutes implies that the principal minors of the Jacobian determinant of order r have the sign $(-1)^r$, or equivalently the determinant of the negative of the Jacobian matrix has all of its principal minors positive. Gale and Nikaido proved that a mapping with such a Jacobian over any interval in $\mathbf{R}^n$ is invertible, which implies that the price vector that corresponds to 0 excess demand is unique. On the other hand, Dierker (1972) used a theorem of differential topology to prove that boundary conditions can be combined with local stability to give uniqueness.

We will first consider the Gale-Nikaido theorem, which has applications to problems of uniqueness other than proving competitive equilibrium to be unique. Indeed, the problem that stimulated their research was factor price equalization in world trade, or the uniqueness of factor prices given goods prices.

A square matrix A is said to be a *P-matrix* if all its principal minors are positive. The first result is purely algebraic.

LEMMA 37 *If A is a P-matrix, then $Ax \leq 0$ and $x \geq 0$ imply $x = 0$.*

Proof The result is immediate if the order of A is 1. Assume that it is true when the order of A is equal to $n - 1$. Let x satisfy the hypothesis and $x \neq 0$ hold. There are two cases.

Case 1. Suppose that some x_i, say x_1, is 0. Let $x_{(1)} = (x_2, \cdots, x_n)$ and $A_1 = [a_{ij}]$, $i, j = 2, \cdots, n$. Then A_1 is a *P*-matrix, and by assumption, $A_1 x_{(1)} \leq 0$ and $x_{(1)} \geq 0$. The induction hypothesis implies $x_{(1)} = 0$, so $x = 0$.

Case 2. Suppose $x > 0$ holds. Since A is a *P*-matrix, A^{-1} has a positive diagonal. Let a_i^{-1} be the ith column of A^{-1}. There is $\lambda_i > 0$ such that $y = x - \lambda_i a_i^{-1} \geq 0$ and $y_k = 0$ for some k. Then $Ay = Ax - \lambda_i A a_i^{-1} = Ax - \lambda_i \delta^i \leq 0$, where $\delta_i^i = 1$ and $\delta_j^i = 0$ for $j \neq i$. From case 1, $y = 0$. Since i is arbitrary and $x = \lambda_i a_i^{-1}$, all the columns of A^{-1} are proportional so that A^{-1} is singular, which is a contradiction. Therefore no such x can exist. ∎

Let $S_n = \{x \in \mathbf{R}^n \mid x \geq 0 \text{ and } \sum_i x_i = 1\}$.

COROLLARY 1   *If A is a P-matrix of order n, there is λ such that $(Ax)_i \geq \lambda > 0$ for some i for any $x \in S_n$.*

Proof Let $y = Ax$ where $x \in S_n$. Let $\eta(x) = \max y_i$, $i = 1, \cdots, n$. Then $\eta(x)$ attains a minimum value λ over the compact set S_n. Moreover, by lemma 37, $\lambda > 0$. ∎

Let cone (A) be the convex cone spanned by the columns of A.

COROLLARY 2   *If A is a P-matrix, there is x such that $x > 0$ and $Ax > 0$. If $a_{ij} \leq 0$ for $i \neq j$, then A has a dominant diagonal.*

Proof Let A be of order n. Lemma 37 is equivalent to the proposition that A is a *P*-matrix implies cone $(A) \cap \mathbf{R}_-^n = \{0\}$. Also cone (A^T) contains an interior point, since A^T is nonsingular as a *P*-matrix.

Let $\bar{y}$ lie in the interior of cone (A^T). Since A^T is a *P*-matrix, $A^T y \leq 0$ and $y \geq 0$ implies $y = 0$. Define $S = \{z \mid z \in \text{cone } (A^T) \text{ and } \bar{y}z = 1\}$. S is convex and compact by lemma 3. Also $S \cap \mathbf{R}_-^n = \emptyset$. Since S is compact and R_-^n is closed, by a separation theorem (Berge 1963, p. 163), there is $x \neq 0$ and μ such that $xz < \mu$ for all $z \varepsilon R_-^n$ and $xz > \mu$ for $z \in S$. It follows from the first inequality that $\mu > 0$ and $x \geq 0$. Then the second inequality implies that $xz > 0$ for $z \in \text{cone}(A^T) \backslash \{0\}$. That is, $x^T A^T w > 0$ for all $w \geq 0, w \neq 0$, or $Ax > 0$. By continuity, x may be chosen so that $x > 0$. Suppose that A satisfies $a_{ij} \leq 0$ for $i \neq j$. Then $Ax > 0$ implies that A^T

has a dominant diagonal. Then, by the proof of theorem 3.1, A has a dominant diagonal. ∎

In other words, not only is it true for a P-matrix A that cone $(A) \cap \mathbf{R}^n_- = \{0\}$ but cone $(A) \cap \operatorname{int} \mathbf{R}^n_+ \neq \emptyset$. It was proved by Hawkins and Simon (1949) that the matrix of a simple Leontief model $\mathscr{L}$, which is a P-matrix, has a nonnegative inverse. Note that corollary 2 implies that a Leontief matrix that satisfies the Hawkins-Simon conditions has a dominant diagonal. Then theorem 3.1 implies that it has a nonnegative inverse. Thus the Gale-Nikaido theorem provides an alternative proof of the Hawkins-Simon theorem.

An open interval $I = (p, q)$ in $\mathbf{R}^n$ is $\{x \mid p < x < q\}$. If F is a differentiable mapping of an open interval I of $\mathbf{R}^n$ into $\mathbf{R}^n$, write $F'(x)$ for the Jacobian $[F_{ij}]$ of F at x. By applying lemma 36 to the Jacobian, a weak form of monotonicity can be proved for nonlinear maps.

LEMMA 38   *If $F'(x)$ is a P-matrix for all x in an open interval I, then for any a and x in I, $x \geq a$ and $F(x) \leq F(a)$ implies $a = x$.*

Proof   For $n = 1$, F is a strictly monotone function, and the result is clear. Assume that the result holds for $n - 1$. Without loss of generality, assume $a = 0$ and $F(0) = 0$. Let X be the set of solutions to $x \geq 0$, $F(x) \leq 0$, $x \in I$. Then, by differentiability,

$$\lim_{x \to 0} \left(\frac{F(x)}{|x|} - \frac{F'(0) \cdot x}{|x|} \right) = 0. \tag{8}$$

By corollary 1, the second term in parentheses of (8) has some coordinate less than or equal to $\lambda < 0$ for any $x \geq 0$ and $\neq 0$. But $|x|$ sufficiently small implies that the left side of (8) is less than λ in absolute value. Thus $F(x)$ has a positive coordinate. In other words, $F(x) \leq 0$ has no solution for $x \geq 0$ and $|x|$ small. Therefore 0 is an isolated point of X.

Let $\bar{X} = X \backslash \{0\}$. Since X is closed and 0 is isolated in X, $\bar{X}$ is closed. Since $\bar{X} \subset I$, it is also bounded. The theorem is proved if it is shown that $\bar{X}$ is empty. If $\bar{X} \neq \emptyset$, there is $\bar{x}$ such that no $x \in \bar{X}$ satisfies $x \leq \bar{x}$ other than $\bar{x}$ itself. There are two cases to consider to establish the lemma.

Case 1. $\bar{x} > 0$.

By corollary 2, there is $x < 0$ such that $F'(\bar{x}) \cdot x < 0$. For x sufficiently small, $x' = \bar{x} + x > 0$. Since $\bar{x} > x' > 0$, $x' \in I$. But, for x small, $F(x') \cong F(\bar{x}) + F'(\bar{x}) \cdot x < F(\bar{x})$. Therefore $x' \in \bar{X}$ in contradiction to the minimality of $\bar{x}$. In other words $\bar{x} > 0$ cannot hold.

Case 2. $\bar{x}_i = 0$, for some i, say $i = 1$.

Define F^* on $\mathbf{R}^{n-1}$ by $F_i^*(x_2, \cdots, x_n) = F_i(0, x_2, \cdots, x_n)$ for $i = 2, \cdots, n$. F^* is then defined on an interval and $F^{*\prime}$ is a P-matrix. But $F_i^*(0) = F_i(0)$ and $0 \geq F_i(\bar{x}) = F_i^*(\bar{x}_2, \cdots, \bar{x}_n)$, $i = 2, \cdots, n$. Since $\bar{x} \geq 0$ by the induction hypothesis, $\bar{x}_i = 0$, $i = 2, \cdots, n$. Thus $\bar{x} = 0$ in contradiction to the assumption that $\bar{x} \in \bar{X}$. In other words, $\bar{x}_i = 0$ for some i is not possible either.

Since case 1 and case 2 exhaust the possible cases, we may conclude that $\bar{X}$ is empty. ∎

We will show that the weak monotonicity of nonlinear maps whose Jacobians are P-matrices implies that these maps are univalent over intervals where this condition holds. Say that a mapping is differentiable if there are continuous first-order partial derivatives over the domain of the mapping.

THEOREM 5   *If F is a differentiable mapping of an open interval $I \subset R^n$ into R^n, and the Jacobian $F'(x)$ is a P-matrix for all $x \in I$, F is univalent in I.*

Proof   Suppose that there are x, $y \in I$ and $F(x) = F(y)$. Without loss of generality, we may assume $x_i \leq y_i$ for $i \leq k$, $x_i > y_i$ for $i > k$. Define the transformation D on I by $D(z_1, \cdots, z_n) = (z_1, \cdots, z_k, -z_{k+1}, \cdots, -z_n)$, that is,

$$D = \begin{bmatrix} I_k & 0 \\ 0 & -I_{n-k} \end{bmatrix},$$

where I_k is the identity matrix of order k. Then D is univalent and $D^{-1} = D$. Also D applied to I gives an open interval. Let $Dx = x'$, $Dy = y'$. Define $H = D \circ F \circ D$. Then $H(x') = D \circ F(x) = D \circ F(y) = H(y')$. Also H' is a P-matrix, since in every principal minor there is an equal number of sign changes in rows and columns between F' and H'. Therefore by lemma 38, $x' = y'$. This implies $x = y$. ∎

One form of the factor price equalization problem is the inversion of a set of cost functions to find the goods prices implied by a vector of factor prices when the number of goods equals the number of factors. Consider the cost functions

$$\pi_i = g_i(w_1, \cdots, w_n), \qquad i = 1, \cdots, n. \tag{9}$$

Assume that $\partial g_i/\partial w_j$ is well defined and continuous for $w \in \mathbf{R}_+^n \setminus \{0\}$. Assume that the Jacobian $[g_{ij}]$ of g is a P-matrix over an open interval $I = (0, z)$ where $z > 0$. Then theorem 5 implies that the functions

$$w_j(\pi) = g_j^{-1}(\pi_1, \cdots, \pi_n), \qquad j = 1, \cdots, n,$$

exist and are continuous over $R = g(I)$ where $I \subset \mathbf{R}_+^n \setminus \{0\}$. Suppose that the open interval I may be chosen arbitrarily in $\mathbf{R}_+^n$. Assume that we can ignore transport costs, and there are no impediments to trade. Suppose that the conditions of supply for the factors determine that factor prices must be positive in a competitive equilibrium. Then, if production functions and thus cost functions are the same in two countries and if all n goods are produced in both countries, given a vector of goods prices $p > 0$ the factor prices in each country must be equal to $g^{-1}(p)$ in a competitive equilibrium.

On the other hand, we may consider a system of excess demand functions

$$x_i = e_i(p_1, \cdots, p_{n-1}, 1), \qquad i = 1, \cdots, n-1. \tag{10}$$

The numéraire commodity is omitted since $x_n = -\sum_{i=1}^{n-1} p_i x_i$ by Walras' Law. The excess demand functions define a differentiable mapping of int $\mathbf{R}_+^{n-1}$ into $\mathbf{R}^{n-1}$. Assume that in competitive equilibrium the price vector $\bar{p}$ must be positive. If the Jacobian $[-e_{ij}]_{n-1}^1$ of $-e$ is a P-matrix over an open interval $I \subset \mathbf{R}_+^n$ where $0 \in R = e(I)$, then theorem 5 implies that the equilibrium price $\bar{p} = e^{-1}(0)$ is unique.

An alternative approach to the uniqueness problem is by way of differential topology. This approach was first used by Dierker (1972). We will adapt an argument due to Varian (1975). Let $S = \{p \mid \sum_{i=1}^n p_i^2 = 1$, $p_i > 0$, for all $i\}$. For $z, w \in S$ let $d(z, w)$ be the length of the shortest arc on S between z and w. Define $S' = \{p \mid p \in S, p_i > \delta > 0$, for all $i\}$. Define $S'' = \{p \mid p \in S, d(p, S') \leq \delta/2\}$.

LEMMA 39 S'' is a smooth manifold with boundary.

Proof   It is clear that S'' is a smooth manifold (Milnor 1965) if it has a smooth boundary. This means that each boundary point p of S'' is supported relative to S'' by a unique vector lying in the tangent space to S at that point. That is, at each boundary point p of S'' there is a unique vector s in TS_p, the tangent space of S at p, such that $sq \leq sp$ for all $q \in S''$. By its definition S' is a convex subset of S in the generalized sense in which shortest arcs in S take the place of chords. Consequently the shortest arc c on S linking p to S' is unique. Then s is the tangent to c, pointing away from S'', at the point where c meets S''. Thus s is unique. ∎

Let $z(p)$ be an excess supply function that is well defined for $p \in S$. $z(p) = -e(p)$. Introduce

ASSUMPTION 22 $z(p)$ is continuously differentiable for $p > 0$.

ASSUMPTION 23 $p \in S$ and $p_i < \delta$ implies $z_j(p) < 0$ for some j.

ASSUMPTION 24 $z(p) = 0$ implies $|z_{ij}(p)|_{n-1}^1 \neq 0$ for $p \in S$.

ASSUMPTION 25 $p \cdot z(p) = 0$.

LEMMA 40 $z(p)$ *defines a smooth vector field on S''.*

Proof Since S'' lies in the surface of a sphere the tangent space TS_p'' of S'' at p is the affine subspace containing p and orthogonal to p. Then from assumption 25, $z(p)$ is an element of TS_p''. Therefore by assumption 22, $z(p)$ defines a smooth vector field on S'' (Milnor 1965). ∎

If $z(p) = 0$ for $p \in S$, define the *index* $\iota_z(p)$ of z at p to be sign $|z_{ij}(p)|_{n-1}^1$. Let D^n denote the n-dimensional disk. We quote a lemma of Hopf (Milnor 1965).

LEMMA 41   *Let v be a smooth vector field on D^{n-1} which maps D^{n-1} into R^{n-1}. Suppose that $v(p)$ points out of D^{n-1} on the boundary and has isolated zeros $p^1, \cdots, p^k, k \geq 1$. If $|v_{ij}| \neq 0$ for any p^i, then $\sum_{i=1}^{k} \iota_v(p^i) = 1$.*

With the help of lemma 41, we may prove a uniqueness result for a system of excess demand functions.

THEOREM 6   *Under assumptions 22 through 25, if $|z_{ij}|_{n-1}^1$ has the same sign, different from 0, at all zeros of $z(p)$ for $p \in S''$, there is only one zero of $z(p)$ in S''.*

Proof S'' is diffeomorphic to the $(n-1)$-dimensional disk D^{n-1}. Therefore the conclusion follows from an application of lemma 41. ∎

Let us say that a differential equation system has local linear stability if it has a stable linearization. Local linear stability implies local stability by lemma 2.11.

COROLLARY 1   *If all equilibria of $e(p)$ have local linear stability, the equilibrium is unique.*

Proof The determinant of the matrix $[z_{ij}(p)]_{n-1}^1$ is equal to the product of its characteristic roots. If $\bar{p}$ is an equilibrium, local linear stability implies that all characteristic roots of $J_n(\bar{p}) = -[z_{ij}(p)]_{n-1}^1$ have negative real parts. Thus the characteristic roots of $[z_{ij}(p)]_{n-1}^1$ have positive real parts. Since complex roots come in conjugate pairs, stability implies that the product of the characteristic roots of $[z_{ij}(p)]_{n-1}^1$ at the equilibrium is positive and the sign of $|z_{ij}(p)|_{n-1}^1$ at an equilibrium is positive. Then the sum of the indexes $\iota_z(p)$ over the competitive equilibria is equal to the number of equilibria. Since, by lemma 41, this sum is 1, there is only one equilibrium. ∎

Lemma 41 has another rather odd consequence which was noticed by Varian.

PROPOSITION   *If the number of goods is even, the equilibrium cannot be completely unstable if it is unique.*

Proof By lemma 41, $\iota_z(\bar{p}) = 1$ if the equilibrium $\bar{p}$ is unique. Let the λ_i be the roots of $J_n(\bar{p})$. By complete instability, $\mathscr{R}(\lambda_i) > 0$, where $\mathscr{R}(\lambda_i)$ is the real part of λ_i. Then the real parts of the roots of $[z_{ij}]_{n-1}^1$ have the sign -1. But this implies that $\iota_z(\bar{p}) = (-1)^{n-1} = -1$, which contradicts lemma 41 since the equilibrium is unique. ∎

Theorem 6 is a valid example of Samuelson's correspondence principle (Samuelson 1947, p. 258), which says that the assumption of stability has consequences for statics. Benhabib and Nishimura have also shown how to apply Hopf's lemma to establish the uniqueness of stationary optimal paths in capital accumulation problems (Benhabib and Nishimura 1979), and Nishimura to prove that factor prices are equalized (Nishimura 1981).

Appendix A: Existence of a Zero of the Excess Demand Functions

In the case of the exchange economy or in the case of the economy of firms it is possible for the excess demand correspondences to be ordinary functions and even to be continuously differentiable. Then, if there is free disposal and a boundary condition is met, the equilibria must occur in the interior of the price simplex. In the interior it is possible to assume that the Jacobian of the excess demand functions is well defined everywhere. We can then prove that a zero of these functions exists when the Jacobian bordered with the price vector is nonsingular for positive prices. This is equivalent to proving that a competitive equilibrium exists for the special case. This result was stated by Barbolla and Corchon (1989). However, they proved a somewhat weaker result that assumed that the numéraire is a gross substitute for the aggregate of other goods.

Consider

ASSUMPTION 26   The Jacobian $J(p)$ of the excess demand functions $e(p)$ is well defined for all $p \in \mathbf{R}^n_{++}$.

ASSUMPTION 27   If $p^v \to p$, $p^v \in R^n_{++}$, $v = 1, 2, \cdots$, where $p_i = 0$ for some i then $|e(p^v)| \to \infty$.

ASSUMPTION 28 $\begin{bmatrix} J(p) & p \\ p^T & 0 \end{bmatrix}$ is nonsingular for all $p \in \mathbf{R}^n_{++}$.

ASSUMPTION 29 $p \cdot e(p) = 0$ for all $p \in \mathbf{R}^n_{++}$.

ASSUMPTION 30 $e(p)$ is homogeneous of degree 0.

The meaning of assumption 28 is found in the implication that $J(p)$ has rank $n - 1$, so market excess demand cannot remain constant when relative prices change by a small amount. To see this, consider an orthogonal basis, say p and q, for a two-dimensional null space of $J(p)$. Then consider $\begin{bmatrix} J(p) & p \\ p & 0 \end{bmatrix} \begin{pmatrix} q \\ 0 \end{pmatrix} = 0$. This contradicts assumption 28 if $q \neq 0$. Thus there is no null space of $J(p)$ of dimension greater than 1. However, $J(p)p = 0$ by assumption 30 which implies that the rank of $J(p)$ is $n - 1$.

THEOREM 7   *With assumptions 26 through 30 there is $p \in S_n$ such that $e(p) = 0$.*

Proof   Walras' Law, assumption 29, implies that $p^T J(p) = -e(p)$. Let $S_n = \{p \mid \sum_{i=1}^n p_i = 1, p_i \geq 0\}$. Consider the problem:

I.   Minimize $E(p) = \sum_{i=1}^n e_i^2(p)$ over S_n.

Let $S'_n(\delta) = \{p \mid p \in S_n$ and $p_i > \delta$ for all i where $0 < \delta < 1\}$. We will need

LEMMA 42 δ *may be chosen small enough so that the minimum of* $E(p)$ *in* S_n *must lie in* $S_n'(\delta)$.

Proof For any δ with $0 < \delta < 1$ the set $S_n \backslash S_n'(\delta)$ is compact. Then the continuous function $E(p)$ attains its minimum in $S_n \backslash S_n'(\delta)$. Suppose that the minimum does not exceed $E(p')$ for $p' = (1/n, \cdots, 1/n)$ however small δ is chosen. Then a convergent sequence of price vectors p^v may be found such that $p^v \to p \in$ boundary S_n and $|e(p^v)| \to \infty$ does not hold, in contradiction to assumption 27. Therefore there must be a δ satisfying the condition of the lemma. ∎

A problem that is equivalent to I is to minimize the Lagrangian expression $L(p) = 1/2 \sum_1^n (e_i(p))^2 - \lambda(\sum_1^n p_i - 1)$ with respect to p under the constraint $\sum_{i=1}^n p_i = 1$. The first-order necessary conditions are

I. $e^T(p) \cdot [e_{ij}]_n^1 = \lambda(1, \cdots, 1)$,

II. $\sum_{i=1}^n p_i = 1$.

Multiplying condition I on the right by p, we see that the left side is 0 by homogeneity and the right side is λ by condition II. Therefore $\lambda = 0$. Then the necessary conditions require that $e^T(p) \cdot J(p) = e^T(p) \cdot [e_{ij}]_n^1 = 0$. On the other hand, $p \cdot e(p) = 0$ by assumption 29. Therefore $(e^T(p), 0) \begin{bmatrix} J(p) & p \\ p & 0 \end{bmatrix} = 0$, which violates assumption 28 unless $e(p) = 0$. Therefore the minimum of $e(p)^2$ in $S_n'(\delta)$ is achieved at prices $\bar{p}$ where $e(\bar{p}) = 0$. ∎

The $\bar{p}$ that gives $e(\bar{p}) = 0$ and which exists by theorem 7 is by definition an equilibrium of the economy with the excess demand functions $e(p)$. An example of such an economy is the exchange economy whose agents have excess demand functions with indecomposable Jacobians that satisfy the gross substitute condition as in theorem 16 of appendix A, chapter 4. Excess demand functions that satisfy these conditions are implied by Cobb-Douglas utility functions.

7 Competitive Equilibrium over Time

Implicitly the earlier chapters were concerned with competitive equilibrium over time. One only needs to treat goods at different times as different goods and assume a market at the initial time for all the goods over the finite or infinite horizon. Then all the theory of the earlier chapters applies. However, there are several reasons to go beyond those discussions. Time introduces a special structure into the set of goods, since a whole list of goods may be repeated at each time except for the change in the time subscript. Then it is natural to consider how the relative quantities of goods change as time passes. This leads to the subjects of capital accumulation and economic fluctuations. Also there is no natural horizon, so one is led to consider an infinite sequence of times. The earlier discussions may no longer apply except for the part that deals with markets having an infinite set of commodities. Finally, once the time structure has been recognized, it becomes less reasonable to assume that all goods are traded in a single market at the initial date. The realistic market structure may be a sequence of markets that reach temporary equilibria. This market structure cannot be studied without introducing assets, including money and debts. The analysis then extends beyond the bounds of what I am calling classical general equilibrium theory (see Magill and Quinzii 1996). Moreover, since economic agents do not have lives of infinite length, realism may lead to a model in which the traders in a market at any one time represent overlapping generations of people (see Samuelson 1958; Balasko, Cass, and Shell 1980).

The only type of stability analysis in chapter 2 is concerned with the stability of a tâtonnement, which is concerned with the search for equilibrium through adjustments in price and excess demand that precede the establishment of equilibrium. In this chapter we are concerned with the pattern that the equilibrium arrived at the initial date assumes over time. Another interpretation is to suppose that the future is known and correct prices are foreseen. Then the number of markets is not important. Finally we will consider the existence and stability properties of paths of capital accumulation when the market is greatly simplified. The market will have but one consumer, or at best a population of identical consumers who live forever. On the other hand, when everyone discounts the future at the same rate, it may be shown by a proper choice of a "representative" consumer that this model can represent a competitive equilibrium with perfect foresight even when consumers do not have the same tastes (Bewley 1982). Moreover, if periodwise discount factors depend positively on utility levels, it may be shown that discount factors of different consumers converge over time (Lucas and Stokey 1984). The significant restrictions are the assumptions that expectations are correct and that consumers live forever. Sometimes it is argued that indefinite life is a reasonable assumption for households who are interested in the welfare of their descendants. Also correct expectations may be regarded as an approximation to "rational expectations." Rational expectations are correct in the more limited sense that a correct probability distribution of future prices is inferred from current information, including current prices.

We will not be concerned in this chapter with the convergence of the market from a set of disequilibrium values for prices and quantities to equilibrium values. In other words, the tâtonnement stability problem of chapter 2 will not be addressed. However, the problem that remains may be described as a problem of stability. Under what conditions will it happen that a path of capital accumulation with correct foresight converges to a given path over time independently of the initial stocks of goods when the tastes of consumers and the technology are assumed to be constant over time? This question is answered by the so-called turnpike theorems. We may also ask under what conditions equilibrium or optimal paths over time exist. It should not be surprising that these questions have new aspects in circumstances where additional structure is present.

7.1 The von Neumann Model

The modern theory of capital accumulation begins with two papers, one by Ramsey (1928) on optimal saving and one by von Neumann (1937) on proportional expansion at a maximal rate. The von Neumann model has limited interest as an economic model in its own right. However, it laid the groundwork for the analysis of equilibrium in models of capital accumulation with many sectors and many methods of production. Before von Neumann there were no rigorous models of equilibrium over time in which the technology presented a choice of techniques.

The von Neumann model treats labor as a produced good in the manner of the classical economists of the early nineteenth century and ignores the limited supply of land. Also the von Neumann model assumes that the maximal growth rate will be attained in equilibrium. This model is not consistent with an economy guided by the utility of consumption. The Ramsey model, on the other hand, has a single produced good and a single production function, and there is a utility function for consumption. In order to achieve a multisector model with greater economic interest, it is necessary to marry the von Neumann model with the Ramsey model. This was done by Gale (1967) and McKenzie (1968).

Let $B = [b_{ij}]$, $i = 1, \cdots, n$, $j = 1, \cdots, m$, where $b_{ij} \geq 0$ is the quantity of the ith good produced per unit level of the jth process. Let $A = [a_{ij}]$, where $a_{ij} \geq 0$ is the quantity of the ith good consumed per unit level of the jth process. Make the following assumptions.

ASSUMPTION 1 For each i, there is some j where $b_{ij} > 0$. (Any good is producible.)

ASSUMPTION 2 For each j, there is some i where $a_{ij} > 0$. (No free lunch.)

Let $\bar{\sigma} = \max \sigma$ such that $(B - \sigma A)x \geq 0$ for some $x \geq 0$, $x \neq 0$.

ASSUMPTION 3 If $(B - \bar{\sigma}A)x \geq 0$, $x \geq 0$, $x \neq 0$, then $Bx > 0$.

A *von Neumann model* $\mathcal{N}$ is given by two $n \times m$ matrices A and B that satisfy assumptions 1, 2, and 3. Let x be an m-vector of activity levels and p an n-vector of prices. Let σ be a positive real number. A triple (σ^*, x^*, p^*) is an equilibrium for $\mathcal{N}$ provided that

I. $(B - \sigma^* A)x^* \geq 0$.

II. $p^*(B - \sigma^* A) \leq 0$.

III. $p^* B x^* > 0$, where $p^* \geq 0$ and $x^* \geq 0$.

THEOREM 1 *Any von Neumann model $\mathcal{N}$ has an equilibrium (σ^*, x^*, p^*). The set of equilibrium price vectors p^* is convex and the set of equilibrium capital stock vectors x^* is convex.*

Proof Let $\sigma^* = \max \sigma$ such that $(B - \sigma A)x \geq 0$ for some $x \in S_m = \{x \mid x \geq 0, \sum_{j=1}^{m} x_j = 1\}$. Let x^* satisfy

$$(B - \sigma^* A)x^* = y^* \geq 0, \qquad x^* \in S_m. \tag{1}$$

By assumption 1 such a $\sigma^* > 0$ exists.

Let $W = \{y \mid y = (B - \sigma^* A)x, x \in S_m\}$. $W \subset \mathbf{R}^n$ is closed, convex, and bounded, since it is a linear transform of S_m. The fact that σ^* is maximal implies $W \cap \text{int } \mathbf{R}_+^n = \emptyset$. Therefore, by a separation theorem for disjoint convex sets (Berge 1963, p. 163), there is (β, p^*) such that $p^* y \leq \beta$ for $y \in W$ and $p^* y \geq \beta$ for $y \in \text{int } \mathbf{R}_+^n$, where β is a real number, $p^* \in \mathbf{R}^n$,

$p^* \neq 0$. The existence of points $y \in \text{int } \mathbf{R}_+^n$ that are arbitrarily near 0 implies that $\beta \leq 0$. Also $p^*y \geq \beta$ for all $y \in \text{int } \mathbf{R}_+^n$ implies $p^* \geq 0$. Then $y^* \in W$, $y^* \geq 0$, implies $\beta \geq 0$, so $\beta = 0$.

We may choose $p^* \in S_n = \{p \mid p \geq 0, \sum_{i=1}^n p_i = 1\}$. By considering $x^i \in S_m$ where $x_j^i = 0$, $j \neq i$, we see that $p^*y \leq 0$ for $y \in W$ implies that

$$p^*(B - \sigma^*A) \leq 0. \tag{2}$$

Also by assumption 3, and (2), we have

$$p^*Bx^* > 0. \tag{3}$$

But (1), (2), and (3) are just the conditions I, II, and III respectively of an equilibrium of $\mathcal{N}$. The convexity of the equilibrium price and activity vectors is immediate from the linearity of the conditions defining the equilibrium. ∎

Theorem 1 is illustrated in figure 7.1.

PROPOSITION 1   If (σ^*, x^*, p^*) is an equilibrium for $\mathcal{N}$, and $y^* = (B - \sigma^*A)x^*$, then $p_i^* > 0$ implies that $y_i^* = 0$, and $y_i^* > 0$ implies that $p_i^* = 0$.

Proof   Multiply condition I on the left by p^* and II on the right by x^*. This gives $p^*(B - \sigma^*A)x^* = 0$. Thus $p^*y^* = 0$, from which the conclusion follows. ∎

PROPOSITION 2   If (σ^*, x^*, p^*) is an equilibrium for $\mathcal{N}$, then $\sigma^* = $ maximum σ such that $(B - \sigma A)x \geq 0$ for some $x \in S_m$. Also $\sigma^* = \min \sigma$ such that $p(B - \sigma A) \leq 0$ for some $p \in S_n$.

Proof   Let σ' be the maximum σ satisfying $(B - \sigma A)x \geq 0$. We must show that $\sigma^* < \sigma'$ implies that σ^* cannot appear in an equilibrium. Let σ' be the maximum σ satisfying $(B - \sigma A)x \geq 0$. Then $p^*Ax^* > 0$ holds, since $p^*(B - \sigma^*A)x^* = 0$ by proposition 1 and $p^*Bx^* > 0$ by condition III of equilibrium. By $p^*Ax^* > 0$ and $\sigma^* < \sigma'$, it follows that $p^*(B - \sigma'A)x^* < 0$ must hold. But we have $(B - \sigma'A)x' \geq 0$ by the feasibility condition and $p^* \geq 0$ by condition III of competitive equilibrium. This implies that $p^*(B - \sigma'A)x^* \geq 0$, which is a contradiction. ∎

Also we must show $\sigma < \sigma^*$ implies that $p(B - \sigma A) \leq 0$ cannot hold for any $p \in S_n$. But $\sigma < \sigma^*$ implies $(B - \sigma A)x^* > 0$, since $Bx^* > 0$ by assumption 3 and $(B - \sigma^*A)x^* \geq 0$ by condition I of equilibrium. There-

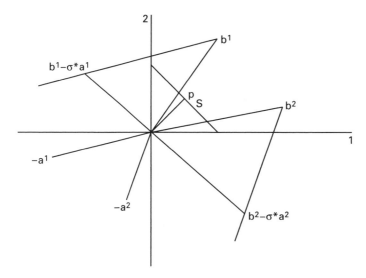

Figure 7.1
The output matrix $B = [b^1 b^2]$. The input matrix $A = [a^1 a^2]$. σ^* is the maximal rate of expansion. S is the unit simplex. p is an equilibrium price vector.

fore $p(B - \sigma A)x^* > 0$ for all $p \in S_n$. In other words, $(p(B - \sigma A))_j > 0$ for some j for any $p \in S_n$ in contradiction to condition II of equilibrium. ■

The proofs of theorem 1, and proposition 2, allow σ^* to be characterized as the maximal expansion factor for $\mathcal{N}$ and σ^{*-1} as the maximal discount factor. Or setting $\sigma^* = 1 + r$, $\sigma^{*-1} = 1/(1 + i)$, we may say that the maximal growth rate is r and the minimum interest rate is i, where $i = r$.

This is essentially the theorem proved by von Neumann (1937). Assumption 3 was introduced by Gale (1956) for a model given by a production set that is a closed convex cone with vertex at the origin. The production set implied by the matrices A and B is a convex polyhedral cone. Condition III of equilibrium was introduced by Kemeny, Morgenstern, and Thompson (1956) in a model where assumption 3 is omitted and, as a consequence, there may be multiple equilibria. Its effect is to eliminate from consideration equilibria that are uninteresting from the economic viewpoint. Only when condition III is satisfied will an equilibrium of the von Neumann model serve as a turnpike, that is, as an asymptote for efficient paths of capital accumulation (McKenzie 1967, p. 56).

Each activity in the von Neumann model converts capital stocks at the beginning of a period into capital stocks at the end of the period. This type of production was introduced in chapter 3 in the generalized Leontief model. In that model the capital goods used in production but not entirely used up in a single period are included in the output of an activity. However, in the generalized Leontief model there are also labor inputs and a current flow of intermediate products, including services, supplied by other activities. Also in each activity there is only one good with an output exceeding the initial stock. Thus a von Neumann activity does not correspond to activities as they are usually described. Rather they represent linear combinations of such activities that must be chosen so that the intermediate products needed during the period as well as the consumption goods required by the workers during the period are produced internally. In the appendix we will show how the generalized Leontief model of chapter 3 may be turned into a von Neumann model (McKenzie 1963).

7.2   Turnpike Theorems for the von Neumann Model

We consider efficient paths of capital accumulation where the objective is to accumulate over a finite number of periods the largest possible final stock of capital goods in fixed proportions. Theorems of this type were first proved by Dorfman, Samuelson, and Solow (1958). Since the paths considered are not limited to stationary paths, the simple model of expansion is no longer adequate. All production possibilities must be considered. The *production set* Y is defined by

$$Y = \{(-w, z) \mid -Ax \geq -w, Bx \geq z, \text{ for some } w, z, x \geq 0\}.$$

A *path of capital accumulation* in the von Neumann model $\mathcal{N}$ is a sequence $\{y^t\}$, $y^t \geq 0$, $t = 0, \cdots, T$, of capital stocks such that $(-y^t, y^{t+1}) \in Y$ for $t = 0, \cdots, T - 1$. The choice of 0 as the initial time is arbitrary. It is immediate that Y is a closed, convex cone with vertex 0. Also make

ASSUMPTION 4 $y^0 > 0$.

The price vectors lie in Y^*, the dual cone to Y, which is defined by

$$Y^* = \{(p, q) \mid -pw + qz \leq 0 \text{ for all } (-w, z) \in Y\}.$$

Since w is unbounded above and z is unbounded below, it is clear that $(p,q) \in Y^*$ implies that $(p,q) \geq 0$. With any $(p,q) \in Y^*$ we may associate a face $F(p,q)$ of the production cone Y that is defined by

$$F(p,q) = \{(-w,z) \,|\, (-w,z) \in Y \text{ and } -pw + qz = 0\}.$$

$F(p,q)$ is a closed convex cone with vertex 0. $F(p,q) \neq \emptyset$, since $0 \in F(p,q)$.

Let $P = \{p \,|\, p(B - \sigma^* A) \leq 0 \text{ and } p \in S_n\}$, where σ^* is the growth factor of a von Neumann equilibrium. Consider $p^* \in$ interior P relative to the smallest affine subspace that contains P. The face F^* of Y given by $F(\sigma^* p^*, p^*)$ has special interest since it is an asymptote in terms of angular distance for efficient paths of capital accumulation, or equivalently normalized paths in terms of Euclidean distance. F^* is called the *von Neumann facet* of Y. Its existence is implied by theorem 1 and the definition of a von Neumann equilibrium.

LEMMA 1 F^* *is unique and satisfies* $F^* = \bigcap_{p \in P} F(\sigma^* p, p)$.

Proof   By proposition 2, σ^* is the maximum value of σ that can appear in an equilibrium. Also by proposition 2 σ^* is the minimum value of σ that can appear in an equilibrium. Thus σ^* is unique. Since $p^* \in$ relative interior P and P is convex, for any $p \in P$, $p \neq p^*$, there is (β, p') with $p' \in P$ such that $p^* = \beta p + (1 - \beta)p'$, $0 < \beta < 1$. Thus $-\sigma^* p^* w + p^* z = 0$ implies that $-\sigma^* pw + pz = 0$ for any $p \in P$. Therefore $F^* = \bigcap_{p \in P} F(\sigma^* p, p)$. This shows that F^* is also unique.   ∎

The linearity of the von Neumann model leads us to define an angular distance function. Define $\alpha(u,v) = |(u/|u| - v/|v|)|$ for $u, v \neq 0$, where $|\cdot|$ is the sum of the absolute values of the components. Define the angular distance from a point to a set $C \neq \emptyset$ by $\alpha(u,C) = \inf \alpha(u,v)$ for $v \in C$. A result due to Radner (1961) is

LEMMA 2   *For any* $\varepsilon > 0$ *there is* $\delta < 1$ *such that* $(-w,z) \in Y$ *and* $\alpha((-w,z), F^*) > \varepsilon$ *implies that* $-\delta\sigma^* p^* w + p^* z \leq 0$.

Proof $V = \{z \,|\, (-w,z) \in Y \text{ and } w \in S_n\}$ is bounded. To see this, assume that there is $(-w^s, z^s)$, $w^s \in S_n$ and $|z^s| \to \infty$, $s = 1, 2, \cdots$. Consider $(-w^{s'}, z^{s'})$, where $w^{s'} = w^s/|z^s|$, $z^{s'} = z^s/|z^s|$. This sequence is bounded, and there is an accumulation point $(-\bar{w}, \bar{z}) \in Y$ by closedness of Y. Also $|\bar{z}| = 1$. But $\bar{w} = 0$, which implies by assumption 2 that $\bar{z} = 0$. Since this is a contradiction, we conclude that V is bounded.

Now suppose that there is $\varepsilon > 0$ and a sequence $(-w^s, z^s) \in Y$ such that $\alpha((-w^s, z^s), F^*) \geq \varepsilon$, but $p^* z^s / p^* w^s \to \sigma^*$, $s = 1, 2, \cdots$. By definition of P and the fact that $p^* \in P$, it follows that $(\sigma^* p^*, p^*) \cdot (-w^s, z^s) \leq 0$. Thus, if $p^* w^s = 0$ holds, $p^* z^s = 0$ holds, which implies that $(-w^s, z^s) \in F^*$. Since this contradicts the assumption that $\alpha((-w^s, z^s), F^*) \geq \varepsilon$, $p^* w^s > 0$ must hold. Let $w^{s'} = w^s / |w^s|$, $z^{s'} = z^s / |w^s|$. $(-w^{s'}, z^{s'})$ is bounded since it lies in V. There is an accumulation point $(-\bar{w}, \bar{z}) \in Y$. Then $-\sigma^* p^* \bar{w} + p^* \bar{z} = 0$ and $(-\bar{w}, \bar{z}) \in F^*$, which again is a contradiction of the assumption. This shows that no sequence $p^* z^s / p^* w^s$ converging to σ^* can exist. Since $p^* z / p^* w \leq \sigma^*$ always holds for $(-w, z) \in Y$, it follows that there is $\delta < 1$ such that $p^* z / p^* w \leq \delta \sigma^*$.   ∎

Let $\bar{y} \neq 0$ be a given vector in $\mathbf{R}^n_+$. Define $\rho(y)$ by $\rho(y) = \min(y_i / \bar{y}_i)$ over i such that $\bar{y}_i \neq 0$. We will say that a T period path $(y^0, \cdots, y^T)$ in the von Neumann model is a *maximal path* if for any alternative path $(w^0, \cdots, w^T)$ with $w^0 = y^0$, $\rho(y^T) \geq \rho(w^T)$. An alternative definition of an equilibrium for a von Neumann model $\mathcal{N}$ is that (σ^*, y^*, p^*) is an equilibrium if $(-y^*, \sigma^* y^*) \in F(\sigma^* p^*, p^*)$ and $p^* y^* > 0$. It is easily seen that this definition is equivalent to the earlier one.

We may now prove the fundamental turnpike theorem for the von Neumann model.

THEOREM 2   *Suppose that $\mathcal{N}$ satisfies assumptions 1, 2, and 4 but not necessarily assumption 3. Let $(y^0, \cdots, y^T)$ be a maximal path of T periods. Let (σ^*, y^*, p^*) be an equilibrium for $\mathcal{N}$, where $p^* \bar{y} > 0$ and $\bar{y}_i > 0$ implies $y_i^* > 0$. Then, for any $\varepsilon > 0$, there is N such that the number of periods in which $\alpha((-y^t, y^{t+1}), F^*) > \varepsilon$ cannot exceed N for any T.*

Proof   Choose $y^* \leq y^0$ with $y_i^* = y_i^0$ for some $y_i^0 \neq 0$. Then $(y^0, \sigma^* y^*, \cdots, \sigma^{*T} y^*)$ is a T period path. By lemma 2, there is $\delta < 1$ such that

$$\alpha((-y^t, y^{t+1}), F^*) > \varepsilon \quad \text{implies} \quad \delta \sigma^* p^* y^t \geq p^* y^{t+1}. \tag{4}$$

For all t we have by choice of p^*

$$\sigma^* p^* y^t \geq p^* y^{t+1}.$$

Multiply the tth inequality by σ^{*T-t} and sum the inequalities using the appropriate inequality in each period. If (4) holds for τ periods, this gives

$$\delta^\tau \sigma^{*T} p^* y^0 \geq p^* y^T. \tag{5}$$

But $(y^0, \cdots, y^T)$ maximal implies

$$\rho(y^T) \geq \rho(\sigma^{*T} y^*) = \sigma^{*T} \rho(y^*), \tag{6}$$

and $y_i^* > 0$ for $\bar{y}_i > 0$ implies $\rho(y^*) > 0$.

Choose p^* such that $p_i^* \geq 1/\bar{y}_i$ for some i for which $p_i^* > 0$ and $\bar{y}_i > 0$. Then, for $z \geq 0$,

$$p^* z \geq \frac{z_i}{\bar{y}_i} \geq \rho(z). \tag{7}$$

Combining (5), (6), and (7),

$$\sigma^{*T} \rho(y^*) \leq \rho(y^T) \leq p^* y^T \leq \delta^\tau \sigma^{*T} p^* y^0. \tag{8}$$

The first and last terms of (8) give $\rho(y^*)/p^* y^0 \leq \delta^\tau$. Therefore we may choose N such that $\delta^N < \rho(y^*)/p^* y^0$. Note that the value of δ, and therefore N, depends on ε. ∎

Figure 7.2 shows a case where the von Neumann facet F^* is one dimensional.

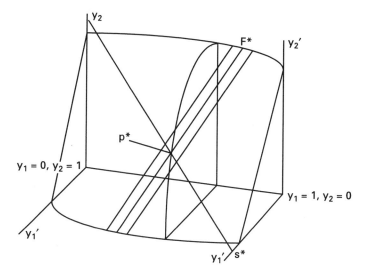

Figure 7.2
The von Neumann turnpike with neoclassical technology. $p^* = (q, p_1, p_2)$ and $q = \sigma^*(p_2 - p_1)$. The origin is labeled by $y_1 = 1$, $y_2 = 0$.

Note that assumption 3 was not used for the turnpike theorem. As a result there may be more than one equilibrium. Indeed, given any good, there is an equilibrium associated with the supremum of the rate at which this good may be accumulated along a balanced growth path, that is, a path in which $y^{t+1} = \sigma y^t$ for all t and some $\sigma > 0$ (McKenzie 1967). However, these equilibria need not be distinct. At the smallest such rate of balanced growth all goods may be accumulated, but those goods that are overproduced will have 0 prices. Theorem 2 will apply when all goods appearing in positive amounts in the vector that defines the objective are produced in an equilibrium and at least one of these goods has a positive price in this equilibrium. However, there are borderline cases in which the supremum is not attained or where all the goods in the objective have zero prices at the equilibrium in which these goods are accumulated at the maximal rate. There are turnpike theorems (with more complicated statements) even for these cases (McKenzie 1967).

Theorem 2 proves the maximal paths to be close to the smallest facet of the production cone on which an equilibrium lies. If this facet is a ray, then the proportions in which the capital stocks are accumulated along a maximal path approach the proportions of the appropriate equilibrium capital stock vector. Even if the von Neumann facet is larger than a ray the maximal path may still converge to a ray (in angular distance) that lies on the facet on which the equilibrium lies. This will be true if the facet is stable in the sense that any path that lies on the facet for an indefinite period must approach an equilibrium ray on the facet (see McKenzie 1963, 1967; Inada 1964).

7.3   A Generalized Ramsey Growth Model

From the viewpoint of economics the von Neumann model has several undesirable features. The objective is pure accumulation, and the horizon is finite and even arbitrary. It treats labor as available in unlimited quantities so long as provision is made for the workers' subsistence. In the Dorfman, Samuelson, and Solow (1958) turnpike theorem for the von Neumann model, the objective does not depend on consumers' utility. Also the model is stationary in the sense that the technology does not change over time. On the other hand, it is a multisector model in which the relative composition of the capital stock is crucial. The model we will now describe is a generalization to many goods of the one sector model introduced by Ramsey in 1928 in order to discuss the optimal rate of saving. In this model the horizon is chosen to be infinite to recognize the difficulty of choosing a finite horizon in a convincing way and to recognize the interest of the current generation in its descendents. The objective is stated in terms of consumers' utility, and the limited supply of labor and natural resources is allowed for. It is possible in this model to let technology and utility functions vary over time, although we will not pursue this generalizaton. The first asymptotic theorem for a Ramsey model with more than one sector was proved by Atsumi (1965).

The periodwise utility function is written $u(x, y)$, where x is the vector of initial stocks and y is the vector of terminal stocks in a unit period. Then $u(x, y)$ represents the maximum utility achievable in one period given the end conditions x and y. It is possible to derive such a function from a utility $u(c)$ defined on a per capita consumption vector c, and a neoclassical production function $f(x)$ normalized on one unit of labor with consumption given by $c = f(x) - y$. This is the way the one-sector Ramsey model was treated by Koopmans (1965) and Cass (1966). However, in a period model the total quantities consumed, given by c, cannot adequately represent a stream of consumption over the unit period, which should have a definite time structure derived from optimizing over the set of feasible streams. On the other hand, in the continuous time model the assumption that utility is separable and additive over time is particularly unrealistic. I call this period model the Malinvaud model (1953), although he did not introduce utility but only considered efficiency of production over time.

There is a set $D \subset \mathbf{R}_+^{2n}$ on which the function u is defined. D reflects the technology as well as the subsistence requirements of the consumers. The function u maps D into $\mathbf{R}$. Let φ be a concave function defined on a convex set S. Let $\psi(w, \varepsilon) = \sup \varphi(z)$ for $|w - z| \leq \varepsilon > 0$, z in S, $z \neq w$, $w \in$ relative boundary S. φ is said to be *closed* (Fenchel 1953, p. 78) if $\varphi(w) = \lim \sup \psi(w, \varepsilon)$ as $\varepsilon \to 0$ when $w \in S$, and $\psi(w, \varepsilon) \to -\infty$ otherwise (also see Rockafellar 1970, p. 308). We introduce the following assumptions

ASSUMPTION 5 The utility function u is concave, closed, and not constant. The set D is convex

ASSUMPTION 6 There is $\zeta > 0$ and $\xi < 1$ such that $|x| \geq \zeta$ implies for any $(x, y) \in D$ that $|y| < \xi|x|$.

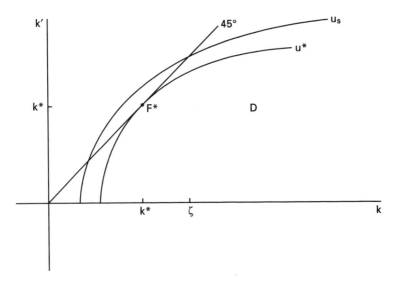

Figure 7.3
The Ramsey model without discounting. The k axis represents initial stocks. The k' axis represents terminal stocks. ζ is maximal sustainable stock. u^* is maximal sustainable utility. F^* is the (trivial) von Neumann facet. u_s bounds D.

ASSUMPTION 7   If $(x, y) \in D$, then $(z, w) \in D$ for all $z \geq x$, $0 \leq w \leq y$, and $u(z, w) \geq u(x, y)$ holds.

ASSUMPTION 8   There is $(\bar{x}, \bar{y}) \in D$ for which $\bar{y} > \bar{x}$ holds.

Figure 7.3 represents a Ramsey model with one capital good.

We will say that a sequence of capital stocks $k^0, k^1, \ldots$, is a *path of capital accumulation* if $(k^{t-1}, k^t) \in D$ for all t. The path may be finite or infinite. Assumption 6 implies that paths will be bounded. Assumption 7 allows for free disposal of capital stocks. Assumption 8 asserts that an *expansible stock* exists, that is, a stock that may be increased in every component. This describes a multisector Ramsey model without discounting of future utility, which is stationary, that is, utility functions and technology do not change over time. We will first be concerned with finite paths of accumulation where both initial capital stocks and terminal capital stocks are specified in the manner of end conditions in the calculus of variations. When the horizon is finite the objective is to maximize the sum of periodwise utilities over the accumulation period. This is in contrast to the objective described in the von Neumann model, which is to maximize the size of the terminal capital stocks. A path $(k^0, \cdots, k^T)$ is an *optimal path* if $\sum_1^T u(k^{t-1}, k^t) \geq \sum_1^T u(k'^{t-1}, k'^t)$ for any path $(k'^0, \cdots, k'^T)$ with $k'^0 = k^0$ and $k'^T = k^T$. In order to study the asymptotic properties of optimal paths, we consider stationary paths along which sustainable utility is maximized. We obtain a stationary price sequence $p^t = p$, $t = 0, \cdots, T$, with $p \in \mathbf{R}^n$, that supports the stationary path in a sense similar to the support of a competitive equilibrium.

LEMMA 3   *There is $p \geq 0$ such that $u(x, y) + py - px \leq \bar{u}$ for all $(x, y) \in D$, where $\bar{u} = \max u(x, x)$ for $(x, x) \in D$.*

Proof   Define the set $V = \{v \,|\, v = y - x, \text{ for } (x, y) \in D\}$. Free disposal and the existence of an expansible stock imply that $0 \in$ interior V. Indeed, $y' - x' = v' \in V$ if $(x, y) \in D$ and $x < x' < y$ and $x < y' < y$. We will show that $y - x \geq v$ for given $v \in V$ implies that (x, y) is bounded. By their definitions as capital stocks, x and y are bounded below. Suppose there is $v \in V$ such that $D_v = \{(x, y) \in D \,|\, y - x \geq v\}$ is not bounded above. Let $(x^s, y^s) \in D_v$ be such that $|x^s| + |y^s| \to \infty$ as $s \to \infty$. If x^s is unbounded, y^s is unbounded, since $y^s \geq x^s + v$ and v is fixed. This contradicts assumption 6. Therefore x^s is bounded. If y^s is unbounded, by free disposal, assumption 7, x^s unbounded is also possible in contradiction to x^s bounded. Therefore D_v is bounded.

Define $f(v) = \sup u(x, y)$ for $(x, y) \in D_v$. Since u is concave and closed by assumption 5 and D_v is bounded, the sup is attained for any $v \in V$. Let $W = \{(u, v) \,|\, u \leq f(v) \text{ and } v \in V\}$. Maximum sustainable utility is $\bar{u} = f(0)$. We may also choose $\bar{u} = 0$. W is convex since f is concave, and $(\bar{u}, 0)$ is a boundary point of W. By a separation theorem (Berge 1963, p. 245), there is $(\pi, p) \in \mathbf{R}^{n+1}$ and $(\pi, p) \neq 0$ such that $\pi u + pv \leq \pi \bar{u}$ for all $(u, v) \in W$. Since V is unbounded below by assumption 7, $p \geq 0$. Suppose $\pi \leq 0$. Then $pv \leq \pi(\bar{u} - u)$ for all $(u, v) \in W$. However, for $v > 0$, the definition of $\bar{u}$ implies that $(\bar{u} - u) \geq 0$. Since 0 is interior to V, this leads to contradiction unless $(\pi, p) = 0$. Thus $\pi > 0$ must hold, and we may choose (π, p) so that $\pi = 1$.   ∎

Let $u(k, k) = \bar{u}$ realize the maximal sustainable utility of lemma 3. Let p be the vector shown to exist in lemma 3. Then the path $\{k^t\}$, $t = 0, \cdots, T$, with $k^t = k$ for all t is said to be *supported* by the price sequence $\{p^t\}$, $t = 0, \cdots, T$, where $p^t = p$ for all t. Any such path $\{k^t\}$ may be shown to be optimal with the end conditions $k^0 = k$ and $k^T = k$ for any finite value of T. However, the corresponding infinite path need not have the optimality properties for infinite paths, which will be defined in the next section. Let G be the graph of u. That is, $G = \{(u, x, y) \mid u = u(x, y)\}$. G lies in $\mathbf{R}^{2n+1}$. By analogy to the von Neumann facet of the production cone in the von Neumann model, define the von Neumann facet F^* of the graph G of u to be the set $F^* = \{(x, y) \mid u(x, y) + py - px = \bar{u}\}$. F^* is the projection on the subspace of goods along the utility axis of a set of points (u, x, y) lying in the graph G of u, where G is supported by the vector $(1, -p, p)$. Since $\bar{u}$ is unique by its definition F^* is unique, although the stocks realizing $\bar{u}$ need not be unique. For any $(x, y) \in D$ the *value loss* $\delta(x, y)$ relative to F^* is defined by

$$\delta(x, y) = \bar{u} - u(x, y) - py + px \geq 0.$$

We will prove a result analogous to the Radner lemma for the von Neumann model, lemma 2. This lemma was first proved by Atsumi (1965) for the two good case and used to establish a turnpike theorem. For any vector u and set C let the distance of u from C be $d(u, C) = $ infimum $|u - v|$ for $v \in C$. The function d is continuous.

LEMMA 4   *Let ζ be as in assumption 6. For any $\varepsilon > 0$ there is $\delta > 0$ such that $d((x, y), F^*) > \varepsilon$ implies $\delta(x, y) > \delta$ for any $(x, y) \in D$ with $|x| < \zeta$.*

Proof   Suppose the lemma is false. Then there is a sequence (x^s, y^s) with $d((x^s, y^s), F^*) > \varepsilon$ for all s where $\delta(x^s, y^s) \to 0$ and $|x^s| \leq \zeta$. Since $|x^s|$ is bounded, by assumption 6 the sequence (x^s, y^s) is bounded and there is a point of accumulation $(\bar{x}, \bar{y})$ for which $\delta(\bar{x}, \bar{y}) = 0$. Since $\delta(x^s, y^s) \to 0$, $u(x^s, y^s)$ is bounded along the sequence. By closedness of u on D, $(\bar{x}, \bar{y}) \in D$. Then $(\bar{x}, \bar{y}) \in F^*$ in contradiction to $d((x^s, y^s), F^*) > \varepsilon$ for all s. Thus the lemma must be true.   ■

In order to carry out a proof of a turnpike theorem on the same lines as the proof of theorem 2, it is necessary to show that a path exists from the initial stocks that reaches a path that realizes maximal sustainable utility. In the proof of the turnpike theorem for the von Neumann model, this lemma was not needed since a path of balanced growth at the maximal rate could be reached by disposal. Since the maximal path is now given by a point rather than by a ray, disposal may not work. The appropriate lemma was proved by Gale (1967). The comparison of utility sums is not affected if an arbitrary constant is added to the utility function u. Therefore without loss of generality, we may choose the utility function u so that $u(\bar{k}, \bar{k}) = \bar{u} = 0$, where $\bar{k}$ is a stock that achieves maximal sustainable utility. If $(x, x) \in D$, we say that x is a *sustainable stock*.

LEMMA 5 *If x is an expansible stock and k is a sustainable stock, there is a path $\{k^t\}$, $t = 0, 1, \cdots$, such that $k^0 = x$ and $k^t \to k$ as $t \to \infty$. If $k = \bar{k}$, then $\sum_1^\infty u(k^{t-1}, k^t) > -\infty$.*

Proof Consider $\alpha^t(x, y) + (1 - \alpha^t)(k, k) = (k^t, k^{t+1'})$ where $y > x$, $0 < \alpha < 1$, and $t = 0, 1, \cdots$. For $t = 0$, $(k^t, k^{t+1'}) = (x, y)$ and, as $t \to \infty$, $(k^t, k^{t+1'}) \to (k, k)$. But $k^{t+1'} = k - \alpha^t(k - y)$ and $k^{t+1} = k - \alpha^{t+1}(k - x)$. Then $k^{t+1'} > k^{t+1}$ if $y - \alpha x > (k - \alpha k)$. This holds for α near 1 since $y > x$. Therefore by free disposal we may replace $(k^t, k^{t+1'})$ by (k^t, k^{t+1}), and $\{k^t\}$ is an infinite path approaching k.

If $k = \bar{k}$, by concavity of u

$$u(k^t, k^{t+1'}) \geq (1 - \alpha^t)u(\bar{k}, \bar{k}) + \alpha^t u(x, y) = \alpha^t u(x, y).$$

Using free disposal and summing gives $\sum_0^\infty u(k^t, k^{t+1}) \geq u(x, y)/(1 - \alpha)$. ∎

COROLLARY *If k^0 is expansible and k is expansible, then for some T there is an accumulation path $\{k^t\}$, $t = 0, 1, \cdots, T$, such that $k^T = k$.*

Proof By the assumption that k is expansible, there is $k' > k$ such that $(k, k') \in D$. By lemma 5, for any $\varepsilon > 0$ there is a path $\{k^t\}$ from k^0 and a time T such that $|k^T - k'| < \varepsilon$. Again, by free disposal for small ε, a new k^T may be chosen equal to k. ∎

In preparation for applying the value loss lemma we need

LEMMA 6 *If $\{k^t\}$, $t = 0, 1, \cdots$, is a path $|k^t| \leq \max(|k^0|, \zeta)$ for all t.*

Proof Assumption 6 implies that $|k^t|$ falls monotonically to a level below ζ if $|k^t| > \zeta$. If $|k^0| \leq \zeta$, assumption 6 implies that $|k^t| \leq \zeta$ holds for all t. ∎

We now add

ASSUMPTION 9 There is an expansible stock $\bar{k}$ with $u(\bar{k}, \bar{k}) = 0$, where 0 is maximal sustainable utility.

With lemma 4 and the corollary to lemma 5 we can prove a turnpike theorem for the multisector Ramsey model.

THEOREM 3 *Let k^0 and k be expansible stocks. Given assumptions 5 through 9, for large T there is an optimal path $\{k^t\}$, $t = 0, 1, \cdots, T$, with $k^T = k$. Moreover, given any $\varepsilon > 0$ there is N, independent of T, such that $d((k^t, k^{t+1}), F^*) > \varepsilon$ holds for not more than N periods.*

Proof The corollary to lemma 5 implies that a path exists from k^0 to $k^T = k$ for large T. Lemma 6 implies that the set of all T period paths from k^0 to k is bounded. Since u is concave, it is continuous in the interior of D. Therefore, since u is closed a T period path, $\{k^{*t}\}$ exists with $\sum_1^T u(k^{*t-1}, k^{*t})$ maximal over all paths satisfying these end conditions. By assumption 9, there is a stationary path $\{k^t\}$ with $k^t = \bar{k}$ for all t where $u(\bar{k}, \bar{k}) = 0$ and $\bar{k}$ is expansible. Also from the definitions $(\bar{k}, \bar{k})$ lies on F^*. Since $\bar{k}$ is expansible, by the corollary to lemma 5 there is a path of N_0 periods leading from k^0 to $\bar{k}$. Since k is expansible, there is also a path of N_1 periods leading from $\bar{k}$ to k. Therefore we may define a *comparison path* $\{k''^t\}$ for which $k''^0 = k^0$, $k''^t = \bar{k}$ for $N_0 \le t \le T - N_1$, and $k''^T = k$. Then

$$\sum_1^T u(k^{*t-1}, k^{*t}) \ge u_0 + u_1, \tag{9}$$

where u_0 and u_1 are the utility sums for the N_0 first and N_1 last periods. On the other hand, lemma 3 implies

$$u(k^{*t-1}, k^{*t}) \le -p \cdot (k^{*t} - k^{*t-1}). \tag{10}$$

By lemma 6, k^{*t} is bounded over all t independently of T. Therefore lemma 4 implies for $d(F^*, (k^{*t-1}, k^{*t})) > \varepsilon > 0$ there is $\delta > 0$ such that

$$u(k^{*t-1}, k^{*t}) \le -p \cdot (k^{*t} - k^{*t-1}) - \delta. \tag{11}$$

By summing (10) and (11) over the periods to which they apply and substituting in (9), we obtain

$$u_0 + u_1 \le \sum_1^T u(k^{*t-1}, k^{*t}) \le -p \cdot (k - k^0) - \tau\delta,$$

where $d(F^*, (k^{*t-1}, k^{*t})) > \varepsilon$ for τ periods. Note that both τ and δ are nonnegative. Then

$$\tau \le \delta^{-1}(-u_0 - u_1 - p \cdot (k - k^0)). \tag{12}$$

Therefore N may be chosen equal to the right-hand side of (12). ∎

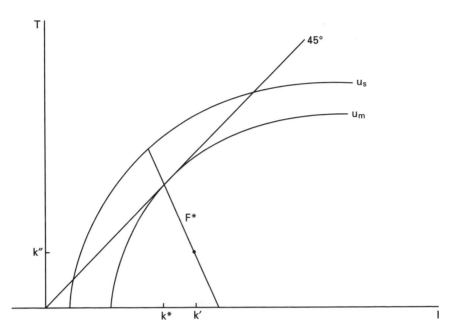

Figure 7.4
I labels the axis of initial capital stocks and *T* the axis of terminal capital stocks. k' to k'' is a path that cannot be continued on F^*, which is the von Neumann facet. k^* is the stationary optimal path. No other paths on F^* can be continued indefinitely.

As in the case of the turnpike theorem in the von Neumann model, the convergence of the optimal path can be extended to a convergence on F^* if F^* is stable in the sense that any path that remains on F^* indefinitely must converge to a stationary path on F^* (see McKenzie 1968). The facet F^* in figure 7.4 is stable in this sense.

7.4 Turnpike Theorems over an Infinite Horizon

As mentioned in the introduction to this chapter, there is no natural way to select a finite horizon. Therefore many theorists have argued that the most natural assumption to use is an infinite horizon even when no one believes that an infinite future will be realized. This was the assumption used by Ramsey in his paper of 1928.

If the horizon is to be infinite, it is useful to give a definition of the objective function that takes account of the possibility that the sum

$\sum_{t=1}^{n} u_t(k^{t-1}, k^t)$ diverges to infinity as $n \to \infty$. Two definitions will be given. The stronger definition characterizes an optimal path. We will say that an infinite path $\{k^t\}$ *catches up to* a path $\{k''\}$ if for any $\varepsilon > 0$ there is $T(\varepsilon)$ such that $\sum_1^T (u(k''^{t-1}, k'') - u(k^{t-1}, k^t)) < \varepsilon$ for all $T > T(\varepsilon)$. Then an infinite path is *optimal* if it catches up to any alternative path, starting from the same initial stocks. In other words, an infinite path is optimal if it is asymptotically as good as any other path from the same initial stocks when they are compared by means of their initial segments.

We will say that an infinite path $\{k^t\}$ *overtakes* a path $\{k''\}$ if there is $\varepsilon > 0$ and $T(\varepsilon)$ such that $\sum_{t=1}^{T}(u(k^{t-1}, k^t) - u(k''^{t-1}, k'')) > \varepsilon$ for all $T > T(\varepsilon)$. An infinite path is *maximal* in the Ramsey model if there is no path from the same initial stocks that overtakes it. In other words, a maximal path does not become permanently worse than any alternative path when they are compared by means of their initial segments. Definitions of this type were first given by Atsumi (1965) and von Weizsäcker (1965). They were refined by Gale (1967) and Brock (1970).

The convergence of infinite optimal paths to an optimal stationary path may be proved in a simple way if assumption 5 is strengthened to

ASSUMPTION 10   The utility function u is strictly concave and closed. The set D is convex

It is a consequence of assumption 10 that a stationary stock $\bar{k}$ realizing the maximum sustainable utility is unique and the infinite path $\{k^t\}$ with $k^t = \bar{k}$ for all t is optimal from the initial stock k. On assumptions 6, 7, 8, and 10 it is then possible to prove that all infinite optimal paths from an expansible stock converge to $\bar{k}$ as $t \to \infty$. This result may be proved using the prices supporting the stationary optimal path in a manner similar to the proof of the turnpike theorem of section 7.3. However, a proof may also be made in primal terms without introducing support prices. The proof using prices and value losses due to departures from the stationary optimal path exploits the property of a concave function u that for any point (u, x, y) in the graph G of u there is a hyperplane $H(x, y)$ passing through (u, x, y) such that $H(x, y)$ lies entirely above G (apply cor. 2, p. 245, of Berge 1963) taking the convex set C to be the set of points on and below G). In the proof $H(x, y)$ is defined as the hyperplane through (u, x, y) that is orthogonal to the prices $(1, -p, p)$ given by lemma 3. However, there is a corresponding property that may also be the basis of a proof. This is that the line segment L stretching between any two points

(u, x, y) and (v, z, w) that lie in G has the property that L lies entirely below G. The primal proof exploits this property. We first demonstrate the optimality of the stationary path based on the stock that realizes maximal sustainable utility.

LEMMA 7   *There is a unique capital stock $\bar{k}$ that realizes maximum sustainable utility and the infinite path $\{k^t\}$ with $k^t = \bar{k}$ for $t = 0, 1, \ldots$, is optimal.*

Proof It was shown in the proof of lemma 3 that maximal sustainable utility is attained in the Ramsey model. If $u(x, y)$ with $y \geq x$ satisfies $u(x, y) \geq u(z, w)$ for any $(z, w) \in D$ with $w \geq z$, then by free disposal, assumption 7, $u(x, x) \geq u(z, w)$ for any $(z, w) \in D$ with $w \geq z$. Thus there must be a maximal point on the diagonal of D. Suppose that a point (x, x) and any other point (z, w) both realized the maximum sustainable utility $\bar{u}$. Then by strict concavity $u((x + z)/2, (x + w)/2) > \bar{u}$ would hold, which is a contradiction.

By lemma 3, there is $p \geq 0$ such that $u(z, w) + pw - pz \leq \bar{u} = 0$ for all $(z, w) \in D$, and by strict concavity, assumption 10, the inequality is strict if $(z, w) \neq (\bar{k}, \bar{k})$. Let (k^t) be any infinite path with $k^0 = \bar{k}$. Again, we choose u so that $\bar{u} = 0$. Then

$$u(k^{t-1}, k^t) = pk^{t-1} - pk^t - \delta_t, \tag{13}$$

where $\delta_t \geq 0$ and $\delta_t > 0$ if $(k^{t-1}, k^t) \neq (\bar{k}, \bar{k})$. Summing (13) from $t = 1$ to T gives

$$\sum_1^T u(k^{t-1}, k^t) = p\bar{k} - pk^T - \sum_1^T \delta_t. \tag{14}$$

Unless $k^T \to \bar{k}$, lemma 4 implies that $\sum_1^T \delta_t \to \infty$ as $T \to \infty$, and the right side of (14) is negative for large T, or $\sum_1^T u(k^{t-1}, k^t) < 0$ for large T. On the other hand, if $k^T \to \bar{k}$ in the limit, the right side of (14) is negative unless $k^t = \bar{k}$ for all t. Therefore $\sum_1^T u(k^{t-1}, k^t) \leq 0$ and equality only holds if $k^t = \bar{k}$ for all k^t. Thus $k^t = \bar{k}$ for all t is the unique optimal path from $\bar{k}$. ∎

The result of lemma 7 depends on the uniqueness of the stock providing maximal sustainable utility which is implied by strict concavity of u. Otherwise, it may be possible to dominate a path realizing maximal sustainable utility by reducing the capital stock in one period while afterward continuing to realize maximal sustainable utility.

Recall that the utility function u is chosen to satisfy the condition $u(\bar{k}, \bar{k}) = 0$. Let us define K as the set of initial stocks x for which there are infinite paths $\{k^t\}$ with $\liminf \sum_1^T u(k^{t-1}, k^t) > -\infty$ and $k^0 = x$. Also define the *value function* $V(x)$ for $x \in K$ by $V(x) = \sup(\liminf \sum_1^T u(k^{t-1}, k^t))$ over all paths $\{k^t\}$ with $k^0 = x$. V is allowed to assume the value ∞. We may state

LEMMA 8   *If x is expansible, then $x \in K$. Assume that $\bar{k} \in$ relative interior K. Then $x \in K$ implies $V(x) < \infty$.*

Proof   Since $u(\bar{k}, \bar{k}) = \bar{u} = 0$, we have $V(\bar{k}) = 0$. The first statement of the lemma is immediate from lemma 5. For the second statement note that the function V is concave from the concavity of u. Also K is convex from the convexity of D and the concavity of V. Therefore for any $x \in K$ it is possible to express $\bar{k}$ by $\bar{k} = \alpha x + (1 - \alpha)y$ where $y \in K$. If $V(x) = \infty$ held then $V(\bar{k}) = \infty$ would hold by the concavity of V. This contradicts $V(\bar{k}) = 0$.   ∎

We are now able to prove an asymptotic theorem for infinite optimal paths.

THEOREM 4   *Given assumptions 6, 7, 8, 9, and 10, let $\bar{k}$ be the unique stock that realizes maximum sustainable utility in a stationary path where $\bar{k} \in$ relative interior K. Let $\{k^t\}$ be an optimal program that is arbitrary, except that $k^0 \in K$. Then for any $\varepsilon > 0$ there is a number $N(\varepsilon)$ such that $|k^t - \bar{k}| > \varepsilon$ can hold for at most $N(\varepsilon)$ periods.*

Proof   Let $k^{\prime\prime} = 1/2(\bar{k} + k^t)$. By convexity of K, $k^{\prime\prime} \in K$, and by strict concavity of u, for any $\varepsilon > 0$ there is $\delta > 0$ such that $|(k^t, k^{t+1}) - (\bar{k}, \bar{k})| > \varepsilon$ implies that

$$u(k^{\prime\prime}, k^{\prime\prime+1}) = u(\tfrac{1}{2}(k^t + \bar{k}, k^{t+1} + \bar{k})) \geq \tfrac{1}{2}(u(k^t, k^{t+1}) + u(\bar{k}, \bar{k})) + \delta$$

$$= \tfrac{1}{2}u(k^t, k^{t+1}) + \delta. \tag{15}$$

Let $N(\varepsilon)$ be the number of times $|(k^t, k^{t+1}) - (\bar{k}, \bar{k})| > \varepsilon$ holds. Summing utility over the paths, (15) implies that

$$V(k^{\prime 0}) \geq \tfrac{1}{2}V(k^0) + N(\varepsilon)\delta. \tag{16}$$

We use the fact that optimal paths realize the value of the initial stock. Also $\liminf_{T \to \infty} \sum_{t=1}^{T} u(k'^{t-1}, k'^{t}) = V(k'^{0})$. Then (16) implies that

$$N(\varepsilon) \leq \delta^{-1}(V(k'^{0}) - \tfrac{1}{2}V(k^{0})).$$

$V(k'^{0}) < \infty$ by lemma 8 and $k^{0} \in K$ implies that $V(k^{0}) > -\infty$. Thus the right side of (16) is finite. ∎

The asymptotic theorem has been proved with the optimal stationary path as a turnpike. However, the logic of the argument extends beyond this. It can be applied to a utility function $u_t(k^{t-1}, k^{t})$ which is not constant over time. A definition of uniform strict concavity is given in section 7.6. The result is that all optimal paths from initial stocks in K converge together if the utility function is uniformly strictly concave along one of the paths that starts from an initial stock relative interior to K. The extension to this more general case involves no new principles (McKenzie 1986, p. 1308). We may also note that a parallel theorem can be proved for convergence to the von Neumann facet when only concavity of u is assumed.

7.5   The Generalized Ramsey Model with Discounting

Up to this point we have not allowed for the possibility that future utilities are discounted in the Ramsey model in which a sum of periodwise utilities is the objective. However, this type of myopia has often been treated as the normal condition of utility maximizers, for example, in the work of Irving Fisher (1930), although Ramsey along with some of his Cambridge predecessors took the view that discounting is inappropriate when it is applied to the utilities of future generations. An interesting case to consider is got by setting $u_t = \rho^t u$, where ρ is less than 1. In this case it becomes nontrivial to prove that an optimal path exists with a stationary capital stock. Our proof uses a fixed point theorem. Also a turnpike theorem becomes more difficult to prove, and no proof had been found long after turnpike theorems were proved for the undiscounted case. The first results were obtained by Cass and Shell (1976) and Scheinkman (1976).

The model where the utility function on capital stocks is constant over time, which implies that technology and utility are constant except for the presence of the discount factor, is referred to as the *quasi-stationary model*. In place of assumptions 5 and 8 we now have

ASSUMPTION 11   The utility function $u_t = \rho^t u$ for $0 < \rho < 1$. Also u is concave, closed, and not constant. The set D is convex.

ASSUMPTION 12   There is $(\bar{x}, \bar{y}) \in D$ for which $\bar{y} > \rho^{-1}\bar{x}$ holds.

Assumptions 6 and 7 are retained. The existence of a stationary optimal path in a quasi-stationary model was first proved by Peleg and Ryder (1974). The proof used here is from McKenzie (1986).

Let Δ be the set $\{x \mid x \geq 0 \text{ and } |x| \leq \zeta\}$ where ζ is given by assumption 6. Then Δ is a compact convex subset of $\mathbf{R}_+^n$. For any $x \in \Delta$ define

$$f(x) = \{(z, w) \mid \rho w - z \geq (\rho - 1)x \text{ for } (z, w) \in D\}.$$

It is sometimes helpful to consider the equivalent definition

$$f(x) = \{(z, w) \mid w - \rho^{-1}z \geq (1 - \rho^{-1})x \text{ for } (z, w) \in D\}.$$

Then it is natural to describe the set $f(x)$ in terms of the generalized slope ρ^{-1} of a map from the input space to the output space defined by $(e, -\rho^{-1}e)$, where $e = (1, \cdots, 1)$. That is to say, the set $f(x)$ is the set of all points of D that lie above the hyperplane through (x, x) that is orthogonal to $(e, -\rho^{-1}e)$.

LEMMA 9 $f(x)$ is nonempty, convex, closed, and bounded.

Proof   By assumption 12, we have $\bar{y} > \rho^{-1}\bar{x}$. This implies that $e(\bar{y} - \rho^{-1}\bar{x}) > e(\bar{x} - \rho^{-1}\bar{x})$. Therefore the point $(\bar{x}, \bar{y})$ lies in $f(x)$, and $f(x)$ is not empty. Since D is convex and closed, $f(x)$ is convex and closed since it is defined by linear inequalities. If $(z, w) \in f(x)$, the definition of f implies that

$$|z| \leq \rho|w| + (1 - \rho)|x|, \qquad\qquad (17)$$

where $0 < \rho < 1$. Suppose $|z| \geq \zeta$ holds. Then $|w| < |z|$. Substituting in (17), $|z| < \rho|z| + (1 - \rho)|x|$, or $|z| < |x|$. Since $|x| \leq \zeta$ by definition of Δ, this gives a contradiction. Thus z is bounded. This implies that (z, w) is bounded by assumption 6 and free disposal, assumption 7.   ∎

For a set $U \subset D$ let

$$g(U) = \{(z, w) \in U \mid u(z, w) \geq u(z', w') \text{ for all } (z', w') \in U\}. \qquad (18)$$

LEMMA 10   *The set $g(f(x))$ for $x \in \Delta$ is compact, convex, and not empty.*

Proof Consider $g(f(x))$ for $x \in \Delta$. Since u is concave and closed by assumption 11 and $f(x)$ is compact by lemma 9, the set $W = \{(z, w) \in f(x) \mid u(z, w) \geq u(\bar{x}, \bar{y})\}$ is compact and not empty since it contains $(\bar{x}, \bar{y})$. Since u is closed, $u(z, w)$ achieves its maximum on W and the set of maximizers is closed and bounded. But the maximizers of $u(z, w)$ on W are also the maximizers of $u(z, w)$ on $f(x)$. Thus $g(f(x))$ is compact and not empty. Since $u(z, w)$ is concave $g(f(x))$ is convex. ∎

Let $h(U)$ for U contained in D be the set $\{z \mid (z, w) \in U\}$. Thus $h(U)$ is the projection of U on Δ along the first factor of the Cartesian product $\mathbf{R}^n \times \mathbf{R}^n$. Finally define $F = h \circ g \circ f$. Then F maps Δ into the set of nonempty, convex, compact subsets of Δ.

LEMMA 11   *The correspondence f is lower semicontinous on Δ.*

Proof The proof is analogous to the proof in chapter 2 that the budget correspondence is lower semicontinuous. Let $x^s \to x$, $s = 1, 2, \cdots$, where $x^s \in \Delta$. Suppose $(z, w) \in f(x)$. We show that there is $(z^s, w^s) \in f(x^s)$ and $(z^s, w^s) \to (z, w)$. Consider $(z^s, w^s) = \alpha_s(z, w) + (1 - \alpha_s)(\bar{x}, \bar{y})$, $0 \leq \alpha_s \leq 1$ and α_s maximal for $(z^s, w^s) \in f(x^s)$. Since $(\bar{x}, \bar{y}) \in f(x^s)$, all s, and $f(x^s)$ is convex, α_s exists. Let α be a limit point of α_s as $s \to \infty$. I claim $\alpha = 1$. Suppose not. Consider $(z', w') = \alpha(z, w) + (1 - \alpha)(\bar{x}, \bar{y})$ with $\alpha < 1$. Since $(z, w) \in f(x)$ and $(\bar{x}, \bar{y})$ satisfies the condition to be in $f(x)$ with strict inequality, it follows that for some $\delta > 0$, $\rho w' - z' > (\rho - 1)x + \delta$ must hold. Then for large s, $\rho w^s - z^s > (\rho - 1)x^s + \delta$ holds and α_s is not maximal contradicting the hypothesis. However, $\alpha > 1$ is impossible since $0 \leq \alpha_s \leq 1$. Therefore $\alpha = 1$ must hold. ∎

We will prove that $g \circ f$ is upper semicontinuous by a proof analogous to the proof in chapter 6 that the consumer demand correspondence is upper semicontinuous. The set $f(x)$ replaces the budget set of the consumer and u replaces the consumers preference correspondence.

LEMMA 12   *The correspondence $g \circ f$ is upper semicontinuous.*

Proof Let $x^s \to x$ and $(z^s, w^s) \to (z, w)$, where $(z^s, w^s) \in (g \circ f)(x^s)$. Note that (z, w) must lie in D. Otherwise, $u(z^s, w^s) \to -\infty$ and $u(\bar{x}, \bar{y}) > u(z^s, w^s)$ holds for s large in contradiction to the definition of $g \circ f$. We must show that $(z, w) \in (g \circ f)(x)$. If not, there is $(z', w') \in f(x)$ and $u(z', w') > u(z, w)$. Since f is lower semicontinuous by lemma 11, there is

$(z'^s, w'^s) \to (z', w')$, where $(z^{s\prime}, w^{s\prime}) \in f(x^s)$. Using the construction of the proof of lemma 11, the sequence (z'^s, w'^s) may be chosen so that it lies on a line through (z', w'). By concavity and closedness of u, u is continuous on a line segment in D (Fenchel 1953, p. 78; Rockefellar 1970, p. 84). Therefore $u(z', w') = \lim u(z'^s, w'^s)$ as $s \to \infty$. But $u(z^s, w^s) \geq u(z'^s, w'^s)$, all s and $u(z, w) \geq \limsup u(z^s, w^s)$ by the closedness of u. Therefore $u(z, w) \geq \lim u(z'^s, w'^s) = u(z', w')$ in contradiction to the hypothesis. Thus there is no such (z', w'), and (z, w) is a maximizer of u in $f(x)$. This means that the graph of $g \circ f$ is closed. Since $g \circ f$ has compact range, $g \circ f$ is upper semicontinuous (Berge 1963, p. 112). ■

LEMMA 13   *There is $x \in \Delta$ such that $x \in F(x)$.*

Proof The mapping h is continuous and $g \circ f$ is upper semicontinuous by lemma 12. Therefore F is upper semicontinuous (Berge 1963, p. 113). Since Δ is compact and convex and F maps Δ into convex subsets, the lemma follows from the Kakutani fixed point theorem (Berge 1963, p. 174). ■

In figure 7.5 the mapping F sends k into k', and at the fixed point $k = k'$. The line segment $[0, \zeta]$ is Δ.

One should note the difference between the distinguishing properties of a capital stock $x \in F(x)$ and a capital stock that realizes maximal sustainable utility. The capital stock $x \in F(x)$ is the stock of a stationary path, but (x, x) does not maximize utility over the set of stationary paths but rather over the set of (z, w) such that $\rho w - z \geq (\rho - 1)x$. However if $\rho = 1$ the definitions become identical. We will prove the analogue of lemma 3 in the wider context.

LEMMA 14   *Assume that $\rho < 1$. If $x \in F(x)$, then there is $q \in R^n$, $q \geq 0$, such that $u(z, w) + qw - \rho^{-1}qz \leq u(x, x) + (1 - \rho^{-1})qx$, for all $(z, w) \in D$.*

Proof Let $V(\rho) = \{v \mid v = \rho w - z, (z, w) \in D\}$. Assumption 12 implies that $v' \in V(\rho)$ where $v' = \rho \bar{y} - \bar{x} > 0$. Then $(\rho - 1)x \in$ interior $V(\rho)$ since $(\rho - 1)x \leq 0$ and v is unbounded below by assumption 7. For $v \in V$ let $D_v(\rho) = \{(z, w) \in D \mid \rho w - z \geq v\}$. The boundedness of $D_v(\rho)$ follows from the argument used to bound D_v in the proof of lemma 3.

Define $\varphi(v) = \sup u(x, y)$ for $(x, y) \in D_v(\rho)$, $v \in V$. Since $D_v(\rho)$ is bounded and u is closed the supremum is attained. Let $U = \{(u, v) \mid u \leq \varphi(v)$ for $v \in V(\rho)\}$. U is convex and interior $U \neq \emptyset$. Consider $x \in$

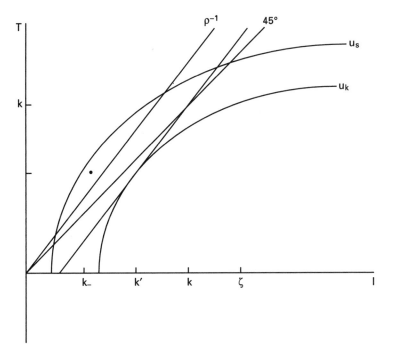

Figure 7.5
The line labeled ρ^{-1} has slope ρ^{-1} and passes through the origin. k_- can be expanded in a ratio larger than ρ^{-1}. u_k is the highest level of utility achievable above the line with slope ρ^{-1} that passes through the point (k, k). The map F sends points of $(0 - \zeta)$ into convex subsets of $(0 - \zeta)$. A fixed point is the capital stock of a stationary optimal path, for example, if $k = k'$.

$F(x)$. Let $\bar{v} = (\rho - 1)x$ and $\bar{u} = \varphi(\bar{v})$. Then $(\bar{u}, \bar{v}) \in$ boundary U. Therefore, by a separation theorem for convex sets (Berge 1963, p. 245), there is $(\pi, r) \neq 0$ such that

$$\pi u + rv \le \pi \bar{u} + r\bar{v} \tag{19}$$

for all $(u, v) \in U$. Since v is unbounded below for given u, we have $r \ge 0$. If $\pi \le 0$, consider $r(v - \bar{v}) \le \pi(\bar{u} - u)$ for all $v \in V(\rho)$, $u = \phi(v)$. For $v > \bar{v}$, we have $u \le \bar{u}$, by the definition of $\bar{u}$ and assumption 7. Since $\bar{v} \in$ interior $V(\rho)$, this leads to contradiction unless $(\pi, \rho) = 0$. Therefore $\pi > 0$. Choose (π, r) so that $\pi = 1$. Then $u + rv \le \bar{u} + (\rho - 1)rx$, all $(u, v) \in U$. Putting $q = \rho r$ gives the result sought. ∎

The existence of a stationary optimal path may now be established.

THEOREM 5   *Given assumptions 6, 7, 11, and 12, if $p < 1$ and $x \in F(x)$ the path $\{k^t\}$ with $k^t = x$ for all t is optimal.*

Proof Suppose that $\{k^t\}$ is a path with $k^0 = x$. Then with q from lemma 14 we have

$$p^t(u(k^{t-1}, k^t) - u(x, x)) \leq p^t q(x - k^t) + p^{t-1} q(k^{t-1} - x).$$

Or summing over t

$$\sum_1^T p^t(u(k^{t-1}, k^t) - u(x, x)) \leq p^T q(x - k^T) + q(k^0 - x). \tag{20}$$

However, k^T is bounded by lemma 6, and $x = k^0$. Therefore the right side of (20) converges to 0 as $T \to \infty$ and $\limsup \sum_1^T p^t(u(k^{t-1}, k^t) - u(x, x)) \leq 0$. Therefore $\{k^t\}$ with $k^t = x$ for all t is an optimal path from x. ∎

Note that the proof fails if $p = 1$. However, it may be recovered if $k^T \to x$ as $T \to \infty$. This is implied by theorem 3 when strict concavity holds for u.

The periodwise utility $u(k^{t-1}, k^t)$ is bounded above from the boundedness of k^t and the closedness of u. Thus the sum $\sum_1^T p^t u(k^{t-1}, k^t)$ converges to a finite number *or* $-\infty$ as $t \to \infty$, and the sum $\sum_1^T p^t u(x, x)$ also converges to a finite number even without normalizing $u(x, x)$ to be 0. So in the quasi-stationary case the overtaking objective is equivalent to the usual objective and the generalization to overtaking is not needed. In recent years less attention has been given to the models without discounting. However some environmentalists do not accept the discounting of future utilities when it leads to the exhaustion of resources which are renewable. Thus the practice of discounting in setting social objectives is condemned by that group.

7.6   A Turnpike Theorem for the Quasi-stationary Model

Turnpike results are much harder to reach in the Ramsey model with discounting than in the Ramsey model without discounting. The reason is apparent. Our argument for the Ramsey turnpike for a finite horizon used the utility achieved on a comparison path to provide a floor for the utility achieved on an optimal path. But departure from the von Neumann facet for an indefinite period causes a shortfall in the utility sum achieved which is unbounded. Unless convergence to the facet occurs, a contradiction arises when the utility sum on the optimal path falls below the utility sum on the comparison path. However, if utility is discounted, the value losses will be bounded, so it becomes necessary to use a more subtle argument as well as accept a weaker conclusion. Also in the primal argument that we used for the case of an infinite horizon, a crucial step in the proof involves an unbounded utility gain by an intermediate path. However, the gain is no longer unbounded when utility is discounted. A way around these difficulties was first found by Cass and Shell (1976) and by Scheinkman (1976).

We will prove a turnpike theorem for the discounted Ramsey model by extending the utility gain method to the discounted case using a technique suggested by the work of Bewley (1982). However, the primary result will be convergence of an optimal path to an arbitrary neighborhood of the stationary optimal path rather than asymptotic convergence to the stationary optimal path. We follow the argument of McKenzie (1982). The set of sustainable stocks is $\Sigma = \{x \mid (x, x) \in D\}$. Define $\bar{\Delta} = \{x \mid x \in \Sigma$ and $u(x, x) \geq u(\bar{x}, \bar{y})\}$, where $(\bar{x}, \bar{y}) \in D$ and $\bar{y} > \rho^{-1}\bar{x}$ with ρ the discount factor for utility. We retain assumptions 6 and 7 and assume

ASSUMPTION 13   The utility function $u_t = \rho^t u$ for $0 < \bar{\rho} \leq \rho \leq 1$, where u maps D into $\mathbf{R}$. Also u is concave and closed, and uniformly strictly concave over the set of (x, x) with $x \in \bar{\Delta}$. The set D is convex.

ASSUMPTION 14   There is $(\bar{x}, \bar{y}) \in D$ for which $\bar{y} > \bar{\rho}^{-1}\bar{x}$ holds.

The condition of *uniform strict concavity* for u over all (x, x) with $x \in \bar{\Delta}$ means that for any (x, x) with $x \in \bar{\Delta}$ and any $(w, z) \in D$, the following holds. For any $\varepsilon > 0$ there is $\delta > 0$ such that $|(x, x) - (w, z)| > \varepsilon$ implies $u(1/2(x, x) + 1/2(w, z)) - 1/2(u(x, x) + u(w, z)) > \delta$.

LEMMA 15 $\bar{\Delta}$ *is compact and not empty.*

Proof $\bar{\Delta}$ is not empty since free disposal implies that it contains $\bar{x}$. $\bar{\Delta}$ is bounded since $|x| > \zeta$ implies by assumption 6 that $(x, x) \notin D$ and so $x \notin \Sigma$. To see that $\bar{\Delta}$ is closed, let $x^s \to x$, $s = 1, 2, \cdots$, with $x^s \in \bar{\Delta}$. Since $u(x^s, x^s) \geq u(\bar{x}, \bar{y})$ and u is closed, it follows that $(x, x) \in D$ and $u(x, x) \geq u(\bar{x}, \bar{y})$. ∎

Let $(\bar{k}, \bar{k})$ satisfy $u(\bar{k}, \bar{k}) = \bar{u} \geq u(z, w)$ for $(z, w) \in D$ and $w \geq z$. Lemma 15 and free disposal imply that such a point exists. Strict concavity of u at (x, x) with $x \in \bar{\Delta}$ implies that $\bar{k}$ is unique. We will refer to $\bar{k}$ as the optimal stationary stock. Finally we will assume

ASSUMPTION 15 *The optimal stationary stock $\bar{k}$ is expansible. Also $\bar{\Delta}$ is relative interior to Σ the set of sustainable stocks.*

The only stationary optimal paths $\{k^t\}$, $t = 0, 1, \cdots$, that will concern us are those that satisfy the condition that $k^t = x$ for all t and $u(x, x) \geq u(z, w)$ for all (z, w) for which $\rho w - z \geq (\rho - 1)x$. We will refer to these stationary paths as *nontrivial*. We will say that a capital stock x is *sufficient* if there is a finite path $\{k^t\}$, $t = 0, 1, \cdots, T$, such that $k^0 = x$ and k^T is expansible (that is, there is $(k^T, y) \in D$ with $y > k^T$). The trivial stationary paths may arise when $(x, x) \in D$ but x is not sufficient. A preliminary step to the turnpike theorem is to show that the set of nontrivial optimal stationary stocks k^ρ converge uniformly to the optimal stationary stock $\bar{k}$ as $\rho \to 1$ (Scheinkman 1976).

LEMMA 16 *A nontrivial optimal stationary stock k^ρ lies in $\bar{\Delta}$ if $1 \geq \rho \geq \bar{\rho}$. If $\rho \to 1$ with $\rho < 1$ then $\sup|k^\rho - \bar{k}| \to 0$ where the sup is taken over the set of k^ρ that appear in nontrivial optimal stationary paths.*

Proof Let $f'(x, \rho) = \{(z, w) \mid \rho w - z \geq (\rho - 1)x$ for $(z, w) \in D\}$. Then $\bar{\rho}\bar{y} - \bar{x} > 0$ while $(\rho - 1)x \leq 0$, so $(\bar{x}, \bar{y}) \in f'(x, \rho)$. Since $u(k^\rho, k^\rho) \geq u(z, w)$ for any $(z, w) \in f'(k^\rho, \rho)$, this implies from the definition of $\bar{\Delta}$ that $k^\rho \in \bar{\Delta}$.

A small modification of the proof of lemma 11 establishes the lower semicontinuity of f' in x and ρ. For any $(z, w) \in f'(x, \rho)$ one considers the sequence $(z^s, w^s) \in f'(x^s, \rho^s)$ that is closest to (z, w) as $x^s \to x$ and $\rho^s \to \rho$, where $1 \geq \rho \geq \bar{\rho}$. As before, it may be shown that $(z^s, w^s) \to (z, w)$ and lower semicontinuity follows. Then the argument of lemma 12 applies to show that $g \circ f'$ is upper semicontinuous.

The capital stock k^ρ of a nontrivial stationary optimal path satisfies $k^\rho \in F(k^\rho)$ from its definition. Suppose there were a sequence $\rho_s \to 1$, $s = 1, 2, \cdots$, converging to 1 from below and a sequence $k^{\rho_s} \in F(k^{\rho_s})$, such that $|k^{\rho_s} - \bar{k}| \geq \varepsilon > 0$ for $s = 1, 2, \cdots$. Let k' be a point of accumulation of the k^{ρ_s}. The upper semicontinuity of $g \circ f'(k, \rho)$ implies that $k' \in g \circ f'(k', 1)$. But $\rho = 1$ implies that (k', k') maximizes sustainable utility. Then $u(k', k') \geq u(\bar{k}, \bar{k})$ and $k' \neq \bar{k}$ in contradiction to the uniqueness of the element (x, x) with $x \in \bar{\Delta}$ that maximizes sustainable utility. Thus no such sequence can exist. ∎

We choose the origin of utility by setting $u(\bar{k}, \bar{k}) = 0$. This has no effect on the comparison of paths. Let $V^\rho(x) = \sup(\lim \sum_{t=1}^{T} \rho^t u(k^{t-1}, k^t)$ as $T \to \infty)$ where the supremum is taken over all paths $\{k^t\}$ with $k^0 = x$. The limits exist since lemma 6 implies that the paths are bounded. Thus $u(k^{t-1}, k^t)$ is bounded above and the sum of the positive terms in the series $\{u(k^{t-1}, k^t)\}$ exists since $0 < \rho < 1$. Then the limit of the full sum exists and is finite *or* $-\infty$. V^ρ is the value function for the discount factor ρ.

LEMMA 17   *If x is sufficient $V^\rho(x)$ is bounded for $\bar{\rho} \le \rho \le 1$.*

Proof   By lemma 3 there is p such that

$$u(\bar{k}, \bar{k}) \ge u(k^{t-1}, k^t) + pk^t - pk^{t-1}.$$

Since $u(\bar{k}, \bar{k}) = 0$ this implies that

$$u(k^{t-1}, k^t) \le p(k^{t-1} - k^t). \tag{21}$$

Multiplying (21) through by ρ^t and summing from $t = 1$ to $t = T$ gives

$$\sum_{t=1}^{T} \rho^t u(k^{t-1}, k^t) \le \sum_{t=1}^{T} \rho^t p(k^{t-1} - k^t)$$

$$= \rho p k^0 + \sum_{t=1}^{T-1} \rho^t (\rho - 1) p k^t - \rho^T p k^T \le \rho p k^0. \tag{22}$$

The first expression of (22) is bounded above by pk^0 over $\rho \le 1$ independently of T. Thus $V^\rho(x)$ is bounded above for $\bar{\rho} \le \rho \le 1$.

To show that $V^\rho(x)$ is bounded below, note that x sufficient implies that there is a path $\{x^t\}$, $t = 0, 1, \cdots, T$, where $x^0 = x$ and x^T is expansible. Let $y > x^T$ hold where $(x, y) \in D$. Then from the proof of lemma 5 there is an infinite path $\{x^t\}$, $t = T, T+1, \cdots$, where $x^{T+\tau} = \alpha^\tau x^T + (1 - \alpha^\tau)\bar{k}$, with $0 < \alpha < 1$, and $u(x^{T+\tau}, x^{T+\tau+1}) \ge \alpha^\tau u(x^T, y) + (1 - \alpha^\tau)u(\bar{k}, \bar{k}) = \alpha^\tau u(x^T, y)$. Then $\sum_{t=T}^{\infty} \rho^t u(x^t, x^{t+1}) \ge (\rho^T/(1 - \rho\alpha)) \cdot u(x^T, y)$. The last expression is bounded below uniformly for ρ satisfying $0 < \bar{\rho} \le \rho \le 1$. Since the utility accumulated in the first T periods is finite for $\rho \le 1$, it follows that $V^\rho(x)$ is bounded below uniformly for $\bar{\rho} \le \rho \le 1$. ∎

Next we show that the sustainable stocks that lie in $\bar{\Delta}$ are actually uniformly expansible. Write $e = (1, \cdots, 1)$.

LEMMA 18   *Given $x \in \bar{\Delta}$ there is $\varepsilon > 0$ such that $(x, x + \varepsilon e) \in D$.*

Proof Since $\bar{k}$ is expansible by assumption 15, there is ε' such that $(\bar{k}, \bar{k} + \varepsilon' e) \in D$. The convexity of D implies that Σ is convex. Since $\bar{\Delta} \subset$ relative interior Σ by assumption 15, any (x, x) with $x \in \bar{\Delta}$ may be expressed as $(x, x) = \alpha(y, y) + (1 - \alpha)(\bar{k}, \bar{k})$ for some α with $0 \leq \alpha < 1$ and some (y, y) with $y \in \Sigma$. Then $(x, x + (1 - \alpha)\varepsilon' e) = \alpha(y, y) + (1 - \alpha) \cdot (\bar{k}, \bar{k} + \varepsilon' e) \in D$. Choose $\varepsilon = (1 - \alpha)\varepsilon'$.   ∎

The neighborhood turnpike theorem is

THEOREM 6 (McKenzie 1981)   *Make assumptions 6, 7, 13, 14, and 15. Let $\{k^t\}$, $k^t = k^\rho$, $t = 0, 1, \cdots$, be a nontrivial stationary optimal path for $\bar{\rho} \leq \rho \leq 1$. Assume that x is sufficient. If $\{k^t(\rho)\}$, $t = 0, 1, \cdots$, is an optimal path with $k^0 = x$, given any $\varepsilon > 0$ there is $\rho' > 0$ and T such that $|k^t(\rho) - k^\rho| < \varepsilon$ for all $t > T$ and all ρ with $\rho' \leq \rho \leq 1$.*

Proof We will represent $\{k^t(\rho)\}$ as an element $k(\rho)$ of the Banach space $l_\infty^n = \{y = (y_1, y_2, \cdots) \mid y_t \in \mathbf{R}^n \text{ and } |y_t| \leq \beta \text{ for some } \beta \geq 0, \text{ for all } t \geq 0\}$.

Let $k''^t(\rho) = \frac{1}{2}(k^t(\rho) + k^\rho)$. Define the *utility gain* in period t by

$$g_t(k(\rho), k^\rho) = u(k''^{t-1}(\rho), k''^t(\rho)) - \tfrac{1}{2}(u(k^{t-1}(\rho), k^t(\rho)) + u(k^\rho, k^\rho)).$$

By the concavity of u, we have $g_t(k(\rho), k^\rho) \geq 0$.

Define the Liapounov function

$$G_t(k(\rho), k^\rho) = \sum_{\tau=1}^{\infty} \rho^\tau g_{t+\tau}(k(\rho), k^\rho).$$

Then

$$G_{t+1}(k(\rho), k^\rho) - G_t(k(\rho), k^\rho) = \sum_{\tau=1}^{\infty} \rho^\tau g_{t+\tau+1} - \sum_{\tau=1}^{\infty} \rho^\tau g_{t+\tau},$$

where the arguments of the g functions are omitted. Thus we have

$$G_{t+1} - G_t = (\rho^{-1} - 1)G_t - g_{t+1}, \tag{23}$$

omitting the arguments $(k(\rho), k^\rho)$ of both G and g functions. For any $\delta > 0$ we may choose ρ close enough to 1 to give $(\rho^{-1} - 1)G_0 < \delta$ provided that $G_0(k(\rho), k^\rho)$ is bounded as $\rho \to 1$. This is proved in

LEMMA 19 $G_0(k(\rho), k^\rho)$ *is bounded for ρ near 1, $\rho \leq 1$.*

Proof Since $k^0(\rho) = x$ we have

$$G_0(k(\rho), k^\rho) = V^\rho(\tfrac{1}{2}(x + k^\rho)) - \tfrac{1}{2}(V^\rho(x) + V^\rho(k^\rho)).$$

$V^\rho(x)$ is bounded by lemma 17 since x is sufficient. Also $V^\rho(1/2(x + k^\rho))$ is bounded above by the first part of the proof of lemma 17. Since, by lemma 16, all $k^\rho \to \bar{k}$ uniformly as $\rho \to 1$, it is enough to bound $V^\rho(k^\rho)$ in a neighborhood B of $\bar{k}$ relative to Σ. Since for ρ near 1 lemma 16 implies that $k^\rho \in \bar{\Delta}$, which is relative interior to Σ, we may choose $B = \{x \,|\, x \in \bar{\Delta}\}$. Then, by lemma 18, for an $\varepsilon > 0$, we have $(k^\rho, k^\rho + \varepsilon e) \in D$ for any $k^\rho \in B$. Then the proof of lemma 17 implies, for a small $\varepsilon' > 0$, that $V^\rho(k^\rho) \geq (\rho/(1 - \rho\alpha))u(k^\rho, k^\rho + \varepsilon'e)$ where $0 < \alpha < 1$. However, $u(k^\rho, k^\rho + \varepsilon'e)$ converges to $u(\bar{k}, \bar{k} + \varepsilon'e)$ as $\rho \to 1$. Since $(\bar{k}, \bar{k} + \varepsilon'e)$ is interior to D for small ε', $u(\bar{k}, \bar{k} + \varepsilon'e)$ is finite and $u(k^\rho, k^\rho + \varepsilon'e)$ is bounded below as $\rho \to 1$. Therefore $V^\rho(k^\rho)$ is bounded below as $\rho \to 1$. Then G_0 is bounded above. On the other hand, $G_0 \geq 0$ follows from the concavity of u. Therefore G_0 is bounded. ∎

By lemma 19, for any $\delta > 0$ we may choose ρ so that $(\rho^{-1} - 1)G_0 < \delta$. A first step to establish G_t as a Liapounov function is to show for any $\varepsilon > 0$ that there is $\delta > 0$ such that the left side of (23) when $t = 0$ is less than $-\delta$ if $|k^0(\rho) - k^\rho| > \varepsilon$. However, this follows since $|(k^0(\rho), k^1(\rho)) - (k^\rho, k^\rho)| > \varepsilon$ implies $g_1(k(\rho), k^\rho) > 2\delta$ for some $\delta > 0$ by strict concavity of u at (k^ρ, k^ρ) uniformly for $k^\rho \in \bar{\Delta}$. Thus, for any $\varepsilon > 0$, $G_1 - G_0 < -\delta$ may be guaranteed for some $\delta > 0$ when k_0 is different from k^ρ by at least ε by choosing ρ near enough to 1.

The argument continues by induction. Suppose $G_{t+1} - G_t < -\delta$ and $(\rho^{-1} - 1)G_t < \delta$, relations that have been established for $t = 0$. Then

$$(\rho^{-1} - 1)G_{t+1} < (\rho^{-1} - 1)G_t < \delta.$$

On the other hand, if $|(k^{t+1}(\rho), k^{t+2}(\rho)) - (k^\rho, k^\rho)| > \varepsilon$ holds, then, as in the argument above, by strict concavity $g_{t+2} > 2\delta$ holds, so using (23) again, we have $G_{t+2} - G_{t+1} < -\delta$. In other words, $G_{t+1} - G_t < -\delta$ continues to hold for $t \geq 0$ so long as $k^t(\rho)$ remains outside an ε-neighborhood of k^ρ. By summing these inequalities, we then obtain

$$G_T(k(\rho), k^\rho) \leq G_0 - T\delta \tag{24}$$

if $k^t(\rho)$ is outside the ε-neighborhood of k^ρ from $t = 0$ until $t = T$. Since G_T is nonnegative, by its definition the inequality (24) forces $k^t(\rho)$ eventually to enter the ε-neighborhood to avoid contradiction. Note that if the argument holds for ρ', it holds uniformly for all ρ such that $\rho' \leq \rho \leq 1$. Also for a given ρ with $\rho' \leq \rho < 1$, all nontrivial stationary optimal paths k^ρ must lie in the ε-neighborhood of any one of them. On the other hand, with the assumption of strict concavity when $\rho = 1$, there is a unique stationary optimal path whose capital stock is the unique stock maximizing sustainable utility.

We have shown that paths cannot stay outside any neighborhood U of k^ρ indefinitely. However, to complete the proof, we must show that once a path has entered U, there is a neighborhood W that it cannot leave. For this purpose another lemma is needed.

LEMMA 20   *If $k(\rho)$ is an optimal path from k^0 then for any $\delta > 0$ there is $\varepsilon > 0$ such that $|(k^0, k^1(\rho)) - (k^\rho, k^\rho)| < \varepsilon$ implies $G_0(k(\rho), k^\rho) < \delta$, uniformly for $\bar{\rho} \leq \rho \leq 1$ and all nontrivial stationary paths for ρ.*

Proof   By the definition of G_0 and the feasibility of the intermediate path

$$\begin{aligned}
G_0(k(\rho), k^\rho) &\leq u(\tfrac{1}{2}(k^0 + k^\rho), \tfrac{1}{2}(k^1(\rho) + k^\rho)) \\
&\quad - \tfrac{1}{2}(u(k^0, k^1(\rho)) + u(k^\rho, k^\rho)) \\
&\quad + \rho V^\rho(\tfrac{1}{2}(k^1(\rho) + k^\rho)) \\
&\quad - \tfrac{1}{2}(\rho(V^\rho(k^1(\rho)) + V^\rho(k^\rho)).
\end{aligned} \tag{25}$$

By lemma 16, we have $k^\rho \in \bar{\Delta}$. Since $\bar{\Delta}$ is compact and relative interior to the set of sustainable stocks by assumption 15, uniform concavity of u implies that u is uniformly continuous over (x, x) with $x \in \bar{\Delta}$. Then from (25) it follows that G_0 is small for $(k^0, k^1(\rho))$ near (k^ρ, k^ρ), provided that $V^\rho(k^{1\prime}(\rho)) \to V^\rho(k^\rho)$ when $k'(\rho)$ is an optimal path from $k^{0\prime}$ and $(k^{0\prime}, k^{1\prime}(\rho)) \to (k^\rho, k^\rho)$. However, lemma 18 implies that k^ρ is uniformly expansible for $\bar{\rho} \leq \rho \leq 1$. Expansibility of k^ρ and free disposal imply that $(k^\rho, k^{1\prime}(\rho)) \in D$ for $k^{1\prime}(\rho)$ near k^ρ. This implies

$$u(k^\rho, k^\rho) + \rho V^\rho(k^\rho) \geq u(k^\rho, k^{1\prime}(\rho)) + \rho V^\rho(k^{1\prime}(\rho)).$$

Therefore $V^\rho(k^{1\prime}(\rho)) \leq V^\rho(k^\rho) + \varepsilon$ may be assured for any assigned $\varepsilon > 0$ for any ρ, $\bar{\rho} \leq \rho \leq 1$, and any k^ρ by bringing $(k^{0\prime}, k^{1\prime}(\rho))$ near to (k^ρ, k^ρ).

This argument may be repeated for a switch from $k^{0\prime}$ to k^ρ. Let $\bar{\Delta}'$ be a compact set contained in the relative interior of Σ, the set of sustainable stocks, having $\bar{\Delta}$ in its interior relative to Σ (see Berge 1963, p. 68). The argument of lemma 18 may be applied to $\bar{\Delta}'$ to show that x is uniformly expansible for $x \in \bar{\Delta}'$ for all ρ with $\bar{\rho} \leq \rho \leq 1$. Then k^ρ may be reached from $k^{\prime 0}$ near k^ρ. This gives $V^\rho(k^\rho) \leq V^\rho(k^{\prime 1}(\rho)) + \varepsilon$ for any assigned $\varepsilon > 0$ when $(k^{\prime 0}, k^{\prime 1}(\rho))$ is sufficiently near (k^ρ, k^ρ). Thus $V^\rho(k^{1\prime}(\rho)) \to V^\rho(k^\rho)$ as needed. ∎

We may now complete the proof of theorem 6. Given any $\varepsilon > 0$ we have shown that there is ρ' such that the optimal path from a sufficient x may be brought within ε of any k^ρ for any ρ with $\rho' \leq \rho < 1$. To complete the proof, we must show that given any $\varepsilon' > 0$ it is possible to choose ε so small that once the path has become within ε of k^ρ it must lie within $\varepsilon' > 0$ of k^ρ thereafter. Choose $\eta < \rho G_0$. By uniform strict concavity in $\bar{\Delta}$, assumption 13, given ε' there is η so small that $|(k^{t+1}(\rho), k^{t+2}(\rho)) - (k^\rho, k^\rho)| > \varepsilon'$ implies

$$G_{t+1} \geq \rho g_{t+2} \geq \rho^{-1}\eta \tag{26}$$

uniformly for all k^ρ and all ρ with $\bar{\rho} \leq \rho \leq 1$. Relation (23) implies

$$G_{t+1} \leq \rho^{-1}G_t. \tag{27}$$

By lemma 20, for any $\eta > 0$ there is an $\varepsilon > 0$ such that $|(k^t(\rho), k^{t+1}(\rho)) - (k^\rho, k^\rho)| \leq \varepsilon$ implies that $G_t < \eta$. Inserting this bound for G_t into (27) gives a contradiction of (26). Therefore, if $(k^t(\rho), k^{t+1}(\rho))$ lies in the ε-neighborhood of (k^ρ, k^ρ), it must be that $(k^{t+1}(\rho), k^{t+2}(\rho))$ lies within ε' of (k^ρ, k^ρ). If $(k^{t+1}(\rho), k^{t+2}(\rho))$ is not within ε of (k^ρ, k^ρ), the first part of the proof implies that G_τ decreases for $\tau > t + 1$ until $(k^\tau(\rho), k^{\tau+1}(\rho))$ is within ε of (k^ρ, k^ρ) once more. Moreover the fact that G_τ is decreasing means from (26) and (27) that $(k^\tau(\rho), k^{\tau+1}(\rho))$ cannot leave the neighborhood of (k^ρ, k^ρ) defined by ε'. The choices of constants is first ε', then η, and finally ε. These choices are consistent. Somewhat more detail for the proof may be found in the proof of lemma 35 below, which is parallel to this proof with the additional complication that the welfare function depends on the discount factor ρ. ∎

Of course, if $\rho = 1$ convergence occurs for all values of ε'. That is, the optimal path converges to k^ρ as we already know from theorem 4. For ρ sufficiently near 1 it is also possible to prove a neighborhood turnpike theorem for the von Neumann facet $F(\rho)$ even though F is not trivial. Moreover this result may be extended to a neighborhood theorem for an optimal stationary stock $k(\rho)$ when $k(\rho)$ is unique and $F(\rho)$ is stable. Finally, with some conditions of negative definiteness for the Hessian matrix of u, the stability can be extended to asymptotic convergence of the optimal path to $k(\rho)$ (see McKenzie 1983).

7.7 The Turnpike in Competitive Equilibrium

It is possible to extend the Ramsey turnpike theorem to provide a turnpike theorem for the competitive equilibrium of the model with an infinite horizon for which existence of equilibrium was proved in chapter 6. Since the turnpike theorem was proved for a model in which separability over time is assumed both for consumer's utility and for production, the model in which the competitive turnpike theorem is proved will not have the generality of the model described in chapter 6. In the existence theorem neither of these assumptions was made. We will also make the further assumption that future utility is discounted by a constant factor, which is the same for all consumers. Models of this type were first developed by Bewley (1982) and Yano (1984).

The existence theorem will be applied to an economy with the production sector used by Malinvaud (1953) in a study of efficiency for infinite programs. In this economy, production has a property of separability between time periods. We also introduce a consumers' sector where separability between time periods is assumed. The economy then has a kind of Markov property since the possibilities of production and trading in any period depend only on the state of the economy at that time. The state of the economy is given by the stock of capital, the technology, the consumption possibility sets, and consumer's preferences. In this model, as a model of competitive equilibria, it is not possible to concentrate only on preferences over trades since trades would include trades in assets, which have no current utility. Such trades must consider the utilities that accrue in the future and depend on the liquidation of assets. Since we will deal with competitive equilibria as well as optimal paths of accumulation, it is necessary to identify goods that are consumed within the period and provide utility. The technology set, the possibility sets for consumption, and the consumer preferences are unchanging over time. On the consumers' side, this may reflect a set of families whose characteristics do not change from one generation to another. On the production side, although production possibilities do not change, feasible outputs may be affected by capital accumulation. We will use the assumption that the social production set is a convex cone, recalling that this production set may represent an economy of firms when entrepreneurial factors are introduced.

The commodity space is the space s^n with the product topology defined in section 6.4. In this section it is convenient to place time indexes on most symbols as subscripts rather than as superscripts. This should cause no confusion. Separability in the production sector is represented by setting $Y = \sum_{t=1}^{\infty} \bar{Y}_t$, where $\bar{Y}_t$ lies in s^n and contains vectors of the form $y^t = (0, \cdots, 0, -k_{t-1}, v_t, 0, \cdots)$. The vector $k_{t-1} \in \mathbf{R}_+^n$ represents capital stocks available at the beginning of the tth period and $v_t \in \mathbf{R}_+^n$ represents outputs during the tth period, including terminal capital stocks and inputs of goods and services supplied by consumers. Let the set Y_t be the set of all $y(t) = (-k_{t-1}, v_t) \in \mathbf{R}_-^n \times \mathbf{R}^n$ for which there is $y^t \in \bar{Y}_t$ with $y^t = (0, \cdots, 0, -k_{t-1}, v_t, 0, \cdots)$. The initial capital stocks k_0 are inputs for the production processes of the first period. Outputs $v_t = k_t + y_t$, where k_t are terminal stocks at time t and y_t, are goods and services either taken by consumers or provided by consumers in the period from $t-1$ to t. We call this the tth period.

Possible consumption sets are $C^h = \sum_{t=0}^{\infty} \bar{C}_t^h$, where $\bar{C}_t^h$ contains vectors of the form $x^{ht} = (0, \cdots, 0, x_t^h, 0, \cdots)$. However, $\bar{C}_0^h = \{(-k_0^h, 0, \cdots)\}$ represents the provision of initial stocks. Also $C = \sum_{h=1}^{H} C^h$, and C_t is the projection of C on tth period goods. Negative components of x_t^h are quantities of goods and services provided by the hth consumer during the tth period and positive components of x_t^h are quantities of goods and services received by the consumer during the tth period. We assume that some components of x_t^h are necessarily negative. These are included in $x_t^{1h} \in \mathbf{R}_-^{n_1}$ and the remaining components are included in $x_t^{2h} \in \mathbf{R}^{n_2}$ where $\mathbf{R}^n = \mathbf{R}^{n_1} \times \mathbf{R}^{n_2}$ with $n_1, n_2 > 0$ and $n_1 + n_2 = n$. Then we may write $x_t^h = (x_t^{1h}, x_t^{2h})$.

The initial capital stocks are allocated among consumers, that is, $k_0 = \sum_{h=1}^{H} k_0^h$. Subsequent capital stocks need not be explicitly allocated since only their values are relevant and the value of a consumer's holding of capital stocks is implied by the value of his initial stocks and his consumption in earlier periods. The capital stocks are timed at regular intervals which define the periods. Periodwise utility functions u_t^h are defined on the tth period consumption set C_t^h for the hth consumer. A strict preference relation $\mathscr{P}^h$ is defined on streams of consumption by $z \mathscr{P}^h x$ if $\sum_{t=1}^{\infty} u_t^h(z_t) > \sum_{t=1}^{\infty} u_t^h(x_t)$. The definition of u_t^h will imply that these sums are finite. Weak preference and indifference, $\mathscr{R}^h$ and $\mathscr{I}^h$, are defined in terms of $\mathscr{P}^h$ in the same way as before. The definition of a periodwise consumption possibility set and this definition of the preference relation is the meaning of separability in utility. Irreducibility and strong irreducibility have the definitions given earlier. Let $e = (e_0, e_1, \cdots)$, where $e_t = (1, \cdots, 1) \in \mathbf{R}^n$.

ASSUMPTION 16   The periodwise production set $Y_t \subset \mathbf{R}_-^n \times \mathbf{R}^n$, $t = 1, 2, \cdots$, is a closed convex cone with vertex at the origin. Also $Y_t = Y_s$, all s and t. If $y(t) = (-k_{t-1}, v_t) \in Y_t$, then $k'_{t-1} \geq k_{t-1}$ and $v'_t \leq v_t$ implies that $(-k'_{t-1}, v'_t) \in Y_t$

ASSUMPTION 17   Let $(-k_{t-1}, v_t) \in Y_t$, where $v_t = k_t + y_t$. Then $y_t^1 = 0$ and $k_{t-1} = 0$ imply $v_t = 0$. Also there is $\zeta > 0$ such that $|k_{t-1}| > \zeta$ and $y_t \in C_t$ implies $|k_t| < \xi |k_{t-1}|$ for $\xi < 1$.

ASSUMPTION 18   The periodwise consumption set $C_t^h \subset \mathbf{R}^n$ is convex, closed, and bounded below by $\bar{z}$ for all h. Also $C_t^h = C_s^h$ for all h and s, t.

Let $P = \{\rho \mid 0 < \rho < 1\}$.

ASSUMPTION 19   The utility function $u_t^h = \rho^t u^h$, where $\rho \in P$ and (by an abuse of notation) u^h is a real-valued function on C_t^h, $t = 1, 2, \cdots$, that is concave, continuous, and bounded. If $x_t \in C_t^h$ and $z_t \geq x_t$, then $z_t \in C_t^h$ and $u^h(z_t) \geq u^h(x_t)$. If $z_t > x_t$, then $u^h(z_t) > u^h(x_t)$.

The Malinvaud economy $\mathscr{E}_m$ is given by $(Y_t, C_{t-1}^1, \cdots, C_{t-1}^H, \rho, u^1, \cdots, u^H)$, $t = 1, 2, \cdots$.

ASSUMPTION 20   The economy $\mathscr{E}_m$ is strongly irreducible.

Given initial stocks $k_0 = \sum_{h \in H'} k_0^h$ a *feasible path for H'* is a sequence $(-k_{t-1}, v_t) \in Y_t$ for $t = 1, 2, \cdots$, such that $v_t = (k_t + y_t)$ and $y_t = \sum_{h \in H'} y_t^h$ with $y_t^h \in C_t^h$ for $t = 0, 1, \cdots$, and $H' \subset H$. Then $\{y_t^h\}$ is a *feasible path of consumption* for H'. A stock k_{t-1} is *expansible* if there is $(-k_{t-1}, v_t) \in Y_t$ with $v_t = (y_t + k_t)$, $y_t \in C_t$, and $k_t > k_{t-1}$ relative to the goods subspace S_g. If $k_t \geq k_{t-1}$, the stock k_{t-1} is said to be *sustainable*. These ideas also apply to individual capital stocks k_t^h with $y_t \in C_t^h$.

ASSUMPTION 21   For all h the individual capital stocks k_0^h are sustainable for $\{h\}$. The total capital stock k_0 is expansible for H. For any h and t there are δ and $\alpha > 0$ such that $(k_t^h, k_t^h + \delta e_{g,t+1} + y_{t+1}^h) \in Y_{t+1}$ implies $(k_t^h, k_t^h + y_{t+1}^h + \alpha e) \in Y_{t+1}$. Also, if $\{y_t^h\}$, $t = 0, 1, \cdots$, is a feasible path of consumption for h, for any $\tau \geq 0$ there is $(k_\tau^h, \bar{k}_{\tau+1}^h + \bar{y}_{\tau+1}^h) \in Y_{t+1}$ where $\bar{k}_{\tau+1}^h = k_\tau^h$ and $\bar{y}_{\tau+1}^h \in C_{\tau+1}^h$.

The last part of assumpton 21 says that along a path of consumption feasible for h each capital stock is sustainable while providing a consumption that is constant and lies in the set of possible consumption bundles for h.

Define $U^h(z, p) = \sum_{t=1}^{\infty} p^t u^h(z_t)$ for $z \in C^h$ and $p \in P$. We first prove

LEMMA 21   *The function U^h is concave in z, continuous, and bounded on C^h for given $p \in P$.*

Proof   The assumption that u^h is bounded and $0 < p < 1$ implies that U^h is well defined and bounded. Concavity is an immediate consequence of the concavity of u^h. For continuity it is sufficient to show that for any neighborhood V of $v = U^h(z, p)$ there is an open neighborhood Z of (z, p) relative to $C^h \times P$ in the topology of s^n such that $(z', p') \in Z$ implies $U^h(z', p') \in V$. We may assume that V contains all $v' \in \mathbf{R}$ such that $|v - v'| < \varepsilon > 0$. In the product topology all but a finite number of the factors of an open set must be unrestricted. Choose small open neighborhoods W_t of z_t, relative to C_t^h, for $1 < t < T$, and a neighborhood R of p in P. Then the open set $Z = \prod_{t=1}^{T} W_t \times \prod_{t>T} C_t^h \times R$ is a neighborhood of (z, p). The W_t, R, and T may be chosen so that $(z', p) \in Z$ implies that $\sum_{t=1}^{T} p'^t |u^h(z_t') - u^h(z_t)| < \varepsilon/2$ and $\sum_{t=T+1}^{\infty} p'^t b < \varepsilon/2$, where b is an upper bound on $|u^h(w_t)|$ for $w_t \in C_t^h$ for all t. It is implied by the continuity and boundedness of u and the fact that $p < 1$ that these choices can be made and define a neighborhood Z of (z, p) relative to $C^h \times P$ that maps into V under U^h.   ∎

We first prove the existence of a competitive equilibrium.

THEOREM 7   *Under assumptions 16 through 21 the economy $\mathscr{E}_m$ has a competitive equilibrium.*

Proof Existence of competitive equilibrium follows from theorem 6.4 if we can show that assumptions 6.16 to 6.21 are implied by assumptions 16 through 21. The first part of assumption 6.16 is the same as assumption 16 in view of the definition of Y. The second part follows from assumption 17 since $y \in Y$ and $y \neq 0$ implies that $y(t) \in Y_t$ and $y(t) \neq 0$ for some t. Therefore $y(t) = (-k_{t-1}, x_t^1 + x_t^2 + k_t)$, and either $-k_{t-1} \neq 0$, or $x_t^1 \leq 0$, $x_t^1 \neq 0$, for some t. Recall that $x_t^1 \leq 0$ represents services provided by consumers in period t. In either case $-y$ does not satisfy the definition of Y. Thus Y cannot contain a straight line. The assumption that Y_t is constant could be replaced by an assumption of variation within limits, but this would complicate the extension of the turnpike theorem. By the usual boundedness argument when certain factors are necessary for production, we have that k_0 given and x_1 bounded below implies that v_1 is bounded above. Thus k_1 is bounded. Then, by induction, v_t is bounded in every period. Thus y_t is bounded in every period. This is boundedness of y in the topology of s^n which implies assumption 6.17. Assumption 6.18 is immediate by assumption 18. Again the constancy assumption of assumption 18 could be replaced by an assumption of variation within limits that would complicate the argument. Transitivity, convexity, and monotonicity of $\mathscr{P}^h$ is immediate from assumption 19. The other parts of assumption 6.19 are established in

LEMMA 22   *P^h is open valued and has open lower sections in s^n and R^h is the closure of P^h in s^n.*

Proof Suppose $z\mathscr{P}^h x$ holds. Then $U^h(z, \rho) > U^h(x, \rho)$. Since U^h is continuous by lemma 21 there is a neighborhood W of z relative to C^h such that $z' \in W$ implies $U^h(z', \rho) > U^h(x, \rho)$. Since z is arbitrary, $P^h(x)$ is open. A similar argument shows that the lower section of P^h at x is also open. Since x is arbitrarily chosen from C^h, we have established that P^h is open valued and has open lower sections. The continuity of U^h and the fact that C^h is closed imply that $R^h(x)$ is closed. Since there are preferred points for any $x \in C^h$ by monotonicity, $R^h(x)$ is the closure of $P^h(x)$ for any $x \in C^h$. ∎

Assumption 20 is the same as assumption 6.20.

LEMMA 23   *Assumptions 16, 18, 19, and 21 imply assumption 6.21.*

Proof The initial capital stock k_0^h is sustainable by assumption 21. This implies that the consumption path $\{\bar{x}_t^h\}$ with $\bar{x}_t^h \in C_t^h$ with $x_t^h = x_1^h$ for

$t \geq 1$ is feasible with $k_t^h = k_0^h$ for all t. In other words, $0 \in C^h - Y$, thus satisfying the first requirement of assumption 6.21. Consider $y(t) \in Y_t$, where $y(t) = (k_{t-1}, v_t)$ and $v_t = (k_t + y_t)$. Since k_0 is expansible, by the second part of assumption 21, it is feasible to hold k_t constant and equal to k_0 in every period while y_t is increased in all components in every period. This satisfies the second part of assumption 6.21. To verify the last statement of assumption 6.21, note that by the third part of assumption 21, additional capital stocks at time 0 makes possible an expansion of all outputs at time 1. Then, by the last part of assumption 21, at any period τ on a feasible consumption path y^h for h there is $(k_\tau^h, k_{\tau+1}^h + \bar{y}_{\tau+1}^h) \in Y_t$ with $k_{\tau+1}^h = k_\tau^h$ and $\bar{y}_{\tau+1}^h \in C_{\tau+1}^h$. These assumptions together imply for some $\delta > 0$ and $\alpha > 0$ that there is a path $^\tau \bar{w}^h$ with $w^h(1) = (k_0^h + \delta e_{g0}, k_1^h + y_1^h + \alpha e_1) \in Y_1$, $w^h(t) = y^h(t)$ for $1 < t \leq \tau$, and $w(t) = (k_t^h, \bar{k}_{t+1}^h + \bar{w}_{t+1}^h) \in Y_t$ with $\bar{k}_{t+1}^h = k_t^h \bar{w}_t^h = \bar{w}_{t+1}^h \in C_{t+1}^h$ for any $t \geq \tau$. Then $^\tau w^h = (k_0^h + \delta e_{g0}, y_1^h + \alpha e_1, y_2^h, \cdots, y_\tau^h, \bar{w}_{\tau+1}^h, \cdots)$ is a feasible consumption path for h. Moreover $^\tau w^h \in P^h(y^h)$ since $\delta < 1$. Now, as $\tau \to \infty$, $^\tau w^h \to (k_0^h + \delta e_{g0}, y_1^h + \alpha e_1, y_2^h, \cdots)$. Since u^h is bounded by assumption 19, we have that $U^h(w) \to U^h(y_1^h + \alpha e_1, y_2^h, \cdots)$ as $\tau \to \infty$. This implies, for large enough τ, that $^\tau w^h - y^h \in R^h(y) - Y$, which satisfies the last part of assumption 6.21. The verification of the assumptions of theorem 6.4 completes the proof of theorem 7. ∎

Let $p = (p_0, p_1, \cdots)$ with $p_t \in \mathbf{R}^n$. Recall that $p \in l_1^n$ and $p \geq 0$. Let $px = \sum_{t=0}^{\infty} p_t x_t$, when the sum exists as a finite number or $+\infty$. A *competitive equilibrium* for the economy $\mathscr{E}_m$ is given by a list $(p, y, x^1, \cdots, x^H)$ as in section 6.4. In the case of $\mathscr{E}_m$ it is convenient to restate the equilibrium conditions in the following equivalent form.

I. $px \leq 0$ and $U^h(z, \rho) > U^h(x, \rho)$ implies $pz > 0$.

II. $y(t) \in Y_t$ and $(p_{t-1}, p_t) \cdot y(t) = 0$. Also $(p_{t-1}, p_t) \cdot z(t) \leq 0$ for all $z(t) \in Y_t$.

III. $\sum_{h \in I} x^h = y$.

The definition of $\mathscr{P}^h$ in terms of U^h implies that I is equivalent to I as defined in section 6.4. Separability in production and the definition of Y implies that II is equivalent in $\mathscr{E}_m$ to II from section 6.4. Finally III is unchanged.

Let $H^h(m) = \{z \mid z \in C^h \text{ and } pz \leq m\}$. By lemma 6.35, we have that pz is well defined as a finite number or $+\infty$. Thus $H^h(m)$ is well defined. By condition I, the competitive equilibrium consumption stream x^h for the hth consumer satisfies the condition that $U^h(x^h, p)$ maximizes $U^h(z, p)$ over $H^h(0)$. Let $g(m) = \sup U^h(z, p)$ over $H^h(m)$. The supremum is finite since $U^h(z, p)$ is bounded over C^h by lemma 21. Let $I = \{m \mid \text{there is } z \in C^h \text{ and } pz \leq m\}$. The epigraph G of $g(m)$ is defined for $m \in I$ by $G = \{(v, m) \mid v \leq g(m)\}$. The concavity of g implies that G is convex. Consider the point $(v^*, 0)$ in G where $v^* = g(0)$. This is a boundary point of G, and therefore by a separation theorem (Berge 1963, p. 163), there is a vector $(\gamma^h, \mu) \neq 0$ such that $\gamma^h v - \mu m \leq \gamma^h v^*$ for all $(v, m) \in G$. Equivalently $\mu m \geq \gamma^h(v - v^*)$. Irreduciblility with assumption 21 implies that a cheaper point at equilibrium prices p exists in C^h. That is, there is $m < 0$ with $m \in I$. The definition of v^* implies that m and $(v - v^*)$ have the same signs. Thus γ^h and μ must have the same signs as well. But, if these signs were negative, the fact that v is unbounded below by the definition of G, while m is bounded below, since C^h is bounded below, would lead to a contradiction. Therefore it must be that $\mu > 0$ and $\gamma^h > 0$. We may choose (γ^h, μ) so that $\mu = 1$. Then we have $v^* = g(0) \geq g(m) - (1/\gamma^h)m$. In other words,

$$U^h(x^h, p) \geq U^h(z^h, p) - \left(\frac{1}{\gamma^h}\right)pz^h \qquad \text{for any } z^h \in C^h. \tag{28}$$

Finally, by choice of p, we may obtain $\sum_{h=1}^{H} \gamma^h = 1$. It is customary to refer to $1/\gamma^h$ as the marginal utility of wealth for the hth consumer. Let $\gamma = (\gamma^1, \cdots, \gamma^H)$. We denote by S_H the unit simplex in $\mathbf{R}^H$. By choice of p we obtain $\gamma \in S_H$ where γ is derived from a competitive equilibrium with discount factor $\rho \in P$.

Since the discount factor ρ may vary, we will write $U^h(z, \rho)$ for the utility of a consumption stream. Recall $C = \sum_{h=1}^{H} C^h$. Define a *social welfare function* W for $z \in C$, any $\gamma \in S_H$, and $0 < \rho < 1$ by $W(z, \gamma, \rho) = \max \sum_{h=1}^{H} \gamma^h U^h(z^h, \rho)$ over all $z^h \in C^h$ such that $\sum_{h=1}^{H} z^h = z$.

LEMMA 24 *At a competitive equilibrium with the consumption vectors $(x^1, \cdots, x^H)$ and the marginal utilities of wealth given by $1/\gamma^h$, the welfare function $W(x, \gamma, \rho) = \sum_{h=1}^{H} \gamma^h U^h(x^h, \rho)$.*

Proof Let $\{z^h\}$ be any other allocation of x. Multiply the inequalities (28) by γ^h and sum. Since $\sum_{h=1}^{H} z^h = \sum_{h=1}^{H} x^h$, we have $\sum_{h=1}^{H} pz^h = 0$. Thus $\sum_{h=1}^{H} \gamma^h U^h(z^h, \rho) \leq \sum_{h=1}^{H} \gamma^h U^h(x^h, \rho)$. This shows that

$\sum_{h=1}^{H} \gamma^h U^h(x^h, p)$ maximizes the weighted utility sum over all possible allocations and thus equals the welfare function for the given output. ∎

LEMMA 25   *At a competitive equilibrium $W(x, \gamma, p)$ maximizes the welfare function over all $y \in Y \cap C$.*

Proof The profit condition II of competitive equilibrium requires $(p_{t-1}, p_t) \cdot z(t) \leq 0$ for all $z(t) \in Y_t$ when p are the equilibrium prices. However, summing (28) over h, we find that $W(z, \gamma, p) > W(x, \gamma, p)$ implies $pz > 0$. Since $Y = \sum_{t=1}^{\infty} \overline{Y}_t$, this is inconsistent with the profit condition. Thus no such z exists. ∎

Define the correspondence Γ mapping C into $\tilde{C} = \prod_{h=1}^{H} C^h$ by $\Gamma(z) = \{(z^1, \cdots, z^H) \,|\, z^h \in C^h$ for all h and $\sum_{h=1}^{H} z^h = z\}$. We first prove

LEMMA 26   *Γ is continuous in the product topology.*

Proof Let V be an arbitrary open neighborhood of $\tilde{z} \in \tilde{C} = \prod_{h=1}^{H} C^h$ in the product topology relative to $\tilde{C}$. We must first show that Γ is lower semicontinuous at z. That is, there is a neighborhood U of $z = \sum_{h=1}^{H} z^h$ relative to $C = \sum_{h=1}^{H} C^h$ such that $z' \in U$ implies that $\Gamma(z') \cap V$ is not empty (Berge 1963, p. 109). If $\tilde{z}$ is an element of the open set V, then for no more than a finite number of indexes (h, t) we have $z_t^h \in V_t^h$, where V_t^h is an open set properly contained in C_t^h, and for the remaining indexes $V_t^h = C_t^h$. Similarly the open set U has no more than a finite number of indexes t such that $z \in U$ implies $z_t \in U_t$, where U_t is an open set properly contained in C_t while for the remaining indexes $U_t = C_t$. We must select the U_t so that $z_t' \in U_t$ implies that there is $\tilde{z}' \in \Gamma(z')$ with $z_t'^h \in V_t^h$ for all h and t. For h and t such that $V_t^h \neq C_t^h$ we may assume, with no loss of generality, that $V_t^h = \{z_t'^h \in C_t^h \,|\, |z_t^h - z_t'^h| < \varepsilon > 0\}$ for an appropriate ε. For all t such that $V_t^h \neq C_t^h$ for some h, let $U_t = \{z_t' \in C_t \,|\, |z_t' - z_t| < \delta > 0\}$. Since there is only a finite number of such (h, t), it is possible to choose δ so small that for every $z_t' \in U_t$ there is a distribution $\tilde{z}' \in \Gamma(z')$ with $z_t'^h \in V_t^h$. Therefore Γ is lower semicontinuous (see Berge 1963, p. 109).

To see that Γ is upper semicontinuous, suppose that $\tilde{x}^s \in \Gamma(x^s)$, and let $\tilde{x}^s$ converge pointwise to $\tilde{y}$ and x^s converge pointwise to w. It follows from the continuity of addition that $\tilde{y} \in \Gamma(w)$. Thus Γ is a closed correspondence. Since the range of Γ over a compact neighborhood of x is compact Γ is upper semicontinuous (Berge 1963, p. 112). ∎

LEMMA 27 $W(x, \gamma, \rho)$ *is concave on C for fixed (γ, ρ) and continuous on* $C \times S_H \times P$.

Proof Let

$$W(z, \gamma, \rho) = \sum_{h=1}^{H} \gamma^h U^h(z^h, \rho)$$

and $W(z', \gamma, \rho) = \sum_{h=1}^{H} \gamma^h U^h(z'^h, \rho)$. Let $z'' = \alpha z + (1 - \alpha)z'$, $0 \le \alpha \le 1$. By lemma 21, U^h is concave for all h. Therefore

$$W(z'', \gamma, \rho) = \sum_{h=1}^{H} \gamma^h U^h(z''^h, \rho) \ge \alpha W(z, \gamma, \rho) + (1 - \alpha) W(z', \gamma, \rho),$$

and it follows that W is concave on C.

Consider $z^s, \gamma^s, \rho^s \to z, \gamma, \rho$, for $s = 1, 2, \cdots$, where $z^s \in C$, $\gamma^s \in S_H$, $\rho \in P$. Suppose $W(z^s, \gamma^s, \rho^s) = \sum_{h=1}^{H} \gamma^{hs} U^h(z^{hs}, \rho^s)$. Since z^{hs} is bounded below by $\bar{z}$ and $z^s = \sum_{h=1}^{H} z^{hs} \to z$, it follows that z^{hs} is bounded. Since C^h is closed a subsequence, $\{z^{hs}\}$ (retain notation) converges to a limit $z^h \in C^h$ for all h. By lemma 21, U^h is continuous on $C^h \times P$. Therefore $\sum_{h=1}^{H} \gamma^{hs} U^h(z^{hs}, \rho^s) = W(z^s, \gamma^s, \rho^s)$ converges to $\sum_{h=1}^{H} \gamma^h U^h(z^h, \rho)$ along the subsequence.

Let $\tilde{w}$ be an arbitrary element of $\Gamma(z)$, and consider $\sum_{h=1}^{H} \gamma^h U^h(w^h, \rho)$. Since Γ is lower semicontinuous by lemma 26, along the subsequence there are $w^{hs} \to w^h$ where $w^{hs} \in C^h$ and $\sum_{h=1}^{H} w^{hs} = z^s$. Continuity of U^h implies $U^h(w^{hs}, \rho^s) \to U^h(w^h, \rho^s)$. However,

$$\sum_{h=1}^{H} \gamma^{hs} U^h(w^{hs}, \rho^s) \le \sum_{h=1}^{H} \gamma^{hs} U^h(z^{hs}, \rho^s).$$

Therefore $\sum_{h=1}^{H} \gamma^h U^h(w^h, \rho) \le \sum_{h=1}^{H} \gamma^h U^h(z^h, \rho)$. Thus

$$W(z, \gamma, \rho) = \sum_{h=1}^{H} \gamma^h U^h(z^h, \rho),$$

and $W(z^s, \gamma^s, \rho^s) \to W(z, \gamma, \rho)$. This means that W is continuous over $C \times S_H \times P$. ∎

The definition of Y as the sum of the $\bar{Y}_t$ implies that if $x \in Y$, then for each t there is $(-k_{t-1}, x_t + k_t) \in Y_t$. Let $F(k_{t-1}, k_t) = \{z_t \mid (-k_{t-1}, z_t + k_t) \in Y_t$ and $z_t \in C_t\}$. Define the periodwise welfare function $w(k_{t-1}, k_t, \gamma) = \max \sum_{h=1}^{H} \gamma^h u^h(z_t^h)$ for $\sum_{h=1}^{H} z_t^h = z_t \in F(k_{t-1}, k_t)$. These definitions are independent of t since Y_t and C_t are independent of t. The maximum exists at some $x_t \in F(k_{t-1}, k_t)$ since $F(k_{t-1}, k_t)$ is compact by an argument parallel to the proof of lemma 6.19 and u^h is continuous by assumption 19 for all h and t. At a competitive equilibrium with discount factor ρ, welfare weights γ, and consumption vector $x \in Y \cap C$ we have, by lemma 25, $W(x, \gamma, \rho) \geq W(z, \gamma, \rho)$ for all $z \in Y \cap C$. Then the fact that $\sum_{h=1}^{H} \gamma^h u^h(x_t^h) = w(k_{t-1}, k_t, \gamma)$ implies, from the definition of W, that $W(x, \gamma, \rho) = \sum_{t=1}^{\infty} \rho^t w(k_{t-1}, k_t, \gamma)$. Moreover $W(x, \gamma, \rho) \geq W(z, \gamma, \rho)$ implies that

$$\sum_{t=1}^{\infty} \rho^t w(k_{t-1}, k_t, \gamma) \geq \sum_{t=1}^{\infty} \rho^t w(k_{t-1}', k_t', \gamma)$$

for any other choice of $\{k_t'\}_{t=0}^{\infty}$, with $k_0' = k_0$, for which $w(k_{t-1}', k_t', \gamma)$ is well defined. This is the condition for a path of capital accumulation to be optimal in the argument of section 7.6 when the discount factor is ρ. To prove that the path of capital accumulation for a competitive equilibrium satisfies a turnpike theorem, we must look for a set of assumptions that are consistent with both the assumptions used to establish the competitive equilibrium and the assumptions that imply a turnpike for optimal paths. The assumptions must now be made for the welfare functions $W(x, \gamma, \rho)$ uniformly for all the ρ and γ involved in the competitive equilibria for which the turnpike theorem is to be proved.

The assumptions used for the turnpike theorem are 6, 7, 13, 14, and 15. Assumption 6 is the second part of assumption 17. Assumption 7 or free disposal of capital stocks is implied by the second part of assumption 16. Define the set D_t by $D_t = \{(k_{t-1}, k_t) \mid \text{there is } z_t \in C_t \text{ and } (-k_{t-1}, z_t + k_t) \in Y_t\}$. From the assumptions on C_t and Y_t we have convexity of D_t and $D_t = D$ for all t. To establish the assumption 13 in the generality needed we first prove

LEMMA 28   *If (k_{t-1}, k_t) is relative interior to D_t the correspondence F is continuous at (k_{t-1}, k_t).*

Proof If $(-k_{t-1}^s, x_t^s + k_t^s) \in Y_t$ and $x_t^s \in C_t$, and $(-k_{t-1}^s, x_t^s + k_t^{\prime s})$, $s = 1, 2, \cdots$, converges to $(-k_{t-1}, x + k_t)$, then $(-k_{t-1}, x_t + k_t) \in Y_t$ and $x_t \in C_t$ by closedness of Y_t and C_t. Also $x_t \in F(k_{t-1}, k_t)$ by definition of F. Thus F is closed. Since it is also bounded (see lemmas 6.1 and 6.19), it is upper semicontinuous (Berge 1963, p. 112).

We must show that F is lower semicontinuous when the interiority condition is met. Let $S_\varepsilon(x_t)$ be a closed ball of radius ε about x_t, where $x_t \in F(k_{t-1}, k_t)$. We must show for a sufficiently small neighborhood U of $(k_{t-1}, k_t) \in$ relative interior D_t that if $(k_{t-1}', k_t') \in U$, it follows that $S_\varepsilon(x_t) \cap U \neq \emptyset$. Let x_t' be the element of $F(k_{t-1}', k_t')$ closest to x_t. Let the Euclidean distance between x_t' and x_t equal η. Choose the largest α with $0 \leq \alpha \leq 1$ so that $\alpha\eta \leq \varepsilon$. Then $x_t'' = \alpha x_t' + (1 - \alpha)x_t \in S_\varepsilon(x_t)$. Since D_t is convex and $(k_{t-1}, k_t) \in$ relative interior D_t, for small U, we have $(k_{t-1}'', k_t'') = \alpha(k_{t-1}', k_t') + (1 - \alpha)(k_{t-1}, k_t) \in D_t$. It follows by concavity of F and free disposal that $x_t'' \in F(k_{t-1}'', k_t'')$. Since x_t' is bounded by classic arguments given assumptions 17 and 18, α is bounded above 0 as (k_{t-1}', k_t') ranges over U. Let α^* be a lower bound of α over U. Then the set of $(k_{t-1}'', k_t'') \in S_\delta(k_{t-1}, k_t)$ for $\delta \leq \alpha^*\varepsilon$ is a closed neighborhood U of (k_{t-1}, k_t). Moreover, by construction, the points $x_t'' \in F(k_{t-1}'', k_t'')$ for any $(k_{t-1}'', k_t'') \in U$ lie in $S_\varepsilon(x_t)$. This shows that F is lower semicontinuous at (k_{t-1}, k_t). ∎

We may now prove

LEMMA 29 *The periodwise welfare function* $w(k_{t-1}, k_t, \gamma)$ *is concave and continuous for* (k_{t-1}, k_t, γ) *in the relative interior of* D *and* $\gamma \in S_H$.

Proof Let $u_t(\tilde{z}_t, \gamma) = \sum_{h=1}^H \gamma^h u_t^h(z_t^h)$. Let $\tilde{C}_t = \prod_{h=1}^H C_t^h$. By assumption 19, we have u_t^h continuous in C_t^h. Therefore u_t is continuous in $\tilde{C}_t \times S_H$. Define Γ_t mapping C_t into $\tilde{C}_t$ by $\Gamma_t(z_t) = \{\tilde{z}_t \mid \sum_{h=1}^H z_t^h = z_t\}$. Recall that $w(k_{t-1}, k_t, \gamma) = \max u_t(\tilde{z}_t, \gamma)$ over $\tilde{z}_t \in \Gamma_t(z_t)$ over all $z_t \in F(k_{t-1}, k_t)$. Assume $(k_{t-1}^s, k_t^s, \gamma^s) \to (k_{t-1}, k_t, \gamma)$ for $s = 1, 2, \cdots$. Let $w(k_{t-1}^s, k_t^s, \gamma^s) = u_t(\tilde{z}_t^s, \gamma^s)$. Since the $\tilde{z}_t^s$ lie in a compact set, there is a subsequence (save notation) converging to $\tilde{z}_t$. Then, by the upper semicontinuity of $\Gamma_t \circ F$, it follows that $\tilde{z}_t \in \Gamma_t \circ F(k_{t-1}, k_t)$. Let $\tilde{z}_t'$ be an arbitrary element of $\Gamma_t \circ F(k_{t-1}', k_t')$. Since, by lemmas 26 and 28, $\Gamma_t \circ F$ is lower semicontinuous, if $\tilde{z}_t' \in \Gamma_t \circ F(k_{t-1}, k_t)$, there is a sequence $\tilde{z}_t'^s \to \tilde{z}_t'$ where $\tilde{z}_t'^s \in \Gamma_t \circ F(k_{t-1}^s, k_t^s)$. Then $u_t(\tilde{z}_t^s, \gamma) \geq u_t(\tilde{z}_t'^s, \gamma)$ for each s. By the continuity of u_t, we have $u_t(\tilde{z}_t, \gamma) \geq u_t(\tilde{z}_t', \gamma)$. Since (k_{t-1}', k_t', γ) and $\tilde{z}_t'$ are arbitrary choices, it follows that $w(k_{t-1}, k_t, \gamma) = u_t(\tilde{z}_t, \gamma)$. Therefore w is continuous in the relative interior of D. Also see the Theorem of the Maximum (Berge 1963, p. 116). ∎

Continuity implies closedness. Thus assumption 13 is implied, except for strict concavity of w on $\bar{\Delta}$. We define $\bar{\Delta}(\gamma)$ relative to Σ analogously to the definition of $\bar{\Delta}$. We will prove that there is $(\bar{k}_{t-1}, \bar{k}_t)$ satisfying $\bar{k}_t > \bar{\rho}^{-1}\bar{k}_{t-1}$. Define $\bar{\Delta}(\gamma) = \{(k_{t-1}, k_t) \mid k_{t-1} = k_t \in \Sigma$ such that $w(k_{t-1}, k_t, \gamma) \geq w(\bar{k}_{t-1}, \bar{k}_t, \gamma)\}$. The argument γ is needed since the welfare function w depends on the utility weights. Uniform strict concavity of $w(k_{t-1}, k_t)$ over all $k_{t-1} = k_t \in \bar{\Delta}(\gamma)$ will be assumed directly. That $\bar{\Delta}(\gamma)$ is not empty will be proved in lemma 30 below. Since services cannot be stored, capital stocks k_t lie in the subspace S_g of $\mathbf{R}^n$ spanned by the coordinate axes for goods. Thus k_t is an n-vector whose services coordinates are equal to 0. Assumption 17 implies that S_g has dimension less than n. Then Σ is contained in the nonnegative orthant of S_g, which is a proper subspace of $\mathbf{R}^n$. However, to show that it is not empty, we require that sustainable and expansible stocks (relative to S_g) exist. In the light of free disposal it is sufficient to prove that expansible stocks exist. This will establish assumption 14.

LEMMA 30   *In the Malinvaud economy $\mathscr{E}_m$ there is $\bar{\rho} < 1$ and $(\bar{k}_{t-1}, \bar{k}_t) \in D$ such that $\bar{k}_{t-1} > \bar{\rho}^{-1}\bar{k}_t$ relative to S_g.*

Proof   It follows from assumption 21 that there is $y \in Y$ and $z \in C$ with $y - z > \delta e > 0$. Then, by reducing consumption, capital stocks may be increased in any period t by δe_{gt}, where $e_{gt} \in S_g$ has all goods components equal to 1 and other components equal to 0. Thus D is not empty. By convexity, the average initial capital stocks k_a and terminal capital stocks k'_a over the period of accumulation from 1 to T also give an element $(k_a, k'_a) \in D$. Since the capital stocks are bounded along the path and every terminal stock is also an initial stock, k_a and k'_a are arbitrarily close for large T. Since D is closed and every terminal stock k_t can be increased by δe_{gt}, it follows that k'_a can be increased by δe_g. Since k_a can be made arbitrarily close to k'_a by choice of T, it follows that in the limit, for any ratio $\sigma < \text{minimum}_i(k_a + \delta e_g)_i / \kappa$ where i indexes capital stocks and κ is an upper bound on capital stocks, there are capital stocks which are expansible in the ratio σ. Thus $\bar{\rho} < 1$ may be chosen with $\bar{\rho}^{-1} < \sigma$. ∎

Let $\gamma(\rho)$ be an arbitrary selection from the γ which appear in a competitive equilibrium with the discount factor ρ. Lemma 30 together with free disposal implies that $\bar{\Delta}(\gamma)$ is not empty for any $\gamma = \gamma(\rho)$ when $\bar{\rho} \geq \rho < 1$. Moreover $\bar{\Delta}(\gamma)$ is closed since w is continuous, and Y_t and C_t^h are closed. It is also bounded by assumption 17, and thus it is compact (see lemma 15). The maximum of $w(k_t, k_{t-1}, \gamma)$ on $\bar{\Delta}(\gamma)$ is achieved by the continuity of w. Let this maximum be attained at $(k^1(\gamma), k^1(\gamma))$. Then $k^1(\gamma)$ is the stock of the unique nontrivial optimal stationary path for $\rho = 1$ by the assumption of strict concavity of w on $\bar{\Delta}(\gamma)$. Assumption 15 will be made explicitly in addition to the assumptions 16 through 21. The additional assumptions involve notions that are special to the reduced welfare function $w(k_{t-1}, k_t, \gamma)$. The function w depends jointly on the utility functions and the production technology.

Let $k_t = k^{\rho}(\gamma)$, $t = 0, 1, \cdots$, be a nontrivial stationary optimal path for $\bar{\rho} \leq \rho < 1$.

ASSUMPTION 22   The function $w(k_{t-1}, k_t, \gamma)$ is uniformly strictly concave for $k_{t-1} = k_t$ with $k_{t-1} \in \bar{\Delta}(\gamma)$ over all $\gamma \in \gamma(\rho)$ with $1 > \rho \geq \bar{\rho}$.

Assumption 22 is a strengthened version of the concavity assumption in assumption 13. We make the revised version of assumption 15 directly as

ASSUMPTION 23   An optimal stationary stock $k^1(\gamma)$ is expansible relative to S_g. Also $\bar{\Delta}(\gamma)$, for all $\gamma \in \gamma(\rho)$ with $1 > \rho \geq \bar{\rho}$, is contained in the relative interior of Σ, the set of sustainable stocks.

Using lemmas 15 and 18 we see that assumption 23 also implies the following proposition:

PROPOSITION 3   Let $k^{\rho}(\gamma)$ be the stock of a stationary optimal path. Then there is $\eta > 0$ and $\varepsilon > 0$ such that $|k_t - k^{\rho}(\gamma)| < \eta$ implies that $(k_t, k_t + \varepsilon e_g) \in D$ for $\bar{\rho} < \rho < 1$ and $\gamma \in \gamma(\rho)$.

We may now state

THEOREM 8   *Make assumptions 16 through 23.*

i. *A competitive equilibrium path exists for any ρ with $0 < \rho < 1$.*

ii. *There is a choice of $\bar{\rho} < 1$ such that a competitive equilibrium path $(p, y, x^1, \cdots, x^h)$ for any ρ with $1 > \rho > \bar{\rho}$ defines an optimal growth program for the objective function $W(x, \gamma(\rho), \rho)$.*

iii. *Given an ε-ball $S_{\varepsilon}(k^{\rho})$ relative to S_g about $k^{\rho} = k^{\rho}(\gamma(\rho))$, there are $\rho' > \bar{\rho}$ and T such that $k_t(\gamma(\rho), \rho) \in S_{\varepsilon}(k^{\rho})$ for all $t > T$ and all ρ with $\rho' < \rho < 1$.*

Proof The existence of a competitive equilibrium path is provided by theorem 7. The competitive equilibrium path is an optimal path for the welfare function $W(z, \gamma(\rho), \rho)$ by lemma 25 given the initial stock of capital k_0. It should be noted that the utility weights γ^h depend on the distribution $\{k_0^h\}$ of the initial stock as well as on ρ and the particular equilibrium given $\{k_0^h\}$ and ρ. Then theorem 8 says that the capital stock sequence $\{k_t(\gamma(\rho), \rho)\}$ converges to a neighborhood of $k^\rho(\gamma(\rho))$, a capital stock vector for a stationary optimal path for the welfare function $W(z, \gamma(\rho), \rho)$ when ρ is sufficiently near to 1. If γ were constant when ρ changes so that the welfare function is $W(z, \gamma, \rho)$, Theorem 6 would imply that the turnpike property holds when ρ is sufficiently near to 1. However, the welfare function also depends on ρ through the function $\gamma(\rho)$. Recall that $\gamma(\rho)$ has been defined as a choice from the γ that appears in a competitive equilibrium with the discount factor ρ. As a consequence of the dependence of γ on ρ, we must return to the proof of theorem 6 and show that under our assumptions there is ρ' such that the argument for the turnpike holds for $W(z, \gamma, \rho)$ uniformly for $\gamma \in \gamma(\rho)$ and $1 > \rho > \rho'$.

First we must generalize lemma 17 so that the value functions are bounded uniformly as the welfare functions vary with ρ. For this purpose we will bound uniformly the prices that support the stationary optimal paths $k^\rho(\gamma)$. It is implied by lemma 14 and theorem 5 that given $\rho \in P$ and $\gamma \in S_H$, there is $p^\rho(\gamma) \in \mathbf{R}^n$ such that

$$w(k^\rho(\gamma), k^\rho(\gamma)) + (1 - \rho^{-1})p^\rho(\gamma)k^\rho(\gamma)$$

$$\geq w(k_{t-1}, k_t) + p^\rho(\gamma)k_t - \rho^{-1}p^\rho(\gamma)k_{t-1} \tag{29}$$

for all $(k_{t-1}, k_t) \in D$. Applying the definition of the value function to the present context with $\rho \in P$ gives

$$V(k, \gamma(\rho), \rho) = \sup\left(\lim \sum_{t=1}^{T} \rho^t w(k_{t-1}, k_t, \gamma(\rho)) \text{ as } T \to \infty\right).$$

The supremum is taken over all paths with initial stock $k_0 = k$. To prove that $V(k_0, \gamma(\rho), \rho)$ is bounded above, we need to prove that the prices $p^\rho(\gamma)$ are uniformly bounded for ρ near 1 and $\gamma \in \gamma(\rho)$ where $\gamma(\rho)$ are utility weights derived from competitive equilibria. Write $k^\rho(\gamma)$ for $k^\rho(\gamma(\rho))$.

LEMMA 31   *Let $k_t(\gamma(\rho), \rho) = k^\rho(\gamma)$, all $t \geq 0$, be a stationary optimal path of capital accumulation for the welfare function based on utility weights*

$\gamma(\rho)$. Let $p^\rho(\gamma)$ be support prices for $k^\rho(\gamma)$. Then $p^\rho(\gamma)$ is uniformly bounded as $\rho \to 1$.

Proof Suppose that there is a subsequence ρ^s (preserve notation) such that $\rho^s \to 1$ and $|p^{\rho^s}(\gamma^s)| \to \infty$ as $s \to \infty$. Let $\gamma^s = \gamma(\rho^s)$ in (30). Divide (30) through by $|p^{\rho^s}(\gamma^s)|$, and consider a further subsequence (preserve notation) for which $p^{\rho^s}(\gamma^s)/|p^{\rho^s}(\gamma^s)| \to p$. From (30) we obtain $0 \geq p(k_t - k_{t-1})$ for all $(k_{t-1}, k_t) \in D$, where $p \geq 0$, $p \neq 0$. This contradicts lemma 30. Thus no such sequence exists. ∎

The proof that the value function is bounded is similar to the proof given in lemma 5 where the utility function is constant except for discounting.

LEMMA 32 *If the capital accumulation path $k(\gamma(\rho))$ corresponds to a competitive equilibrium allocation $x(\gamma(\rho))$, then $V(k_0, \gamma(\rho), \rho)$ is bounded for $\rho \in P$ as $\rho \to 1$.*

Proof Let $k^\rho(\gamma)$ be the capital stock of a nontrivial stationary optimal path. Let $k_t(\gamma(\rho))$, $t = 0, 1, \cdots$, be a path of capital accumulation that is consistent with a competitive equilibrium path from initial stocks k_0 when the discount factor is ρ. We will write p^ρ for $p^\rho(\gamma(\rho))$ and suppress $\gamma(\rho)$ in the expressions for w and k. Given ρ subtract $w(k^\rho, k^\rho)/H\gamma^h(\rho)$ from each u^h so that, saving the notation, the normalized $w(k^\rho, k^\rho) = 0$. This has no effect on the comparison of paths for a particular ρ. Then multiplying (29) through by ρ^t gives

$$\rho^t p^\rho k^\rho - \rho^{t-1} p^\rho k^\rho \geq \rho^t w(k_{t-1}(\rho), k_t(\rho))$$
$$+ \rho^t p^\rho (k_t(\rho) - \rho^{t-1} p^\rho k_{t-1}(\rho)). \tag{30}$$

Summing (30) from $t = 1$ to $t = \infty$, and applying the definition of V, gives

$$V(k_0, \gamma(\rho), \rho) = \lim_{T \to \infty} \sum_{t=1}^{T} \rho^t w(k_{t-1}(\rho), k_t(\rho)) \leq p^\rho(k_0 - k^\rho). \tag{31}$$

Thus we have $V(k_0, \gamma(\rho), \rho) < p^\rho k_0$. Then $V(k_0, \gamma(\rho), \rho)$ is uniformly bounded above as $\rho \to 1$ since p^ρ is bounded as $\rho \to 1$ by lemma 31.

To show that $V(k_0, \gamma(\rho), \rho)$ is bounded below note that k_0 is expansible by assumption 21. Thus $V(k_0, \gamma(\rho), \rho) \geq \sum_1^\infty \rho^t w(k_{t-1}(\rho), k_t(\rho))$ where $w(k_{t-1}(\rho), k_t(\rho)) = w(k_0, k_1(\rho))$ for all t. Also the capital stock $k(\rho)$ of a stationary optimal path is expansible by proposition 3. Thus by the corollary to to lemma 6.18 there is a path from k_0 to $k^T = k^p(\gamma)$. Since $w(k^p, k^p) = 0$, we have

$$V(k_0, \gamma(\rho), \rho) \geq \sum_{t=0}^{T-1} \rho^t w(k_t, k_{t+1}, \gamma(\rho)).$$

Suppose that there is a sequence $\rho^s \to 1$ for which $w(k_t, k_{t+1}, \gamma(\rho^s)) \to -\infty$ for some t with $0 \leq t \leq T$. Since γ lies in a compact set, there is a subsequence for which $\gamma(\rho^s)$ (retain notation) converges to $\bar{\gamma}$. Since the $w(k_t, k_{t+1}, \gamma(\rho^s))$ is a continuous function of γ, this implies that $w(k_t, k_{t+1}, \bar{\gamma})$ is not well defined, contradicting the fact that $(k_t, k_{t+1}) \in D$. Thus no such sequence exists, and $w(k_t, k_{t+1}, \gamma(\rho^s))$ is bounded below as $\rho^s \to 1$. ∎

Let $k_t'(\rho) = \frac{1}{2}(k_t(\rho) + k^p)$. Analogously to the utility gain, define the *welfare gain* in period t by

$$g_t(k(\rho), k^p) = w(k_{t-1}'(\rho), k_t'(\rho)) - \frac{1}{2}(w(k_{t-1}(\rho), k_t(\rho)) + w(k^p, k^p)).$$

Concavity of w implies that $g_t(k(\rho), k^p) \geq 0$. The welfare gain is relative to k^p, which may be arbitrarily chosen from the set of k^p consistent with ρ and $\gamma(\rho)$. Recall that $\gamma(\rho)$ is derived from the marginal utilities of income consistent with a competitive equilibrium where ρ is the discount factor. For notational simplicity these relations are not always explicitly recognized. Define the Liapounov function $G_t(k(\rho), k^p) = \sum_{\tau=1}^{\infty} \rho^\tau g_{t+\tau}(k(\rho), k^p, \gamma(\rho))$. Then

$$G_{t+1}(k(\rho), k^p) - G_t(k(\rho), k^p) = \sum_{\tau=1}^{\infty} \rho^\tau g_{t+\tau+1} - \sum_{\tau=1}^{\infty} \rho^\tau g_{t+\tau},$$

where the arguments of the g functions are omitted. Thus, omitting the arguments $(k(\rho), k^p)$ of both G and g functions, we have

$$G_{t+1} - G_t = (\rho^{-1} - 1)G_t - g_{t+1}. \tag{32}$$

For any $\delta > 0$ we may choose ρ close enough to 1 to give $(\rho^{-1} - 1)G_0 < \delta$ provided that $G_0(k(\rho), k^p)$ is bounded as $\rho \to 1$. This is proved in

LEMMA 33   *Then $G_0(k(\rho), k^p)$ is bounded as $\rho \to 1$, $\rho < 1$.*

Proof The proof follows the lines of the proof of lemma 19. Write $V^p(k)$ for $V(k, \gamma(\rho), \rho)$. Then, as in the proof of lemma 19,

$$G_0(k(\rho), k^p) = V^p(\tfrac{1}{2}(k_0 + k^p)) - \tfrac{1}{2}(V^p(k_0) + V^p(k^p)).$$

We note that $G_0 \geq 0$ follows from $g_t \geq 0$. Thus boundedness below is immediate and only boundedness above needs to be proved. $V^p(k_0)$ is bounded below by lemma 32 since k_0 is expansible. Also $V^p(1/2(k_0 + k^p))$ is bounded above by the first part of the proof of lemma 32. Since $w(k^p, k^p, \gamma(\rho)) = 0$ by the normalization at $\gamma(\rho)$, we have that $V^p(k^p) = 0$ as well. Therefore G_0 is bounded above. ∎

To show that the path of a competitive equilibrium must enter an arbitrary ε-neighborhood of k^p for ρ sufficiently close to 1, we must prove that the Liapounov function $G_t(k(\rho), k^p)$ decreases by at least $\delta > 0$ each period that the path is outside the ε-neighborhood.

LEMMA 34 *Along a competitive equilibrium path, given any $\varepsilon > 0$, there is ρ' such that if $\rho \geq \rho'$, there is $T \geq 0$, where $|(k_T(\rho), k_{T+1}(\rho)) - (k^p, k^p)| \leq \varepsilon$.*

Proof Since $G_0(k(\rho), k^p)$ is bounded as $\rho \to 1$ by lemma 33, for any $\delta > 0$ we may choose ρ near enough to 1 so that $(\rho^{-1} - 1)G_0 < \delta$. A first step to establish G_t as a Liapounov function is to show for any ε that there is $\delta > 0$ such that the left side of (32) when $t = 0$ is less than $-\delta$ when $|k_0 - k^p| > \varepsilon$. However, this follows since $|(k_0, k_1(\rho)) - (k^p, k^p)| > \varepsilon$ implies $g_1(k(\rho), k^p) > 2\delta$ for some $\delta > 0$ by assumption 22. Thus $G_1 - G_0 < -\delta$ may be guaranteed for some $\delta > 0$ when k_0 is outside the ε-neighborhood of k^p by choosing $\rho \geq \rho'$ where ρ' is near enough to 1.

The argument continues by induction. Suppose $G_{t+1} - G_t < -\delta$ and $(\rho^{-1} - 1)G_t < \delta$, relations that have been established for $t = 0$. Then, if $\rho \geq \rho'$, we have

$$(\rho^{-1} - 1)G_{t+1} < (\rho^{-1} - 1)G_t < \delta.$$

On the other hand, if $|(k_{t+1}(\rho), k_{t+2}(\rho)) - (k^p, k^p)| > \varepsilon$ holds then, as in the argument above, by uniform strict concavity $g_{t+2} > 2\delta$ holds, so using (32) again, we have $G_{t+2} - G_{t+1} < -\delta$. In other words, $G_{t+1} - G_t < -\delta$ continues to hold for $t \geq 0$ so long as $(k_t(\rho), k_{t+1}(\rho))$ remains outside an ε-neighborhood of (k^p, k^p). By summing these inequalities, we then obtain

$$G_\tau(k(\rho), k^\rho) \le G_0(k(\rho), k^\rho) - \tau\delta, \tag{33}$$

if $(k_t(\rho), k_{t+1})$ is outside the ε-neighborhood of (k^ρ, k^ρ) from $t = 0$ until $t = \tau$. Since G_T is nonnegative by its definition, to avoid contradiction with the inequality (33), $(k_t(\rho), k_{t+1}(\rho))$ must enter the ε-neighborhood at a time $T \le G_0(k(\rho), k^\rho)/\delta$. ■

Note that the argument holds for uniformly for all ρ with $\rho' \le \rho < 1$. Also given ρ with $\rho' \le \rho < 1$ all nontrivial stationary optimal paths (k^ρ, k^ρ) must lie in the ε-neighborhood of any one of them.

We have shown that paths cannot stay outside any neighborhood U of (k^ρ, k^ρ) indefinitely. However to complete the proof, we must show that once a path has entered U there is a neighborhood W that it cannot leave. For this purpose another lemma is needed. In the lemma it is understood that the welfare function is defined by ρ and $\gamma(\rho)$.

LEMMA 35 *If $k(\rho)$ is an optimal path from k_0, then for any $\delta > 0$ there is $\varepsilon > 0$ such that $|(k_0, k_1(\rho)) - (k^\rho, k^\rho)| < \varepsilon$ implies that $G_0(k(\rho), k^\rho) < \delta$, uniformly for $\bar\rho \le \rho < 1$ and all nontrivial stationary optimal paths for ρ.*

Proof By the definition of G_0 and the feasibility of the intermediate path, we have

$$G_0(k(\rho), k^\rho) \le w(\tfrac{1}{2}(k_0 + k^\rho), \tfrac{1}{2}(k_1(\rho) + k^\rho))$$
$$- \tfrac{1}{2}(w(k_0, k_1(\rho)) + w(k^\rho, k^\rho))$$
$$+ \rho V^\rho(\tfrac{1}{2}(k_1(\rho) + k^\rho)) - \tfrac{1}{2}\rho(V^\rho(k_1(\rho)) + V^\rho(k^\rho)). \tag{34}$$

It is implied by lemma 16 and the definition of k^ρ that $w(k^\rho, k^\rho) \ge w(\bar k_{t-1}, \bar k_t)$ for all k^ρ, $\bar\rho \le \rho < 1$. Thus $k^\rho \in \bar\Delta(\gamma(\rho))$. By assumption 23, we have that $\bar\Delta(\gamma)$ is relative interior to the set Σ of sustainable stocks and, by assumption 22, w is uniformly strictly concave over $\bar\Delta(\gamma)$ for all $\gamma \in \gamma(\rho)$ with $1 > \rho \ge \bar\rho$. This implies that $w(k_{t-1}, k_t, \gamma)$ is uniformly continuous with respect to (k_{t-1}, k_t) over all $k_{t-1} = k_t \in \bar\Delta(\gamma)$ and all $\gamma(\rho)$ with $1 > \rho \ge \bar\rho$. Suppose that $(k_0', k_1') \to (k^\rho, k^\rho)$ implies $V^\rho(k_1') \to V^\rho(k^\rho)$. Then from (34) it follows that G_0 is small for $(k_0', k_1'(\rho))$ near (k^ρ, k^ρ). However, proposition 3 and lemma 16 imply that k^ρ is uniformly expansible for ρ with $\bar\rho \le \rho < 1$ and $\gamma = \gamma(\rho)$. Expansibility of k^ρ and free disposal imply that $(k^\rho, k_1'(\rho)) \in D$ for $k_1'(\rho)$ near k^ρ. This implies

$$w(k^\rho, k^\rho) + \rho V^\rho(k^\rho) \ge w(k^\rho, k_1'(\rho)) + \rho V^\rho(k_1'(\rho)).$$

Therefore $V^\rho(k_1'(\rho)) \le V^\rho(k^\rho) + \varepsilon$ may be assured for any assigned $\varepsilon > 0$ for any ρ, $\bar{\rho} \le \rho < 1$, and any k^ρ by bringing $(k'^0, k'^1(\rho))$ near to (k^ρ, k^ρ).

This argument may be repeated for a switch from k_0' to k^ρ. Let Σ' be a compact set contained in the relative interior of Σ having $\bar{\Delta}(\gamma(\rho))$ in its interior relative to Σ (see Berge 1963, p. 68). Then, using the proof of lemma 18, we find that k is uniformly expansible over all $k \in \Sigma'$ for all ρ and $\gamma(\rho)$ with $\bar{\rho} \le \rho < 1$. Therefore k^ρ may be reached from k_0' sufficiently near k^ρ. This gives $V^\rho(k^\rho) \le V^\rho(k_1'(\rho)) + \varepsilon$ for any assigned $\varepsilon > 0$ when $(k_0', k_1'(\rho))$ is sufficiently near (k^ρ, k^ρ). Thus $V^\rho(k_1'(\rho)) \to V^\rho(k^\rho)$ as needed. ∎

We may now complete the proof of theorem 8. Choose an arbitrary $\varepsilon > 0$. We have seen that there is ρ' such that the optimal path may be brought within ε of any k^ρ for any ρ and $\gamma(\rho)$ where $\rho' \le \rho < 1$. To complete the proof, we must show that given any $\varepsilon' > 0$ it is possible to choose ε so small that once the path has become within ε of (k^ρ, k^ρ) it must lie within $\varepsilon' > 0$ of (k^ρ, k^ρ) thereafter. By strict concavity, assumption 22, given ε' we may choose η so small that $|(k_{t+1}(\rho), k_{t+2}(\rho)) - (k^\rho, k^\rho)| > \varepsilon'$ implies

$$G_{t+1} \ge \rho g_{t+2} \ge \rho^{-1}\eta \tag{35}$$

uniformly for all k^ρ and all ρ with $\rho' \le \rho < 1$. Since $g_{t+1} \ge 0$ relation (32) implies

$$G_{t+1} \le \rho^{-1} G_t. \tag{36}$$

By lemma 35, for any $\eta > 0$ there is an $\varepsilon > 0$ such that $|(k_t(\rho), k_{t+1}(\rho)) - (k^\rho, k^\rho)| \le \varepsilon$ implies that $G_t < \eta$. Inserting this value for G_t into (36) gives a contradiction of (35). Therefore, if $(k_t(\rho), k_{t+1}(\rho))$ lies in the ε-neighborhood of (k^ρ, k^ρ), (35) cannot hold and $(k_{t+1}(\rho), k_{t+2}(\rho))$ must lie within ε' of (k^ρ, k^ρ). On the other hand, if $(k_{t+1}(\rho), k_{t+2}(\rho))$ is not within ε of (k^ρ, k^ρ), we have

$$G_{t+2} < G_{t+1} \le \rho^{-1} G_t < \rho^{-1}\eta. \tag{37}$$

The first inequality is implied by (32), since we assume $\rho \ge \rho'$, and the path is outside the ε-neighborhood. The second is (36) since the path at that time is within the ε-neighborhood. The third holds from the choice of ε.

From (32) we derive

$$\rho G_{t+3} = G_{t+2} - \rho g_{t+3}. \tag{38}$$

Substituting from (37) for G_{t+2} in (38), and taking account of the fact that $G_{t+3} \geq 0$, gives $\rho g_{t+3} < \rho^{-1}\eta$. Therefore the condition for G_{t+2} analogous to (35) cannot hold, which implies that $(k_{t+2}(\rho), k_{t+3}(\rho))$ lies within ε' of (k^ρ, k^ρ). This argument may be repeated for $G_{t+\tau}$ for $\tau = 3, 4, \cdots$. Thus the path does not leave the ε'-neighborhood of (k^ρ) so long as it is outside the ε-neighborhood. The first part of the proof implies that G_τ decreases for $\tau > t + 1$ until $(k_\tau(\rho), k_{\tau+1}(\rho))$ is within the ε-neighborhood of (k^ρ, k^ρ) once more. Then the entire argument may be repeated. Therefore $(k^\tau(\rho), k^{\tau+1}(\rho))$ cannot leave the neighborhood of (k^ρ, k^ρ) defined by ε' as $\tau \to \infty$. This completes the proof of theorem 8. ∎

It may be helpful to review the logical order in which the choices are made in the proof. First ε' is chosen arbitrarily. Then η is chosen to give (35). Then ε is chosen to give $G_t < \eta$. These choices are uniform over ρ such that $\bar{\rho} \leq \rho < 1$. Finally ρ' is chosen to cause convergence of the optimal path to the ε-neighborhood of k^ρ for all $\rho \geq \rho'$, $\rho < 1$. These choices can be made consistently.

For ρ sufficiently near 1, it is also possible to prove a neighborhood turnpike theorem for the von Neumann facet $F(\rho)$ when $F(\rho)$ is not trivial. Moreover this result may be extended to a neighborhood theorem for an optimal stationary stock k^ρ when k^ρ is unique and $F(\rho)$ is stable. Finally with some conditions of negative definiteness for the Hessian matrix of u the stability can be extended to asymptotic convergence of the optimal path to k^ρ (see McKenzie 1982).

The convergence of the capital stock vector k_t of the competitive equilibrium to a neighborhood of a capital stock vector k^ρ does not obviously imply the convergence of the consumption vectors x_t to a neighborhood of consumption vectors. However, we will be able to show that such a convergence is implied to a neighborhood, which may be arbitrarily small, of the set consisting of all the lists of periodwise consumption vectors $\tilde{z}_t = (z_t^1, \cdots, z_t^H)$ that satisfy $\sum_{h=1}^{H} \gamma^h u^h(z_t^h) = w(k^\rho, k^\rho)$.

Define a correspondence φ which maps D into $\mathbf{R}^{nH}$ by $\tilde{y}_t \in \varphi(k_{t-1}, k_t)$ if $\tilde{y}_t$ realizes $w(k_{t-1}, k_t)$. Recall that $w(k_{t-1}, k_t)$ equals $\max \sum_{h=1}^{H} \gamma^h u_t^h(z_t^h)$ over $\tilde{z}_t$ where $\tilde{z}_t \in \Gamma \circ F(k_{t-1}, k_t)$.

LEMMA 36   *The correspondence φ is upper semicontinuous at $(k_{t-1}, k_t) \in$ relative interior D.*

Proof   The correspondence $\Gamma \circ F$ is continuous at (k_{t-1}, k_t) by lemmas 26 and 28. Let $(k_{t-1}^s, k_t^s) \to (k_{t-1}, k_t) \in$ relative interior D, $s = 1, 2, \cdots$. Suppose that $\tilde{y}_t^s \in \varphi(k_{t-1}^s, k_t^s)$ and that $\tilde{y}_t^s \to \tilde{y}_t \in \Gamma \circ F(k_{t-1}, k_t)$. Then $w(k_{t-1}^s, k_t^s) = \sum_{h=1}^{H} \gamma^h u_t^h(y_t^{sh}) \to \sum_{h=1}^{H} \gamma^h u_t^h(y_t^h)$. Consider any other $\tilde{z}_t \in \Gamma \circ F(k_{t-1}, k_t)$. By the lower semicontinuity of $\Gamma \circ F$ there is a sequence

$$\tilde{z}_t^s \in \Gamma \circ F(k_{t-1}^{\prime s}, k_t^{\prime s}) \to \tilde{z}_t \in \Gamma \circ F(k_{t-1}^{\prime}, k_t^{\prime}).$$

Since $\tilde{y}_t^s$ realizes $\varphi(k_{t-1}^s, k_t^s)$, we have $\sum_{h=1}^{H} \gamma^h u_t^h(y_t^{sh}) \geq \sum_{h=1}^{H} \gamma^h u_t^h(z_t^{sh})$. Therefore by the continuity of u_t^h it follows that

$$\sum_{h=1}^{H} \gamma^h u_t^h(y_t^h) \geq \sum_{h=1}^{H} \gamma^h u_t^h(z_t^h).$$

Since $\tilde{z}_t$ is arbitrarily chosen, this shows that $\tilde{y}_t \in \varphi(k_{t-1}, k_t)$ or ϕ is upper semicontinuous. This argument is parallel to that proving that demand functions are upper semicontinuous. (See the theorem of the maximum in Berge 1963, p. 116.)   ■

Lemma 36 allows us to prove the convergence of the consumption vectors along a competitive equilibrium path.

THEOREM 9   *Make the assumptions of theorem 8. Let (k_{t-1}, k_t), $t = 1, 2, \cdots$, be the capital stock vectors of a competitive equilibrium path. Let $W(z, \gamma(\rho))$ be the welfare function for which this path is an optimal path of accumulation. Then there is a choice of $\bar{p} < 1$ in the economy E_m such that for any ρ with $1 > \rho > \bar{p}$ a competitive equilibrium path $(p, y, x^1, \cdots, x^h)$ from the initial stock $k_0 = \sum_{h=1}^{H} k_0^h$ defines an optimal growth program for the objective function $W(x, \gamma(\rho))$. For any $\varepsilon > 0$ let $S_\varepsilon(\varphi(k^\rho, k^\rho))$ be the set of vectors $\tilde{z}_t$ that lie within ε of $\varphi(k^\rho, k^\rho)$. Then there are $\rho^{\prime} < \rho < 1$ and T such that $\tilde{x}_t \in S_\varepsilon(\varphi(k^\rho, k^\rho))$ for all $t > T$ and all ρ with $\rho^{\prime} < \rho < 1$.*

Proof   By theorem 8 given any δ and ρ with $\rho^{\prime} < \rho < 1$ we may chose T so that $k_t \in S_\delta(k^\rho)$ for $t > T$. By lemma 16, we have that $(k^\rho, k^\rho) \in$ relative interior D. Then φ is upper semicontinuous at $\varphi(k^\rho, k^\rho)$ by lemma 36. This implies for any open neighborhood V of $\varphi(k^\rho, k^\rho)$ that there is an open neighborhood U of (k^ρ, k^ρ) in the relative interior of D such that

$(k_{t-1}, k_t) \in U$ implies that $\varphi(k_{t-1}, k_t) \in V$. Therefore for any $\varepsilon > 0$ we may choose δ small enough that $S_\varepsilon(\varphi(k^p, k^p))$ contains all $\varphi(k'_{t-1}, k'_t)$ for k'_{t-1} and k'_t in $S_\delta(k^p)$. It follows for $t > T$ and $p' < p < 1$ that $\tilde{x}_t$ must lie in $S_\varepsilon(\varphi(k^p, k^p))$. ∎

Appendix: A Leontief Model with Capital Coefficients as a von Neumann Model

We will modify the Leontief model with capital stocks presented in chapter 3 to represent a von Neumann model (see McKenzie 1963). It is convenient to normalize activities on outputs rather than on labor inputs in this model. Let a_j be the jth column of the matrix A which is $n \times n$, where n is the number of material goods and the number of industries; a_j is the vector of material goods consumed in a certain production process that is possible for the jth industry. This consumption must occur from the stocks of goods available at the start of the period. Unlike the model of chapter 3, current flows during a period are not modeled. Let b_j be the jth column of the matrix B also $n \times n$, where b_j is the vector of capital needed at the start of a period of production where this production process is used for the jth industry. Let D_j be a set of (a_j, b_j) that can appear together in a production process of the jth industry.

ASSUMPTION 24 D_j is compact, convex, and not empty.

ASSUMPTION 25 $b_j \geq a_j \geq 0$, $\neq 0$, for all $(a_j, b_j) \in D_j$.

Let $\mathscr{D}$ be the set of all (A, B) whose columns lie in D_j for all j. Define a transformation set T in $\mathbf{R}^{2n}$ as all $(y', -y)$ such that

$$\begin{bmatrix} I - A + B \\ -B \end{bmatrix} x \geq \begin{pmatrix} y' \\ -y \end{pmatrix} \tag{A1}$$

for some $x \geq 0$ and some $(A, B) \in \mathscr{D}$. T is a closed convex cone. Note that $I - A + B$ is greater than or equal to I, so $y' = 0$ implies that $x = 0$. Therefore $T \cap R_+^{2n} = (0, 0)$. The stocks of goods available at the beginning of the period appear in $y \geq 0$, and the stocks available at the end of the period appear in $y' \geq 0$. The weak inequality in (A1) implies that goods are freely disposable. An input–output combination $(y', -y) \in T$ is said to be efficient if $(z, -w) - (y', -y) \geq 0$, $\neq 0$, implies that $(z, -w) \notin T$.

Any input–output of this model must involve the use of an activity from every industry whose good is being produced. Then the technology in use can always be expressed in the form of (A1) with some choice of (A, B). The using up of durable capital is represented as a destruction of a part of the stock of durable capital by the production process. We also make

ASSUMPTION 26   There are $(a_j, b_j) \in D_j$, $j = 1, \cdots, n$, such that $(I - A)$ has a quasidominant diagonal which is positive. Moreover $(I - A)x > 0$ for some $x > 0$ implies that B is indecomposable.

LEMMA 37   *For given A, B with $(a_j, b_j) \in D_j$, $j = 1, \cdots, n$, all stocks can expand together if and only if $(I - A)$ has a quasidominant diagonal.*

Proof   By (A1) we have

$$(I - A)x + Bx \geq y', \quad -Bx \geq -y.$$

Suppose that it is possible for all stocks to expand together. Then $(I - A)x \geq y' - Bx \geq y' - y$, with $y - y' > 0$. Therefore $(I - A)^T$ has a quasidominant diagonal. This implies by the proof of theorem 3.1 that $(I - A)$ has one also. Now suppose that $(I - A)$ has a quasidominant diagonal. Consider $(I - A - (1 - \alpha)B)x = z$. For $\alpha > 1$ and near enough to 1, $(I - A - (1 - \alpha)B)$ also has a quasidominant diagonal. Thus x exists for any $z \geq 0$. Put $y = Bx$ and $y' = \alpha y + z$. For $z \geq 0$, all stocks are expanding.   ∎

A von Neumann equilibrium (α, x, y, p) in this model is defined by the following conditions. There is $(A^*, B^*) \in D$ and (α, x, y, y') with $y' = \alpha y$, $\alpha > 0$ such that

I. $(I - A^* + B^*)x - \alpha B^* x \geq 0$.

II. $p^T(I - A + B) - \alpha p^T B \leq 0$ for any $(A, B) \in D$.

III. $p^T(I - A^* + B^*)x > 0$, where $p \geq 0$ and $x \geq 0$.

LEMMA 38   *Let α^* be the maximum of α such that there is y for which (A1) is satisfied with $y' = \alpha y$. Then there is p such that*

$$(p^T, \alpha p^T) \begin{bmatrix} I - A + B \\ -B \end{bmatrix} \leq 0 \tag{A2}$$

for all $(A, B) \in D$ with equality for an (A^*, B^*) that realizes $(\alpha y, -y)$.

Proof If α^* is the supremum of expansion rates for the model there is a sequence (A^s, B^s) of choices of technology that realize growth rates $\alpha^s \to \alpha^*$. By assumption 24, we also have $(A^{s'}, B^{s'}) \to (A^*, B^*)$ for a subsequence. Then (A^*, B^*) realizes the growth rate α^*. This means there is $x \geq 0$ and a choice of (A, B) such that $y' \geq \alpha^* y$, and no such x and (A, B) exist for $\alpha > \alpha^*$. Let $W = \{z \mid z = y' - \alpha^* y$ for $(y', -y) \in T\}$. Since α^* realizes maximal growth, $W \cap \mathbf{R}_+^n \neq 0$. As in the proof of theorem 1 the maximality of α^* implies $(W \cap \operatorname{int} \mathbf{R}_+^n) = \emptyset$. Otherwise, (A1) could be satisfied with $\alpha > \alpha^*$. Then as before there is (β, p^*) such that $p^* z \leq \beta$ for $z \in W$ and $p^* z \geq \beta$ for $y \in \operatorname{int} \mathbf{R}_+^n$, where β is a real number, $p^* \in \mathbf{R}^n$, $p^* \neq 0$, and $z \in \mathbf{R}^n$. The existence of points $z \in \operatorname{int} \mathbf{R}_+^n$ that are arbitrarily near 0 implies $\beta \leq 0$. Also $p^* z \geq 0$ for all $y \in \operatorname{interior} \mathbf{R}_+^n$ implies $p^* \geq 0$. Since z^* realizes the growth rate α^*, there is $z^* \in W$, $z^* \geq 0$. Therefore $\beta \geq 0$, and so $\beta = 0$. Also $p^* z \leq 0$ for all $z \in W$. Therefore $z_i^* > 0$ implies $p_i^* = 0$ or $p^* z^* = 0$. This is equivalent to (A2) with equality for an (A^*, B^*) that realizes the growth rate α^*. That is, $p^* \alpha^* y - p^* y \leq 0$ for all choices of (A, B) and $x \geq 0$ in (A1) with equality for (A^*, B^*) and some $x^* \geq 0$. ∎

We may now prove

THEOREM 10 *Make assumptions 24, 25, and 26 for a Leontief model that satisfies relations (A1). There is a von Neumann equilibrium (α^*, x, y, p) for this model where $y > 0$, $p > 0$, and $\alpha^* > 1$. There is no von Neumann equilibrium for growth factor different from α. The set of equilibria for α^* is convex.*

Proof Let (A, B) realize the maximal growth rate α^*. By assumption 26 and lemma 37, we have $\alpha^* > 1$. This means that all stocks that appear in y are expanding. Also B is indecomposable by assumption 26, which implies that all stocks are needed for this production. Therefore y is positive.

It is convenient to define $\bar{A} = B(I - A)^{-1}$. Let $\bar{x} = (I - A)x$. Since stocks are expanding $(I - A)^{-1}$ exists by lemma 37 and $(I - A)x > 0$ holds. Then the model (A1) can be written

$$\begin{bmatrix} I + \bar{A} \\ -\bar{A} \end{bmatrix} \bar{x} \geq \begin{pmatrix} y' \\ -y \end{pmatrix} \tag{A3}$$

for $\bar{x} > 0$. In particular, the form (A2) is possible for $(\alpha y, -y) \in T$, where y is a positive stock expanding by the factor α. By lemma 38, there are prices $(p, \alpha^* p)$ which satisfy (A2) with equality for the (A, B) that realizes the growth rate α^*. For the $\bar{A}$ derived from this (A, B) these prices will satisfy

$$(p^T, \alpha^* p^T) \begin{bmatrix} I + \bar{A} \\ -\bar{A} \end{bmatrix} = 0. \tag{A4}$$

Suppose $p_i = 0$ for some i. Let δ_i have $\delta_{ii} = 1$, $\delta_{ij} = 0$, $j \neq i$, for $\delta_i \in \mathcal{R}^n$. Suppose there is i such that $p_i = 0$. Then $-p \cdot \bar{a}_i + \alpha^{-1} p \cdot (\delta_i + \bar{a}_i) < 0$ for this i, since $\bar{A}$ is indecomposable and $\alpha > 1$. This contradicts (A4). Therefore $p_i = 0$ cannot occur and $p > 0$ must hold.

Relations (A3) and (A4), together with $\alpha > 1$, $x > 0$, $y > 0$, and $p > 0$, imply all the conditions I through III for a von Neumann equilibrium. There cannot be a second growth factor α with a von Neumann equilibrium since $\alpha < \alpha^*$ implies that the input–output $(\alpha^* y, -y)$ belonging to α^* would earn a profit at the prices $(p, \alpha p)$ belonging to the equilibrium with the growth factor α. The linearity of the equilibrium conditions implies that for a given α the set of equilibria is convex. ∎

With stronger assumptions in the Leontief model we can show that the equilibrium is unique. We will say that a set $S \subset \mathbf{R}^{2n}$ is *relatively strictly convex* if it is strictly convex in the smallest affine subspace containing it. The new assumptions are

ASSUMPTION 24′ D_j is compact, *relatively strictly* convex, and not empty.

ASSUMPTION 26′   There are $(a_j, b_j) \in D_j$, $j = 1, \cdots, n$ such that $(I - A)$ has a quasidominant diagonal. Moreover $(I - A)x > 0$ for some $x > 0$ implies that B is indecomposable *and nonsingular*.

THEOREM 11   *Under assumptions 24′, 25, and 26′ the von Neumann ray and the von Neumann price vector are unique in a von Neumann equilibrium.*

Proof Let α be the growth factor, p the price vector, x the activities vector, and y the capital stock vector of a von Neumann equilibrium. Let the processes in use in this von Neumann equilibrium be given by (A, B). With assumption 24′, relative strict convexity of the D_j, equations (A4) imply that (A, B) is unique. Then $(I - A + B)x \geq \alpha y$ and $-Bx \geq -y$. Since all goods are produced, $(I - A)$ is nonsingular with a dominant diagonal by lemma 37, and we may rewrite these relations in the form of

(A3), $(I + \bar{A})\bar{x} \geq \alpha y$ and $-\bar{A}\bar{x} \geq -y$. However, theorem 10 implies that $p > 0$. If these relations did not hold with equality, there would be a contradiction of (A4). Then $\bar{x} = \bar{A}^{-1}y$, or

$$(I + \bar{A}^{-1})y = \alpha y,$$

where $\bar{A} = B(I + A)^{-1} \geq 0$. $\bar{A}^{-1}$ exists by the nonsingularity of B asserted in assumption 26'.

Thus y is a characteristic vector of $(I + \bar{A}^{-1})$ and α is the corresponding characteristic root. Since $\bar{A}$ is nonnegative and indecomposable with a positive diagonal, it follows from theorem 3.3 that it has a unique positive characteristic ray with a corresponding positive characteristic root. Moreover no other characteristic root has a nonnegative characteristic vector, and by Frobenius theory (Gantmacher 1977, p. 69) the positive root of $\bar{A}$ is simple. However, $\bar{A}$ and $(I + \bar{A}^{-1})$ have the same characteristic vectors. Therefore y is unique up to multiplication by a positive constant and α is the only characteristic root with a nonnegative characteristic vector. An analogous argument shows that $p > 0$ lies in the unique nonnegative characteristic ray of $(I + \bar{A}^{-1})$ on the left. ∎

A von Neumann facet F^* is the set of $(y', -y)$ that satisfy (A1) with equality with the A and B proper to a von Neumann ray. Since $\alpha > 1$, these are also the $(y', -y)$ which satisfy (3) with equality. In the present case, by theorem 11, the von Neumann facet is unique. If a path $\{y'\}$, $t = 0, 1, \cdots n$, lies in the von Neumann facet, it must satisfy the difference equation

$$y^{t+1} = (I + \bar{A}^{-1})y^t \tag{A5}$$

for $t = (0, 1, \cdots, n - 1)$. The discussion is somewhat simpler if we define a matrix $C = \alpha^{-1}(I + \bar{A}^{-1})$, whose unique positive root is equal to 1. Then the solution corresponding to y is $z = \alpha^{-1}y$ and (A5) becomes

$$z^{t+1} = Cz^t. \tag{A6}$$

The von Neumann facet will be stable in the sense of convergence of all paths on the facet to the unique von Neumann ray if α is a simple root of C and all roots λ_i of C other than α satisfy $|\lambda_i| < \alpha$ or $|\lambda_i| > \alpha$. In order to prove that the von Neumann facet is stable, we must make a further assumption. Let A, B, α belong to the unique von Neumann equilibrium of a model that satisfies assumptions 24', 25, and 26'.

ASSUMPTION 27 $I - A + B$ is nonsingular. Furthermore, if λ is a characteristic root of $(I + \bar{A}^{-1})$ and $|\lambda| = \alpha$, then $\lambda = a$.

THEOREM 12   *Under assumptions 24', 25, 26', and 27 there is a unique von Neumann facet F^* and F^* is stable.*

Proof   The uniqueness of the facet is implied by theorem 11. By definition of the facet, a path y^t that remains on the facet must satisfy the first order difference equation (A5).

Convergence to the ray (z) of the new paths is equivalent to the convergence to the ray (y) of the old paths. The characteristic roots of C are the characteristic roots of $(I - \bar{A}^{-1})$ divided by α. Thus the root corresponding to the growth factor α of the von Neumann equilibrium is 1. We will consider C as a transformation on the n-dimensional vector space $\mathscr{C}^n$ over the complex numbers which is the extension of $\mathscr{R}^n$ (see Gantmacher 1959, p. 282). The space $\mathscr{C}^n$ can be expressed as the sum of disjoint subspaces S_1, S_2, and S_3, that are invariant under application of C, where S_1 is spanned by vectors w that satisfy the relation $(C - \lambda_i I)^n w = 0$ for some λ_i with $|\lambda_i| = 1$, S_2 is spanned by vectors w that satisfy the relation $(C - \lambda_i I)^n w = 0$ for some λ_i with $|\lambda_i| < 1$, and S_3 is spanned by vectors w that satisfy this relation for some λ_i with $|\lambda_i| > 1$. S_1 is one dimensional since $|\lambda_i| = 1$ implies $\lambda_i = 1$ by assumption 27 and 1 is a simple root by the Frobenius theory.

The initial stocks z^0 of a path on the von Neumann facet may be expressed as $z^0 = \beta_1 z + \beta_2 w_2^0 + \beta_3 w_3^0$, where $w_2^0 \in S_2$ and $w_3^0 \in S_3$. Then, by (A6), $z^t = \beta_1 z + \beta_2 w_2^t + \beta_3 w_3^t$ where $|w_2^t| \to 0$ and $|w_3^t| \to \infty$ unless $w_3^0 = 0$. However, p is a characteristic vector of C on the left with the characteristic root 1. Consider

$$p(C - \lambda_i I)w = p \cdot (1 - \lambda_i)w \neq 0.$$

Also

$$p(C - \lambda_i I)w = p \cdot (\lambda_i - \lambda_i)w = 0$$

when w is one of the basis vectors of S_2 corresponding to the characteristic root λ_i. This is a contradiction unless $pw = 0$. Thus $pw = 0$ must hold for all vectors $w \in S_2$. Similarly $pw = 0$ for all vectors $w \in S_3$. Since z is a vector of capital stocks, it is nonnegative. Therefore w_3^0 must have a negative component in order for $pw_3^0 = 0$ to hold. But $|w_3^t| \to \infty$, so z^t cannot continue to be nonnegative for large t. This is a contradiction, which implies that $w_3^0 = 0$. Therefore for any path $\{y^t\}$ on the von Neumann facet it must be that $\alpha^{-t} y^t \to \beta_1 z$. This means that $d(y^t, \alpha^t \beta_1 z) \to 0$, where d is the angular distance defined in section 7.2. ∎

It is possible to go further and show that an infinite path that converges to the von Neumann facet in angular distance must also converge in angular distance to a path that remains on the facet indefinitely, and therefore must converge in angular distance to the vector of stocks of the von Neumann equilibrium (see McKenzie 1963).

References

Alexandroff, D. 1939. Almost everywhere existence of the second differential of a convex function and some properties of convex surfaces connected with it. *Leningrad State University Annals, Mathematical Series* 6: 3–35 (in Russian).

Allingham, Michael. 1975. *General Equilibrium.* Wiley, New York.

Arrow, Kenneth J. 1951. An extension of the basic theorems of classical welfare economics. In *Proceedings of the Second Berkeley Symposium on Mathematical Statistics and Probability,* edited by J. Neyman. University of California Press, Berkeley.

Arrow, Kenneth J. 1990. Certainty Equivalence and Inequivalence for Prices. In *Value and Capital: Fifty Years Later,* edited by L. W. McKenzie and S. Zamagni. Macmillan, London.

Arrow, Kenneth J., H. D. Block, and Leo Hurwicz. 1959. On the stability of the competitive equilibrium II. *Econometrica* 27: 82–109.

Arrow, Kenneth J., and Gerard Debreu. 1954. Existence of an equilibrium for a competitive economy. *Econometrica* 22: 265–90.

Arrow, Kenneth J., and Alain Enthoven. 1956. A theorem on expectations and the stability of equilibrium. *Econometrica* 24: 288–93.

Arrow, Kenneth J., and F. H. Hahn. 1971. *General Competitive Analysis.* Holden-Day, San Francisco.

Arrow, Kenneth J., and Leo Hurwicz. 1958. On the stability of the competitive equilibrium. *Econometrica* 26: 522–52.

Arrow, Kenneth J., and Leo Hurwicz. 1960. Competitive stability under weak gross substitutability: The "Euclidean distance approach." *International Economic Review* 1: 38–49.

Arrow, Kenneth J., and Leo Hurwicz. 1962. Competitive stability under weak gross substitutability: Nonlinear price adjustment and adaptive expectations. *International Economic Review* 3: 233–55.

Arrow, Kenneth J., and Marc Nerlove. 1958. A note on expectations and stability. *Econometrica* 26: 297–305.

Atsumi, Hiroshi. 1965. Neoclassical growth and the efficient program of capital accumulation. *Review of Economic Studies* 32: 127–36.

Atsumi, Hiroshi. 1969. The efficient capital programme for a maintainable utility level. *Review of Economic Studies* 36: 263–87.

Balasko, Yves, David Cass, and Karl Shell. 1980. Existence of competitive equilibrium in a general overlapping-generations model. *Journal of Economic Theory* 23: 307–322.

Barbolla, Rosa, and Luis C. Corchon. 1989. An elementary proof of the existence of a competitive equilibrium in a special case. *Quarterly Journal of Economics* 104: 76–85.

Becker, Robert A., and John H. Boyd III. 1997. *Capital Theory, Equilibrium Analysis and Recursive Utility.* Blackwell, Oxford.

Bellman, R. 1970. *Introduction to Matrix Analysis.* McGraw-Hill, New York.

Benhabib, Jess, and Kazuo Nishimura. 1979. The hopf bifurcation and the existence and stability of closed orbits in multisector models of optimal economic growth. *Journal of Economic Theory* 21: 284–306.

Berge, Claude. 1963. *Topological Spaces.* Oliver and Boyd, Edinburgh. Reprinted 1997, Dover, New York.

Bewley, Truman. 1982. An integration of equilibrium theory and turnpike theory. *Journal of Mathematical Economics* 10: 233–68.

Birkhoff, Garrett, and Saunders MacLane. 1965. *A Survey of Modern Algebra,* 3rd ed. Macmillan, New York.

Black, J., and Y. Morimoto. 1968. A note on quadratic forms positive definite under linear constraints. *Economica* NS 35: 205–206.

Border, Kim C. 1985. *Fixed Point Theorems with Applications to Economics and Game Theory*. Cambridge University Press, Cambridge.

Boyd, John H. III, and Lionel W. McKenzie. 1993. The existence of competitive equilibrium over an infinite horizon with production and general consumption sets. *International Economic Review* 34: 1–20.

Brock, William. 1970. On existence of weakly maximal programmes in a multi-sector economy. *Review of Economic Studies* 37: 275–80.

Brock, William, and Leonard J. Mirman. 1972. Optimal economic growth and uncertainty: The discounted case. *Journal of Economic Theory* 4: 479–513.

Browning, M., and P. A. Chiappori. 1998. Efficient intra-household allocations: A general characterization and empirical tests. *Econometrica* 66: 1241–78.

Cass, David. 1966. Optimum growth in an aggregative model of capital accumulation: A turnpike theorem. *Econometrica* 34: 833–50.

Cass, David, and Karl Shell. 1976. The structure and stability of competitive dynamical systems. *Journal of Economic Theory* 12: 31–70.

Choquet, G. 1962. Ensembles et cônes convexes faiblement complets. *Comptes Rendus de l'Academie des Sciences* 254: 1908–10.

Coddington, E. A., and N. Levinson. 1955. *Theory of Ordinary Differential Equations*. McGraw-Hill, New York.

Courant, R. 1936. *Differential and Integral Calculus*, vol. 2. Interscience, New York.

Debreu, Gerard. 1952. Definite and semidefinite quadratic forms. *Econometrica* 20: 295–300.

Debreu, Gerard. 1954. *Representation of a Preference Ordering by a Numerical Function, in Decision Processes*, edited by R. M. Thrall, C. H. Coombs, and R. L. Davis. Wiley, New York.

Debreu, Gerard. 1959. *Theory of Value*. Wiley, New York.

Debreu, Gerard. 1970. Economies with a finite set of equilibria. *Econometrica* 38: 387–92.

Debreu, Gerard. 1972. Smooth preferences. *Econometrica* 40: 603–15.

Debreu, Gerard. 1974. Excess demand functions. *Journal of Mathematical Economics* 1: 15–21.

Debreu, Gerard, and Herbert Scarf. 1963. A limit theorem on the core of an economy. *International Economic Review* 4: 235–46.

Dierker, E. 1972. Two remarks on the number of equilibria of an economy. *Econometrica* 50: 867–81.

Dieudonné, Jacques. 1960. *Foundations of Modern Analysis*. Academic Press, New York.

Diewert, W. E. 1977. Generalized Slutsky conditions for aggregate consumer demand functions. *Journal of Economic Theory* 15: 353–62.

Dorfman, Robert, Paul Samuelson, and Robert Solow. 1958. *Linear Programming and Economic Analysis*. McGraw-Hill, New York.

Dunford, Nelson, and Jacob T. Schwartz. 1966. *Linear Operators, Part I: General Theory*. Interscience, New York.

Edgeworth, Francis Y. 1881. *Mathematical Psychics*. Kegan Paul, London.

Fenchel, W. 1953. Convex cones, sets, and functions. Mimeo. Department of Mathematics, Princeton University, Princeton.

Fisher, Irving. 1930. *The Theory of Interest*. Macmillan, New York.

Gale, David. 1956. The closed linear model of production. In *Linear Inequalities and Related Systems*, edited by H. W. Kuhn and A. W. Tucker. Princeton University Press, Princeton.

Gale, David. 1960. A note on revealed preference. *Economica* NS 27: 348–54.

Gale, David. 1967. On optimal development in a multi-sector economy. *Review of Economic Studies* 34: 1–18.

Gale, David, and Andreu Mas-Colell. 1975. An equilibrium existence theorem for a general model without ordered preferences. *Journal of Mathematical Economics* 2: 9–16.

Gale, David, and Hukukane Nikaido. 1965. The Jacobian matrix and global univalence of mappings. *Mathematische Annalen* 159(2): 81–93.

Gantmacher, F. R. 1959. *Application of the Theory of Matrices*. Interscience, New York.

Gantmacher, F. R. 1977. *The Theory of Matrices*. Chelsea, New York.

Grandmont, Jean-Michel. 1990. Temporary equilibrium: Money, expectations, and dynamics. In *Value and Capital: Fifty Years Later*, edited by L. W. McKenzie and S. Zamagni. Macmillan, London.

Grandmont, Jean-Michel. 1998. Expectations formation and stability of large socioeconomic systems. *Econometrica* 66: 741–83.

Graves, Lawrence M. 1956. *The Theory of Functions of Real Variables*, 2d ed. McGraw-Hill, New York.

Green, Jerry. 1977. The nonexistence of informational equilibria. *Review of Economic Studies* 44: 451–63.

Hartman, P. 1964. *Ordinary Differential Equations*. Wiley, New York.

Hawkins, David, and Herbert Simon. 1949. Note: Some conditions of macroeconomic stability. *Econometrica* 17: 245–48.

Hicks, John R. 1939. *Value and Capital*. Oxford University Press, Oxford. Second edition, 1946.

Hildenbrand, Werner. 1983. On the "law of demand." *Econometrica* 51: 997–1019.

Hildenbrand, Werner, and Michael Jerison. 1989. The demand theory of the weak axioms of revealed preference. *Economics Letters* 29: 209–13.

Hurwicz, Leonid, and Hirofumi Uzawa. 1971. On the integrability of demand functions. In *Preferences, Utility, and Demand*, edited by J. Chipman, L. Hurwicz, M. Richter, and H. Sonnenschein. Harcourt, Brace, Jovanovich, New York.

Inada, Ken-ichi. 1964. Some structural characteristics of turnpike theorems. *Review of Economic Studies* 31: 43–58.

Jaffe, W. 1954. Translator and editor. *Elements of Pure Economics* by Leon Walras. George Allen and Unwin, London.

Kaganovich, Michael. 1998. Sustained endogenous growth with decreasing returns and heterogeneous capital. *Journal of Economic Dynamics and Control* 22: 1575–1602.

Kehoe, Timothy. 1985. Multiplicity of equilibria and comparative statics. *Quarterly Journal of Economics* 100: 119–47.

Kelley, J. L., and Isaak Namioka. 1963. *Linear Topological Spaces*. D. Van Nostrand, Princeton, NJ.

Kemeny, J. G., Oscar Morgenstern, and G. L. Thompson. 1956. A generalization of the von Neumann model of an expanding economy. *Econometrica* 24: 115–35.

Koopmans, Tjalling C. 1957. *Three Essays on the State of Economic Science*. McGraw-Hill, New York.

Koopmans, Tjalling C. 1965. The concept of optimal growth, in the econometric approach to development planning. *Pontificae Academiae Scientiarum Scripta Varia*, no. 28. North-Holland, Amsterdam.

Kusumoto, Sho-Ichiro. 1976. Extensions of the Le Chatelier-Samuelson principle and their applications to analytical economics—constraints and economic analysis. *Econometrica* 44(3): 509–36.

La Salle, J., and S. Lefshetz. 1961. *Stability by Lyapounov's Direct Method with Applications*. Academic Press, New York.

Leontief, Wassily. 1941. *The Structure of American Economy, 1919–1929*. Harvard University Press, Cambridge.

Leontief, Wassily. 1953. *Studies in the Structure of the American Economy*. Oxford University Press, Oxford.

Lucas, Robert, and Stokey, Nancy. 1984. Optimal growth with many consumers. *Journal of Economic Theory* 7: 188–209.

Majumdar, Mukul, and Tapan Mitra. 1994. Robust ergodic chaos in discounted dynamic optimization models. *Economic Theory* 4: 649–76.

Magill, Michael, and Martine Quinzii. 1996. *Theory of Incomplete Markets*, vol. 1. MIT Press, Cambridge.

Malinvaud, Edmond. 1953. Capital accumulation and efficient allocation of resources. *Econometrica* 21: 233–68.

Mas-Colell, Andreu. 1974. An equilibrium existence theorem without complete or transitive preferences. *Journal of Mathematical Economics* 1: 237–46.

Mas-Colell, Andreu. 1983. Notes on price and quantity tâtonnement dynamics. *Models of Economic Dynamics*, edited by H. Sonnenschein. Springer-Verlag, New York.

Mas-Colell, Andreu. 1991. On the uniqueness of equilibrium once again. In *Equilibrium Theory and Applications*, edited by W. A. Barnett et al. Cambridge University Press, Cambridge.

McKenzie, Lionel W. 1954. On equilibrium in Graham's model of world trade and other competitive systems. *Econometrica* 22: 147–61.

McKenzie, Lionel W. 1956–57. Demand theory without a utility index. *Review of Economic Studies* 24: 185–89.

McKenzie, Lionel W. 1957. An elementary analysis of the Leontief system. *Econometrica* 25: 456–62.

McKenzie, Lionel W. 1959. On the existence of general equilibrium for a competitive market. *Econometrica* 27: 54–71.

McKenzie, Lionel W. 1960a. Matrices with dominant diagonals and economic theory. In *Mathematical Methods in the Social Sciences*. Stanford University Press, Stanford, CA.

McKenzie, Lionel W. 1960b. Stability of equilibrium and the value of positive excess demand. *Econometrica* 28: 606–17.

McKenzie, Lionel W. 1963. Turnpike theorems for a generalized Leontief model. *Econometrica* 31: 165–80.

McKenzie, Lionel W. 1967. Maximal paths in the von Neumann model. In *Activity Analysis in the Theory of Growth and Planning*, edited by E. Malinvaud and M. O. L. Bacharach. Macmillan, London.

McKenzie, Lionel W. 1968. Accumulation programs of maximum utility and the von Neumann facet. In *Value, Capital, and Growth*, edited by J. N. Wolfe. Edinburgh University Press, Edinburgh.

McKenzie, Lionel W. 1981. The classical theorem on existence of competitive equilibrium. *Econometrica* 49: 819–41.

McKenzie, Lionel W. 1982. A primal route to the turnpike and Liapounov stability. *Journal of Economic Theory* 27: 194–209.

McKenzie, Lionel W. 1983. Turnpike theory, discounted utility, and the von Neumann facet. *Journal of Economic Theory* 30: 330–52.

McKenzie, Lionel W. 1986. Optimal economic growth, turnpike theorems and comparative dynamics. In *Handbook of Mathematical Economics*, vol. 3, edited by K. J. Arrow and M. D. Intriligator. North-Holland, Amsterdam.

McKenzie, Lionel W. 1988. A limit theorem on the core. *Economics Letters* 27: 7–9.

McKenzie, Lionel. 1990. A limit theorem on the core: Addendum. *Economics Letters* 32: 109–10.

McKenzie, Lionel, and Tomoichi Shinotsuka. 1991. A limit theorem on the core. Addendum II. *Economics Letters* 37: 331.

Michael, E. 1956. Continuous selections I. *Annals of Mathematics* 63: 361–82.

Milgrom, Paul, and John Roberts. 1994. Comparing equilibria. *American Economic Review* 84: 441–59.

Milnor, J. W. 1965. *Topology from the Differentiable Viewpoint*. University Press of Virginia, Charlottesville.

Mirrlees, James A. 1969. The dynamic non-substitution theorem. *Review of Economic Studies* 36: 67–76.

Moore, James. 1975. The existence of "compensated equilibrium" and the structure of the Pareto efficiency frontier. *International Economic Review* 15: 267–300.

Morishima, Michio. 1952. On the law of change of price-system in an economy which contains complementary commodities. *Osaka Economic Papers* 1: 101–13.

Morishima, Michio. 1964. *Equilibrium, Stability, and Growth: A Multisectoral Analysis*. Oxford University Press, Oxford.

Muir, Thomas, and William H. Metzler. 1960. *A Treatise on the Theory of Determinants*. Dover, New York.

Mukherji, Anjan. 1973. In the sensitivity of stability results to the choice of numéraire. *Review of Economic Studies* 40: 427–33.

Mukherji, Anjan. 1974. The Edgeworth-Uzawa barter stabilizes prices. *International Economic Review* 15: 236–41.

Mukherji, Anjan. 1975. On the Hicksian laws of comparative statics and the correspondence principle. *Keio Economic Studies* 12: 41–50.

Mukherji, Anjan. 1989. On tâtonnement processes. Working paper. Jawaharlal Nehru University, New Delhi, India.

Negishi, Takashi. 1960. Welfare economics and existence of an equilibrium for a competitive economy. *Metroeonomica* 12: 92–97.

Nishimura, Kazuo. 1981. Kuhn's intensity hypothesis revisited. *Review of Economic Studies* 48: 351–54.

Nishimura, Kazuo, and Gerhard Sorger. 1999. Non-linear dynamics in the infinite time horizon model. *Journal of Economics Survey* 13: 619–52.

Pareto, Vilfredo. 1909. *Manuel d'Économie Politique*. Giard et Brière, Paris.

Peleg, B., and Yaari, M. E. 1970. Markets with countably many commodities. *International Economic Review* 11: 359–77.

Peleg, Bezalel, and Ryder, Harl, Jr. 1974. The modified golden rule of a multi-sector economy. *Journal of Mathematical Economics* 1: 193–98.

Poinsot, Louis. 1803. *Elements de Statique*, 9th ed. Bachelier, Paris, 1848.

Prescott, Edward C., and Robert E. Lucas, Jr. 1972. A note on price systems in infinite dimensional space. *International Economic Review* 13: 416–22.

Quirk, James, and Rubin Saposnik. 1968. *Introduction to General Equilibrium Theory and Welfare Economics*. McGraw-Hill, New York.

Rader, Trout. 1972. General equilibrium theory with complementary factors. *Journal of Economic Theory* 4: 372–80.

Radner, Roy. 1961. Paths of economic growth that are optimal with regard only to final states. *Review of Economic Studies* 28: 98–104.

Radner, Roy. 1972. Existence of equilibrium of plans, prices and price expectations in a sequence of markets. *Econometrica* 40: 289–304.

Ramsey, Frank. 1928. A Mathematical Theory of Savings. *Economic Journal* 38: 543–59.

Rockafellar, R. T. 1970. *Convex Analysis*. Princeton University Press, Princeton.

Roy, René. 1947. La distribution du revenu entre les divers biens. *Econometrica* 15: 205–25.

Samuelson, Paul A. 1947. *Foundations of Economic Analysis*. Harvard University Press, Cambridge.

Samuelson, Paul A. 1951. Abstract of a theorem concerning substitutability in open Leontief models. In *Activity Analysis of Production and Allocation*, edited by T. C. Koopmans. Wiley, New York.

Samuelson, Paul A. 1958. An exact consumption-loan model of interest with or without the social contrivance of money. *Journal of Political Economy* 66: 467–82.

Samuelson, Paul A. 1961. A new theorem on non-substitution. In *Money, Growth, and Methodology and Other Essays in Honor of Joseph Eckerman*, edited by Hugo Hegeland. CWK Gleerup, Lund.

Scarf, Herbert. 1960. Some examples of global instability of the competitive equilibrium. *International Economic Review* 1: 157–72.

Scarf, Herbert. 1967. The core of an *n*-person game. *Econometrica* 35: 50–69.

Scarf, Herbert. 1973. *The Computation of Economic Equilibria*. Yale University Press, New Haven.

Scheinkman, José. 1976. On optimal steady states of *n*-sector growth models when utility is discounted. *Journal of Economic Theory* 12: 11–20.

Smith, Adam. 1776. *An Inquiry into the Nature and Causes of the Wealth of Nations*, edited by E. Cannan. Methuen. London, 1950.

Solow, Robert. 1952. On the structure of linear models. *Econometrica* 20: 29–46.

Sonnenschein, Hugo. 1971. Demand theory without transitive preference with applications to the theory of competitive equilibrium. In *Preferences, Utility, and Demand*, edited by J. Chipman, L. Hurwicz, M. Richter, and H. Sonnenschein. Harcourt, Brace, Jovanovich, New York.

Sonnenschein, Hugo. 1972. Market excess demand functions. *Econometrica* 40: 549–63.

Starr, Ross M. 1969. Quasi-equilibria in markets with non-convex preferences. *Econometrica* 37: 25–38.

Stiglitz, Joseph E. 1970. Non-substitution theorems with durable capital goods. *Review of Economic Studies* 37: 543–52.

Stokey, Nancy L., and Robert Lucas, with Edward C. Prescott. 1989. *Recursive Methods in Econmic Dynamics.* Harvard University Press, Cambridge.

Uzawa, Hirofumi. 1958. The Kuhn-Tucker theorem in concave programming. *Studies in Linear and Non-Linear Programming*, edited by K. Arrow, L. Hurwicz, and H. Uzawa. Stanford University Press, Stanford, CA.

Uzawa, Hirofumi. 1971. Preference and rational choice in the theory of consumption. In *Preferences, Utility, and Demand*, edited by J. Chipman, L. Hurwicz, M. Richter, and H. Sonnenschein. Harcourt, Brace, Jovanovich, New York.

Varian, Hal R. 1975. A third remark on the number of equilibria of an economy. *Econometrica* 43: 985–86.

von Neumann, John. 1937. Über ein Ökonomisches Gleichungssystem und eine Verallgemeinerung des Brouwerschen Fixpunktsatzes. *Ergebnisse eines Mathematischen Kolloquiums* 8: 73–83. Translated as "A model of general economic equilibrium," *Review of Economic Studies* 12: 1–9.

von Weizsäcker, Christian C. 1965. Existence of optimal programs of accumulation for an infinite time horizon. *Review of Economic Studies* 32: 95–104.

Wald, Abraham. 1934–35. Über die Productionsgleichungen der ökonomischen Wertlehre. *Ergebnisse eines mathematischen Kolloquium* 7: 1–6. Translated by William Baumol as "On the production equations of economic value theory, part II" in *Precursors in Mathematical Economics*, edited by W. J. Baumol and S. M. Goldfeld. London School of Economics. 1968.

Walras, Léon. 1874–77. *Eléments d'Économie Politique Pure.* Corbaz, Lausanne. Translated by W. Jaffe as *Elements of Pure Economics.* George Allen and Unwin, London, from the 1926 definitive edition; 1954, Orion, New York.

Wilson, Charles A. 1977. A model of insurance markets with incomplete information. *Journal of Economic Theory* 16: 167–207.

Wilson, Edwin B. 1911. *Advanced Calculus.* Ginn, Boston.

Yano, Makoto. 1984. Competitive equilibria on turnpikes in a McKenzie economy, I: A neighborhood turnpike theorem. *International Economic Review* 25: 695–71.

Index of Economist Citations

Subject Index